CHINA
The Politics of Revolutionary Reintegration

POLITICAL MAP OF CHINA

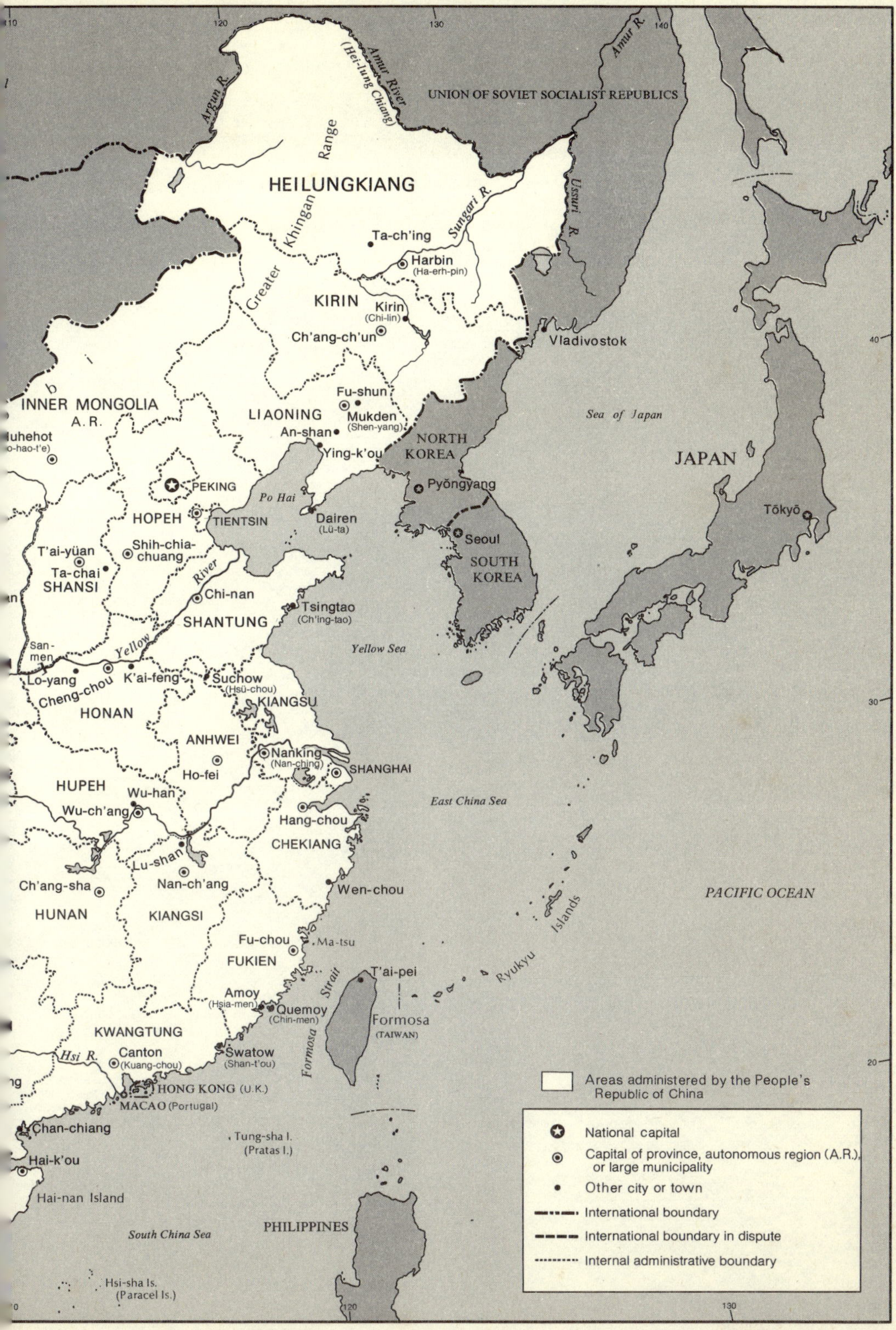
UNION OF SOVIET SOCIALIST REPUBLICS
Amur R.
Argun R.
Amur River (Hei-lung Chiang)
Greater Khingan Range
HEILUNGKIANG
Sungari R.
Ussuri R.
Ta-ch'ing
Harbin (Ha-erh-pin)
KIRIN
Kirin (Chi-lin)
Ch'ang-ch'un
Vladivostok
INNER MONGOLIA A. R.
Fu-shun
LIAONING
Mukden (Shen-yang)
An-shan
Ying-k'ou
NORTH KOREA
Sea of Japan
JAPAN
PEKING
HOPEH
TIENTSIN
Po Hai
Dairen (Lü-ta)
Pyŏngyang
Seoul
SOUTH KOREA
Tōkyō
T'ai-yüan
Ta-chai
SHANSI
Shih-chia-chuang
Chi-nan
SHANTUNG
Tsingtao (Ch'ing-tao)
Yellow River
Yellow Sea
San-men
Lo-yang
Cheng-chou
K'ai-feng
Suchow (Hsü-chou)
KIANGSU
HONAN
ANHWEI
Ho-fei
Nanking (Nan-ching)
SHANGHAI
HUPEH
Wu-han
Wu-ch'ang
Hang-chou
CHEKIANG
East China Sea
Lu-shan
Nan-ch'ang
Ch'ang-sha
HUNAN
KIANGSI
Wen-chou
PACIFIC OCEAN
Ryukyu Islands
Fu-chou
Ma-tsu
FUKIEN
T'ai-pei
Formosa Strait
Amoy (Hsia-men)
Quemoy (Chin-men)
Formosa (TAIWAN)
KWANGTUNG
Hsi R.
Canton (Kuang-chou)
Swatow (Shan-t'ou)
HONG KONG (U.K.)
MACAO (Portugal)
Chan-chiang
Hai-k'ou
Hai-nan Island
Tung-sha I. (Pratas I.)
South China Sea
PHILIPPINES
Hsi-sha Is. (Paracel Is.)
Areas administered by the People's Republic of China
National capital
Capital of province, autonomous region (A.R.), or large municipality
Other city or town
International boundary
International boundary in dispute
Internal administrative boundary
110
120
130
140
40
30
20

CHINA
THE POLITICS OF REVOLUTIONARY REINTEGRATION

James D. Seymour

NEW YORK UNIVERSITY

THOMAS Y. CROWELL COMPANY
New York
Established 1834

Copyright © 1976 by Thomas Y. Crowell Company, Inc.
All Rights Reserved. Except for use in a review, the
reproduction or utilization of this work in any form or by
any electronic, mechanical, or other means, now known or
hereafter invented, including photocopying and recording,
and in any information storage and retrieval system is
forbidden without the written permission of the publisher.
Published simultaneously in Canada by Fitzhenry &
Whiteside, Ltd., Toronto.

Library of Congress Cataloging in Publication Data
Seymour, James D.
  China—the politics of revolutionary reintegration.

  Bibliography: p.
  Includes index.
  1. China—Politics and government—1949–
I. Title.
JQ1504.S49   1976   301.5'92'0951   75-35743

ISBN 0-690-00852-X

Thomas Y. Crowell Company
666 Fifth Avenue
New York, New York 10019

Design by Mina Greenstein
The Chinese calligraphy on the cover is by Vee Edwards.
The author's seal on the half-title page is imprinted
from a chop carved by Hu Fu.

Manufactured in the United States of America

For my Mother and Father

Contents

CHRONOLOGY OF CHINESE HISTORY	xi
PREFACE	xv
NOTE ON PRONUNCIATION	xvii

1 Introduction — 1
  China and Political Science — 2
  Historical Background — 10
  Overview of the People's Republic — 19

2 Informal Political Culture — 25
  Popular Political Culture — 26
  Elite Political Culture — 40

3 Formal Political Culture: Law — 67
  Philosophical Background — 68
  Modern Legal Development: Issues — 79
  Informal Law — 97
  Crime and Political Crime — 101

4 Leadership and Participation — 105
  Theories of Leadership — 106

	Elite and Mass	117
	The Leadership Role of the Center	139
5	**Political Communications and Socialization**	**153**
	Political Socialization	154
	Models	156
	Political Communications and Chinese Culture	160
	Vertical and Horizontal Communications	163
	The Media	166
	Feedback	173
	Bureaucracy	178
6	**Integrative Models**	**183**
	The Subcontinent	189
	Regions and Provinces	197
	Localities	202
7	**Homogeneity**	**221**
	Bridging Life-styles	222
	Equality	232
8	**External Politics**	**245**
	Values and Interests	246
	Relations among Socialist States	251
	China as a Model	255
	The Primacy of Politics	258
	Communicating Requirements and Intentions	263
	International Integration	272
9	**Conclusion: The Cellular Polity**	**281**

APPENDIX A:
THE CONSTITUTION OF THE PEOPLE'S
REPUBLIC OF CHINA · 287

APPENDIX B:
CONSTITUTION OF THE COMMUNIST PARTY
OF CHINA · 297

BIBLIOGRAPHY · 303

AUTHOR INDEX · 313

SUBJECT INDEX · 319

Chinese History

From Earliest Times to 1949

SHANG DYNASTY   dates unknown
CHOU DYNASTY: 1122?–256 B.C.

    Western Chou   1122?–771 B.C. ⎰ "Spring and Autumn,"
    Eastern Chou   770–256 B.C. ⎱   722–481
                                                            Warring States, 403–221

CH'IN PERIOD   221–207

HAN DYNASTIES: 206 B.C.–A.D. 220

"SIX DYNASTIES": 220–588   (Period of disunion)

  1. Three Kingdoms 220–265
  2. Chin
      Western   265–316
      Eastern   316–419

        South ·   *North*
  3. Liu Sung   420–478   "Sixteen Kingdoms," 304–439
  4. Southern Ch'i 479–501   Including 5 hsien-pi
  5. Liang   502–556   (Mongol)
  6. Ch'en   557–588   3 Chinese, 3 Hsiung-nu
                                                  (Turkic),
                                           3 Ti, 1 Chieh, and 1 Tibetan
                                    Northern Wei, 386–534
                                        (Topa/Mongol)
                                 E. Wei–N. Ch'i–N. Chou
                                 534–550–577–581

xii   *Chronology*

SUI DYNASTY   589–618   (Sui founded 581 in North)
T'ANG DYNASTY   618–906
FIVE DYNASTIES AND SUNG DYNASTY
(periods of disunion):

Chinese		*Non-Chinese*	
Five Dynasties	907–960	Liao (Khitan/Mongol)	907–1125
Northern Sung	960–1126	Chin (Jurchen/Manchu)	1115–1234
Southern Sung	1127–1279	Yuan in North: (Mongol)	1260–

YUAN DYNASTY   1280–1368   (Mongol)
MING DYNASTY   1368–1644
CH'ING DYNASTY   1644–1912   (Manchu)
REPUBLIC OF CHINA   1911–
PEOPLE'S REPUBLIC   1949–

Events since 1949

1949 Civil War ends with Communist victory
      Mao Tse-tung visits Moscow

1950 Sino-Soviet alliance and trade agreements
      Laws concerning marriage and women's liberation, land reform, taxation, commerce, etc.
      Korean War begins

1951 Intellectuals subjected to thought reform
      Three-Anti Campaign; 5 percent of state bureaucrats punished
      Five-Anti Campaign; 450,000 businesses investigated, many people sent to prison camps

1952 Nationalization of private enterprises completed

1953 First Five Year Plan begins
      Mutual Aid Teams established in countryside
      Korean War ends

1954	First National People's Congress. National Constitution adopted
1954–1955	Separatist struggle in Manchuria defeated. Kao Kang purged
1955	Party recruits farmers Su-fan campaign against dissidents Rural collectivization begun
1956	Socialism declared "basically achieved" Thaw begins for intellectuals Eighth Party Congress. New Party constitution adopted
1957	"Hundred Flowers" denouement, followed by reaction against intellectuals Anti-rightist and hsia-fang movements
1958	Great Leap Forward begins Communes established, then modified Economic decentralization
1959	Revolt in Tibet; Dalai Lama flees to India Liu Shao-ch'i succeeds Mao-tung as Chairman of Republic Defense Minister P'eng Teh-huai replaced by Lin Piao
1960	Open break with the Soviet Union Production team becomes agricultural accounting unit
1961	Economic and intellectual liberalization
1962	Height of Liu Shao-ch'i's power
1962–1966	Socialist Education Movement
1964–1965	Last National People's Congress until 1975
1965	Ranks abolished in People's Liberation Armed Services Beginning of Great Proletarian Cultural Revolution
1966–1967	Major Cultural Revolution struggles
1966	Liu Shao-ch'i, Teng Hsiao-p'ing ousted Mao Tse-tung's "May 7" directive on social homogeneity
1967	"Ultra-Left" phase of Cultural Revolution
1968	Revolutionary committees established Beginning of urban youth to countryside movement

Chronology

1969	Ninth Party Congress; new Party constitution adopted
1969–1970	Return to normalcy
1971	U.S. table tennis team visits China; beginning of "Ping Pong diplomacy"
	Peking government given China seat in United Nations
	Attempted coup by Lin Piao; Lin dies in plane crash
1972	U.S. President Richard Nixon visits China
	Rehabilitation of victims of Cultural Revolution begins
1973	Tenth Party Congress; new Party constitution adopted
1974	High tide of campaign against Confucius and Lin Piao
1975	Fourth National People's Congress. New national constitution adopted
	Two hundred ninety-three "Kuomintang war criminals" released from prison

Preface

"There is all the difference in the world between thinking about China as exotic—an old way of annexing China to the domain of Western consciousness—and thinking about exoticism in China, which is a universal subject."[1] These words were spoken by Joseph R. Levenson in 1969, before America's rediscovery of China. Many Americans have traveled there since then and returned to tell their countrymen "what China is." Unfortunately, the result has been to once again annex a romanticized version of Cathay to our consciousness.[2] True, there has been much writing about China that is scholarly and profound, but too often writers judge China in terms of Western goals and ideas of social organization.

This book strives to focus upon the real China, as it has been, as it is, and as it strives to become. In order to limit our subject to a manageable scope, I have selected the theme of *political integration*, interpreting this concept broadly enough to give a reasonably comprehensive picture of Chinese politics. More important, it provides a focus on China with a minimum of distortion caused by our own cul-

[1] Joseph R. Levenson, *Revolution and Cosmopolitanism: The Western Stage and the Chinese Stages* (Berkeley: University of California Press, 1971), p. 2.
[2] Past American impressions of China are described and analyzed in Harold R. Isaacs, *Images of Asia: American Views of China and India* (New York: Capricorn, 1962). Originally published in 1958 under the title *Scratches on Our Minds*.

tural and temporal bias. The reader will discover parallels with our own political environment, as well as things that are completely foreign. Exotic or not, China is part of the human experience, a universal subject that is a part of us all. So is political integration. It is hoped that in this text its significance will extend beyond the field of Sinology.

The Chinese are a rural people, and the story of Chinese politics is essentially the story of farmers, how they make collective decisions, and how they are led. In touching only lightly upon cities, I have been influenced by the antiurban bias of the Maoists. Since the political and ecological role of the cities remains unresolved, nothing very definitive could be written about them here. It seems wiser to concentrate on what is the "real" China, both statistically and in the eyes of the leaders. As for the cities, we must wait for the proverbial dust to settle.[3]

In the study of contemporary China, there is one last caution: "disinformation," to use Washington's term. The Chinese governments, as well as the United States, have propagated information that is false, and concealed much that is true. Naturally, I believe all information I have selected to be reliable. No doubt the ideologues and power seekers on all sides have rationalized their conduct to their own satisfaction as a prerequisite to some higher philosophical or social good. I am convinced that all peoples are victimized by these practices. To the extent that distortions occur in this book, I can only express my sad apologies.

This has been an independent project. It received no funding. The book is not the product of any "think tank" (although I profited immeasurably from my association with various groups centered at Columbia University, such as the University Seminar on Modern China). It is hoped that the advantages of such independence will be judged to outweigh the obvious disadvantages.

Independence, of course, does not mean isolation. Although the cited acknowledgments indicate something of the scope of resources from which I have benefited, neither the citations nor any list of names which I could assemble here could adequately convey my debt to the many whose intellect and fund of knowledge have affected this book. Suffice it to acknowledge my gratitude to all of the people who have contributed in their various ways to whatever merit may inhere in this work.

[3] On the cities, see works cited p. 204 note 79, and also the more recent account by Ross Terrill, *Flowers on an Iron Tree: Five Cities of China* (Boston: Atlantic-Little Brown, 1975).

Note on Pronunciation

None of the various commonly-used systems for romanizing Chinese makes the language very accessible to English-speaking people. The most widely-used system is Wade-Giles. In 1975 there was some discussion in China of replacing this system with the *p'in-yin* method. Although *p'in-yin has* been used for certain purposes within China for some time, the idea of extending its use to transliteration in foreign-language material was finally discontinued, and the Wade-Giles system continues to be used. Thus, it is used in this book (although I hope that some day a more transparent system such as Yale's will come into general use).

The most important thing to remember about the Wade-Giles system is that an initial consonant *when followed by an apostrophe* is pronounced as it appears. An initial consonant which is *not* followed by an apostrophe is pronounced soft (unaspirated). In such cases, initial *ch, k, p,* and *t* are pronounced respectively: *j, g, b,* and *d. J* is pronounced *r*. Vowels are pronounced somewhat as in Italian (c*a*lm, *e*nd, mach*i*ne, t*u*be).

CHINA
The Politics of Revolutionary Reintegration

ONE

Introduction

> *Our politics ... must be infinite, reaching to both ends of time and leading a thousand million men from their fathers to their sons, in lines neither broken nor tangled. You [nineteenth-century Westerners] who know so many things do not know the most ancient and powerful; you rage with desire for what is immediate and you destroy your fathers and your sons together.*
>
> ANONYMOUS[1]

> *The imperial Government was very much like the fire-extinguishing equipment of a well-ordered office building: a well-organized system which represents constant expense but which has little to do with the daily life of the inhabitants; when it is active the safety of the inhabitants is already endangered.*
>
> ANONYMOUS[2]

IN THIS CHAPTER we embark on an examination of China as social scientists see it, paying particular attention to the phenomenon of political development. First we shall look at political development as a concept. Then we will survey the political institutions of China's imperial epoch. We shall conclude with a brief overview of the history

---

Many of the bibliographic citations in the footnotes throughout this book are in abbreviated form. Explanations of abbreviated titles may be found on pp. 303–4 in the Bibliography, and full references for shortened footnotes are listed alphabetically by author in the text of the Bibliography (pp. 304–12).

[1] Valéry.
[2] Mu, p. 61.

of Chinese communism. The reader may be justified in omitting a part of this chapter, depending upon his or her knowledge and goals. In particular, a reader with little background or interest in academic problems relating to social science theory may be well advised to ignore or at least postpone the first part.

China and Political Science

Most political science in recent decades has been in some sense comparative, and we do well to pursue this tradition even though studying a single country. Of course, we cannot be very explicit about the bases of comparison ("controls"), and often the comparisons will be implicit.

In general, there are four models with which modern China invites comparison. The first is the one most Chinese have in mind: traditional China. Foreigners should remember that the average Chinese compares the present political environment not with that of another country, but with what he or she recalls or has been told about China's national past. The social scientist also does well to engage in such diachronic analysis—one location across time—for it provides a set of constants different from those inherent in transnational analysis. The second model is the one that China's elite often use as the basis of comparison: the Soviet Union, at first an emulatory model, but after much disillusionment, a negative one. The third type of comparison is probably of greatest interest to social scientists: China and other, less-developed countries. In terms of political development, the third world may well comprise the most relevant control for purposes of measuring China's development. Finally, the model most readers will inevitably bring with them to the study of China: their own country. If that country is one of the developed states of the North Atlantic[3] region, the contrasts will be more notable than the similarities, but far comparisons are not necessarily less instructive than near ones. One should bear in mind, however, that perceived peculiarity may in fact be a reflection of one's *own* idiosyncracies, and draw value judgments with caution.

---

[3] The term North Atlantic will be used in this book in preference to the more vague "West." The countries which we will have in mind as falling under this rubrick are the English-speaking ones as well as northwestern Europe. The Latin world is generally excluded (though France is not). The North Atlantic does not comprise a single culture (e.g., it embraces the two distinct legal traditions, English and Napoleonic), but there has been considerable interaction and cross fertilization throughout it. Visitors among these countries find more that is familiar than strange.

In recent times, the ancient nation of China has been undergoing *tumultuous social change*, which has transformed both the nation's culture and political system. In the late 1940s this change began to be *guided* from above, but was nonetheless *accepted* (with varying degrees of enthusiasm) by the general population. Therefore we may say that China has been a *revolutionary* society. A dilemma, however, confronts the social scientist: What are the essential aspects of social change which require study? Should China be viewed primarily as a "developing" society? If so, we should look for a general improvement in social efficiency and a greater general level of productivity. Should we focus on the question of "modernization," and thus look for signs of increasing specialization in the lives of the people? Or should we be concerned rather with basic questions of social justice, emphasizing the distribution of benefits and the responsiveness of government to social needs?

None of these approaches to understanding a society is invalid. The decision regarding which road to follow is not a scientific one, but rather one derived from the investigator's own cultural underpinnings. The problem of values is one we can never escape entirely, but we can attempt to identify those biases in our thinking, engendered by our own cultural background and by our own times, which may predispose us to anticipate and distort. Thus, we should not consider irrelevant to political development any kind of change which has no Western parallel, and we should not reject as anachronistic any event which in the West may have occurred prior to the Renaissance, or may not yet have taken place. In short, the discipline of political science may require some deparochialization to enable us to understand a polity such as China. To this end, we will not often refer to such common social science themes as development and modernization. (In China, the latter term is even used epithetically.[4]) Rather, we shall strive to use relatively value-free terminology in building our main theme of political *integration* (or, more precisely, *re*integration, because China traditionally enjoyed some degree of integration).

The word *integration* has been used in different ways and to describe dissimilar phenomena. For some, integration is simply the denouement of modernization. According to C. E. Black,

> Integrated societies differ from those in the preceding phase of eco-

---

[4] This is particularly true in the expression "modern revisionism," used to describe the Soviet model. Of course, "modern" and "modernize" have often been used pejoratively in English, also.

nomic and social transformation in their structure of political power. Personal power tends to become institutionalized through bureaucratization, and the exercise of power is divided into many specialties and shared by many people. . . .

In a reasonably well integrated society institutions work effectively, people are in general agreement as to ends and means, and violence and disorder are kept at a low level.[5]

Others use the term in less general ways, with varying degrees of precision and finitude. While this lack of consensus on the meaning of integration may allow us flexibility in using the term, the scientific validity of any concept depends not only upon the universality of its relevance, but also upon how precisely and consistently it describes reality.

As with most of the political scientist's tools, the integration theorist owes a substantial debt to disciplines other than political science. The roots of modern integration theory are to be found in the work of the French sociologist Emile Durkheim.[6] Durkheim saw *repressive law* and *mechanical solidarity* being superseded by *restitutive law* and *organic solidarity*. These latter (which presupposed mutual consent) facilitated the division of labor, specialization, and reciprocity. Repressive law required that everyone's conduct follow established patterns; restitutive law permitted their dissimilar, unorchestrated activities to be integrated on a complementary basis.

Since Durkheim, integration theory has developed in a number of directions. Some have viewed integration as primarily *normative*. This has been true of Talcott Parsons, especially in his earlier works,[7] and the idea has been developed by Edward Shils[8] and Robert Angell.[9] Simply stated, their view holds that a society is integrated to the extent that people follow its norms.

Normative consensus continues to be the foundation of political

---

[5] Black, pp. 83, 27.

[6] Emile Durkheim, *The Division of Labor in Society* (1893; reprint ed., Glencoe, Ill.: Free Press, 1964).

[7] Talcott Parsons, *The Structure of Social Action: A Study in Social Theory with Special Reference to a Group of Recent European Writers* (New York: McGraw-Hill, 1937).

[8] Edward Shils, "The Theory of Mass Society," *Diogenes* 39 (1962): 45–66.

[9] Robert C. Angell, "The Moral Integration of American Cities," *American Journal of Sociology*, vol. 57, no. 1, pt. 2 (1951): 1–140; *Free Society and Moral Crisis* (Ann Arbor: University of Michigan, 1958, 1965); "Social Integration," *International Encyclopedia of the Social Sciences* (New York: Macmillan, 1968), 7: 380–86.

integration for some theorists.[10] For others, integration is a more general *cultural* phenomenon. In its most extreme form,[11] their view holds that all elements in a culture are interrelated; customs, institutions, and values are never mutually irrelevant, and all cultures are intrinsically integrated. Although most anthropologists would take the more restrained view that there are varying degrees of cultural integration, the idea that a society owes its general integration largely to its culture has been accepted by many political scientists.[12] For Karl Deutsch, integration is virtually equated with culture, and it is achieved through cultural assimilation (the acquisition of a common language, for example) and mobilization (indoctrination by the media, and so on).[13] The communications model which he builds,[14] however, would seem to reveal less about what integration is than about how it is attained.

This problem is partially met by the *functional* approach to integration, a view which holds that political mechanisms and factors are seen in terms of their functionality or dysfunctionality. Parsons[15] sees integration as one of a society's four subsystems, the other three being adaptation, pattern maintenance, and goal attainment. Deutsch elaborates upon this, giving substance to Parsons's model by assigning specific social institutions to each function.[16] This does not take us very far in our quest to understand integration, for we are still led to understand that it is comprised of "culture, religion, education, and mass communication." Nevertheless, functionalism is a promising approach to conceptualizing and utilizing integration. If one assumes that integration exists when two elements interact or influence each other, it follows that integration will vary directly with the volume of such interaction. Conversely, if a unit is capable of being detached without

[10] Claude Ake, *A Theory of Political Integration* (Homewood, Ill.: Dorsey, 1967), p. 1.
[11] Bronislaw Malinowski, "Culture," *Encyclopedia of the Social Sciences* (New York: Macmillan, 1931), p. 625.
[12] This has led some to exclude many material factors as integrators. According to one writer, "a disintegrative effect is produced by environmental objects that can be claimed and acquired by single persons or special interest groups—a piece of land, a controversial privilege, a position of power...." Herman Weilemann, "The Interlocking of Nation and Personality Structure," in *Nation-Building*, ed. Karl W. Deutsch and William J. Foltz (New York: Atherton, 1963), p. 40.
[13] Deutsch, "Integration," p. 190.
[14] Karl W. Deutsch, *The Nerves of Government: Models of Political Communication and Control* (New York: Free Press, 1966).
[15] Talcott Parsons, *Essays in Sociological Theory* (Glencoe: Free Press, 1949).
[16] Deutsch, "Integration."

affecting the whole, it is extrinsically unintegrated. An added variable will be the degree of conflict. There would appear to be a relationship between conflict and integration, though probably not one which can be stated in simple terms. Suffice it to say at this point that structured conflict is more integrated than chaotic conflict.

Finally, integration is occasionally treated as a *process*. As such, it does not become a new entity, but we are reminded that integration is more than merely a condition; it is an attaining and maintaining. "By integration," say Parsons and Shils, "we mean the processes by which relations to the environment are mediated in such a way that the distinctive internal properties and boundaries of the system ... are maintained in the face of variability in the external situation."[17] From here, it is a small step to the ideas of disintegration[18] and negative development.[19] On occasion, a society may maximize integration within its given systemic framework, but find itself unable to advance further without fundamental systemic change (revolution). This situation is called *epidevelopment*,[20] a term that can be applied to nineteenth-century China. Such a circumstance requires considerable disintegration, which can then be followed by reintegration along new patterns.

To summarize, when we speak of *integration* we refer to the manner and degree to which parts of a social system (its individuals, groups, and organs) interact and complement each other. The more differentiation and specialization that occur, the more integration required. Although many would use these variables as measures of the "success" of modernization, the reader is urged that as one makes one's intellectual approach to an unfamiliar culture, the formation of value judgments should be postponed until the subject is adequately understood. To cite the economic sphere as an example, one would not want to equate a high gross national product with a satisfactory quality of life, for that is a correlation which each culture is entitled to evaluate for itself. So it is with all aspects of a social system. In politics, we shall want to know how *much* integration exists, but this in itself will not be the basis for any value judgment. One must look further, and evaluate integration qualitatively. How well the performance of a system corresponds with the will (and willingness) of a

[17] Talcott Parsons and Edward Shils, *Toward a General Theory of Social Action* (New York: Harper, 1962), p. 188. Italics eliminated.
[18] Black, p. 27.
[19] Fred Riggs, *Administration in Developing Countries* (Boston: Houghton Mifflin, 1964), pp. 117–221.
[20] The phenomenon of epidevelopment is examined by James C. Hsiung in a forthcoming study.

people, and how that will is determined, should prove much more telling.

The effectiveness of any system is determined by how well the system responds to inputs—to people cashing in their "chips." In a perfect constitutional democracy, those chips are votes. Under pure capitalism the will of the people can be expressed only through the market. The society's dominant system (for example, the economic system) best serves those with the greatest number of or ability to use chips (which, under capitalism, are money). In a society such as China, where the dominant social system is the political system, "the people" are those to whom the political system is designed to respond. Unfortunately, it is more difficult to demonstrate political response than to show the correspondence of will and performance in the marketplace. For China, a land where politics is "in command,"[21] we must consider economics a subordinate subject. One should not infer, however, that economic modernization is unimportant; rather, recognize that at this stage of China's development Maoists are determined that economic modernization should not take place at the expense of sociopolitical transformation, and that they are more willing that the latter interfere with the former than vice versa.

It will be argued in this book that two factors are particularly important as facilitators of political integration. One is a *homogeneous political culture*. This does not mean that all people must think and behave in the same manner, but it does mean that they must understand one another—"speak the same language" in the figurative sense —and not be too often disconcerted by one another's conduct. A common history, ethnic continuities, and normalized communications patterns are all conducive to cultural homogeneity, but they should not be confused with homogeneity itself. If a polity's population is one of compatible political attitudes and behaves in a reasonably predictable manner, then it at least has the potential of maximizing interpersonal activity and minimizing coercion and friction.

The second facilitator of integration is *political participation*.[22] At its most rudimentary level, where individuals are politically aware,

[21] *Cheng-chih kua-shuai*—a common Chinese communist expression. Another similar phrase—*cheng-chih t'u-ch'u*—is also used. Although such expressions describe ideal types better than they describe the reality, it is nonetheless reasonable to consider economics a secondary system, and possibly even a subsystem of politics.

[22] It should perhaps be pointed out that we are discussing the homogeneity of *culture*, not of civilization. In particular, economic heterogeneity need be no bar to political integration.

attend meetings, and occasionally express their views, one might better speak of *political involvement*. The individual is active rather than passive but tends to parrot what he or she has absorbed from the political environment with a minimum of digestion and rethinking. Thus, individual criticism is only superficial, a problem highlighted by a writer in the journal of the Communist party of China, *Red Flag*:[23]

> Everyone says, revolution must be voluntary, and criticism must be based upon the initiative of the masses. Unfortunately, there is some tendency for people to think, "We should criticize when the leadership tells us to criticize." Such an attitude shows a lack of revolutionarity initiative.

On the other hand, true political participation means that there are significant individual inputs into the political system. People have a sense of interest (whether personal or public) and evaluate alternatives presented to them in terms of their interests. But with involvement as well as participation, a person is aware of the political meaning of his or her own and others' expressions and activities.

We shall make use of special terminology to quantify and qualify integration. For quantification, we shall speak of three "degrees" of integration. The greatest degree exists in a highly differentiated society (comprised of specialists) in which individuals and groups are very interdependent—i.e., they cannot function without one another's support. A moderate degree of integration operates when there is some role interchangeability and mutual support, but when that support is withdrawn there is considerable adaptability to the new situation. A still lesser degree of integration might be characterized as *compatibility*. Person A may not need the active support of B, so long as B *tolerates* the activities of A. In short, B has a "veto power" over A, but no more. If such a veto power either does not exist or is never exercised, the condition may be termed *neutral integration*.

There are several ways in which integration can be qualified. First, there are the various types of societal activity—political, economic, cultural, and social (interpersonal). Although we shall deal primarily with the first of these, there is considerable overlap and we shall refer to them all on occasion. Second, there are the vertical and horizontal axes of integration. Vertical axes comprise the relations between the "higher" and "lower" political units, social classes, and so on. Hori-

---

[23] *HC*, 1970, no. 10, p. 58. Loose translation.

zontal integration, on the other hand, denotes the relations among constitutional or socially equivalent people and groups. Interaction among guilds, or among religious groups, among nations, or among villages—each of these is an example of horizontal integration. Finally, there is the most elusive, and yet most important, quality of integration —acceptability. As Karl Deutsch has written:[24]

> To be acceptable as a substitute for special-group facilities—local, national, or even segregated ones—*integrated* facilities must usually be *better* facilities.... They must be better not just in the opinion of distant experts... but also in the experiences and emotions, in the feelings and daily lives of the populations directly concerned.

Thus, we should reemphasize the "will and willingness" aspect of our definition of integration. For *quality* integration to exist, people must *want* to be affected by others in the *way* that they are affected, and they must be at least willing to act in the manner in which others expect them to act. Obviously, "quality" in this sense is not an either-or proposition. If people and groups have to settle for their "second choices," we would still speak of this as integration of reasonable quality. For example, wheat might be acceptable, even though rice might be preferred. Or, Party membership might be denied, but cadre status still conferred. In other words, economic and political systems not only allocate things and conditions that people desire, but they inevitably have to allocate scarcities and undesirables as well. How acceptably this is accomplished is a measure of the quality of integration.

Why, the reader may ask, analyze Chinese politics in terms of *integration*? Is this a concept with which Chinese themselves have shown much concern? The answer is that integration is an often-discussed problem in China, and has been for some time. Clearly, it concerned Sun Yat-sen when he lamented that the Chinese nation was like "loose sand." Interestingly, the Chinese language has no single word the precise equivalent of *integration*. *Chieh-ho* (unite) and *lien-hsi* (connect) are often translated "integration," and properly so, but neither is used in as many contexts as we shall use the word. The test of a concept, however, is not whether it is familiar to the people being analyzed, but whether it enables us to better understand (and perhaps

---

[24] Deutsch, *Nationalism*, p. 171. Emphasis in original. (This statement occurs in the context of international integration, a subject with which we shall not deal until chap 9.)

even predict) their culture and system. As our account of Chinese attitudes toward politics will show, integration is much on the minds of politically articulate Chinese, even though they lack a single term for the phenomenon.

Historical Background

Although political scientists do not address themselves to the same questions as historians, political science is dependent upon historical data. Even at an elementary level, the politics of a country can be understood only contextually—that is, in relation to what went on before, and to what is happening contemporaneously in the broad social and physical environment. For the reader who is new to the subject of China, or whose knowledge is limited to one discipline or period, this section will provide a glimpse of the environment and background against which politics has been conducted in China.

During the second millennium B.C. there existed a homogeneous culture group in North China's Yellow River valley, where the climate and soil are conducive to agriculture (dry grain), provided that the great river can be held in check and predatory neighbors fended off. The population of this group was small in relation to arable land. Even from such limited ecological data, one might predict a reasonably stationary population, enjoying at least minimal security of land tenure. One might also anticipate the emergence of a central authority strong enough to command the resources (especially human) to insure that the waters of the river system, if they did not actually serve farmers, would at least not work to their detriment. Given the probability of crop surpluses, furthermore, one would not be surprised if there emerged a nonagricultural class—an aristocracy, a landowning class, or a merchant-industrial class. And there would have to exist some rudimentary military establishment to provide security.

An examination of the Chou dynastic era (c. 1100–256 B.C.) generally bears out this pattern of political development. A landed aristocracy comprised largely of "knights" controlled the region, and the common people toiled in the fields, rendering agricultural surpluses to their lords. The similarity to European feudalism is in some respects only superficial, but sketched in broad socioeconomic terms the two systems had much in common. Chou's chief claim to distinction is probably the early existence of centralized political control, inspired by hydrological considerations. As the nation expanded to the northern reaches of the Yellow River and south to the Huai River, however, political development failed to keep pace with the needs of the civilization, and fragmentation occurred. As in the case of Europe, the post-feudal need for effective government was met by the formation of a number of unitary states, the internal development of which was spurred by the rivalry among them.

It is generally considered that a "developed polity" must be able to mobilize its population and regulate nature. While we shall have to reexamine this idea of development from time to time, we may accept these criteria for now and observe that a number of Chinese states, prior to the reunification in 221 B.C., possessed many of the hallmarks of development. For security, armies were conscripted and defensive walls erected. The same kind of mobilization also facilitated projects of more immediate benefit to the public. Great waterworks were built to serve irrigation and transportation needs, and to facilitate land reclamation. Such state projects were made possible by new systems of tax collection and monetization. Currencies became vehicles for thriving commerce, often conducted by the same people who collected the taxes. There was thus no clear line between governmental and private commerce, and governments were playing increasing roles in the economy, including state monopolies of essential commodities. With the establishment of "ever-normal granaries," governments endeavored to maintain stability in the agricultural economy.[25] Sometimes even price controls were instituted. Cities grew to populations of hundreds of thousands, and although little is known about their administration, such concentrations of people certainly entailed substantial political and economic organization. Legal systems, and sometimes legal codes,[26] began to appear, bringing a measure of predictability and therefore security to the lives of the people.

It must be emphasized that these developments were primarily intrastate. While there was much emulation of one state by another, and occasional interstate cooperation, the only way integrated development could occur on a wide scale was for pairs or groups of states to consolidate. The reduction in the number of states as a result of conquest and absorption occupies the history of the period during the fourth and third centuries B.C. As often happens, it was not the state with the greatest political sophistication, but rather the one which had concentrated on mobilizing the population and resources for military pursuits, that overcame all rivals and ultimately gave its name to the

---

[25] The first was established in 412 B.C. in Western Wei. Marquis Wen is credited with the achievement.
[26] In the state of Cheng, 536 B.C.

subcontinent.[27] However, the short-lived period of reunification under the Ch'in (221–207) had a lasting impact on China's political development. The most striking achievement was the unification itself; not only did the Ch'in conquer all the Han (ethnic Chinese) states of North China,[28] but it went on to subdue other nations, among them the Vietnamese, whose new homeland (now North Vietnam) soon became a Chinese colony.[29] Unification did not entail simply the physical incorporation of territory into one state, but the creation of an integrated cultural unit to which we can indeed apply the modern term *nation*. China, with its unified systems of writing, weights and measures, road design, and so on, had been established as an indivisible civilization, and any future national disunity was bound to be only temporary.

But the Ch'in had an even more specifically *political* impact than this. The man who presided over the conquest is known as the First Emperor, or Ch'in Shih Huang-ti, and although he failed to found the hoped-for eternal dynasty, he did establish an *imperial office* which survived for over twenty-two centuries. Something of the nature of the position is indicated by the fact that Ch'in Shih Huang-ti occupied a palace half a mile long, and his daily chore of paperwork allegedly amounted to 120 pounds.[30] Through the virtually totalitarian government over which he presided, he wielded tremendous power over the national population (now numbering tens of millions). People were organized into groups of five to ten families, and individuals within the groups were responsible for one another's conduct. The groups were organized in pyramidal fashion, ultimately subject to central authority. The populace could be mobilized to build roads, dig canals, and, in perhaps the greatest human construction effort in history, erect the Great Wall.[31] The fact that hundreds of thousands of corvée

---

[27] *Ch'in* was not used domestically as a name for China after 206 B.C., but the term somehow entered foreign languages.

[28] This still did not include all of what is now thought of as China proper. Much of what is now Hopei Province, for example, was excluded.

[29] The Vietnamese (or *Yüeh*) had occupied much of what is now south and east China. Vietnam (present North Vietnam) was formally annexed by China in 111 B.C., and did not officially gain independence until A.D. 939.

[30] L. C. Goodrich, *A Short History of the Chinese People* (New York: Harper, 1951), p. 34. I have used *paperwork* as a figure of speech only. Paper was not invented until c. A.D. 100. If wood was used, that would help to account for the great weight.

[31] Fragments of the wall had been built prior to the Ch'in period. The Ch'in achievement was in building additional wall to link these. The wall would serve as a defense against nomadic invaders.

laborers toiled on such projects suggests the state's ability to coerce the population. Although unpopular, such crude practices have always been a legitimate means of social mobilization for Chinese rulers. (Around 1974 Ch'in Shih Huang-ti came in for much praise in China's mass media; we shall have more to say about this later.)

Inevitably, however, there was a reaction against such oppressive rule, and after the death of the First Emperor, the Ch'in "dynasty" was replaced by a family which surrounded itself with men of new ideas and a fresh political style. Although it took some time for this dynasty (called Han) to put together a new order, and some features of the Ch'in were retained (the imperial institution, law, authoritarianism), there eventually emerged a new sociopolitical system which was to persist until the twentieth century. This system, which we may term *Confucian*, was one of mankind's most remarkable achievements. The Confucian order, especially if we separate it analytically from the Ch'in legacy and later alien influences, was notable for its civility (as opposed to militarism), and humanism (as opposed to rationalism and materialism). A milieu was created within which a subcontinental unit could retain its cultural integrity until modern times. The flourishing of learning and the arts has been, at least in terms of longevity, unequaled elsewhere. It is difficult to imagine T'ang poets, Sung artists, or even Yüan playwrights being creative in the ways that they were in a less ordered environment, and it is equally difficult to imagine the artistic continuity with the past exhibited during the Ming and Ch'ing periods if social and political institutions had been less viable and enduring. This is not to say that Chinese culture would have been inferior if non-Confucian values and institutions (perhaps militarism, or even commercialism) had predominated, but simply that the artistic achievements would have been more sporadic and dominated by different themes.

All of this is sufficient to whet our curiosity about the social and political institutions that permitted such achievements, but there are other reasons why this subject is important to a study of contemporary Chinese politics. China's political heritage explains much about China today. The Chinese conception of their nation, their attitudes toward the state and toward authority, and even to some extent the political structure, are all influenced by tradition. On the other hand, Chinese communism also represents a revolt against the past, and is, therefore, in a negative way shaped by that past. The next chapter will examine the heritage of political culture, and the extent to which it is a negative or a positive legacy. In the remainder of this section we

ONE: *Introduction*

shall confine ourselves to various broad observations about imperial Chinese political and social organization, with a view to shedding some light on the question of traditionalism and modernism in the Chinese context.

Although during the course of this book we shall have many refinements to suggest concerning how to view the concept of modernization or development, it would be useful at this point to begin setting forth some of the criteria: depersonalization, equality, differentiation, and integration.

By *depersonalization*, we mean that in a developed society, politics is not simply a function of powerful individual will. In the first place, there are constitutional procedures for determining who may exercise power, and in what manner it may be exercised. Rule may be considered highly personalized if leaders are free to act with little regard for the expectations and wishes of other people. Restraints which depersonalize politics may be *normative* (written or unwritten legal restraints) or *political* (the practical necessity of avoiding antagonisms). If a ruler acts in the name of the supernatural, or assumes a godlike aura, he is further detaching himself from social constraints. In this sense, prior to the second century B.C., China was unmodernized, for rulers generally claimed to be responsible to ancestral deities, and some (including the Ch'in emperor) tried to assume divine attributes. But beginning with the Han dynasty, Chinese government was thoroughly secular, and it has for the most part remained so.[32]

In order for a government to be truly impersonal, it must possess two features: law, and nonascriptive offices. Confucian China inherited (albeit with reservations) the institution of law from the Ch'in experiment. Although civilization was considered better served by wise men than by rigid laws, China was never wanting for statutes. Imperial China, then, belongs somewhere in the middle of the legalistic-personalistic scale. (Chap. 3 will be devoted largely to the subject of legal institutions.)

"Nonascriptive" recruitment fills offices on the basis of performance, rather than ascriptively. The reader will recall that prior to the multistate system of the late Chou period, Chinese politics was characterized by a form of feudalism, in that economics and government were dominated by a hereditary (ascriptive) aristocracy. Although there was

---

[32] For a few centuries during and after the Six Dynasties period (220–588), Buddhism did play an important role in Chinese politics.

a tendency for such a system to reemerge at various times even after the first abolition of feudalism in the third century B.C.,[33] in general the only hereditary political office was that of the emperor.[34] While some emperors wielded great power, they customarily relied upon the civil service, which was operative at even the highest levels of government. The civil service was nonascriptive, examination being the preferred means of entry. Questions generally related to the Confucian classics, rarely to practical matters of politics and administration. For this reason (and also because women were excluded), it might be argued that this was still an ascriptive method of elite recruitment. However, the assumption was that the measure of a man was his grasp of and ability to articulate philosophy, and that a good man, so defined, would be a good administrator. At the very least, these examinations tested ability to learn and remember, and they largely insured that official conduct would be governed by the established cultural norms. To this extent, traditional Chinese political recruitment was nonascriptive.

This equality was more stressed in theory than apparent in practice. Every farmer's son was supposed to have an opportunity similar to that of a boy from a scholar-gentry family. He was in fact eligible to sit for the examinations, and if he passed them he would join not only the political but also the socioeconomic elite. If one considers that half the population was excluded by virtue of their sex,[35] and many others because they belonged to one of the less respected professions (merchants, artisans, doctors, monks, and slaves) or ethnic minorities,[36] then one realizes that relatively few were given an opportunity to join the elite. If we consider the long and arduous study, requiring many years that otherwise would be economically productive, we must suspect that the economically disadvantaged would have had little opportunity to gain entry to the elite. Certainly social equality in the modern sense did not exist, and real political participation was limited to a minuscule minority. When we come to social differentiation and integration, we enter an area where considerable conceptual refinement is in order, and much of this book will be devoted to this subject. Clearly,

[33] See Riggs, "Ambivalence," pp. 1–19.
[34] Some military offices were also hereditary, as were many non-Han political offices (both of tribes and of dynasties which ruled China).
[35] We shall elaborate upon the role of women in traditional Chinese society in the next chapter.
[36] Minorities were excluded for cultural, not racial, reasons. Some non-Hans became bureaucrats—sometimes via the Confucian examination system, sometimes otherwise. Naturally, there were more non-Hans in the bureaucracy during periods of non-Han dynastic rule than when the imperial family was of the Han race.

imperial Chinese society was not undifferentiated. Economically, socially, and politically, each man and woman had rather specialized roles to fulfill, and one might already guess that all of this had to be integrated in some sense for the system to survive as long as it did.

Before carrying our overview of Chinese political history down to modern times, there is one subject bridging past and present that should be discussed—the degree of receptiveness of Chinese culture to outside influences. There is a popular tendency to view the world as unidirectional, heading toward a single "'cosmopolitan' culture" (to use Lucian Pye's term),[37] and whether one views this alleged trend in deterministic terms or as the result of interaction and acquisition, we would do well to examine China's adaptability or resistance to external influences and international trends.

China certainly has been no Japan, whose recurrent thirst for alien philosophies, and eagerness to copy the institutions of others, makes the identification of many indigenous features of the civilization difficult. On the other hand, neither was China a "hermit kingdom" (as Korea has been misleadingly called by Westerners). In much the same way as the soils of the great river basins have been periodically refertilized by awesome floods, so was Chinese society occasionally subjected to the trauma of foreign invasion—leaving its civilization sometimes richer, sometimes poorer, but always modified. China acquired the military arts, for example, from its martial neighbors and conquerors. Militarism was a keynote of the Mongols, for one, who also enduringly affected China's performing arts, and added an authoritarian quality to its political institutions.

But China has not had to be *invaded* to be influenced by other nations. Perhaps the greatest impact ever was that of the Western nations from the mid-nineteenth to the mid-twentieth century, though they never seriously contemplated controlling the whole country militarily. There are even examples of entirely benign penetration by alien cultures, as in architecture[38] and religion. Several attempts were made to bring foreign religions to China; perhaps the most strenuous was that of Christian missionaries, who during three widely separated periods undertook to proselytize among the Chinese, each effort ultimately proving unsuccessful.[39] Earlier, the introduction of Buddhism had had a happier fate, for reasons which we shall explore in chapter 2,

[37] Pye, *Aspects*, p. 9.
[38] The characteristic Chinese roof entered China from Indonesia via Vietnam.
[39] T'ang and Ming dynasties, and the mid-nineteenth to mid-twentieth centuries.

but even Buddhism was given a mixed reception. It was necessary to overcome the Confucian bias against foreign ways (if not against foreign people). Mencius had said, "I have heard of using what is Chinese to change what is barbarian, but I have never heard of using what is barbarian to change what is Chinese."[40] It was during a period of major turmoil and disintegration (the Six Dynasties) that Buddhism took root in China, and even then it underwent significant Sinification.

Only one other foreign thought system has had comparable success in China, and it too entered the country during tumultuous times. Did communism, like Buddhism, undergo Sinification? Of course, China was not the kind of setting Marx had had in mind for the achievement of communism, and many adjustments were inevitable. This does not mean that communism would have to yield to the various "feudal" aspects of traditional Chinese culture, something the Chinese Communists have been determined to resist. But as the following remarks by Mao Tse-tung suggest, it is not simply ecology and stage of development which are allowed to influence the creed.

> Being Marxists, Communists are internationalists, but we can put Marxism into practice only when it is integrated with the specific characteristics of our country and acquires a definite national form. The great strength of Marxism-Leninism lies precisely in its integration with the concrete revolutionary practice of all countries. For the Chinese Communist party, it is a matter of learning to apply the theory of Marxism-Leninism to the specific circumstances of China. For the Chinese Communists who are part of the great Chinese nation, flesh of its flesh and blood of its blood, any talk about Marxism in isolation from China's characteristics is merely Marxism in the abstract, Marxism in a vacuum. Hence to apply Marxism concretely in China *so that its every manifestation has an indubitably Chinese character*, i.e., to apply Marxism in the light of China's specific characteristics, becomes a problem which it is urgent for the whole Party to understand and solve. Foreign stereotypes must be abolished, there must be less singing of empty abstract tunes, and dogmatism must be laid to rest; they must be replaced by *the fresh, lively Chinese style and spirit which the common people of China love*. To separate internationalist content from national form is the practice of those who do not understand the first thing about internationalism. We, on the contrary, must link the two

---

[40] Such objections are dealt with by Buddhist apologists in *Hung-ming chi*, which is extracted in W. T. de Bary, *The Buddhist Tradition in India, China, and Japan* (New York: Vintage, 1969), pp. 135–38.

An interesting account of inter-cultural relations is Larry N. Shyu, "National Amalgamation and Cultural Blending in T'ang China," *Hong Kong Baptist College Journal* 1, no. 1 (March 1962): 33–42.

closely. In this matter, there are serious errors in our ranks which should be conscientiously overcome.[41]

These words are asserted to have been written in 1938, but it would be two decades before the "errors" to which Mao referred would be seriously tackled. In the meantime, historical events interceded in the relations between China and the cradle of communism, Soviet Russia. In the 1940s Stalin apparently withdrew his support from the Chinese revolution.[42] The revolution succeeded anyway, but during the 1950s Sino-Soviet relations were not smooth, and the number of Chinese who would blindly imitate Russian ways dwindled. With the complete break between the two countries in the early 1960s, the way was cleared for a Marxist order whose "every manifestation has an indubitably Chinese character."

This brief background should alert us to certain findings in our examination of Chinese politics. First, it is a mistake to view pre-twentieth-century China as politically "undeveloped." Certainly it was not *fully* developed, and its partial development had peculiarities. Development there was, however, and it would profoundly influence the course of further growth. Second, we must reject two conflicting myths about Chinese culture: that it has been entirely discrete, and that it has been highly receptive to foreign influences. The fact is that although, on the whole, Chinese culture has been indigenous, it has always absorbed a certain amount from outside sources. Finally, while Chinese today perceive their politics as entirely novel, we should expect the great weight of tradition, and chronic ecological factors, to have a prominent influence. To a certain degree, this is a matter of vantage point; those on the scene seem to take their history either for

---

[41] Mao, SW, 2: 209 f. Emphasis added. Republication in the 1960s, of course, meant that these views were reaffirmed.

The reference to "internationalist content" and "national form" is curious. The language is obviously intended to echo Stalin's policy regarding the cultures of minority nationalities, which were to be "national in form and socialist in content." Yet Mao, in insisting that it was wrong "to separate internationalist content from national form" seems to be saying that Stalin's principle does not apply in the same way among great nations.

[42] According to Mao, "In 1945, Stalin denied China permission to carry out her revolution, and told us, 'Cooperate with Chiang Kai-shek, and do not engage in civil war. Otherwise, the Republic of China will collapse.' However, we did not oblige, and the revolution succeeded.... [In the winter of 1949–50] I went to Moscow and concluded the Sino-Soviet treaty of alliance. This too was the result of much struggle. Stalin did not wish to sign the treaty.... Only after our resistance to America and support for Korea did Stalin finally come to trust us." *Mainichi shimbun* (Tokyo), March 9, 1967, translated in *CLG*, Spring 1968, p. 6.

granted or as something to be lived down, while we, viewing from afar and with greater perspective, are more aware of the continuities. By referring frequently to primary sources and native commentary, we hope to give the reader the benefit of both perspectives.

Overview of the People's Republic

When the Chinese Communists came to power in 1949, China proper was unified for almost the first time in a century. A war-weary people were eager to accept almost any authority which could restore order. Some people—the poorer farmers—eagerly accepted Communist rule. Others—affluent farmers, businessmen, and intellectuals—were often hesitant but still unresisting. At first, the Communists moved slowly. Permanent governmental institutions were not established for some time, and initial socioeconomic reforms, such as land reform, were moderate. An umbrella organ, the Chinese People's Political Consultative Conference, was established to provide a forum in which various political and cultural groups could hear, though not necessarily be heard. The smaller nationalities occupying vast areas of the hinterland were promised autonomy, at least to the extent of retaining their own cultures. Overseas Chinese were urged to return to help build the New China, and many did. Thus, in reintegrating Chinese society the new leadership sought to embrace and utilize as broad a spectrum of the Chinese population as possible.

Soon, however, it was determined that some elements were unsuitable for integration into the new order because of their anachronistic political and social attitudes. The Chinese Communists had never been basically liberals, and they were not about to permit any obstacles to stand in their way as they pressed forward with their revolution. The educated people were sent to "revolutionary universities" to be reeducated, and the recalcitrant were sometimes subjected to the sophisticated psychological techniques of "brainwashing." Non-Communist organizations (churches, political parties) were reorganized and placed under the direct control of the Communist party's United Front Work Department. Farmers, notwithstanding fairly widespread enthusiasm for the recent land reform program, underwent obligatory collectivism —first mutual aid teams, then cooperatives, then collectives, and finally (in 1958) the communes. In the cities, businesses and labor unions were placed under the supervision of the Communist party, and a pervasive system of social controls was established in all neighborhoods. During the first half of the 1950s, the new regime was obviously fearful of its opponents—the bourgeoisie and "feudal" landlord elements at home, and the foreign enemy, the United States, which seemed to be pressing militarily from the south (Vietnam), the east (Taiwan), and the northeast (Korea).

By the middle of the decade, however, Peking became somewhat more relaxed. The Korean war was ended, the Vietnam question seemed settled, and it became clear that the United States would not participate in any effort by the Chinese Nationalists to invade the mainland. At home, the rocky road to a new order seemed to have been traversed successfully. In 1954 a national constitution was proclaimed, and the structure of government was finally settled. In 1956 the Communist party held its Eighth Congress, declared that socialism had been basically achieved, and drew up a new "constitution" (bylaws) for the Party itself. More and more the Chinese People's Republic was appearing to emulate the Soviet Union, with its dual bureaucracy (Party and government), centralized economy, and strict social controls. But in 1956 Mao Tse-tung decided that restrictions on the free flow of ideas were excessive and counterproductive; the counterrevolutionaries had been safely eliminated from the political scene, and everyone else basically accepted the new order. Mao decided that it would be healthy if people could air their views more freely, and even criticize the Communist party. Thus, he called for the "blooming of the Hundred Flowers" (an allusion to the period of intellectual ferment of the ancient Chou period). At first people were reluctant to speak out, but in the spring of 1957 attacks on Party policies came in torrents. Astounded, Mao called an end to the Hundred Flowers and ordered a rectification campaign against bourgeois rightists—the professional class he had been relying on to modernize China.

Disillusioned with the "experts," Mao turned to the "reds"—the men and women of solid political background. They were to lead the public in a Great Leap Forward (1958–1960), in which harsh economic reality was supposed to be overcome through human will. Through such institutions as the communes, in which all of the energies of the people would be mobilized in a diffuse fashion without the limitations of specialization, communism would be attained ahead of schedule. Unfortunately, these measures failed because of inadequate planning, poor cadre understanding of economics, and bad weather. The communes were reorganized and decentralized, and the authority of the Party hierarchy, which had atrophied during the Leap, was restored. In the early 1960s, China continued in a conservative period of reconstruction. This program proved quite successful, and by the middle of the decade the average Chinese was probably more prosperous than he had ever been.

But Mao Tse-tung and certain of his like-minded colleagues foresaw dangers. Mao did not want his new order to mean that people were simply comfortable and well fed. And he certainly did not want a situation in which the Party elite only filled the roles of the former mandarins, which would be no revolution at all. Tension generated by this and other issues increased until the end of 1965, when China erupted in the Cultural Revolution—Mao's answer to embourgeoisement, bureaucratism, and the decline of public spiritedness. He had decided that introducing new institutions and modes of production had been insufficient. In something of a reversal of basic Marxist principles regarding the relationship between the *base* (class control of the means of production) and the *superstructure* (culture and institutions), Mao decided that for the Chinese revolution to succeed, it would be necessary to attack the flaws of Chinese culture directly—both those deficiencies which had ancient roots, and those which had emerged under the aegis of the Party elite.

In many respects, the issues of the Cultural Revolution are the issues we shall examine later in this book. Suffice it to say that the Cultural Revolution had no formal end, and the issues no clear resolution. This was dramatically revealed by the falling out between Mao and his chief supporter, Defense Minister Lin Piao, in 1971, and the ensuing campaigns against Lin and people identified with him. Several years later the movement was broadened in scope and complexity, as the nation became caught up on the campaign "to criticize Lin Piao and Confucius." There is no simple explanation for these developments. In simultaneously criticizing Lin and Confucius, the Maoists were not pretending that there was substantial similarity between the policies of the two men,[43] nor were they identifying themselves with the policies of the Confucianists' rivals, the Legalists. The Legalists (the term is something of a misnomer)[44] were simply deemed to have been progressives *in their time* because they were thought to have defeated the slave social system, and would have fostered bourgeois society if they had not been defeated by the reactionary Confucianists. However little

[43] It was claimed that Lin Piao had admired some of Confucius's ideas (such as leadership by virtue) and that he echoed certain Confucian slogans ("Restore the rites"). However, such specific links between Lin and Confucius are unconvincing, and were often deemphasized.

[44] See chap. 3.

this may have reflected actual developments in China during the third century B.C.,[45] the basic point that the Legalists were thwarted revolutionaries is valid. As for Lin Piao, while there is nothing in his philosophy to make him as counterrevolutionary as the Confucianists, his attempt to overthrow the personification of the revolution made him *ipso facto* counterrevolutionary.

Lin Piao's allegedly having said that Mao was as despotic as the Legalist emperor Ch'in Shih Huang-ti made it convenient for Maoists to praise legalism. Nevertheless, many of the long historical treatises published referred to Lin either indirectly or not at all. His relevance to abstract evil, ancient or modern, was left for readers to discern with the aid of the well-briefed cadres. There is probably a variety of reasons why Lin figured somewhat superficially in the anti-Confucian campaign. It was easier to attack Confucius, who no longer had a following in China, than to attack Lin, who not only had a following, but whom Mao had for a decade embraced as the heir-apparent. Furthermore, Lin Piao himself was not the real problem, for he was dead. There were, however, many disloyal or philosophically wayward people who could best be attacked by being linked to Lin. Thus, *regional army leaders* who sought power at the expense of the center could be condemned in the name of Lin and/or Confucius, for Lin had led the armed services, and the Confucianists had overturned the Legalist unifiers and sought to fragment China. Because the problem was much larger than Lin, "*only* by criticizing the doctrine of Confucius" could Lin's "ultrarightist" and "counterrevolutionary" line be refuted.[46]

But to think of the campaign as simply a debate concerned with political policies and philosophies would be to overlook other noteworthy aspects. For example, history was not solely a vehicle for discussing the present. Many essays (particularly the earlier ones) were genuinely concerned with matters of historical interpretation.[47] As

---

[45] By non-Communist reckoning, China never had a slave-based society (although some slavery was practiced both before and after the Ch'in period). The feudal system, which had some similarity with that of medieval Europe, was declining around the time of Confucius, and was replaced by the scholar-gentry system. This system the Communists call "feudal," meaning that it was based on land rental. There was no bourgeoisie nor any movement to establish capitalism until the nineteenth century.

[46] *JMJP*, February 2, 1974, *PR*, February 8, 1974, p. 5. Emphasis added.

[47] For example, Kuo Mo-jo, "*Chung-kuo ku-tai shih de fen-ch'i wen-t'i*" [The periodization of ancient Chinese history], *HC*, 1972, no. 7, pp. 56–62; and Yang Jung-kuo, "*Ch'un-ch'iu Chan-kuo shih-ch'i ssu-siang . . .*" [Spring-and-Autumn/Warring States thought . . .], *HC*, 1972, no. 12, pp. 45–54.

politicians seized upon the academic questions and turned them to their own purposes, however, actual historical conditions—both ancient and recent—received rather cavalier treatment. At first, the main interest was in attacking not Lin-types but *conservatives* who had survived the Cultural Revolution or had since been rehabilitated. Even Premier Chou En-lai was an implicit target.[48] These people might have fought back within the philosophical framework of the radicals, but they chose to do otherwise. They turned the argument around and declared that the followers of *Lin* were the "Confucianists" for challenging the new ("Legalist") centralized authority, and promoting personalized leadership ("innate genius"). The reasoning may seem tortuous, and have little to do with the real Lin Piao or the real Confucius, but it was in this form that the campaign was consummated.[49]

The victory of the civilian and moderate elements was signaled on January 1, 1974, with the assignment of new army commanders to most of the military regions. At about the same time, Teng Hsiao-p'ing, who had been the number-two target during the Cultural Revolution, was restored to prominence and became one of China's top leaders. A civilian, in 1975 he received the additional post of chief of staff of the armed services. When the National People's Congress was convened for the first time in a decade, the moderates were very much in control. The Congress lasted only five days—from January 13 to 17, 1975. It was dominated by Chou En-lai, to some a symbol of conservatism, though more accurately seen as a man who could weld a consensus among a fairly broad spectrum. But if the new arrangements and policies had Mao Tse-tung's blessing, there was little indication of the fact. Mao stayed away from the congress for unexplained reasons, one of which may have been a lack of enthusiasm for this thermidor of the Cultural Revolution. The new national constitution (see appendix) which the congress adopted marked a return to established forms and regularized procedures. To what extent the spirit of law and human rights it outlined would be honored in practice only time would tell,

[48] See, for example, "Emperor Ch'in Shih Huang-ti Is a Statesman Dealing a Telling Blow to Slaveowners Who Want to Achieve Restoration," *JMJP*, October 31, 1973, FBIS 1, November 14, 1973, pp. B-3–B-9.

[49] On the anti-Confucian campaign, see Peter R. Moody, Jr., "The New Anti-Confucian Campaign in China: The First Round," *AS*, April 1974, pp. 307–24; Parris Chang, "The Anti-Lin Piao and Confucius Campaign: Its Meaning and Purposes," *AS*, October 1974, pp. 871–86; and John Bryan Starr, "China in 1974: 'Weeding Through the Old to Bring Forth the New,'" *AS*, January 1975, pp. 1–19.

but the release from prison of several hundred former Nationalists in March 1975 indicated confidence regarding both dissension at home and the Formosa problem.[50]

Thus, with the return to normal political procedures marked by the holding of a National People's Congress, and the promulgation of the new constitution, a pattern of national unity emerged. Perhaps in this sense China's leaders are justified in thinking of the mid-1970s as characterized by a Legalist revival.

---

[50] On the prisoner release, see *PR*, March 21, 1975, pp. 11 f.; and *PR*, March 28, 1975, pp. 3 f.

TWO

Informal Political Culture

> Can it be that "national character"
>   is so difficult to change?
> If so, we can more or less guess
>   what our fate will be.
> As is so often said,
>   "It will be the same old story."
>
> LU HSÜN (1925)[1]

> In the past you were concerned with only industry, agriculture, and communications; you have never thought of cultural revolution.... Now we must turn our thoughts to this.
>
> MAO TSE-TUNG (1966)[2]

THE TERM *political culture* refers to the attitudes held by members of a polity which influence their political behavior and which color

---

Much work remains to be done on the subject of popular political culture in China. For an overview of the problem, see Lewis, "Study," which, however, is less concerned with political culture than the title would indicate. Much can be learned about traditional political culture from C. K. Yang, Martin Yang, and the various works of Francis L. K. Hsu. Two controversial studies on political culture under the Communists are Solomon, Mao's Revolution, and Pye, Spirit. Useful for comparative purposes are Lucian W. Pye and Sidney Verba, Political Culture and Political Development (Princeton: Princeton University Press, 1965); Gabriel A. Almond and Sidney Verba, The Civic Culture (Boston: Little, Brown, 1963); and Stuart Fagon, The Transformation of the Political Culture of Cuba (Stanford: Stanford University Press, 1969).

On elite political culture, see SCT and Schram, Political, for general primary material; and for secondary material, see the following: Creel; Holubnychy; Hsiung, Ideology; Levenson; Schurmann; Starr; Tan; and Weber.

[1] "Sudden Notions," *Selected Works of Lu Hsun* (Peking: Foreign Languages Press, 1957), 2:108.

[2] Speech at a Central Committee Work Conference, October 25, 1966, in Mao, *Selections*, p. 15. Translation revised; emphasis added.

the overall nature of a political system. Although political culture, like all culture, is rarely static, it is deeply embedded in people's personalities, and therefore is not generally amenable to abrupt change. This poses a problem for revolutionaries, for it means that the assumption of political power merely marks the beginning of their work. But the fact that political cultures are never ephemeral eases the task of the political scientist somewhat. In studying a revolutionary society, an understanding of cultural inertia provides us with the basis for appreciating many of the problems faced by the new leadership. Unfortunately, culture of any sort is elusive, and political culture of former times or inaccessible places may be difficult to set forth and analyze. Political structures of such polities may be described, social organization can be outlined, historical events may be chronicled—but when it comes to understanding what people have actually thought, we may have only self-conscious assertions of those who were literate and in control of the recording media.

We do well, therefore, to distinguish at the outset between two levels of political culture. At one level there are the normative values, or standards which are set forth in some formal fashion, and adhered to at least (and probably primarily) by an elite or "upper class." This *elite political culture* in China will be the subject of our inquiry in the second half of this chapter. First, we shall examine another level of political culture, that of the people at large. In this enterprise we do not have the benefit (or distraction) of formal ideology, because the masses in China have not had such a political ideology of their own. Of course, there have been formal political values which have been set forth for the common people by others, but we must not assume a priori that these values were indeed important components of the popular political culture. It is the cultural reality which we seek to understand, not the impressions of the official culture's standard-bearers.

Popular Political Culture

In the case of China, although there is a vast literature relevant to the traditional political culture, much of it is indeed self-conscious and elite-oriented. It was written by the literati, a small minority who until this century almost unanimously subscribed to one school of thought. This school was considered so consummatory by its adherents that it did not even have a name. For convenience in English, we call this school of thought *Confucianism*, after the name of the compiler of the earliest body of literature comprising the classics.[3] Can we trust these men when they describe Chinese culture in general, or do they simply idealize what they approve and distort or ignore that which they find less palatable? In particular, what about their views of the masses, from whom they were so far removed socially, and who could not write for themselves? To what extent did *mass* political culture actually reflect that of the elite?

Our problems, then, are legion. Few modern scholars have conducted interviews among the common people, and Confucian scholars, however dedicated, were not anthropologists. They often strove to be objective observers and historians, but they were human and usually wrote for a purpose—perhaps to glorify their times, perhaps to honor the past and by implication indicate their present alienation. From such literature we may be able to infer much about *their* political culture, but they spoke less adequately for others. By "others" we mean the overwhelming majority of the population, not scholars but farmers, not Confucianists but Buddhists, Taoists, and folk religionists. About these people we can frame more questions than we can answer. Merely asking the questions may serve useful purposes, however. For one thing, doing so may stimulate further research. But the questions can serve a still more immediate purpose—that of alerting us to the problems that China's present leaders face as they attempt to bring about cultural transformation. Indeed, the fact that Chinese political culture was not fully understood underlay many of the difficulties which the Communists faced after their assumption of power. Naively, perhaps, they moved directly to questions of economic modernization, erecting political structures, and glossing everyone's vocabularly with Marxist jargon. Apparently, popular political and social behavior did not keep pace with these manifest aspects of the revolution. By the 1960s this problem began to disturb Communist party Chairman Mao Tse-tung deeply (as indicated by the second quotation at the beginning of the chapter), and he undertook to foster a new movement, called—not insignificantly—a *cultural* revolution.

[3] There are usually considered to be five classics in which Confucius had some hand: *Shih Ching* (Book of Songs), *Shu Ching* (Classic of Documents, or Book of History), *I Ching* (Book of Changes), *Ch'un Ch'iu* (Annals, or Spring and Autumn), and *Li Chi* (Record of Rites). The last contains, inter alia, the *Ta Hsüeh* (Great Learning) and the *Chung Yung* (Doctrine of the Mean), both of which are also parts of the Four Books. Completing the Four Books are *The Analects* (*Lun yü*) and *Mencius,* the latter based upon the teachings of Confucius's disciple of the same name. Of all of these, only the *Lun yü* is clearly comprised largely of the words of Confucius, and even it has undergone heavy editing. See also Bibliography, under Confucius.

TWO : *Informal Political Culture*

The first observation to be made about traditional Chinese popular culture is that it was *not* particularly *political*. The concerns of villagers were largely social and economic—maintaining family and clan ties, and sustaining life through agriculture. Government was distant and largely irrelevant to daily concerns. Politics, such as there was, generally was small in scale. Disputes among individuals were settled informally; resort to adjudication was rare. Local public works were performed by social groups, probably the clans, rather than by governmental authority. Popular philosophy was religious or mystical, not political. It often did have an indirect relevance to political and social issues, such as compensating for the shortcomings of Confucianism. Buddhism, for example, was egalitarian—it taught that salvation was available to all, though not in this world. Thus, it served as something of an anodyne for those who could not (or, in some cases would not) participate in the inequitable and perhaps corrupt bureaucratic order. But such approaches make little positive contribution to politics; neither do they help the religionist to distinguish between politics and other areas of concern. It is only when one speaks of the scholar-elite that distinctions between political and nonpolitical culture can be made. For the masses, even purely analytical distinctions along these lines are not very meaningful.

The most notable feature of pre-Communist Chinese society was familism. The *ideal* family was large—multigenerational—and linked to collateral branches through the clan system. Economic considerations, however, limited the size of the *typical* family to about five.[4] The family was the essential economic unit, but the clan (all the families in a village with a surname in common) also had some economic (e.g., communications) and socialization (education) functions. As a result, the clan was quasi-political, and was often about as close to politics as was within the experience of the ordinary Chinese. Government, in the sense of duly-constituted representatives of the national polity, had little meaning for the average man or woman, except as recipient of their taxes. Conversely, the Chinese had little sense of public spiritedness or responsibility toward nonrelatives. Confucius, in discussing what course should be followed by the son of a thief, advised: "The son shields the father, the father shields the son; that is the right way."[5] One result of such familistic attitudes was that there

---

[4] C. K. Yang, *Family*, p. 7. On the Sung period, see Gernet, pp. 146 f.

Sociologists often refer to the type of family common in China as a "stem family." This is comprised of a household of three generations, but not more than one adult couple from any one generation.

[5] Confucius, *Lun yü*, 13:18.

were few moral limits beyond which nonrelatives could not be exploited. Another result was parochialism. Unless a villager happened to belong to a secret society,[6] his associations were limited largely to kinship and village circles. Travel was economically difficult and not culturally sustained. An adage had it that "pleasant are the thousand days at home, but difficult is even half a day spent on the road," and no one envied the man who was obliged to *"li hsiang pei ching"*—turn his back to the well and leave his community.[7]

The socialization process instilled in people certain cultural imperatives. One of these was the requisite of harmony in human affairs. A premium was placed upon conflict avoidance, and violence in particular was rarely legitimate.[8] There was little in the way of competitive athletics (endangering one's body would be an unfilial act), and so that outlet for aggressive impulses was not available. Whether or not this made the individual prone to repressed hatred[9] and gave rise to a "constant undertone of bickering and indirect warfare"[10] in interpersonal relations, as Lucian Pye maintains, it nonetheless did not provide for a psychocultural milieu in which fruitful competition took place. A premium was placed upon conventional, nonupsetting behavior, and any loss of composure was shameful. Obviously, this was hardly conducive either to the development of capitalism or to socialistic revolution. It was not that there was no inclination for conflict, but that so much energy was devoted to repressing conflict that it tended to come in great outbursts which were (and still are) difficult for leaders to control and channel.

Another notable feature of traditional Chinese popular culture was group orientation, as opposed to individualism. Even when one found oneself a member of a nonfamily grouping, a premium was placed upon conforming to group pressures and values. Of course, this is true to some extent in all societies, but the rewards and penalties for individuality vary. In China, responsibilities were assumed by groups, which brooked no challenge from within. Usually, the group was the family, within which work and resources were shared (as they still are). But there were other groups (neighborhood security groups,

---

[6] Secret societies were also an exception to other generalizations we shall make about traditional Chinese society. For example, a relatively egalitarian spirit prevailed within the societies. That they were secret, however, underscores the fact that they lacked legitimacy. Thus, they are a rule-proving exception.

[7] C. K. Yang, *Village*, p. 81.

[8] Children did receive beatings as punishments, but only before adolescence and in private. See Martin Yang, pp. 128 f.

[9] Pye, *Spirit*, p. 67.

[10] Ibid., p. 102.

TWO: *Informal Political Culture*

guilds, religious organizations, and so on), much the same in principle and spirit. Whether this primitive collectivism hindered further political development is perhaps disputable, but there is little doubt that it tended to encourage irresponsibility by making it difficult to assign responsibility. Naturally, the task of a magistrate was simplified if he could hold a group responsible for the misdeeds of an individual, but this system meant that much group effort went into preventing or concealing nonconformity.

Within the collectivity there was a hierarchical ordering, and individuals tended to be passive in the face of authority. Relatives were invariably addressed by titles indicating their relationship. Siblings and cousins, for example, were identified in terms of sex and age relative to one's own. There were over forty distinct kinship terms. Although all of this was rather complicated, presumably providing clear role definition and aiding self-identity, it was comforting to the individual. As one nineteenth-century scholar expressed it:

> Here every man feels that he is both son and father, among thousands and tens of thousands, and is aware of being held fast by the people around him and the dead below him and the people to come. Like a brick in a brick wall, he holds. And this immense sea of individuals has kept the form of a family, in an unbroken line from earliest days.[11]

Thus, the principle of familial hierarchical ordering was also applied in nonkinship situations. There was a tendency to be highly rank-conscious, and although official ranks were nonascriptive, superior–subordinate relationships had a diffuse character. With no background of participatory decision making in the family training-ground, it is not surprising that adults would be passive and obsequious.

Traditional Chinese society was not only authoritarian, it was *male-*authoritarian. Of course, males predominate in most traditional societies, and indeed, this anachronism can be observed in many otherwise developed societies. But, here again, China was special—even among Confucianism-oriented nations. Whereas Vietnam, for example, has a long tradition of heroines in its political history (from the Trung sisters in the first century A.D. to Nguyen Thi Binh), women in China are considered to have played a relatively unsavory role. We can attribute this only in part to the historian's bias.[12] Chinese men in general have

[11] Valéry. (Sentences rearranged; some words omitted.)
[12] See Lien-sheng Yang, "Female Rulers in Imperial China," *HJAS* 23 (1960–61): 47–61.

tended to assume that female ascendancy in the power structure was a national disaster, and while this may have been a self-fulfilling prophecy, it has three thousand years of fairly consistent historical basis.[13] The role of women in politics was a reflection of the role of women in society. Although the *oldest* women wielded considerable authority within households, most women were objects of exploitation. In childhood through middle age (beyond which few survived), there was nothing in the socialization of women that trained them for social assertion, and male treatment of women reinforced this sexist social system.[14] Only with the arrival of Christian missionaries in the nineteenth century did the idea of education of females gain a foothold in China.

In spite of the illiberal spirit of Chinese society, people found various ways for coping with the more disagreeable features of authoritarianism. With personal prestige directly related to proper subordination to legitimate authority, many may have *affected* compliance. The Chinese concern for "face saving" was more than simply a manifestation of the basic human need for respect. Indeed, Chinese make a distinction between the kind of prestige that accompanies success (*mien-tzu*), and the moral reputation that flows from the fulfillment of social obligations (*lien-tzu*); the latter was always more "important." When social obligations are given priority over institutional and political obligations, then the question of face (*lien-tzu*) assumes political relevance. Institutional efficiency could not help but be affected if, in the name of face, men engaged in evasion and ostensible compliance, yet these were considered perfectly appropriate means of dealing with awkward political situations. Indeed, even saving face for a colleague was more important than correcting his errors. The same sometimes went for outsiders, and what Westerners often assumed was duplicity on the part of Chinese was commonly discreet behavior designed to avoid embarrassing the clumsy barbarian.[15]

---

[13] Specifically, a woman (Pao Ssu) is blamed for the fall of the Western Chou state in 771 B.C. The Chou king had so much concern for her good humor that he lit the signal fires and summoned allied armies solely for her amusement. When the troops were really needed, the troops failed to respond. Later, there were a number of empresses and empresses dowager, whose ascendancy often coincided with general dynastic weakness for which historians, probably unjustly, have blamed them.

[14] For a fascinating primary account of the life of a woman in traditional China, see Ida Pruitt, *A Daughter of Han: The Autobiography of a Chinese Working Woman* (New Haven: Yale University Press, 1945).

[15] Hsien Chin Hu (Hsu Hsien-chin), "The Chinese Concepts of 'Face,'" *American Anthropologist*, January–March 1944, pp. 45–65.

TWO: *Informal Political Culture*

A related psychocultural feature is the tendency to show outward submission to the demands of authority, while inwardly at least harboring reservations, even sometimes quietly acting upon them. This was *not* disingenuous or hypocritical, but simply a means of acting out norm compliance formally when not able to substantively. Confucianism sanctioned ritualism for this purpose, but when more than ritual was needed there is evidence that Chinese, faced with the choice between candor and dissimulation, tended to elect the latter. One study, for example, suggests that Chinese find it less disturbing to utter assertions they in fact disagree with than do Americans.[16] The findings of another work (on intellectuals) were consistent with this, in that Westerners in China subject to thought reform after 1949 often underwent sharp but temporary conversion, whereas Chinese most commonly "adapted." The Chinese intellectuals were relatively unaffected by ideological appeals, but when unconvinced about the merit of the Communists' programs they made every effort to adjust to new situations and establish a place for themselves in the society.

> The adapter underwent his share of confusion and identity crisis, but not to the extreme degree of the obviously confused among Westerners; for he was not (except in rare cases) forced to make a sudden transition from one world to another. He often tried to dispel his doubts by behaving like a zealous convert.... In a historical sense, the adapter was following a long-established pattern of Chinese intellectuals: accepting the change in dynasty as part of the order of things, placing his talents at the disposal of the new rulers, and seeing in the reign both good and evil, but not enough good to win his absolute enthusiasm nor enough evil to provoke his unqualified opposition.[17]

Although aliens and natives are not strictly comparable, and intellectuals (about whom we shall have more to say later in the chapter) may be unrepresentative of China as a whole, these findings enhance our impressions about the general problem of credibility and directness. For while a certain amount of circumlocution and courtesy is universal and functional, it would seem that a requirement of modernity would be a reasonable degree of frankness on the part of all

---

[16] See Paul J. Hiniker, "Chinese Reactions to Forced Compliance: Dissonance Reduction or National Character," *The Journal of Social Psychology* 77 (1969): 157–96. Specifically, Hiniker found that his Hong Kong subjects were less apt to undergo dissonance reduction (to alter views to conform with known false assertions) than Americans.

[17] Robert Jay Lifton, *Thought Reform and the Psychology of Totalism: A Study of "Brainwashing" in China* (New York: Norton, 1961), p. 401.

elements of a polity. Certainly in an authoritarian system, nothing can be more debilitating than the subtle subversion of inward reservation and foot-dragging. While the effects of such behavior may be most conspicuous within bureaucracy, it is by no means peculiar to that institution. It is a general cultural trait, a fact which explains Mao Tse-tung's exasperation during his later years. "One who is outwardly compliant but inwardly unsubmissive, says one thing and means another, and speaks in honeyed words to people's faces but plays tricks behind their backs—this is an indication of doubledealing acts."[18] In calling for rational candor, Mao was demanding a fundamental change in China's political culture.

In these ways one *might* have coped with the problems attendant upon the Confucian sociocultural system without departing in any serious way from that system. But for the majority of the population, for whom the elements and the economic system made life extremely harsh, these dodges were often insufficient, and naturally solace was sought in other ways. Without necessarily subscribing to Karl Marx's designation of all religions as "opiates of the people," it must be said that Buddhism, in particular, taught people to accept present miseries in view of what might await them in the next life. In discouraging believers from rebelling against any oppressors or raising demands for reforms,[19] Buddhism, as well as Taoism, played a little-noticed role in sustaining the Confucian political order. This was largely a matter of providing innocuous escapes. Those who found the demands of society unbearable were persuaded to ignore rather than resist them. One does not attempt to alter society and government if one believes that all social and political obligations simply bind one to the painful wheel of life and death.

There is some evidence that governors took advantage of religion to promote docility. According to a commonly held view, as expressed by a seventeenth-century official:

> I have examined carefully into the methods of the ancient rulers. When the people are at peace, they are governed and live according to the proper rules of conduct (*li*), but when troubles arise, punishments

[18] Quoted in Hsiao Ting, "Be Open and Aboveboard, and Don't Intrigue and Conspire," *HC*, 1972, no. 3, FBIS I, March 29, 1972, p. B-3.

[19] On occasion, religions have served as vehicles for revolts, especially when the religions were newly introduced in China. This was true not only of Buddhism, but also of Taoism (Yellow Turbans, first century A.D.; Five Bushels Rice movement, third century A.D.), and Christianity (Taiping Rebellion). However, in general, religion was a benign influence.

TWO: *Informal Political Culture*

must be used. When these penalties are not sufficient to control the people, the sanctions of religion must be employed, for men are frightened by spiritual forces which they cannot see nor hear. We know that Buddha lived in ancient times, and we may employ his teaching, with that of Lao-tze, even though we do not use their names, to reinforce the doctrines of Confucius.... Although the doctrines of the wheels of life (Karma and salvation), of suffering and blessedness, were introduced to deceive the people, yet they were useful in frightening men, in awakening them to the necessity of right behavior, and in checking their sinful desires.[20]

Although this cynical attitude provides us with but a caricature of these great faiths, it enables us to understand why the decline of China's religions was a precondition of political modernization. Unlike the situation in Protestant countries, where religion and modernization were congenial and mutually supportive, in China religion was one of the supports of the old order.

Still, it would be a mistake to view the religious legacy as having entirely negative implications for modernization. In the first place, religion was occasionally associated with (unsuccessful) reform efforts or revolutionary movements.[21] More enduringly, the naturalist quality of popular religion, particularly Taoism and folk religion, may have helped the Chinese to avoid some of the less attractive features of modernization experienced in virtually all of the more developed countries. Although government has been involved in harnessing and controlling waterways for man's protection and benefit for thousands of years, and land has been converted from its natural condition to make it suitable for food crops, the Chinese view has generally been that nature was to be harmonized with, not struggled against. Just as the individual defined his identity in terms of his social environment, so was it necessary for society to maintain a proper relationship with the natural environment.

> Every man here knows that he is nothing apart from this composite earth. Think of the web of our race, and tell me, you [Westerners] who cut your roots and dry your flowers, how is it you still exist? Will it be for long? Our empire is woven of the living, the dead, and nature. It exists because it sets all things in order.[22]

---

[20] John K. Shryock, *The Temples of Anking and Their Cults* (Paris: n.p., 1931), pp. 132 f.
[21] See note 19.
[22] Valéry.

The assumption was that if there was to be any major adjustment between man and nature, man should undergo the adjustment. As the Taoist slogan had put it, "Do not let the artificial obliterate the natural."[23]

In practice, this meant that men evinced great concern for the physical and spiritual impact of their works.[24] "Physical" and "spiritual" are analytical distinctions which we may allow ourselves, although it was probably not one of which many Chinese were aware. Geomancy, in fact, was a synthesis of the two. Before a building was erected or a road laid, it was deemed essential to consult with a geomancer. He would give instructions concerning the *"feng-shui"*— literally "wind and water," but including an analysis of the will and wiles of the spirits. During the past century, these popular concerns have been obstacles to those who would build modern buildings, communications networks, power grids, and the like. Even today, spiritualism and naturalism cause some problem for China's leaders, who have labored hard to overcome the popular fatalistic attitude toward the elements and encourage the belief that it is possible to alter the natural balance in man's favor.[25] On the other hand, the reluctance of most Chinese to accept the essentially Western ideal that nature is to be confronted and overcome ("Subdue the earth" is our biblical mandate[26]) may have facilitated or even brought about the recent efforts to avoid the environmental deterioration and waste which countries elsewhere are experiencing.[27] At any rate, the popular Chinese attitude

---

[23] Herbert A. Giles, *Chuang Tzu: Taoist Philosopher and Chinese Mystic*, 2d rev. ed. (London: Allen and Unwin, 1926), p. 166.

[24] Forests, toward which the Chinese were rather ruthless, were an exception. See Tawney, especially p. 48.

[25] There is some evidence that the practice of consulting with geomancers has continued in recent years. See C. Chen, *Lien-chiang*, p. 49.

[26] Gen. 1:28.

[27] Some examples: Waste is to be avoided; residual materials are to be reused. "Concentrate on Production in Breadth and Depth," *HC*, 1970, no. 12, pp. 51–56, translated in FBIS I, December 10, 1970, pp. B-1–B-7. Transportation facilities are to be constructed with due regard for ecologically sound land use. *JMJP*, May 23, 1971, p. 4, FBIS I, June 16, 1971, p. B-3. There are to be intensive educational efforts to teach people about the ecological relationships between farming and fishing. *PR*, July 30, 1971, pp. 31 ff. See also "Industrial Development and Pollution Control," *China Reconstructs*, February 1973, pp. 2–5.

In 1972 a major campaign was launched to "cover the motherland with trees and turn the earth into a big park." A lengthy article on the subject appeared in the Party journal in March, and was reprinted in newspapers throughout the country. Hua Lin-mo, "Cover the Motherland with Trees," originally published in *HC*, 1972, no. 3, translated in FBIS I, March 9, 1972, pp. B-1–B-7.

toward nature has set China apart from much of the remainder of the world, and influenced its pattern of modern development.

Thus far, we have been speaking of popular culture and society in general terms, with little regard to the pressures for change which may have existed, and to the changes which have actually taken place. A broad overview of the historic development of China reveals that the assertion that China was essentially static and undeveloping does not stand the test of empirical examination,[28] and there were in fact periods of dynamic growth and development. Nevertheless, by the nineteenth century, China was far behind the Western world in terms of economic productivity, social mobility, and political sophistication. Did this relative backwardness create a situation conducive to change? The answer would seem to be that developmental differentials in themselves are insufficient to stimulate progress, and in fact are of little moment in the absence of widespread *awareness* of the lag in development. Aside from consciousness raising, however, there may be other features of a political culture which will encourage or constrict political development and change. Let us now examine China in historical perspective to determine the existence of any traditional popular habit of pressing for the altering of social and political institutions.

Agrarian revolts are not new in China, and several major dynasties (the Hans, T'ang, and Ming) were at least in part products of these. One can hardly say, however, that agrarian revolts provided the impetus for premodern social change in China, even though such change did occur. In the first place, the vast majority of agrarian revolts failed, especially those with radical overtones. There were the movements led by Sun En and Lu Hsün (398–417), Huang Chao and Wang Hsien-chih (874–884), and Li Tzu-ch'eng (1630s and 1640s), and certain other movements during the Sung, Yüan, and Ch'ing periods. The movements which succeeded were either coopted by upperclass elements (Eastern Han, T'ang), or they witnessed the transformation of their leadership into characteristic authoritarian and unegalitarian dynasties (Western Han, Ming).[29] Another factor which deters us from finding substantial revolutionary potential in traditional Chinese political culture is that most of the outstanding social rebellions

---

[28] E.g., the heading "China Never Changed," in Ch'u Chai and Winberg Chai, *The Changing Society of China* (New York: Mentor, 1962), p. 1.

[29] On this subject, see James P. Harrison, *The Communists and Chinese Peasant Rebellions: A Study in the Rewriting of History* (New York: Atheneum, 1969), especially the Appendix, "Sketches of Major Peasant Rebellions," pp. 277–304.

were at the same time revolts against foreign domination. Cases in point are various movements during the Northern Wei and Yüan periods, when China was largely dominated by Mongols,[30] and many revolutionary movements between 1850 and 1950 (the Taipings, Boxers, Republicans, Communists), which were in part reactions to China's domination by Manchus, Westerners, and Japanese.

This leads us to the question of why the Communists, who were the only successful social revolutionaries in two thousand years, did not suffer one of the various fates of their predecessors. Clearly it is insufficient to say that the presence of political corruption, economic stagnation, and foreign imperialism were militating in their favor, for this had been true of many past rebellions. Was it that the Communists were the first leaders with both the personal ability and a viable program, and were thus able to sustain a revolution? Or was Chinese political culture, which had long been susceptible to incipient social movements but which had never had the capacity to consummate them, slowly changing? When the Communist movement was first organized, it was by no means evident to Party leaders that China was ripe for agrarian revolution. One leader, Chang Kuo-t'ao, believed:

> The peasants take no interest in politics. This is common throughout the whole world, but is particularly true in China, for most of the Chinese peasants are smallholders. They are not interested in politics. All they care about is having a true Son of Heaven [emperor] to rule them, and a peaceful, bumper year.[31]

Thus, for a few years the Chinese Communists adhered to the Bolshevik model and largely ignored China's rural populace. But when the revolution failed to develop among the proletariat (or was put down by authorities), some Party leaders found themselves taking another look at the countryside. In 1927 one of them, Mao Tse-tung, visited his native Hunan province and investigated a spontaneous agrarian movement which had broken out there. He concluded that there was great revolutionary potential, and he was particularly interested in the apparent fact that associations which were springing up were dominated by the poorer segment of the rural population.

---

[30] Strictly speaking, the Northern Wei rulers were Toba—distant relatives of the Mongols.
[31] Written in 1922. From J. Ch'en, *Mao . . . Revolution* (1965). Chang had been the presiding officer at the first Communist party congress in 1921, after which he had headed the Communist trade union movement. Later, he left the Party.

TWO: *Informal Political Culture*

> This great mass of poor peasants, or altogether 70 percent of the rural population [Mao wrote], are the backbone of the peasant associations, the vanguard in the overthrow of the feudal forces, and the heroes who have performed the great revolutionary task which for long years was left undone. Without the poor peasant class (the riffraff as the gentry call them), it would have been impossible to bring about the peasant revolutionary situation in the countryside, or to overthrow the local tyrants and evil gentry and complete the democratic revolution. . . . Without the poor peasants there would be no revolution.[32]

But if China had always known rural poverty, the question remains as to why these people had decided to revolt at this time, and from a cultural point of view, why such revolts spread and ultimately succeeded. From our discussion of the history of agrarian revolts, we may infer that although revolution suffered under some cultural constraints, the culture was at least permissive in this regard. The geocultural picture was not uniform, and some of the regions in which the Communists enjoyed relative success had traditions of independence and defiance of central authority.[33] In areas lacking such traditions, other cultural developments were taking place which augured well for revolution. Its potential was becoming increasingly apparent in the more advanced or developed sectors and localities, and especially among the more disadvantaged segments of those areas. In the more remote and relatively backward regions, the revolutionary thrust was almost nonexistent. Thus, the cities contained the most revolutionary pressure, and it was only because the forces of counterrevolution were most effective there that the Communist party enjoyed such ephemeral success. Next came the towns, which, though more stable than the great cities, were less tradition-bound than the countryside.[34] It was the towns, where many youth were exposed to modern ideas and institutions, which spawned most of China's twentieth-century revolutionaries.[35] In villages, especially the remote and isolated ones, people tended to cling to traditional cultural patterns. The people of northern Kiangsi, for example, were found by Mao to be "cold and aloof."[36]

---

[32] Mao, SW, 1: 33.
[33] Hofheinz, "Ecology," p. 73. It is unclear whether these traditions are to be explained in ecological or geographical terms, but it is likely that both of these factors fed independent attitudes.
[34] Lewis, "Study," pp. 509 ff.
[35] Although Mao, for example, was a native of the village of Shaoshan, he attended primary school in the town of Hsianghsiang, and secondary school in the city of Changsha.
[36] Mao, *Hsüan chi*, p. 80; or SW, 1:97 (1928).

In view of the fact that the Communists' successes were in precisely the more backward and inaccessible areas, some writers have maintained that the revolution was dependent upon agitation by urban intellectuals,[37] while others credit the impact of the Japanese invasion in arousing nationalistic sentiment which the Communists exploited, deemphasizing their real revolutionary goals.[38] Still another view considers military control to have been decisive. Of course, all of these factors were significant. But where the Communists had undisputed control, under whatever circumstances, it would appear that they were able to persuade most of the population to accept at least moderately progressive programs.[39] Extreme backwardness, of course, made the job of effecting cultural change more difficult. (Where footbinding was still practiced in the 1930s, the Communists were slow in making inroads.[40]) But elsewhere, if they enjoyed reasonable security from the KMT and warlords, the Communists had considerable success in introducing modern attitudes among the population, who gradually developed new notions of authority, social change, citizenship, and nationhood. In a sense, this was all rather exogenous and lacked spontaneity, but it was nonetheless related to social and economic needs which were both real and felt, and the movement therefore gradually assumed a popular character.

The cultural change which occurred under Communist guidance before 1949, however, was limited by the moderateness of their program at the time and the limited means at their disposal. After the revolution greater strides would be made. As Mao told André Malraux, 1949 represented no consummation.

> Lenin was well aware that at this juncture the revolution is only just beginning. The forces and traditions he was referring to are not only the legacy of the bourgeoisie. They are also our fate. . . . The [Soviet] revisionists confuse cause and effect. . . . You remember Kosygin at the Twenty-third Congress: "Communism means the raising of living standards." Of course! And swimming is a way of putting on trunks! . . . It isn't simply a question of replacing the Tsar with Khrushchev,

---

[37] Tetsuya Kataoka, "Communist Power in a War of National Liberation: The Case of China," *World Politics,* April 1972, p. 426.

[38] Johnson, *Nationalism.*

[39] On the Kiangsi period, see Kim, "Mass Mobilization." For the later period, see Selden, *Yenan.*

nounced in the case of the Kuomintang, which had also been a revolutionary party at one time.

[40] Hofheinz, "Ecology," p. 68. This negative correlation was even more pro-

one bourgeois with another, even if he is called Communist. It's the same thing with women. Of course it was necessary to give them legal equality to begin with! But from there on, everything still remains to be done. The thought, culture, and customs which brought China to where we found her must disappear, and the thought, customs, and culture of proletarian China, which does not yet exist, must emerge. Among the masses, the [modern] Chinese woman does not exist either, but she is beginning to want to exist. To liberate women, moreover, is not to manufacture washing machines—and to liberate their husbands is not to manufacture bicycles or to build the Moscow subway.[41]

The question of who really were the "revisionists" may be subject to debate, inasmuch as Marx, believing that attitudes were a function of economic relations, did not subscribe to the idea of the primacy of culture. But if it is difficult to find in Marx any sanction for the glorification of rural poverty and reliance on propaganda and thought reform, it is just as difficult to use Marx to justify the Soviet emphasis on productivity and elitism as the way of the future. Instead of asking what a true Marxist is, we would more profitably seek to understand the various aspects of revolution and the relative emphasis given each in the various revolutionary models. As a kind of shorthand, we might identify these as the Marxist quadrant (emphasis upon productive relations and class struggle), the Leninist quadrant (organization and coercion), the modernist quadrant (revisionism, or economic development), and the Maoist quadrant (cultural change). While revolutions are comprised of all four, approaches and priorities are defined in terms of the quadrant to which one attaches primacy. Each quadrant has had its champions in China. The story of China's political development in recent years is the story of the contending of these revolutionary models.[42]

Elite Political Culture

We have devoted half of this chapter to mass political culture because of the obvious need to examine the overwhelming majority of China's population in this respect. We discovered that the Chinese populace has been, until recently, fairly passive politically, a posture culturally encouraged. Nevertheless, we confirmed that ordinary Chi-

---

[41] Malraux, pp. 464 f. Translation revised. (The sixth from the last word was *but* instead of *or*. I have assumed that this was an error.)
[42] We shall discuss the Maoist quadrant further in subsequent chapters.

nese, like everyone else in the world, did have a culture, that it was not altogether unrelated to politics, and that it was in many respects independent of any "higher," or elite culture.[43]

When people speak of traditional Chinese culture, however, they are usually referring to the culture of the political elite, or orthodox political attitudes. In the past, whereas the important relationships in the life of the commoner had a biological basis, members of the elite enjoyed relationships with a variety of bases, including cultural and institutional ones. This elite, the scholar-gentry class, gained entry into the prestigious government bureaucracy by mastering the Confucian classics and demonstrating their accomplishment in examinations.[44] Although some of the "higher culture" was absorbed by the population at large, it did not politicize them as it did the elite. A comparable situation has prevailed until recent years. Indeed, during the imperial, republican, and *early* Communist periods, Chinese political culture was largely the political culture of the respective elites.

As with any polity, a major element of the political cultures has been some blend of ideology and myth system. These two terms require some comment. The term *myth*, which has many legitimate applications, is used here in a restricted sense. Whereas in popular parlance a myth is a false belief, and among social scientists the term has sometimes been used to comprise almost *any* belief,[45] here we shall mean by myth a belief which, though vague in its social significance, tends to support anachronistic or otherwise irrelevant values. Most commonly, such myths bind the holder to the past, although we may consider utopian beliefs as similar in function and often similar in content. Myths are not necessarily untrue or degrading, but they tend to preclude consideration of new social arrangements, political behavior, authoritative institutions, or even a strictly pragmatic view of the present. The holder tends to generalize from the alleged past (or conceived future) without distinguishing the present-relevant from the anachronism. Often the past, being sacred, *is* the present, or at least all

---

[43] Here we depart from the view that mass belief systems are necessarily dependent upon elite belief systems. On this question, see Giovanni Sartori, "Politics, Ideology, and Belief Systems," *APSR*, June 1969, p. 407.

[44] To avoid confusion, I am simplifying social history somewhat. Actually, the social status of the Confucian literati was not uniform throughout history (it was rather low during the Six Dynasties and Yüan periods), and bureaucracy was sometimes eclipsed by feudalism. Although not widely available, Riggs's article on this subject is excellent.

[45] R. M. MacIver, *The Web of Government* (New York: Free Press, 1965), p. 4.

that is legitimate in the present; the utopia, being inevitable, is likewise reflected in what is present and legitimate. If one's world view is comprised solely of myths, then one is a romanticist. He is not concerned with verifiable truths; in solving practical problems he will eschew novel approaches. Past-oriented myths (with which we are primarily concerned here), for example, may lead the believer to accept ascriptive relationships as ultimate, for there is little in the past to sanction nonascriptive relationships.

Ideology, as we shall use the term, is to be distinguished from myth on several grounds. Pure ideology (with no mythical component) is nonaffective. It conveys a sense of history which is organic, present-oriented, and places current history in a broad conceptual framework. Because it is present-oriented, it joins knowledge and value—as one writer has said, it "links the cognitive and evaluative perception of one's social condition . . . to a program of collective action for the maintenance, alteration, or transformation of society."[46] We shall, later in this chapter, examine the precise role which ideology has played in the Chinese context. For now we simply note in passing that except in undeveloped polities, ideology plays a much more important role in the political system than myth. It has greater capacity to motivate and constrain *political* behavior, and is a potent integrative force. Ideology not only affects perceptions, it encourages allegiance to the political system and contributions toward common goals (which may be either progressive or conservative).

There are at least two general means by which ideology achieves this. First, ideology is internalized through the socialization process, so that it becomes part of the matrix of attitudes and motivations underlying standard behavior. Second, it legitimizes certain forms of behavior and delegitimizes others. People who adhere to accepted norms thus gain security; those who depart from the norms do so at some risk.[47] (In this respect, ideology is not fundamentally different from myth, though being more rational it is more reliable.[48]) Of course, people often elect to take that risk. Doubtless many leaders in traditional China failed to heed the ideology of the *Tao Te Ching*, which mandated that they give greater concern to the welfare of the people than to their own physical well-being[49] and bear personally the mis-

[46] Mullins, p. 501.
[47] We shall discuss leadership and legitimitization more extensively in chap. 6.
[48] In American political culture one can think of many examples of myths that have affected the security of individuals, such as witchcraft in colonial times, and the more recent myths about communism.
[49] Waley, p. 157.

fortunes of the world.[50] Nevertheless, such ideas set standards for leaders, and he who failed to adhere to them risked losing public and/or (more vital) bureaucratic support.

Insofar as it had sociopolitical relevance, Chinese religion would be considered part of the myth system of the political culture. Buddhism and the common forms of Taoism, for example, were only minimally integrating. In establishing certain cultural norms, and, especially with their anti-conflict bias, they fostered compatibility, but they did little to mobilize, or relate activities. Folk religion and Chinese Christianity, on the other hand, were actually disintegrative. The former fed parochialism and hindered communications.[51] Christianity had been an integrating force in the West, but the Protestant ethic and the social gospel failed to follow it into Chinese culture, and Christianity was divisive there.

Between myth and ideology there is a marginal zone where neither label seems quite adequate. Nationalism, for example, has many of the characteristics of myth, often being backward-looking (a nation is largely defined in terms of the past), ascriptive (based upon ethnicity), and basically affective. It unites a people in the face of an alien foe, but when that factor no longer exists, nationalism does little to solve manifest problems or even direct people's attention to them.[52] Thus, nationalism has been credited with making it possible for the Communists to unite China under their control in the 1940s,[53] but from that point on it was only occasionally useful in maintaining national integration. Indeed, it has in some ways been a profoundly disintegrating force in the People's Republic, because many who are not Han (ethnic Chinese), such as Uigurs and Tibetans, like to think of *themselves* as nations and do not desire integration with Hans. On balance, however, nationalism must be credited with facilitating cohesion, if not throughout China's hinterland, then at least among the elite.[54]

Thus, the distinction we have made between myth and ideology is largely an analytical device, and should not predispose us to expect to

[50] Ibid., p. 238.
[51] Belief in spirits aroused resistance to railroad building, erection of telecommunications lines, etc.
[52] For further discussion of this, see chap. 8.
[53] Johnson, *Nationalism*.
[54] According to Friedrich (p. 90), it is a mistake to speak of nationalism as an ideology. "This term is usually so vague as to have no specific institutional or behavioral content, until converted into a specific ideology." This is a more extreme view than is being taken here. Some mobilized, integrated behavior is fairly regularly associated with nationalism (resistance, for example). Nationalism can have a limited but real integrating effect, and to the extent that it does it should qualify as ideology.

find polities where people adhere exclusively to mythologies or are complete ideologues. China (and perhaps all political cultures) has known a blend of the two. One measure of political development is the extent to which ideology predominates, or is subordinated to myth. The reason for this is that ideology performs certain vital political functions which, if not performed, condemn the polity to backwardness. In order to illustrate these functions, and in order also to help us locate China historically on the myth-ideology continuum, let us undertake a brief overview of the development of the political culture of China's politically significant classes.

During most of China's antiquity (Shang and Chou periods) the political culture which is recorded is classically mythical. Rulers were deemed legitimate by virtue of their ancestry, the men-cum-god dynastic founders. Humane or effective rule was not an end in itself but rather signified proper emulation of ancestral rulers. Indeed, animal and even human sacrifices were made to placate spirits of deceased royalty. There were, of course, examples among the legendary rulers to suggest nonascription and progressive government.[55] But from what we are able to determine about the actual operation of government, we gain a picture of passiveness and ascription,[56] and must conclude that leaders were more concerned with placating the spirits than in addressing themselves systematically to the problems of society. Responsibilities were basically other-worldly rather than public. There was a supreme deity (sometimes called *T'ien*), and unlike the God of the Judeo-Christian tradition, the people did not relate or appeal to him directly. (*T'ien* will be discussed further in chap. 4.) Government, if we may use the term, served as an intermediary, and was more ceremonial than political. Kings claimed mystical power (*te*) and were as much high priests as governors.

In the latter part of the Chou period, however, political culture underwent profound changes. This is strikingly reflected in semantic evolution. The term *t'ien*, which had meant "god," became "heaven," and at the hands of Mencius (c. 372–289 B.C.) came to be used even more figuratively. In reinterpreting some of the ancient myths, Mencius fully secularized the doctrine of the mandate of heaven, as is revealed in this dialogue with his disciple concerning two legendary rulers:

[55] Yü, for example, was credited with regulating the rivers. ("But for Yü," asks the *Tso chuan*, "would we not all be fishes?")

[56] Political power was inherited by sons after the Shang period, when brothers had had priority over sons.

Wan Chang asked, "Is it true that Yao gave the empire [literally, "all under heaven"] to Shun?"

Mencius replied, "No. An emperor [literally, "son of heaven"] cannot give the empire to another man."

"Well, since Shun did acquire the empire, who gave it to him?"

"Heaven gave it to him."

"Did heaven explicitly order the transfer?"

"Heaven does not speak. Its will is revealed in the conduct and affairs [of men]. ... Yao had Shun preside over the sacrifices, and heaven accepted him. Then he had Shun assume control and administer the government. There was then peace among the hundred clans; the people accepted him. ... 'Heaven sees as our people see. Heaven hears as our people hear.' "[57]

Thus, "heaven" now was essentially a figure of speech, and the doctrine of the mandate of heaven had become ideological, not mythical. Similarly, the term *te*, which we noted above had implied magic, came to mean "virtue," an increasingly important requisite of any member of the ruling class. Thus, Confucianism came to possess many of the attributes of ideology.

At the same time, Confucian thought and mores were never able to completely cast off their mythical component, and in some respects Confucianism remained a myth system par excellence. Confucius had taught that men should return to a golden age. His disciples took a cyclical view of history; as dynasties rose and fell, every moment corresponded to a moment in the past. Few Confucianists now contemplated systemic changes in the social order. This had not always been true; in the second century B.C. Confucianism had had a fresh, dynamic quality, and was selected as the basis for a new social order because of the attractiveness of the ideas themselves, not simply because the Master had uttered them. After a time, however, Confucianism became encrusted with myth. History, which for Confucius and his disciples had been a tool for understanding the present, was warped and idealized; the past became an obsession. Scholars labored to "systemize" traditional beliefs and rites to make them fit their mold, and the present ethos and order were justified as reflections of the alleged past. If that past sometimes seemed to become ossified by virtue of the elaborate rituals, Confucius himself bore some responsibility. He had, for example, rejected his disciple's suggestion that a

---

[57] *Mencius*, 5:5. Mencius attributes the last two sentences to the "T'ai shih," part of the *Shu ching*.

particular sacrificial rite be eliminated, saying, "You love the lamb, but I love the rite."[58] Less often remembered was Confucius's exasperation over mindless exercises. ("Rites, rites! Do they mean no more than jades and silks?"[59])

Myths are by no means limited to traditional societies, and may indeed be a necessary feature of any polity. Anyone who undertakes a brief examination of his own political culture will realize that myths abound there.[60] So it is with China today—the Long March, the cave days at Yenan, the Liberation in 1949, the villains purged, Mao's swim in 1966 (the list is almost endless)—all comprise part of the political culture and play some role in effecting cultural homogeneity, but are clearly myths rather than ideology. By themselves they would be insufficient to achieve a significant degree of political integration, but they do have an impact, primarily because they are coordinated with and supportive of the purely ideological aspects of the political culture. Indeed, without the illustrative myths, ideology would be so insipid that it would have little appeal to those of limited education and experience in abstract thought.

But while myths have always been operative in Chinese political culture at all levels of society, for the past two thousand years they have been, as we have seen, more dominant (over ideology) in mass culture than in elite culture. Confucianism was the closest thing traditional China had to an ideology, but Confucianism was the political culture of the elite. After the 1949 revolution, ideology (communism) was still considerably elite-oriented, but less exclusively so than Confucianism had been. Mao Tse-tung still conceived of political culture as playing a special role for the elite (Party), but he thought of *their* political culture in strictly ideological (rather than mythical) terms— embracing a present-oriented study of history, comprised of ideas which were relevant to practice. "No political party," he said, "can possibly lead a great revolutionary movement to victory unless it possesses revolutionary theory and a knowledge of history and has a profound grasp of the practical movement."[61] And it is significant that Mao repeatedly warned against the euhemerizing of Marxism.

> One must respect the classics, but one must not become superstitious about them. Marxism itself was produced by creativity, not imitation.

[58] Confucius, *Lun yü*, 3:17.
[59] Ibid., 17:11.
[60] See note 48.
[61] Shih Chün, p. 16.

...Superstition restrains our mind and prevents us from considering problems freely. When one studies Marxism, it is very dangerous to do it unaudaciously.[62]

As the years passed, Mao became more interested in bridging the gap between the myth-based political culture of the less sophisticated, and the ivory-tower intellectuals in leadership positions and among non-Communist intellectuals.

We are now ready to ask more specifically what roles ideologies have played in Chinese politics. It is possible to discern eight distinct functions: (1) Ideology serves as the basis for social and political organization. (2) It generates a body of ideas and literature which provide the content of political socialization. (3) It offers a method of political analysis. (4) Ideology influences the conduct of citizens and officials, placing them under obligations and limiting their behavior. (5) It provides social cohesion by framing priorities and hopes. (6) Ideology provides the basis of other norms, such as law, in terms of content and function. (7) Its terms and concepts serve as vehicles for communication. Finally, (8) ideology rationalizes and legitimizes behavior and institutions.

Both Confucianism and communism have sanctioned monolithic political *organization*, although Confucianism provided for the autonomy of a rival social organization—the family. Confucianists were usually also tolerant of other thought systems and life-styles, but would not brook strong autonomous organizations, such as churches, which might pose an institutional challenge. Confucianism held that politics should be open to any man, regardless of race or background, provided that he met certain stringent cultural tests. Never questioned (by political philosophers, at least) was Confucius's insistence upon meritocracy. Ability, however, was morally determined; it was not supposed to be measured in terms of practical skills or even statecraft. In discussing the political elite, Confucius had said that men would not do wrong if well read, and that their inner virtue would be reflected by their propriety and practice of rites.[63] Within political organization, men related to each other according to the familial analogue. Although the requirement of loyalty to superiors sometimes resulted in personal

---

[62] Speech at Chengtu, March 22, 1958, in Mao, *Selections*, pp. 46 f. Translation revised.
[63] E.g., Confucius, *Lun yü*, 12:15.

dilemmas of tragic proportions,[64] for Confucian bureaucracy it was the bedrock organizational principle.

Communism, and specifically Leninism, are much more explicit in providing ideological determinants for organization. The cardinal principles are proletarian dictatorship and democratic centralism. The first establishes the relationship between the Party and the public; the second provides for discussion (but no post-decision dissent) *within* the Party.[65] "Proletarian dictatorship" calls for the government to be controlled by a single class (to which extent it resembles the Confucian pattern).[66] Just what social elements comprise this "proletariat," and whether they actually rule, however, are problems which make it somewhat difficult to demonstrate the total subservience of organization to ideology; but the fact that a single party rules in the name of the class does suggest some relevance, especially in view of the fact that the ideology (like Confucianism) justifies the prohibition of rival political forces. Even such integral features of the polity as the governmental and other bureaucracies have effectively been deprived of autonomous power in the name of ideological norms. Government, like the mandarinate, is required to be a meritocracy, although of course new criteria apply. In Mao's words:

> The criterion the Communist party should apply in its cadres policy is whether or not a cadre is resolute in carrying out the Party line, keeps to Party discipline, has close ties with the masses, has the ability to find his bearings independently, and is active, hard-working, and unselfish. This is what "appointing people on their merit" means.[67]

Obviously, it is not only ideology which determines the nature of political organization. Sometimes, in fact, ideology can barely prevent the undermining of organizational principles by special interests or practical necessity—witness the tendency of governmental organs to divide along "red" (political) and "expert" (professional) lines. Furthermore, Chinese leaders have differed among themselves concerning the relationship of ideology to organization, and the role of

---

[64] E.g., see J. Liu, "Yüeh."

[65] The principle applies also to other organizations.

[66] Originally, the dictatorship (democratic) ostensibly represented all classes. However, gradually the term *proletariat* came to imply anyone who supported the Party (and the distinction between *proletarian* and *democratic* was lost).

[67] Quoted in Tang Sheng-ping, "Raise High Our Consciousness of Implanting the Cadre Policy," *JMJP*, May 19, 1972, translated in FBIS I, May 22, 1972, p. B-2. The statement was said to have been made in the early 1930s, but by being quoted was implicitly reaffirmed in 1972.

organization in society. During the 1950s Mao witnessed with chagrin the tendency of ideology to become subordinated to organization, a development for which he would one day hold responsible, among others, his second-in-command, Liu Shao-ch'i. In fact, however, Liu had long insisted upon the primacy of ideology over organization. In 1945, for example, he had criticized

> comrades who, because of their ideological and political weakness and ignorance, have stressed only the organizational aspect of Party building, instead of emphasizing the ideological and political aspects.... They have not used their brains and have been unable to raise organizational leadership to the level of ideological and political leadership. As a result, the Party's organizational work becomes divorced from its ideological and political leadership. This is blindness in Party building.[68]

These remarks illustrate the tendency for political organization to become narrowly based and self-serving. Although this may have come to constitute a greater evil in Mao's eyes than in Liu's, both men considered it basically undesirable, and both saw ideology as the corrective tool.

Ideology can be instrumental in organization largely because it has served as the basis of the participants' *socialization*. In long-established political cultures, most individuals' socialization is accomplished primarily through interaction with family and teachers, and is basically completed by the time of adulthood. Thus, even though Confucianists were generally lacking in missionary zeal, the few Chinese boys who received an education were thoroughly steeped in Confucian values and behavioral patterns at an early age. In revolutionary China, on the other hand, where the new leaders seek to reintegrate society on the basis of a new culture, they find it necessary to resocialize all age groups. The family is no longer considered an important agency for socialization,[69] which is rather accomplished at all ages and is the result of indoctrination as well as "practice"—experience in performing roles in a social system which has been patterned according to Communist principles. There is indeed considerable tension between these two concepts of socialization and knowledge acquisition—being

[68] "Report on the Revised Party Constitution" (June 1945), quoted in Liu Shao-ch'i, *Quotations*, pp. 29 f. Translation revised.
[69] In the heady days of 1958, Mao spoke of how the family was gradually losing its educational and economic functions and would eventually (in thousands of years) disappear. Speech at Chengtu, March 22, 1958, in Mao, *Selections*, p. 47.

T W O : *Informal Political Culture*

told versus learning from doing.[70] Mao, in his writing, always emphasized the role of practice,[71] although the amount of time individuals are required to devote to studying the modern classics[72] might suggest an underlying concern that what people learn from practice may be insufficient and sometimes incorrect. (We shall discuss political socialization further in chap. 5.)

As a person becomes socialized, he learns not only *what* to think, but *how* to think. If he has properly acquired an ideological outlook, then his method of analysis is quite different from that in a world dominated by myth. To begin with, ideology provides guides regarding cognitive approaches to be *avoided*. Confucius, for example, urged agnosticism upon his followers, and recommended against seeking explanations for natural and social phenomena in the realm of the supernatural. "Keeping the spirits at a distance is the better part of wisdom," he said. "One should concentrate on *human* affairs."[73] The classics[74] attempt to establish certain well-ordered criteria to serve as the basis for thought and investigation. The Chinese have always liked to set forth such criteria in numbered categories, as in the "eight points" of the *Great Learning*[75] (extend knowledge, investigate things, and so on). More elaborate, and well demonstrating the effort to integrate the social and natural worlds, are these remarks by an eleventh-century-B.C. prince on the need for man to harmonize with his environment and maintain nature's "constant norms":

> [The nine categories are:] (1) the five agents [discussed below]; (2) reverent attention to the five matters [appearance, speech, vision, hearing, and thought]; (3) earnest devotion to the eight measures of government [food, finance, religious sacrifices, public works, education, justice, diplomacy, and army]; (4) harmonious use of the five regulators [year, month, day, stars and zodiacal signs, and the calendar]; (5) the establishment and use of the royal standard; (6) the discerning use of the three virtues [correctness, mastery through strength, and

---

[70] This question concerning thought and action has long concerned Chinese philosophers. See Nivison, "Problem," especially pp. 119, 141.

[71] See especially "On Practice," in Mao, SW, 1:295–309.

[72] See, for example, Shen Mou-ssu's article in the official Party journal on the need of cadres to study political ideology.

[73] Confucius, *Lin yü*, 6:20. Cf. 11:11.

[74] On the Confucian classics, see note 3. Not all of the classics were written by Confucianists, and not all of the ideas discussed below should be assumed to be Confucian. For our purposes, it is not important to distinguish between what is truly Confucian and what has been added to the culture from non-Confucian sources.

[75] Confucius, et al., *Ta hsüeh*, passim. See note 3.

mastery through weakness]; (7) the intelligent use of the determinators of doubt; (8) the thoughtful use of the various varifications; and (9) the appreciative use of the five felicities [longevity, wealth, health, love of virtue, and a crowning death] and the awing use of the six extremities [premature death, illness, worry, poverty, evil, and weakness].

... The five agents [are] water, fire, wood, metal, and earth. [As to their nature:] Water is the power to soak and descend; fire, to blaze and ascend; wood, to be crooked and straight; metal, to be malleable; and earth, to take seeds and yield crops. That which soaks and descends produces saltiness; that which blazes and ascends produces bitterness; that which is crooked or straight produces sourness; that which is malleable produces acridity; that which takes seeds and yields crops produces sweetness.[76]

Surprisingly, all of this had much to do with the way the Chinese viewed history and politics. The "five agents" were not seen as elements, but as forces which dominate successive units of time. Thus, if a dynasty was characterized by wood, it would be overcome by a "fire" dynasty. Although such thinking is alien to modernists, it represents an attempt to reduce natural and social phenomena to certain basic principles in order to better understand them and cope with them.

One of the best-known intellectual tools of traditional Chinese was the *yin-yang* dichotomy. Here, as was the case with the five agents, was an attempt to comprehend and predict change. According to this concept, everything had its correlate. The metaphysical basis of the social order was most definitively set forth by the great political philosopher Tung Chung-shu (c. 179–c. 104 B.C.):

... If there is the upper, there must be the lower. If there is the left, there must be the right.... If there is cold, there must be heat. If there is day, there must be night. These are all correlates. The yin is the correlate of the yang, the wife of the husband, the subject of the sovereign. There is nothing that does not have a correlate, and in each correlation there is the yin and yang. Thus the relationships between sovereign and subject, father and son, and husband and wife, are all derived from the principles of the yin and yang. The sovereign is yang, the subject is yin; the father is yang, the son is yin; the husband is yang, the wife is yin.[77]

---

[76] Prince of Chi, quoted in the *Shu ching*, translated in De Bary, *SCT*, pp. 98 f.
[77] "Ch'un-ch'iu fan-lu," chap. 53, translated in Fung, *Short History*, pp. 196 f.

TWO : *Informal Political Culture*

All of this was intended to be instructive in terms of understanding social and political relationships. It also suggests something about the unfolding of history: dynasties would rise and fall according to the waxing and waning of yin and yang.

The yin-yang methodology bears certain superficial resemblances to the Marxist dialectic. Both attempt to create an intellectual universe in which phenomena are analyzed in terms of opposites, with history seen as a succession of crises brought about because of the irreconcilability of opposites within the existing milieu. Traditionally, an era was defined in terms of which agent was dominant; if wood (green) had been dominant, it would eventually find itself confronted by metal (white). There would be no stopping the ascendancy of the latter agent. *Today,* it is the primacy of the particular class which matters. In due course, the bourgeoisie (white) was destined to be confronted and overcome by the proletariat (red). But such parallels are somewhat contrived, and it is doubtful that these traditional ways of thinking have done more than make the Chinese subconsciously receptive to the dialectic. Actually, one is more struck by the novelty of the dialectic than by its similarity to yin-yang. Formulators of dialectical theory from Hegel to the present have considered it necessary to choose between idealism (the view that ideas and men's minds determine events) and materialism (economic primacy), a distinction with no relevance for yin-yang. Although with both systems of antitheses an attempt is made to state a systemic relationship between the material and the social, in the case of yin-yang the "material" is nature and the relationship is only stated allegorically, whereas with Marxism dialectical relationships are said to be strictly instrumental.[78]

How is the dialectic used as an analytical tool in China? In the first place, the dialectic as understood by Maoists[79] denies the existence of absolute truth, and thus spares the Chinese the fruitless quest for the perfect program or all-revealing philosophy. Furthermore, for Maoists the contradictions are seen as residing primarily *within* things rather than among them, which suggests that empirical analysis of the thing itself will provide the needed answers and solutions. In a major break from Chinese tradition, which labored under a pervasive fatalism, the emphasis now is on experimentation and problem resolution. Furthermore, whereas formerly the quest was always for harmony, for Mao the correct path now lay in activating contradictions, pressing on even to

[78] Yin-yang is not the only source of the Chinese dialectic. See Holubnychy, especially pp. 29 f.

[79] Lenin was of a different view, insisting upon the existence of absolute truth.

the brink of catastrophe, in order that the relative truth might be revealed. Thus, movements like the Great Leap Forward and the Great Proletarian Cultural Revolution are "correct" not because everything that happens during them is proper and all of their results are beneficial, but because they reveal the condition of society and the nature of the current contradictions, and thus make it possible for the revolution to advance to a new stage.

The concept of the dialectic itself has sometimes been a vehicle for political debate. Most notable has been the dispute between the theory of *conjunction* (*ho erh erh i*, literally "combining two into one"), and *dichotomization* (*i fen wei erh*, literally "one divided into two"). The conjunctive approach was expounded in the early 1960s by Yang Hsien-chen (head of the prestigious Higher Party School[80]). Yang maintained that the common aspects of contradictory elements should be emphasized, which seemed to suggest a politics of reconciliation. His slogan, "Render interests mutual; seek identity without sacrificing difference," implied that although the theory of contradictions remained valid, opposites were compatible.[81] In the mid-1960s this view was officially repudiated, and Yang was purged.[82] Even though the difference between conjunction and dichotomization would appear to be largely a matter of emphasis and style, the only byword since the Cultural Revolution has been *dichotomize*. In addition to emphasizing antagonisms, dichotomization (an analytical device attributed to Mao Tse-tung) calls for broad approaches to specific problems, always looking for the positive and the negative in a non a priori manner. For example, one should always examine one's personal conduct, and be openly critical of one's own shortcomings.

The dialectic is not the only analytical device employed, and one might also explore such ideas as class struggle, empiricism, experiential epistemology, and materialism. But our purpose here is not so much to catalog such tools as to demonstrate that such ideology-derived concepts do indeed function in this manner. As indicated two paragraphs above, they appear to do this in the case of policy decisions by the top leadership. Is this also true for the rank-and-file political actor? Until more on-the-scene interviewing is possible, we

[80] Formerly Marx-Lenin Institute.
[81] Donald Munro, "The Yang Hsien-chen Affair," *CQ*, April 1965, pp. 75–88; Adam Oliver, "Rectification of Mainland China Intellectuals, 1964–65," *AS*, October 1965, pp. 475–90.
[82] Yang's elimination from the political scene was gradual. It seems to have begun before the airing of the conjunction controversy, and was not complete until the time of the Cultural Revolution.

cannot answer this question with certainty, but there is documentary evidence to suggest that this is the case among many local political figures, and even some apparently ordinary citizens. Take, for example, the following statement by a Party secretary for a county in Hopei Province:

> In 1971 I failed to adopt effective measures to deal with the spring drought and popularize in time the good experience of the masses [i.e., certain villages] in overcoming it. Wheat output dropped that year. This failure made me ponder. I studied Lenin's teaching "cognition is the eternal and endless approximation of thought to the object," and Chairman Mao's teachings on dichotomization and on overcoming conceit and complacency. I came to understand that my ideas were a concrete expression of idealist apriorism as well as a big obstacle to carrying out Chairman Mao's revolutionary line. Since then, I have taken up battle against conceit and complacency as an important task in my ideological revolutionization. On three occasions I took the initiative in making self-criticism at study classes run by the county's Party and revolutionary committees.[83]

Such statements, of course, serve a number of purposes and should not automatically be taken at face value. Still, it would seem tenable to assume that with all the emphasis on Maoist methodology (much of which, while new to China, strikes us as common sense), some of the new ideologically inspired approaches and thought processes must be making their imprint.[84]

To say that ideology affects people's political thinking is not quite the same thing as saying that it influences *behavior*. Because of the impossibility of making first-hand observations, any judgments made in this all-important matter can only be at the level of hypothesis. There are, however, a number of reasons to suggest that there is a

[83] Ma Piao, "Use Dialectical Materialist Theory of Knowledge to Guide Revolutionary Practice," NCNA, June 21, 1972, FBIS I, June 22, 1972, p. B-3. Translation slightly revised.

[84] Sometimes the idea of the "Marxist analytical approach" can embrace quasi-ideological thinking, such as nationalism. "The proletariat should always take the Marxist analytical approach in dealing with any matter. Blind faith in anything that is foreign and in the slavish comprador philosophy are the shameful slavish features of the comprador class in semi-colonies. This blind faith must be thoroughly repudiated. Rejection of anything that is foreign, without study and analysis, is a metaphysical approach which also is entirely wrong. What Chairman Mao said about 'Making the old serve the new and making foreign things serve China' is the correct principle which we must uphold." Shih Chun, "Study Some World History," *HC*, 1972, no. 4, FBIS I, April 11, 1972, p. B-4.

causal link between ideology and behavior in both historic and contemporary China. In the first place, in neither culture was ideology thought of in isolation from practice. Rather, behavior has been thought of as a reflection or measure of one's outlook. In traditional China, *li* (propriety, rites) was defined as the "external exemplification of eternal principles."[85] Likewise, today one repeatedly hears that if one divorces theory from practice, one is not a good Maoist. Secondly, there is considerable concurrence to be noted between political philosophy and behavior. Certainly political recruitment, political organization, and the distribution of political power in both traditional and contemporary China have generally reflected the prevailing political philosophy. Confucius's major political principles were that government should be comprised of men of merit, and that government should serve the public welfare. The first requirement was met after a fashion by the civil service examination system. The second involves subjective judgments, but in comparison with other contemporary governments the Chinese leaders were notable in their provision of services which contributed to the general well-being of the people (waterworks, ever-normal granaries, and the like). The affinity between political behavior today and Maoist codes of conduct, while less than total, is nonetheless too apparent to require elaboration. For both periods, however, the question remains whether there is a *causal* relationship between ideology on the one hand and the institutions men decide to build and the way people behave on the other.

Although it is doubtful that any answer to such a question can be the subject of scientific proof, a look at some aspects of Chinese political behavior may provide illumination. It is well known, for example, that Confucianism placed a special premium upon loyalty to one's personal superiors. Loyalty, of course, was not unique to China, but there it was probably given unusual emphasis. It was supposed to be more personalized (rather than institutionally oriented) than in most other polities. Did this ideological imperative actually make Chinese behave differently than men and women at other places and times? There is at least impressionistic evidence that Chinese not only acted somewhat differently, but that there is no nonideological explanation for their behavior. It is true that men were often *forced* to be loyal (disloyalty was sometimes punishable by death[86]), but it is likely that cultural norms were more influential than legal sanctions, especially

---

[85] R. H. Matthews, *Chinese-English Dictionary*, rev. American ed. (Cambridge: Harvard University Press, 1956), p. 567, no. 3886–41.
[86] J. Liu, "Yüeh," p. 291.

in a country where rule of culture prevailed over that of law.[87] It was not out of political, legal, or economic motives that the Sung dynasty official Yüeh Fei, for example, went to extremes to demonstrate his loyalty to the emperor and inculcate a sense of imperial loyalty in his troops—indeed, in these respects his performance proved counterproductive. (When he antagonized the emperor's aides he was arrested and eventually executed, his troops refusing to rescue him because of their loyalty to the throne.[88]) Such compulsive adherence to ideologically derived norms was commonly dysfunctional in both individual and systemic terms.

Another requirement of Confucianism was equality of opportunity. The system's flagrant elitism was quite compatible with the prevailing social philosophy, so long as every man in the respectable classes had an equal chance to prove himself worthy to advance. As we have noted, lack of money deprived most men of the education that was a virtual prerequisite of elite membership. Nevertheless, it was possible for boys from nongentry—even (though rarely) from poor families— to attain degrees and official positions. Confucius himself had set the example by accepting students from all social backgrounds. The principle that "there is no discrimination at the gate of the sages" (*sheng men wu lei*) applied even to race relations, and non-Hans not only sometimes held official positions, but even frequently occupied the throne. (Such great dynasties as the Yüan and Ch'ing were non-Han, and the T'ang imperial family was of mixed blood.) Thus, while China has certainly not been without racial prejudice, at the level of political activity it has been minimal. This would appear to be at least partially attributable to the ideological requirements for interpersonal relationships.

Finally, a word is in order about the relationship between ideology and what was at once the mainstay and the Achilles heel of the traditional Chinese political system—bureaucratism. One could aspire to no higher calling than (in the words of a common slogan) "becoming an official, acting like a lord." With such emphasis upon participation in bureaucracy, it is not surprising that Confucius's insistence that government should serve the people rather than be simply a vehicle for enriching the officeholders would be honored with less than complete regularity. Although officialdom comprised more than sim-

[87] We shall qualify this statement in the following chapter.
[88] In addition to the Liu article, information on Yüeh (also spelled Yo) can be found in Herbert A. Giles, *A Chinese Biographical Dictionary* (London: Quartich, 1898), pp. 949 f.

ply a self-serving autobureaucracy, there was considerable behavior which, in modern parlance, we would have to label corrupt. While it would be difficult to *prove* that traditional Chinese government had more corruption than most governments, few will dispute the assertion. Officials were deliberately underpaid, on the assumption that they could supplement their official incomes with rewards from the people with whom they conducted affairs, and by shrinking the tax receipts before sending them on to the central authorities.[89] But such abuses, if they were considered such, did not interfere with the functioning of the political system as much as did bribes, misappropriations, and patronage.[90] Nepotism was also common as a means of entry into the bureaucracy, though less so as a basis for advancement within the bureaucracy.[91]

Did the prevailing ideology discourage or did it encourage such phenomena? It is true that selflessness was axiomatic, and genuine public service was expected of officials. However, there was no greater moral imperative than filial piety, which inevitably gave rise to divided loyalties. Furthermore, Confucius had been rather permissive in the area of official probity. "Minor transgressions are permissible," he had said, "as long as one is virtuous when it matters."[92] Had early Chinese philosophers possessed some of the puritanism of the more recent ones, one suspects that there might have been somewhat greater checks on political corruption.

Because of this background, China's contemporary leaders have been obliged not only to deal firmly with the more venal aspects of Chinese bureaucratic behavior, but to build safeguards against them into the fabric of their ideology. On one occasion Mao enumerated no less than twenty "manifestations of bureaucracy." One was the complaint that bureaucrats were not properly organizational.

> They employ personal friends; they engage in factionalism; they maintain feudal relationships; they form cliques to further their own private interests; they protect each other, and the individual stands above everything else. These petty officials harm the masses. This is sectarian bureaucracy.[93]

[89] Ch'ü, *Local*, chap. 2.
[90] Gernet, pp. 39, 68, 69 respectively.
[91] An exception during the Ch'ing period was the case of the Manchus (as distinguished from the Hans) whose chances for advancement within the government were enhanced by well-placed relatives. See Robert M. Marsh, "Bureaucratic Constraints on Nepotism in the Ch'ing Period," *JAS*, February 1960, pp. 117–33.
[92] Confucius, *Lun yü*, 19:11.
[93] Mao, *Selections*, p. 43 (Date and occasion unknown.)

TWO : *Informal Political Culture*

On another occasion (an interview with André Malraux) Mao linked the problem directly to traditional Chinese bureaucratic behavior:

> Corruption, law breaking, the arrogance of intellectuals, the wish to do honor to one's family by becoming a white-collar worker and not dirtying one's hands any more, all these stupidities are only symptoms. Inside the party and out. The cause of them is the historical conditions themselves. But also the political conditions.[94]

In other words, the roots of the problem lay in the past, but the problem still existed because it had not been dealt with "politically," i.e., people's thinking had not been adequately reformed.[95]

This brings us to the important question of the relationship among thought, theory, and practice. We noted above that in traditional China, thought and action were not considered in isolation of each other. Today, an intimate relationship between the two continues to be maintained. As it was put by one writer in the Party journal *Red Flag*, "Whether it is necessary to *study* Marxism is essentially a question of whether it is necessary to *practice* Marxism."[96] But then, interestingly, the same writer proceeds to acknowledge that this view is not universally held.

> Some comrades say that they can find no close connection between studying revolutionary theories and solving the specific problems arising from actual work. What they want is to find in the books ready answers for solving specific problems. When they happen to find an answer, they say studying is relevant, but when they cannot find a quick answer to the problem to be solved, they say studying is not relevant. This demonstrates that there are some comrades who still do not fully understand Chairman Mao's principle of combining theory with practice.[97]

This passage suggests that even since the Cultural Revolution there has been a tendency among "some comrades" to eschew ideology in favor of pragmatism.

---

[94] Malraux, p. 460.
[95] In general, observers agree that China has come a long way in the drive to eliminate corruption. See *FEER*, September 6, 1974, p. 27. For reports of instances of corruption, see *FEER*, June 7, 1970, p. 61 (corrupt people in industry executed), and C. Chen, *Lien-chiang*, p. 109 (diverting materials and labor to build a cadre's house).
[96] Emphasis added.
[97] Shen Mou-ssu, p. 10.

Why is it that such tendencies are so anathema to China's authorities? The answer is not simply that ideological backsliding would signal a loss of their control over society, although to some extent this would doubtless be true. More important is the form that national integration would take if the ideology lost its hold on the public, and especially on the elite. Were everyone simply to attend to specific problems in a pragmatic fashion, while losing sight of moral imperatives and the Maoist vision of the good society, then society would be holding together and interacting—i.e., it would be integrated—in a manner much more similar to the Western model than to the Maoist ideal. The tendency would be for marketplace considerations to prevail—an "unseen hand" mediating the privately motivated interactions of people. But the Chinese do not see the choice as lying between this kind of "organic solidarity" (to use Durkheim's term) and "mechanical solidarity" based upon "repressive" law.[98] Instead, the Chinese are intent upon achieving an integrated society on a new basis—psychic (rather than material) motivation, and ideological conformity. The viability of such an order, in which coercion, competition, and formal law are to play minor roles, has yet to be demonstrated, but the experiment is a significant one which warrants respectful watching.

Naturally, not all tenets of either Confucianism or Chinese communism have been equally relevant to actual conduct. Indeed, both ideologies have recognized a special level of ideology which was action-oriented, as opposed to the more ethereal philosophy. Although the distinction between this *practical ideology* and *theory*[99] or *-isms*[100] sometimes becomes blurred,[101] it continues to be adhered to. Today, practical ideology is often referred to by the Chinese as *ssu-hsiang* (thought), although there is no particular semantic consistency. Loosely speaking, we may think of *ssu-hsiang* as the state of mind in which one approaches one's life activities. *Maoist* thought is prescribed as the frame of mind which good citizens should have in a country like China, in transition from a traditional to a developed socialist society. Sometimes the term *ssu-hsiang* is used indistinguishably from the terms for theory, with other terms being employed to denote the link

[98] Emile Durkheim, *The Division of Labor in Society* (New York: Macmillan, 1933), chaps. 2, 3.
[99] *Li lun*.
[100] *-Chu-yi*.
[101] This was especially true from 1965 to 1969, when Mao's thought was often spoken of as theory (Lin Piao, "Long Live . . . ," passim), and unauthorized Red Guard publications referred to it as "Maoism" (a term never officially sanctioned, and now never seen in Chinese).

60   TWO : *Informal Political Culture*

between theory and practice ("orientation," "line," etc.). To quote again from *Red Flag*:

> Linking theory with practice is primarily a function of orientation and line. When one grasps the issue of line, he grasps all actual conditions. Some comrades would only link theory with the practice of their daily work. They ignore the aspects of practice which are of the greatest importance—orientation and line.[102]

"Line" refers to the current general policies of the leadership (which at this time was comprised of Chou En-lai's moderation, as opposed to the militance of the late Lin Piao). It is still "practical ideology," however, and is presented in ideological terms.

> If one ... does not grasp the issue of line, he is "unable to take a comprehensive view of an entire objective process, lacks clear direction and long-range perspective, and is complacent about occasional successes and glimpses of the truth," as Chairman Mao has reminded us in his "On Practice." Such a person becomes a pragmatist who is divorced from proletarian politics, a revolutionary without a clear mind, and loses his bearings in the course of the struggle between the two lines [presumably, the Chou line versus the Lin line].[103]

"Orientation" is also relevant to ideology, and involves one's general understanding of the nature, timing, and direction of the revolution. These are all consistent with and legitimized by pure theory, but are more relevant than the latter to immediate community concerns.[104]

That *political purpose* is derived from ideology is too obvious a point to require extensive documentation, but we would do well to specify the manner in which ideology serves this integrative function. Ideology tends to prevent the disintegration that would ensue from a sense of aimless drifting, fatalism, and hopelessness. As Clifford

---

[102] Shen Mou-ssu, p. 11.
[103] Ibid.
[104] In discussing theory and practical ideology, I have adopted the terminology in Schurmann, *Ideology*, especially p. 23, although much has transpired since the publication of that book to affect our understanding of the terms. For a more recent study, see Hsiung, *Ideology*, which, though in general excellent, probably gives the subject more precision than it warrants. The Chinese Communists deal with these matters in a rather loose manner, and rarely define their terms. Hsiung (who wrote without the benefit of Schurmann's revised version) rejects much of Schurmann's analysis and terminology, though sometimes only by inference. "Any analysis that separates ideology in its 'pure' form from ideology in practice fails to capture the true spirit of *szu-hsiang*." Hsiung, *Ideology*, p. 147.

Geertz has put it, 'Ideology bridges the emotional gap between things as they are and as one would have them to be, . . . insuring the performance of roles that might otherwise be abandoned in despair or apathy."[105] Thus, at the time of the revolution Mao's public statements were brimming with optimism:

> . . . We believe that revolution can change everything, and that before long there will arise a new China with a big population and a great wealth of products where life will be abundant and culture will flourish. All pessimistic views are utterly groundless.[106]

After a century of civil wars and foreign incursions, and centuries of endemic fatalism, the first order of business for any government was to lift the sights of the nation and to persuade it that the conditions of the past were not inevitably the way of the future. Although these grandiose, almost mythical promises were unrealistic, they served a purpose. Indeed, ten years later, with the above predictions unfulfilled (except for the reference to "a big population"), Mao was still insisting that in view of the "tremendous energy of the masses . . . it is possible to accomplish any task whatsoever."[107] While such assertions may eventually generate cynicism among some, as long as minimal progress is visible to many people it is likely that the deliberate fostering of optimism which underlies the official ideology (and indeed, all Marxism) provides vital political cohesion.[108]

Additionally, ideology provides a general framework for social priorities, and ideological indoctrination fosters a public consensus for these. The manner in which priorities are expressed is at once ideological and concrete. It often reflects the Chinese penchant for enumeration. A case in point is the "four firsts," which have been defined officially as follows:

---

[105] In Apter, *Ideology*, p. 55.
[106] Mao, "The Bankruptcy of the Idealist Conception of History," SW, 4: 454. Although it is not indicated in SW, this article originally appeared as a *JMJP* editorial, September 16, 1949.
[107] *HC*, 1958, no. 10, pp. 1 f., quoted in Schram, *Political*, p. 352.
[108] One of the attributes for which Mao's opponents are repeatedly condemned is their alleged pessimism. "How long can we keep the red flag flying?" they are reported to have wondered during the revolutionary struggle. But Mao had "pointed out that the 'principal cause' of theoretical errors of those . . . despondent opportunists . . . was their 'failure to clearly understand that Ch'na is a semicolony being struggled for by many imperialist powers.' " Shih Chün, p. 20. Again, we see that ideology is intended to provide the basis of hope. (The first quotation is attributed to "swindlers like Liu Shao-ch'i," an apparent reference to Lin Piao.)

> First place must be given to man in handling the relationship between man and weapons; to political work in handling the relationship between political and other work; to ideological work in relation to routine tasks in political work; and, in ideological work, to the living ideas in a person's mind, as distinguished from ideas in books. In brief, first place to man, first place to political work, first place to ideological work, and first place to living ideas.... Upholding the "four firsts" makes it possible to give full play to the commanding role of ideology and politics, to consistently promoting the revolutionization of people's thinking....[109]

It will be noted that not only does ideology *establish* the priorities, but ideology itself *is* a priority. In short, there is no "end of ideology" in sight in China, but rather we find an "ideology of ideology."

Since ideology provides a statement of the general aspirations of society, it also underlies the general underpinnings of *other normative systems* than ideology, as well as defining the role of such systems. Ethical codes, rites, law, and the sociopsychological[110] features of a polity all interact with ideology, being influenced by it at least as much as it is by them. Some of these systems will be discussed in later chapters, and here we simply point out the relevance of ideology to them. Likewise, the subject of political *communications* will be dealt with in chapter 5, but we note here in passing the role which ideology has always served in this connection. Traditionally, political communications were often heavily infused with Confucian ritual, or would be couched in terms expressing a general cosmological view. If all was well or not well with the empire, the mandarins would advise the emperor of this by reference to alleged felicitous or ominous natural events. Today the language of politics remains heavily ideological. Also, the connotations of the terms and concepts used is not limited to their surface meanings. If someone is labeled a "class enemy," the public is told much more than what his social position is or about his new status as a political nonperson. Such language conveys a whole ethos wherein politics is comprised of class contention and classes are defined in cultural terms. However, the vocabularly employed is rather limited, which both eases and complicates communications. It facilitates them because of the common vocabulary which people throughout the country can roughly understand. But there is much which can-

---

[109] *PR*, February 26, 1969, p. 11. Initially, the four firsts concerned only the PLA, but they eventually were prescribed for other institutions.

[110] "Ideology provides 'a symbolic outlet' for emotional disturbances generated by social disequalibrium." Geertz, in Apter, *Ideology*, p. 54.

not really be communicated within the framework of rather abstract and therefore ambiguous language. (There are, as we shall see in chap. 5, various ways to circumvent this problem.) On the other hand, language which is abstruse has the advantage of enabling the authorities to communicate to "insiders" who are trained to decode arcane messages, while the uninitiated must wait for explanations. If a communication is a trial balloon, it may be withdrawn with no explanation.[111] Also, this method of communication may reduce the shock of policy reversals. If, for example, the defection of Mao's heir apparent Lin Piao in 1971 had been openly acknowledged at the time, the government might have been in serious difficulty. By gradually expanding the meaning of "revisionism" and hinting at class enemies, the public was allowed to learn of the spectacular events when it was psychologically prepared, and when the government was in a position to forestall any political setback.

Ideology, then, does much more than simply lend authority to phenomena which would transpire without it. In the final analysis, however, it must be acknowledged that often ideology does serve as a tool of legitimization. *Legitimacy* (about which we shall have more to say in chap. 4) is important in any political institution or activity. Sometimes, though, ideology degenerates into mere rationalization, in which case it no longer renders a substantial contribution to the functioning of the political system. Certainly it was unconstructive in the nineteenth century, when ideology often blinded statesmen from reality. In more recent times, there are indications that ideology has sterilized political dialogue almost as often as it has provided a serviceable vehicle for it. One official (of the relatively benign school), asked how he would have reacted if the leftist troublemakers during the Cultural Revolution had caused him difficulties, responded, "If they had quoted Chairman Mao to me, I would have quoted Chairman Mao to them—and I would have won."[112] Such misapplication of ideology must have exasperated Mao. As his close supporter complained in 1968, "The reading of quotations [from Mao's writings] has become nothing but a war of words. [People take the attitude] I will only read passages

---

[111] E.g., the 1970 draft constitution of the People's Republic, which was obtained by Kuomintang agents, but never announced or ratified in China. The text was published in translation by the KMT in *Background on China* (New York: November 4, 1970). (Probably the main reason why the constitution was never promulgated was that it names Lin Piao, who soon turned against Mao, as the latter's "close comrade-in-arms." Art. 26.)

[112] Quoted by Ross Terrill, *Atlantic Monthly*, January 1972, p. 49.

from the quotations which are favorable to me; I will not read anything which is unfavorable to me."[113] From a hint that Mao dropped to André Malraux in 1965, we may infer that this was one of the problems which prompted the launching of the Cultural Revolution. "There is a whole generation of dogmatic youth, and dogma is of less use than cow dung. One can make whatever one likes out of it, even revisionism." It was time, Mao added, to reveal the sorry ideological condition of much of China's youth.[114]

If ideology becomes dysfunctional when it is trifled with, it is equally hazardous for it to become an obsession—a set of *idées fixes* and a dogmatic denial of common sense. As early as 1942, at Yenan, Mao had detailed his concern over this problem.

> Our comrades must understand that we do not study Marxism-Leninism because it is pleasing to the eye, or because it has some mystical value, like the doctrines of the Taoist priests who ascend Mao Shan to learn how to subdue devils and evil spirits. Marxism-Leninism has no beauty, nor has it any mystical value. It is only extremely useful. It seems that right up to the present quite a few have regarded Marxism-Leninism[115] as a ready-made panacea: Once you have it, you can cure all your ills with little effort. This is a type of childish blindness.... Marx, Engels, Lenin, and Stalin have repeatedly said, "Our doctrine is not dogma; it is a guide to action.[116]

This last slogan has been reiterated many times by Mao and others.[117] Mao once even averred that Marx himself had made errors in using theory to understand history and political change.[118] Nonetheless, in a culture where reliance upon canonical authority has long been *de rigueur*, and which still provides safety only for those who can justify

---

[113] Chang Ch'un-ch'iao, speech at Chiao-t'ung University (Shanghai), *Tzu-liao chuan-chi* (Canton), February 10, 1968, *SCMP*, no. 4146, p. 3.

[114] Malraux, p. 467. Translation slightly revised. Cf. Mao's 1959 complaint that some people trotted out the "magic power" of Marxism to criticize the communes. Mao, *In Camera Statements*, p. 52.

[115] In the 1966 version this wording is somewhat diluted. It is now only the *"pieh-tzu"* which should not be treated as panaceas. Mao, *Hsuan chi*, p. 822. *"Pieh-tzu"* is rendered "odd quotations" in *SW*, 3:43. I am unable to confirm the alleged official English translation quoted by Schram, *Political*, p. 179, n. 1, on the basis of the pages he cites in *SW*.

[116] Schram, *Political*, p. 179.

[117] For example, *More on the Differences between Comrade Togliatti and Us* (Peking: Foreign Languages Press, 1963), p. 169. The question of dogmatism is given somewhat defensive treatment in this widely circulated paper.

[118] Mao, *In Camera Statements*, p. 42.

their actions and attitudes in ideological terms, it is perhaps inevitable that dogmatism should continue to be a problem.[119]

Communism, like Confucianism, was originally adopted in China not only as a philosophy of an elite (the Party), but also as a philosophy of elitism. Between 1949 and 1965 communism became, if anything, more elitist than it had been earlier. Mao, always something of an egalitarianist himself, disapproved of the trend and sought to reverse it. His attack on social stratification took many forms. He moved against the institutions (Party and government) and the economic system which were contributing to the problem, but, as the name of the campaign which engulfed China during the late 1960s suggests, most important was making certain correctives in the realm of *culture*. Ideology, comprising part of that culture, was to come in for scrutiny. Although Mao found no need to alter the content of the ideology, he did redirect public attention away from the Leninist tenets, and reemphasized the egalitarianism, puritanism, and populism which he considered more fundamental. In short, Mao's ultimate crusade was directed toward eliminating the distinction between elite political culture and mass political culture.[120]

---

[119] The reader should not be left with the impression that all Chinese leaders have attached equal importance to the role of explicit ideology. It is well to recall, for example, that in the latter part of the 1950s there was a strong demand on the part of "modernists" among the arts, the professions, and in the military, for greater pragmatism in policy formation and execution, with which leaders such as Defense Minister P'eng Teh-huai associated themselves. Mao, we are told, always emphasized the role of ideology. "While opposing P'eng Teh-huai's right opportunist line in 1959, Chairman Mao particularly stressed that it is necessary to defeat the anti-Party, anti-Marxist trend of thought ideologically and theoretically. He called on us to study philosophy and then the history of philosophy in order to criticize empiricism theoretically." Tang Hsiao-wen, "Read a Few Books on the History of Philosophy," *HC*, 1972, no. 2, FBIS I, February 8, 1972, p. B-5.

Even after the Cultural Revolution, it would appear that some Chinese leaders (and not only those on the right) disputed the ideologues and insisted that people should not spend a disproportionate amount of time internalizing political statements. One hardly knows what to make of the assertion, but according to Shen Mou-ssu (p. 13), Lin Piao had parted with Mao over this issue. "Swindlers like Liu Shao-ch'i," Shen wrote (in an apparent reference to Lin Piao), "must be thoroughly criticized for criminally disrupting the study of Marxism-Leninism-Mao Tse-tung Thought. . . ."

[120] This will be further examined in chaps. 4 and 7.

THREE
Formal Political Culture: Law

> Chinese authorities were bound by the doctrine of official responsibility for the administration of justice. When someone was killed, the magistrate was responsible to his superiors that justice and retribution should follow. Nothing could absolve him from his responsibility except the express word of his superior. The way most patent in the world of showing zeal in administering justice was to report that, for a life lost, a life was taken. With the magistrate serving at once as coroner, police superintendent, jail warden, prosecuting attorney, judge, and sheriff, human nature would lead him to wish to bring his cases to a "successful" conclusion.
>
> H. B. MORSE (1910)[1]

> In government, reliance must be placed upon men, rather than upon law.
>
> MAO TSE-TUNG[2]

IN THE PREVIOUS CHAPTER we dealt with certain aspects of "political culture," or politically relevant cultural norms. The type of

---

Two bibliographies on Chinese law are Fu-shun Lin, Chinese Law Past and Present: A Bibliography of Enactments and Commentaries in English Text (New York: East Asian Institute, Columbia University, 1966), and George Ginsburgs, "Soviet Sources on the Law of the Chinese People's Republic," University of Toronto Law Journal 18, no. 2 (1968): 179–97. An interesting bibliographical essay is J. A. Cohen, "New Developments in Western Studies of Chinese Law," JAS, May 1968, pp. 475–83.
On imperial law, see Bodde and Morris; Ch'ü, Law; and Mäding.
For the Republican period, see Ch'ien, and Escarra.

norm which we examined—and in China it is the most important type—is a relatively informal variety enforced largely by social sanctions. Life can be made quite unpleasant for a violator of an informal norm, but the authority of the state will not generally be invoked unless the norm has been made formal—that is, until it becomes, in some sense, *law*.[3]

Philosophical Background

Although the ancient Chinese had experience with legal codes as early as the sixth century B.C.,[4] events of the third century B.C. gave rise to strong objections toward the firm implantation of law. The First Emperor (Ch'in Shih Huang-ti), was one of the most ruthless rulers in world history. Although his accomplishments (the most famous being the completion of the Great Wall) are a matter of historical record and partially account for China's subsequent greatness, he is best remembered for the mass suffering that he caused. For our purposes here, what is significant is that among the various political philosophies current during his youth, the most appealing went by the name of *fa*, a word generally translated "law," though the two words can hardly be equated. Certainly the notion of government under law was little known to statesmen of the *Fa* school, which (bowing to convention) we shall nonetheless refer to as Legalism. This school had its origins in the fourth century B.C.—well after the time of Confucius but before

---

Among the many works on law in the People's Republic, those cited in the Bibliography of this book are: Blaustein; P. Chen; Chugunov; Cohen (two works); and Leng. Some interesting pieces not cited in the Bibliography or elsewhere in the notes are: J. Cohen, "The Party and the Courts: 1949–1959," April 1969, CQ, pp. 120–57; A. Dicks, "A New Model for Chinese Legislation: The 1972 Shipping Regulations," CQ, January 1974, pp. 63–83; D. Finkelstein, "The Language of Communist China's Criminal Law," JAS, May 1968, pp. 503–21; Lectures on the General Principles of Criminal Law in the People's Republic of China (Peking: Fa-lü ch'u-pan she, 1957, translated by JPRS, no. 13331); and Shao-chuan Leng, "The Lawyer in Communist China," Journal of the International Commission of Jurists, Summer 1962.

[1] Morse, 1:116 (paraphrase).
[2] Quoted in the Cantonese Red Guard-type newspaper *Fan P'eng, Lo hei hsien* (Oppose the Black Line of P'eng [Chen] and Lo [Jui-ch'ing]), July 1968. Translated in CLG, Winter 1969–70, p. 7.
[3] States, of course, sometimes prosecute for reasons other than norm violation (e.g., antagonizing officials).
[4] The first known Chinese legal code was promulgated in 536 B.C. in the small state of Cheng. It was a criminal code, and was apparently cast on bronze vessels. See Creel, chap. 26.

Confucianism established itself as the foundation of Chinese politics. Legalism's main spokesmen were Ch'in politicians, whose manner of statecraft was quite Machiavellian. These were militant individuals, whose plans for expanding state power succeeded so well that the state of Ch'in ultimately conquered the remaining states of China and other nations as well. It would not be the last time in world history that men would act lawlessly in the name of the law to change the order of things.

Legalists had to debate with many schools in ancient China, though they did not have to contend with any liberal constitutionalists. Their most formidable opponents were the Confucianists. Legalists did not share the Confucianists' concern for propriety and rites. They did not view society as family-centered, nor did they believe that the state should be modeled after the family and emulate its norms. Human relationships were less important than the relationship between the people and the state. Thus, it was necessary that the people obey rules which the state laid down, rather than simply live according to general principles which had been internalized during the socialization process. Infractions could not be dealt with adequately by social ostracism or similar pressures; instead, punishments had to be authoritative and severe. An exemplary but aloof ruler was insufficient to insure happiness and prosperity throughout the realm; the state must play a positive role in culture and the economy. Indeed, Chinese associate the term *fa* ("law") less with law than with strongly activist government. It is small wonder that the Chinese people, though certainly aware of the many arbitrary and disagreeable features of the Confucian system, would not turn to a system of law for refuge. That alternative may have well served the English—especially the upper classes—but China's gentry, as one Legalist philosopher complained, "by means of letters upset laws."[5]

If it would be a mistake to think of the Legalists as believers in the supremacy of law, it would likewise be erroneous to view their chief opponents as altogether *opposed* to law. It is true that Confucianists were either opposed to *fa*, or else considered certain concessions to Legalist principles a matter of unpleasant necessity. But the *li* (propriety) which they favored over *fa* was not altogether alien to law. Indeed, certain connotations of our word *law* which do not inhere in *fa* are quite relevant to *li*. Certainly *law*, like *li*, connotes a measure of propriety, which distinguishes both words from *fa*. And

[5] Han Fei-tzu, in SCT, p. 147.

while it is too much to freight *li* with all of the connotations of *justice*, certainly more of a sense of decency and *rightness* (recall *Recht, droit*) inheres in *li* than in *fa*. But, whereas the *fa* aspects of law are manifested in the form of governmental commands, and are rather external to the individual, *li* is more a matter of socialization—of following examples set by superiors one respects. *Li* was realized in the form of rites and propriety, but these manifestations were simply indications of an inner commitment to eternal principles.

One other important distinction needs to be made between *li* and *law*. Central to the purpose of law in North Atlantic countries is the protection of individual rights. The idea of people having certain "unalienable" rights (natural law), of being entitled to do anything not prohibited by law, or to protect private interest when not in violation of law, does *not* inhere in *li*. Rather, *li* places primary emphasis upon the individual's maintaining harmonious relations with other people, and toward that end subordinating himself or at least deferring to others. Of course there would be times when people would not conform to *li*, when it might be necessary to fall back upon sanctions provided for under *fa*. But a citizen would rarely volunteer to go to court to attain his "*fa* rights," for *fa* was primarily a matter of punishments, and there was no "civil" law.[6] Indeed, some political philosophers argued that the laws should not even be published, lest people become unduly concerned with their rights, resulting in a litigious lifestyle which would be incompatible with the spirit of *li*. Confucius himself had been a most reluctant judge, favoring instead the elimination of litigation.[7] The fear was that people who appreciated only *fa* would with impunity perpetrate shameful acts which, however immoral, might still be technically legal. Better to inculcate in the people a sense of propriety so that they would be bent on avoiding not punishment but shame, and seek not gain but honor.[8] Such warnings about litigation became something of a self-fulfilling prophecy for later Confucian officials, for they made court procedures as demeaning as possible. Courts were thought of as appropriate for criminals, not as recourse for victims of wrongdoers. Rather than present oneself (on one's knees, if the plantiff were a commoner) before a magistrate, the

---

[6] Kuang-hsü, the last emperor to reign over imperial China, sought to have civil distinguished from criminal law. Although a draft code was prepared, it suffered the same unhappy fate of his other reforms, and China did not have a completed civil code until 1930.
[7] *Lun Yü*, 12:13.
[8] Ibid., 2:3.

aggrieved party usually sought some kind of informal arbitration by a local elder—who probably would know little of *fa,* but as a Confucian literatus would be generally respected for his decency and sense of justice. Fortunately, *li* norms were just about specific and comprehensive enough for this system to operate reasonably effectively.

Li and *fa,* then, were distinct and in some respect antithetical formulations of cultural norms, although various attempts were made to reconcile the two. The T'ang code, for example, purported to incorporate *li* into the *fa*. But except in possibly a few areas, mostly having to do with the affairs of the family (marriage, welfare, inheritance, and so on), the principles grouped under *li* were too imprecise to be administered legalistically, and by their very nature defied bureaucratic application. Nonetheless, the belief that *li* should be taken as primary was held not only by naive idealists, as one might expect. Even the more pessimistic or "realistic" among the Confucian philosophers did not hesitate to subordinate *fa* to *li*. Hsun-tzu (third century B.C.), for example, who started from the premise that human nature was fundamentally evil and required correction,[9] insisted on total reliance upon *li*. The following passage, in which *li* variously refers to ritual, rites, or rules of decorum, is instructive.

> Man is born with desires. If his desires are not satisfied for him, he cannot but seek some means to satisfy them himself. If there are no limits and degrees to his seeking, then he will inevitably fall to wrangling with other men. From wrangling comes disorder and from disorder comes exhaustion. The ancient kings hated such disorder, and therefore they established *li* in order to curb it, to train men's desires and to provide for their satisfaction. They saw to it that desires did not overextend the means for their satisfaction, and material goods did not fall short of what was desired. Thus both desires and goods were looked after and satisfied. This is the origin of *li*.[10]

This is a philosophy of political paternalism, but the state's proper role is seen not so much as active intervention to serve the people's welfare (*fa*) as reducing the people's wants by causing them to be more principled (*li*). Any ruler who placed undue reliance upon commands and regulations, Hsun-tzu believed, would inevitably fail to provide the kind of moral leadership that society would need. Not *fa,* but *li* represented "the highest expression of hierarchical order, the

---

[9] Burton Watson, *Hsün-Tzu: Basic Writings* (New York: Columbia University Press, 1963), pp. 157 ff.
[10] Ibid, p. 123. Translation slightly revised.

basis for strengthening the state, the way in which to create authority, the crux of achievement and respect."[11]

If Hsun-tzu gave low priority to formal law, the less authoritarian wing of Confucianism was even more opposed to Legalism, and of course the rather anarchistic Taoists were totally opposed to it. And while most Chinese intellectuals did not fit neatly and exclusively into philosophic "schools," they nonetheless shared a common bias against Legalism.[12] Exceptions were rare, but one important one deserves mention. Huang Tsung-hsi, the seventeenth-century scholar whose father had been a victim of political persecution, argued against the rarely disputed preference for rule of men rather than laws.

> Only if there are good laws will there be leaders who govern well. Inasmuch as "unlawful laws" fetter people hand and foot, even a person who might be capable of governing well is likely to be suspicious and arbitrary. Of course, a *good* leader will realize the full intent of the law anyway; what law would do additionally is prevent the human suffering which results from rule by tyrants. Thus, I say that only good laws will ensure good rulers.[13]

The notion of "unlawful laws" has a remarkably modern ring—seeds of constitutionalism and judicial review, we might say, had the seeds ever sprouted. It was an almost utopian vision, although (in the typical style of Chinese scholasticism) Huang Tsung-hsi professed to find the golden age in the mythical past. Huang's complaint about Chinese politics was that it had degenerated into a contest for the national treasury, and that successive dynasties had misguidedly relied upon coercive regulations for its protection. This was a perversion of law, which should instead be directed toward benefiting the entire population.

But Huang Tsung-hsi was a maverick, and no philosophy based upon the supremacy of law ever gained general acceptance in China. By and large, even the leaders of the Republic of China have viewed law as an

---

[11] Ibid., p. 71. Translation slightly revised.

[12] An excellent discussion of *li* and *fa* is contained in Benjamin Schwartz, "On Attitudes toward Law in China," in Milton Katz, *Government under Law and the Individual* (Washington, D.C., 1957), reprinted in Cohen, *Criminal Process*, pp. 62–70. One must quarrel, however, with Schwartz's translation of *fa chih* as "rule of law," even though he admits the irony. *Fa chih* simply does not mean "rule of law," but rather "control by law," "governing by law," etc. It is interesting to note that in Japanese the distinction is made between this term (read *hōchi* in Japanese) and *hō no shihai*, which *does* mean "rule of law."

[13] *SCT*, pp. 592 f. Translation revised.

instrument of control, and favored "law and order" in the reactionary sense of the phrase.[14] It was only in the 1930s that a fledgling modern legal system began to function, and this was a time when the principle of government under law was being severly challenged around the world, undoubtedly influencing legal development in China or at least failing to encourage China to institute rule of law. The result was a kind of statism reflecting traditional *fa* authoritarianism. As one apologist for the Republic of China explains it:

> ... Chinese legislators have ... selected precisely those new principles of Western law which are most congenial to the spirit of Chinese tradition. By a fortunate coincidence, the Chinese civil code was produced at a time when Western juristic thought had for several decades been turning away from the extreme individualism of the nineteenth century and heading steadily toward a humanistic and sociological position strikingly similar, in spirit, to the Chinese philosophy of the human-minded and well-integrated individual, who thinks of his duties more than his rights.[15]

So, although the civil and criminal codes of the Republic of China reveal much borrowing of the European legal tradition, the spirit in which these laws were administered have marked a sharp rejection of that influence (from which much of the North Atlantic region has departed at one time or another), and also much carryover of China's Legalist tradition. There were also times, however, when Chiang Kai-shek sought to strike a balance between Legalism and Confucianism—reminding us very much of many Chinese emperors.

> Chinese political philosophy analyzes the relation between ethics and law with the greatest minuteness and clarity. Chinese political philosophy advocates the joint application of ethics and law, though distinguishing between them in their order of application. Chia Yi [second century B.C.] said: "*Li* prohibits a misdeed before it happens; law prosecutes after the occurrence." Tung Chung-shu said: "Virtue first, punishment afterward." These statements mean that ethics comes

---

[14] It is only a coincidence, but the character *fa* is used in transliterating *fascist* into Chinese. It is possible that this reinforces the psychic connection in the Chinese mind. At any rate, Chiang Kai-shek was far from anti-Nazi during the 1930s.
[15] John C. H. Wu, "The Status of the Individual in the Political and Legal Traditions of Old and New China," in *The Chinese Mind*, ed. Charles A. Moore (Honolulu: East-West Center Press, 1967), p. 353.

THREE: *Formal Political Culture: Law*

before the law, but do not imply that there are only ethics to the exclusion of the law.[16]

Chiang made it clear that his conception of law was far from the European idea—that of a legal framework within which a person is free to do what he or she pleases so long as it does not violate the law (*nulla poena sine lege*).

> We must never permit individual interest to interfere with the common interest of the state, nor allow individual "freedom" to encroach upon the "freedom" of others. To seek "freedom" we must first understand its intrinsic nature; to uphold government by law we must first form the habit of obedience to law. Our four hundred and fifty million citizens must each be instilled with this idea of freedom and government by law. Only then can China be established as a state governed by law, and only then will it exist as a solidly organized body of national defense, capable of sharing the responsibility for world peace and the liberation of mankind along with other free and independent countries of the world.[17]

The object, it became clear, was not to have China governed by law so much as it was to have China governed by Chiang Kai-shek. Law, then, was primarily an instrument of control in the *fa* tradition; Chiang never viewed it as constraining the ruling elite.

In the actual legal codes of the Republic of China (still largely in effect on Formosa) one sees the continuing influence of *fa* as well as *li*. Obviously, lawmakers, have wrestled with the ancient problem of reconciling morality and formal law. Statutes abound with clauses (reminiscent of the T'ang code) to the effect that, regardless of the letter of the law, moral considerations are to prevail over legal formalism. For example, Article 72 of the civil code declares void any juristic action which is "contrary to public order or good morals."[18] In addition, judges are given wide discretion in sentencing. Flexibility is always advantageous if the judges are of high professional and moral caliber, but a fledgling legal system in a culture that tolerates corruption will inevitably foster erratic and arbitrary justice. This has certainly been a problem in the Republic of China. On the mainland before 1949, even in cities, traditional practices prevailed over legal

[16] *China's Destiny* (New York: Roy Publishers, 1947), p. 206.
[17] Ibid., pp. 212 f.
[18] Wu (see note 15), p. 353. To some extent, this idea also reflects European codes.

requirements. In the countryside, of course, courts were few and far between.[19] Little was done to educate the public about citizens' legal rights. On the contrary, the official press flaunted the arrest and execution of "bandits," with no apparent awareness that in the absence of martial law even "bandits" are entitled to due process.[20] The situation was no better on Formosa during the first decade of Kuomintang rule. Since the early 1950s, law has played an ever-increasing role, but martial law prevails and opponents of the government are still jailed as "rebels."[21]

In North Atlantic political systems, the heart of policymaking is *legislating*—the laying down of rules for political actors to follow. A study of a North Atlantic political system, therefore, generally pays considerably more attention to the legislative process (including the election of legislators, and the legislative roles of executives and judges) than to the role of enacted law. In this limited sense, then, the study of politics is usually the study of law. There is a tendency to assume that once a law has been enacted it will automatically be carried out. To study the execution process would involve the student in what is to many a relatively dull subject—bureaucracy and administration. True, it is recognized that in exceptional cases the law will be violated rather than followed, but this is assumed to occur primarily on the fringes of society, and is a relatively specialized subject.

To question the adequacy of these preconceptions for the study of Western politics would carry us beyond the scope of this book. But when it comes to the study of Chinese politics, it cannot be emphasized too strongly that such an approach will yield a highly distorted picture. There, politics is also comprised of stating and restating norms, but

---

[19] Ch'ien Tuan-sheng, p. 254.
[20] This is approximately how the legal system in republican China has been described by an eyewitness apologist of the Kuomintang, Franz Michael, in "The Role of Law in Traditional, Nationalist, and Communist China," *CQ*, January 1962, p. 134.
[21] On constitutional developments, see Seymour, "Republic."

When this book went to press it appeared that the Republic of China government was about to commute the sentences of some prisoners, including some political prisoners. (In May 1975 the author served as an emissary to Taipei for the human rights organization Amnesty International to encourage this.) The draft commutation bill was published in *Chung-kuo shih-pao* (Taipei), May 17, 1975. For a commentary by Huang Mo (Mab Huang), see *Sing-tao jih-pao* (New York), May 25, 1975. Additional information will appear in various releases of Amnesty International (London), including an article in the July 1975 newsletter *Amnesty Action* (New York), and late July issues of *Sing-tao jih-pao* (New York and Hong Kong).

legislation in the usual sense of the word does not lie at its heart. If one were only to master the lawmaking activities of legislatures, judges, and administrators, one would have a poor understanding of Chinese politics.

Nevertheless, the law in China asks even more of a citizen than in other countries. In the West, one's primary responsibility is to *refrain from violating* the law. Under normal (nonmartial) circumstances, if a person pays his taxes (which, with sales and withholding taxes, are not easily evaded), the government will otherwise pay little attention. Positive acts required of citizens by law are few and minor—obtaining certain licenses, serving on juries, but not much more.[22] The argument that law plays a greater role in China than in other countries may be surprising, and the assertion could certainly be disputed if law is thought of as statutes and judicial precedents. But if by "law" we mean the rules which political authority requires men to live by, then it can readily be seen that law plays a much more positive role in the life of every Chinese citizen than it does in most other countries.

No sharp line exists between formal political culture (law) and informal political culture, which was discussed in the previous chapter. The gray area between them—general principles which the state propagates but which are realized more through socialization than through law enforcement—is of crucial importance in China. This informal law, as we shall term it, has obvious disadvantages, most of which spring from its vagueness. Uncertainties stem from its lack of precision, which in turn may give rise to arbitrariness and erratic interpretation. On the other hand, informal law has distinct advantages. Once the norms have been internalized by the people, they are largely self-enforcing, with little need for bureaucratic apparatus to apply the law. Furthermore, flexibility permits greater attention to the spirit of the law (rather than to its letter), and also to the *ad hoc* public policy aspect of law, even in judicial proceedings. In a Western court a judge will fall back upon "public policy" in his judicial interpretations only as a last resort. In Communist China, judicial personnel always have Party spokesmen at their sides to remind them of the current line, and advise (or compel) them to render legal judgments consistent with Party policy. Later in this chapter we shall examine the implications of this practice for the integrity of the law and the efficacy of Party policies.

[22] Two "exceptions" that might come to mind are actually not exceptions. The military draft is a martial situation, and compulsory schooling is for minors (noncitizens).

True formal law—clear rules enforced by the state—on the other hand has the opposite set of advantages and disadvantages. In addition, the Chinese leadership is particularly sensitive to the problem of dissonance between formal law (tending to be conservative), and radical or at least popularly responsive politics.

Here is how one textbook on law states the problem:

> Because the masses have been attracted to participate extensively in judicial activities . . . , it has become possible to listen to the demands and reflections of the masses, as well as to understand their sentiments when cases are handled. This is one of the important prerequisites in our correct implementation of Party policy and the law. There are people who merely emphasize "doing things in accordance with the law," thus maintaining that there is no need to consider mass demands. This method of handling cases in isolation is one kind of manifestation of rightist conservative ideology that places no confidence in the masses. The belief that the masses are ignorant about law and cannot present correct opinions is contrary to fact. The masses understand law; they grasp the facts of cases; and in regard to such civil disputes as marriage and property cases, they are often adept at offering suggestions for disposition that are both practical and reasonable. Even in criminal cases, they can also give reasons for severe or light punishment.[23]

When such writers insist that "the masses understand law," they do not mean that knowledge of formal law has penetrated the populace, but that it is legitimate for those who must interpret the law to look to other sources than lawbooks for standards to apply in particular cases.

All of this is not to say that the Chinese leadership is content to allow law to be defined by grass-roots consensus. On the contrary, in their view law in all cultures is an instrument of class rule, and in China the Communist party presumes to speak for that class. Law, furthermore, is still called *fa*, and, just as in imperial times, is considered an instrument of dictatorship and repression—words from which Communists do not shrink when discussing the relations between "the people" and the "enemies of the people."

> Observance of . . . laws and ordinances on the part of the people cannot be equated with observance of . . . laws and ordinances on the

[23] *On the People's Democratic Dictatorship and the People's Democratic Legal System* (Peking: Department of Law, People's University, 1958), translated in *CLG*, Summer 1969, p. 50.

THREE: Formal Political Culture: Law

part of the enemy. The only way to make the enemy very carefully obey our laws is repression.[24]

In many respects, Communists take very much the same attitude toward law that they do toward the state.[25] Both the law and the state are instruments of dictatorship possessed by one or more classes during a particular historic phase. This explains why it was deemed necessary to abolish all Kuomintang laws in 1950. "The law is the ideology of the state, and any ruling class maintains it by force of arms," said the operative directive on that occasion. "Laws, like the state, are merely the tool that protects the interests of a given ruling class."[26] Law, then, has not been viewed as a framework within which all men are equal and free, but rather an instrument for waging class struggle[27] and realizing class interests.[28]

The emphasis upon the informal and political aspects of law should not lead one to conclude that law performs none of the roles in China that it does elsewhere. Legal scholars in China generally agree that formal law is necessary to reduce the element of uncertainty in political and economic life.[29] By providing a peaceful mechanism for resolving

[24] Ibid., p. 34. For a general discussion of the meaning of the application of the law vis à vis "the enemy" and "the people," see pp. 24–36.

[25] The relationship between the two has been the subject of some academic debate. A symposium on this subject was published in *Cheng-fa yen-chiu* in 1964, and translated in *CLG*, Summer 1968, pp. 27–76. (Hereafter, this symposium will be cited as "*CLG*, Summer 1968.")

[26] Cheng P'u, "Thoroughly Destroy the Old Legal System and Eliminate Bourgeois Legal Thought," *Cheng-fa yen-chiu*, 1964, no. 2, translated in *CLG*, Fall 1968, p. 68.

[27] Ibid., pp. 74 f., for a discussion of the judicial system as the focal point of class struggle.

[28] An interesting and somewhat unusual formulation of this issue was expounded by Chang Hung-sheng in 1964. Exploiting societies, he said, have rule by "military suppression and political deceit," whereas under socialism, dictatorship against the enemy and democracy among the people are practiced. "These different kinds of societies and methods of ruling are all realized through the state and law. Study of the laws of the ruling class in using the state and law to wage class struggle forms an indispensable theme in the objects of legal study. These two kinds of laws are organically linked together, permeate one another, affect one another, and are mutually complementary; but they cannot be completely equated. Neither of the two kinds of laws can, in the absence of the other, constitute the comprehensive contents of the particular contradictions of the objects of legal study." *CLG*, Summer 1968, p. 33.

[29] "The broad mass of basic-level cadres and masses ... demand knowledge of all things and the reasons for phenomena; they demand enlightenment on and mastery of the laws of things; they demand to be relieved of the conditions of uncertainty." Hsiang Shih, "New Problems in the Realm of Legal Studies," *Cheng-fa yen-chiu*, 1964, no. 3, translated in *CLG*, Summer 1968, p. 10.

disputes, a legal system also enhances social stability, provided that courts are resorted to in moderation. (There is considerable apprehension that if individuals developed a high degree of awareness of their rights, and became aggressive in asserting them, the result would be highly destabilizing.[30]) It is also realized that law facilitates the assignment of responsibility, and therefore the apportionment of material and psychic rewards for successes, and sanctions in the event of failures. This enhances the power and effectiveness commanded by the state.

Modern Legal Development: Issues

This general discussion of Chinese attitudes toward law has so far taken little note of the fact that many of the issues involved have been the subject of heated debate, and legal policies have had a markedly different color during different periods of the history of Chinese communism. A sketch of the history of the relevant policies and controversies would be helpful at this point, both as background for the remainder of our discussion of law, and also as relevant groundwork for much of what we shall be discussing in the remainder of this book.

As already indicated, the history of law in China prior to 1949 had been rather checkered. Since the third century B.C. it had been associated with the most authoritarian style of government. Never had there developed the notion of law as a normative framework within which all citizens were equal. Certainly law in imperial China never served the interests of the average peasant—geared as it was to protecting the interests of the gentry. In the nineteenth century, with the introduction of Western legal concepts, one might have expected this situation to improve, but China's experience with law continued to be an unhappy one, for it came first in the form of extraterritoriality—the doctrine according to which foreigners in East Asia who came from countries with "advanced" legal systems were governed by the legal principles of their own countries, rather than by local law. The double standards that arose, and the general demise of traditional Chinese law because of its irrelevance to the modern world, gave rise to a general disrespect and suspicion of all law. Although some Kuomintang officials worked diligently to develop a body of law and a judicial structure, their work was undermined by the inability of their party

---

[30] There is some justification for this view. During the period of British colonialism in Asia, an attempt was made to introduce the British legal system, but the resultant volume of litigation was the cause of considerable instability.

80   THREE: *Formal Political Culture: Law*

to control most of the country, and the lack of interest on the part of other Kuomintang officials in instituting the rule of law.

China's present leaders derive their attitudes toward law not only from China's tradition, but also from Marxist doctrine. They have doubtless been influenced by the Bolshevik bias against law as a bourgeois institution,[31] as much as they have been persuaded by Stalin and Vyshinsky that under socialism, law is necessary and indeed reaches its highest point of development. These latter views did not find fertile ground in soviet China during Chinese communism's incubatory period. The leaders of the movement had almost no philosophic understanding of the social role of law, or of the content of existing Chinese law. Nor was there any group of professional lawyers or legal scholars to whom they could turn. As a result, efforts in this area were experimental, somewhat erratic, and never highly developed. Examination of the decades of insurgency does reveal certain patterns, however—in fact, two counterveiling tendencies. The Kiangsi period (1929–34) was characterized by harsh regulations and often brutal handling of enemies. Justice began to be thought of in terms of class struggle, with mass trials held primarily for their educational and mobilizing value. However, these practices appear to have been less than totally successful in assisting the Party in carrying out its political programs. Following the Long March a much milder approach was followed. During the Yenan period (1935–46) legal development was placed under the direction of distinguished jurists who enjoyed some success in their efforts to develop orderly legal procedures, which gained popular respect. Widespread utilization of "people's assessors" brought the courts closer to the people, and amicable settlement of disputes was encouraged through the process of out-of-court conciliation. Mass trials continued to be held, but they were tamer affairs than had been seen in Kiangsi. When zealots demanded excessive punishments, the Party exercised a restraining hand.[32]

In abolishing all Kuomintang laws upon their accession to power,[33] the Chinese Communists attempted to sever all ties with what had been an emerging bourgeois legal tradition. In fact, however, they did not set to work drawing up comprehensive replacement law, and were slow to establish new organs of judicial administration. Through the early 1950s many of the security organs and courts continued to exist

[31] For example, the pre-1920 views of legal theorist Y. B. Pashukanis.
[32] Shao-chuan Leng, "Pre-1949 Development of the Communist Chinese System of Justice," *CQ*, April 1967, pp. 93–114.
[33] See Cheng P'u (note 26).

much as they had before 1949. Not infrequently, these were staffed largely by former Kuomintang officials, who continued to adhere to traditional practices and laws *faute de mieux*. And although the Communists proceeded to develop a formal body of law in certain fields, they continued, consciously or unconsciously, to fall back upon Kuomintang and sometimes even ancient practices. An interesting example of this, the role of confessions in adjudication, is worth examining in some detail.

The Chinese judicial system has always emphasized confession to an extent that is surprising to Westerners. Courts in traditional China sometimes seemed less interested in punishing offenders than in bringing them to an appreciation of their wrongs. Far from having any right against self-incrimination, penalties were commonly increased in cases where the defendant maintained his innocence, while confessions brought reductions or remissions of punishment. True, most legal systems find ways of rewarding cooperative defendants, but the Chinese practice went far beyond "plea bargaining."[34] The intention was to facilitate harmonious human relations and maintain correct relations with the cosmos.[35] Such practice was at marked variance with the North Atlantic legal methods (at least until recent times[36]) where specific penalties for intended socially harmful acts have been mandatory. In China, the original intent was relatively unimportant; what mattered was a defendant's post-apprehension attitude.

From the very beginning of their lawmaking efforts, the Chinese Communists incorporated this concept, albeit secularized. Faced with winning over a skeptical population in Kiangsi, they were quite naturally more concerned with eliciting future cooperation than with punishing ancient infractions, though so-called crimes against the new order could not be ignored. In 1932 the central bureau of the Kiangsi soviet announced its intention to "promulgate articles for the punishment of counterrevolutionary crimes as well as articles dealing with those elements of counterrevolutionary cliques *who voluntarily sur-*

---

[34] The term *tzu-shou* (voluntary surrender and confession) was used at least as early as the second century B.C. until 1957. (Thereafter, the term *tzu-tung t'an-pai* was substituted.) For details on this practice, see W. Allyn Rickett's interesting article, "Voluntary Surrender and Confession in Chinese Law: The Problem of Continuity," *JAS*, August 1971, pp. 797–814.

[35] Where irredeemable injury had been done to the natural order (e.g., parricide), mitigation was not appropriate even if the perpetration had been unintentional or indirect.

[36] In the United States in the 1960s, the pendulum swung so far in the direction of judicial discretion that penalization often became erratic.

THREE: *Formal Political Culture: Law*

render and confess and reform to become new people." Although the code which eventually appeared did not stress confessions, their encouragement by remission of sentences seems to have been common, at least vis à vis the lower classes. By 1934, detailed provisions for confessed criminals appeared in the statutes, although the Communists' expulsion from Kiangsi made such matters moot. After reestablishing themselves in Shensi, increasing thought was given to dealing with people who committed antisocial acts. Rather than emphasizing the mechanical application of the law, the stated object was "winning over" the defendants.[37] As one report on judicial work written at the end of the Yenan period stated:

> In regard to sentencing, the Border Region has adopted a policy of leniency. We must exert every effort to win over every prisoner who can be won over. It must be realized that to win over to the side of the revolution a criminal who has formerly opposed and harmed the revolution is to decrease to some extent the strength of the counterrevolution and increase that of the revolution. For this reason it cannot be otherwise in the Border Region. We absolutely must not apply the death penalty lightly. But when, because of political conditions of our relations with the masses, we must apply the death penalty, we absolutely cannot permit any relaxation or leniency.[38]

We see, then, that leniency in the eyes of the Chinese Communists has served a somewhat different purpose than it has in the West, where considerations of administrative efficiency and also an abstract sense of justice predominate.[39] In China, the rationale has been that the interests of the social (or cosmic) order should determine how culprits should be treated. The Communists have carried this one step further: the interests of society require that everything be done to encourage the accused to be "saved."

---

[37] Rickett (see note 34), p. 805.
[38] Ibid.
[39] "The Purpose of the system of voluntary confession in the criminal law of the People's Republic of China is to use political means to win over most of the counterrevolutionary and other criminals by exhorting them to repent for their criminal acts so they may be remolded through education and become laboring citizens in a socialist society. As is true of all criminal law in the People's Republic of China, the system of voluntary confession is designed to serve the construction of a socialist society. Thus we have been able to exhort counterrevolutionary and other criminals to repent and to confess their crimes in large numbers...." Ning Han-lin, "Voluntary Confession in the Criminal Law of the People's Republic of China," *Cheng-fa yen-chiu*, 1957, no. 4, translated in *CLG*, Spring 1969, pp. 16 f.

> In our country, the number of crimes solved is about the same as the number committed. There is no need, therefore, to use reduction of, or exemption from, punishment as bait to induce counterrevolutionary or ordinary criminals to make voluntary confessions. This demonstrates that the system of voluntary confession emanates from the historical mission of the proletariat and its political party to re-form the world, and is designed to induce those people who are opposed to being remodeled to accept it willingly.[40]

Statutes are replete with provisions for reduction or remission of punishment for confessed offenders, and courts seem to have regularly granted such treatment. At the same time, sentences have often been stiffened for those who refuse to confess (with much judicial miscarriage undoubtedly resulting).[41]

The same legal spirit was conspicuous in the late 1960s (although by this time the ancient terminology had been reformed). Even Chief of State Liu Shao-ch'i was compelled to confess his errors three times, his first two confessions having been deemed insufficiently sincere.[42] Some astute readers of the political winds came forth with early and earnest recantation without waiting to have it extracted from them. This was especially true of ordinary cadres, but a few high officials (Ch'en Yi, Kuo Mo-jo) avoided some of the excesses of the Cultural Revolution by timely confessions. All of these developments illustrate that punishment in China is not an end in itself, and that to an extent greater than elsewhere aids the maintenance of social norms, which are considered best served when wrongdoers simply confess and reform.[43]

If the special place of confessions in Chinese judicial proceedings was less than revolutionary, however, there was much else that was. The campaign against counterrevolutionaries in the early 1950s was a truly tumultuous affair, though it was not without legalistic trappings. Numerous regulations were handed down by Peking to judicial cadres on how businessmen, for example, were to be treated. These were more precise regarding what the overall results of the drive were to be than how individual accused persons were to be dealt with. As

---

[40] Ibid.
[41] Ibid., p. 19, cautions against abuses.
[42] Parts of Liu Shao-ch'i's confession of October 23, 1966, appeared in the April 1967 issue of *Atlas*; the confession of July 9, 1967, in *SCMP*, no. 4037, October 9, 1967; and that of c. August 1, 1967, in *CLG*, Spring 1968.
[43] On this question, see also Cohen, *Criminal Process*, pp. 371 ff.

a result, large numbers of bourgeois men and women were convicted (800,000 in the first half of 1951 alone); only a small fraction were acquitted.[44]

By 1954, however, the new government was prepared to wind down the campaign against bourgeois elements, and to regularize judicial practices. Doubtless this came about because the new regime had survived its first few years, had eliminated its most serious opponents, and had built up a corps of trained cadres who understood and could carry out the new laws and regulations, and administer the new judicial system. This turning to a more formal model of law was celebrated by the promulgation of a constitution in 1954, which mandated that "all personnel of organs of state must be loyal to the system of people's democracy, observe the Constitution and the law, and strive to serve the people."[45] There ensued a period of almost three years of what comes closest in the Chinese Communist experience to constitutional government. As we examine the formal Chinese legal practices in this chapter, it is generally to the mid-1950s that we refer.

We may assume that during this period the constitutional experiment had widespread support at all levels. Although it is possible that Mao Tse-tung was not quite as enthusiastic about the constitution as was his deputy Liu Shao-ch'i, there is no reason to assume that there was any substantial difference between the two men at this time. For his part, Liu praised the constitution, within whose framework "the people of the entire country [were to] unite to build a socialist society. ... Every person and every organ of state, without exception, must observe the Constitution."[46] Years later, after his fall from grace, Liu's critics recalled that he had advocated the establishment of a "comprehensive legal system," which, they argued, had been tantamount to establishing bourgeois law and restoring capitalism. With due allowance for hyperbole, there is doubtless some truth to the charge that by 1954 Liu had sought to downgrade the state's role as a dictatorial instrument. The time had come, he apparently believed, for regularization. "Thus, the organs related to dictatorship should be commensurately reduced, though their quality must be enhanced and the work should be done more meticulously."[47]

---

[44] Many of those convicted were executed, including some who did not have the benefit of a trial. On the loss of life during this period, see note 92.

[45] Article 18. Quotations from the 1954 Constitution are all taken from *Constitution of the People's Republic of China* (Peking: Foreign Languages Press, 1961).

[46] Liu Shao-ch'i, *Quotations*, p. 64.

[47] "Liu Shao-ch'i's Role in Political and Legal Work," *Cheng-fa kung-she*, April 1967, translated in *CLG*, Spring 1968, pp. 69 f.

The practice of quasi-constitutional government and bureaucratic normalization was a success if measured in terms of stability and progress in modernization of the economy and political institutions. Viewed in terms of cultural and social revolution, however, this system of formal law came to constitute a serious roadblock. Thus, the constitutional experiment was brought to an abrupt end in June 1957, after many people (particularly intellectuals), persuaded of their legal rights, indulged in what the leadership determined to be an unacceptable orgy of liberalism and negativism. The story of the Hundred Flowers movement is too familiar to require repetition here, but we should point out that the affair had special meaning for legal development. For those who advocated the formal model of law, Hundred Flowers was a major test, and the result was a major setback. The original idea to permit relatively free expression had been predicated upon the assumption that a mature Party and state could now be relied upon to keep society moving on its Marxist course, and that some criticism would be healthy and stimulating. Mao's confidence on this score is well known, and Liu Shao-ch'i also proclaimed that citizens were free to undertake any action and make any statement, so long as the constitution and laws were not violated.[48]

But when the intellectuals began to speak out, one of the first things to become apparent was how imperfectly the formal model of law had been realized.[49] Numerous complaints from members of the legal profession demonstrated this. Often men of bourgeois background, they complained about the heavy-handedness of Party control, and the fact that China still lacked a comprehensive legal system.[50] The more radical view, on the other hand, was that the legal system had already produced too much rigidity, and the prospects for revolution within a constitutional framework, always dubious, now appeared nil. Thus, in mid-1957 China's leaders decided to sidetrack the development of a formal legal system, and all efforts were bent upon completing the informal model.

The new tone in Chinese politics was set by Mao's famous Six Points, which were made public on June 18, 1957.[51] The next year, when the

---

[48] Liu Shao-ch'i, *Quotations*, pp. 64 f.

[49] Note, for example, that there are very few lawyers in China. See Shao-chuan Leng, "The Lawyer in Communist China," *Journal of the International Commission of Jurists*, Summer 1962.

[50] See, for example, NCNA, May 11, 1957, in *SCMP*, no. 1543.

[51] *CCPDA*, p. 290. The six points were published as part of the Hundred Flowers speech ("On the Correct Handling of Contradictions among the People"), which had been delivered on February 27 but not published until June. It is likely that the Six Points were not in the original speech, however.

relevance of the Six Points was explained to judicial personnel and law students in a textbook,[52] they were rearranged and given somewhat altered emphases. In fact, although they continued to be referred to as the *Six* Points, only five were reiterated. The points, in order as listed in the textbook, were as follows:

It is necessary to obey the leadership of the party absolutely and to implement thoroughly the mass line. (Mao's fifth point.) Only the party, with the benefit of ideology and contact with the masses, it was explained, was in a position to "correctly prescribe the basic lines of legal construction and the concrete tasks in every period." This applied both to legislative and judicial activities, as well as other legal activities of the state.

Consolidation of the people's democratic dictatorship. (Mao's third point.) Inasmuch as the word *dictatorship* had not appeared in the body of the 1954 Constitution,[53] one might have expected the writers of the textbook to ignore that document on this point. Instead, however, they quoted from Articles One and Nineteen in the constitution concerning the *democratic* nature of the People's Republic, insisting (in something of a non sequitur) that the principle of dictatorship was thus "saliently embodied" in the constitution. The effort appears to have been to preserve constitutional legitimacy, while *de facto* discarding many of the provisions of the constitution.

Protection and development of the socialist system of ownership and safeguarding socialist and communist construction. This had been Mao's second point, although he had referred only to socialist, not communist construction. The socialist transformation was supposed to have been basically completed in 1956, and was already part of the law of the land. That upholding socialism was part of the responsibility of the legal community went without saying. The addition of the word *communist* (which implied severing wage rates from productivity) would appear to be a manifestation of the heady atmosphere of the Great Leap Forward.

Uniting the people of the various nationalities. For some reason Mao's first point became the last point here. Suppression of counterrevolutionaries (which in this context meant stamping out any ethnic separatist movements) was "the main cutting edge of the people's democratic legal system."

Also dutifully included was Mao's last point, concerning world peace

---

[52] *CLG*, Summer 1969, pp. 18 ff.
[53] The preamble to the constitution did mention that in 1949 "the People's Republic of China—a people's democratic dictatorship" had been founded.

and international socialist solidarity. Although it was insisted that this was one of the "basic principles of the people's democratic legal system," it was not made clear in just what way this was so. Perhaps it was intended as a reminder that lawyers (especially international lawyers) whose early experience involved Western-style law were to emulate the Soviet model instead.[54]

Not surprisingly, developments in the field of formal law during the ensuing years (as the Chief Justice delicately put it) "fell behind the development of the situation."[55] In 1964 a writer in the journal *Politics and Law* lamented that "nothing has been done" in the area of legal studies.[56] The reason for this state of affairs was that informal law was being emphasized at the expense of formal law. This situation would continue for at least another decade, although the Great Proletarian Cultural Revolution marked the temporary breakdown of even informal law. It was, after all, a *cultural* revolution, and law is an aspect of culture. At times the Maoist press went so far as to advocate the dissolution of law. *People's Daily* came out explicitly in favor of "lawlessness," proclaiming that only in such a spirit could revolutionaries control their destiny. In an apparent reference to those desiring a return to law and order, the newspaper likened revolutionaries to "the Monkey King [in a traditional Chinese novel] who turns the heavenly palace upside down. We will destroy your 'law,' smash your 'world,' rebel against you and seize your power."[57] In 1967 the chief procurator[58] was opposed in a rally, and the following year the president of the Supreme Court[59] reportedly was driven to suicide. In this atmosphere, the courts and procurate appeared to cease functioning, although the final stage of the Cultural Revolution was punctuated by

---

[54] The omission of Mao's fourth point, concerning democratic centralism, is quite unaccountable. Perhaps it was an oversight or editorial error. It is possible, but less likely, that it foreshadowed the antibureaucratic spirit of the Cultural Revolution.

[55] Hsieh Chueh-tsai, "Report on the Work of the Supreme People's Courts" (December 26, 1964), *Main Documents of the First Session of the Third National People's Congress* (Peking: Foreign Languages Press, 1965), p. 58.

[56] Hsiang Shih, "New Problems in the Realm of Legal Studies," *Cheng-fa yen-chiu*, 1964, no. 3, translated in *CLG*, Summer 1968, p. 5.

[57] Quoted in Schapiro and Lewis, "The Roles of the Monolithic Party...," in Lewis, *Party*, p. 138.

[58] Chang Ting-ch'eng. *Mainichi shimbun* (Tokyo), June 15, 1967; FBIS I, June 15, 1967, p. C-3.

[59] Yang Hsiu-feng. This information was said to have appeared in a Red Guard newspaper, and was broadcast by radio Taipei, August 5, 1968; FBIS I, August 6, 1968, p. B-6.

an occasional show trial designed to demonstrate the return to relative normalcy.[60]

The handling of legal affairs in the 1970s, however, has hardly been "normal" in the sense of resembling the pre-Cultural Revolution situation.[61] Unfortunately, so little has been observed or revealed about the subject that it is difficult to present a general picture of China's judicial life.[62] Apparently, the local revolutionary committee exercises a supervisory role. The revolutionary committee appoints a legal subcommittee comprised of "people's lawyers" (sometimes former judicial personnel), which operates within or in conjunction with the public security bureau (police). All legal matters fall within the purview of the legal subcommittee except those pertaining to land reform (now essentially a moot issue) and counterrevolutionaries (who are dealt with by a special military court). "People's lawyers," who may serve on or under the subcommittee, sometimes undergo a crash educational program to give them some understanding of the law and its ideological basis.

When a crime is reported, the legal subcommittee orders that an investigation be conducted by people's lawyers, who may be joined by other citizens as deemed appropriate. Sometimes a workers' or farmers' organization appoints a representative to participate in the investigation. Minor infractions are generally disposed of without trial, the emphasis being on reforming the perpetrator. If a trial is held, it normally is a small affair held in a commune or workplace (not a formal courtroom), with a group of citizens hearing and deciding the issues. Usually there are no professional prosecutors or lawyers present, and there are no tenured judges. Trials are generally presided over by a member of the revolutionary committee (but the status-term *judge* has been dropped). Party policies (doubtless *ex cathedra*) play a more important role than statutory provisions, but great emphasis is also

---

[60] During the Cultural Revolution various Red Guard groups conducted kangaroo trials, but this practice was not condoned by the Maoist leadership.

[61] Most of the information in the following three paragraphs is taken from the accounts by Cheng Huan (*FEER*, January 22, 1972, pp. 14 f.) and Gerde Ruge (*Die Welt*, May 20, 1974; and *CQ*, March 1975). Information about civil trials can be found also in Stanley Lubman, "A Divorce Trial—Peking Style," *Wall Street Journal*, June 5, 1973.

[62] On the difficulties visitors to China have in obtaining information on this subject, see the account of Yale law professor Leon Lipson, *Yale Alumni Magazine*, October 1974, p. 28. Lipson was not permitted to interview anyone in the judicial field. In addition, he was told that in China there are no violations of public order (a claim which was subsequently retracted without elaboration).

placed upon the role of public opinion and community standards.[63] If the case is of special interest, political significance, or educational value, documents may be disseminated among the public. These will be considered in small group discussions, and the court is then sent opinions concerning how the accused should be dealt with. In handing down verdicts and meting out punishments, such opinions are supposed to be seriously heeded. Indeed, legal officials insist that one purpose of a trial is to appease the anger of the masses.

Although sometimes this may result in excessive sentences, there is a variety of means by which punishments may be mitigated. Probably most common is for the convicted person to appeal to the provincial appellate court (although this runs the risk of implying lack of contrition). In serious cases, especially where the death sentence is involved, there will be a review by authorities in Peking. Whatever the procedural route, the final judgment, like the original accusation, is usually based less upon formal law than upon political or informal legal considerations. True, there are some indications that the pendulum may be swinging back toward a somewhat more formal legal model. (One often hears favorable reference to such phrases as "according to law" and "rules and regulations."[64]) On the other hand, following the promulgation of the 1975 National Constitution it was announced that all old formal laws were deemed to have been repealed. Unless and until the old laws are again recognized or new ones formulated, informality will necessarily continue.

Perhaps the revival of constitutionalism itself is to be taken as a sign of renewed reliance upon formal law. However, the 1975 National

---

[63] In the West, fact and law alone are supposed to determine the outcome of cases. However, it is generally recognized that juries have a legitimate role in applying community standards to judicial proceedings. In a rare Memphis, Tennessee, case, where the city had made no provision for trial by jury, a judge allowed those who happened to be present in the courtroom (including some people awaiting to be tried) to decide whether a woman was guilty of assault. (She was found innocent.) *New York Times,* March 20, 1975.

[64] On the importance of adhering to regulations (especially in economic enterprises), see "Report on Shenyang Plant Instituting Rational Rules," Peking radio, December 5, 1970, in FBIS I, December 8, 1970, pp. B-1–B-6; "Take Line as the Key Link in Establishing and Perfecting Rational Regulations and Rules," Peking radio, June 1, 1972, in FBIS I, June 5, 1972, pp. B-4–B-7; and "Raise Our Consciousness of the Struggle between the Two Lines and Improve Product Quality," Peking radio, November 14, 1972, in FBIS I, November 20, 1972, pp. B-1 f. According to the latter account, "After the broad masses had criticized the theory 'rules and regulations are omnipotent' in the Greek Proletarian Cultural Revolution, swindlers like Liu Shao-ch'i [i.e., Lin Piao] interfered with enterprise management from the left by claiming that 'rules and regulations are useless.' In claiming this, they were vainly attempting to negate enterprise management."

Constitution is quite brief (one-third the length of the instrument it replaced), and its provisions loose. Nonetheless, the constitution does provide for the enactment of legislation (by the National People's Congress), and such laws are to be binding upon the government as well as upon the people. (See Appendix A, National Constitution, Arts. 17, 20, and 26.) The constitution gives citizens the right to make complaints to the government concerning official illegal conduct (Art. 27). Obstruction of complaints or retaliation is expressly forbidden. If given life, such clauses could effect the realization of government under law. However, similar provisions in the 1954 Constitution (e.g., Art. 97) were largely inoperative.

The national constitution should probably be looked upon as a general philosophical statement rather than as the core of a body of formal law. It begins with the assertion that China is a socialist dictatorship (not a "people's democracy" as it had been termed in the 1954 Constitution). This is intended to reflect the achievement of socialism, and the essential elimination of the old bourgeoisie. True, classes and class contradictions were assumed to persist, the continued suppression of "traitors and counterrevolutionaries" is called for (Art. 14), and public security organs have the authority to make arrests (Art. 28). But on balance the constitution conveys a sense of optimism that the people can be trusted to uphold socialism and support the Party. Not only are they accorded the usual rights (Arts. 26–30), but the right to speak freely (Art. 13) and to strike (Art. 28) are particularly stressed. The latter, it was announced at the time of promulgation, was being inserted into the document at Mao Tse-tung's own behest.[65]

Although the tension between "democracy" and "centralism" is implicitly recognized (Art. 3), the constitution falls short in providing guidelines for the mediation of this tension.

> Speaking out freely, airing views fully, holding great debates and writing big-character posters are new forms of carrying on Socialist revolution created by the masses of the people. The state shall ensure to the masses the right to use these forms to create a political situation in which there are both centralism and democracy, both discipline and freedom, both unity of will and personal ease of mind and liveliness, and so help consolidate the leadership of the Communist party of China over the state and consolidate the dictatorship of the proletariat. (ART. 13)

---

[65] Chang Ch'un-ch'iao, "Report on the Revision of the Constitution," *PR*, January 24, 1975, p. 19.

Thus, for all the assurances of popular rights, it is made clear that the Communist party is reasserting itself.

> The Communist party of China is the core of leadership of the whole Chinese people. The working class exercises leadership over the state through its vanguard, the Communist party of China.... (ART. 2)

Although Article 3 provides for the election and recall of delegates to people's congresses, the term "democratic consultation" is also used, suggesting selection by something other than popular vote. The local political leadership—the revolutionary committee—is chosen indirectly (Art. 23), and must be approved by the next higher level of government (Art. 22). Thus, the Constitution of 1975 would appear to legislate a shift away from the grass-roots politics of the Cultural Revolution period, and a return to the more traditional Leninist model, based upon centralized political control.[66]

Although Chinese law remains predominantly informal, China has not had quite the dearth of formal law that is often believed. Early in the 1950s there was considerable discussion within the Communist party concerning how legalistic or formal a course should be taken. Some urged the early preparation of comprehensive codes, while others sought maximum flexibility and minimal formal law. The result was a compromise. The line that was adopted rejected the entreaties of both the "legal stabilizers" (formalists), and the "legal nihilists" (who believed that formal legal institutions were for the presocialist stage only and should be discarded as China approached socialism). In practice, the middle course meant that there would be some written law, and some areas where cadres would simply rely upon their general understanding of Communist goals and Party policy.

The following is a partial list of the more important laws which were formally enacted (by 1954, in most instances):

Corruption Suppression
Court Organization
Elections
Labor and Trade Unions

---

[66] For negative Soviet reaction to the 1975 Constitution, see James Clarity's account in the *New York Times*, February 6, 1975. For a more positive account, see Tsien Tche-hao, "La Nouvelle Constitution et la révolution: La solution des contradictions," *NC*, May 1975, pp. 9–16.

THREE: *Formal Political Culture: Law*

    Land Reform
    Marriage
    Police Organization
    Procuratorate Organization
    Reform through Labor
    Residents Committee Organization
    Security Administration Punishment
    Security Stations
    Street Offices

It is clear that in general these laws primarily had organizational and educational (propaganda) functions. Largely absent are general criminal, civil, and procedural codes, although some of the above statutes fall partially within these areas. It is known that other draft codes (e.g., criminal) were prepared but never enacted. According to one Soviet scholar, these "codes" are often referred to by judicial personnel for guidance.[67] All of this tends to demonstrate and confirm the Communists' preference for informal law.

The legal profession in general—largely comprised of non-Communists—was not at all happy with these arrangements. The Hundred Flowers episode of 1957 revealed that a large segment of the profession was dissatisfied with the vagueness of the law and with the interference in the administration of law by the Party. And if we are to believe the charges made during the Cultural Revolution a decade later, some Party leaders reflected similar dissension. As early as 1954, we are told, Liu Shao-ch'i, Lo Jui-ch'ing, and P'eng Chen had begun to

> madly oppose Chairman Mao's revolutionary line. They have disregarded the difference between the dictatorship of the proletariat and that of the capitalist class and have endeavored to continue the illegitimate legal tradition by pushing on with the feudal, capitalist, and revisionist legal system. They have lined up the reactionary legal authorities of the capitalist class, together with whom they plot conspiracy. By deliberate planning, they have nurtured poisonous weeds. They have openly advocated that "law has the nature of continuity" and that "the old laws of the Kuomintang may be continued." Therefore, under the guidance of Liu Shao-ch'i, they formed an organization to systematize the law. P'eng Chen was the man ostensibly in charge of the whole thing. In 1954, they threw out to the public the

[67] G. S. Ostroumov, "Politico-juridical Ideology and the Crisis of Power in China," *Sovetskoe gosudarstvo i pravo*, 1967, no. 6, translated in *CLG*, Fall 1968, p. 11.

"Procuratorate Organization Law," the "Court Organization Law," and so forth. Thereafter, they manufactured the public opinion that called for the "improvement of the legal system" and handed out, with various modifications, the whole set of feudal, capitalist, and revisionist laws...."[68]

With due allowance for hyperbole, there would appear to be some substance to the charge of attempts to systematize the law.[69] Especially during 1956, Liu seems to have urged that political struggle be waged within the legal framework, and that even struggle against counterrevolutionaries "should be waged in accordance with the legal system." To facilitate this, Liu reportedly urged the expeditious drafting and adoption of criminal and civil codes, and their wide publication.[70]

Law codes are meaningful only to the extent of the pervasiveness of their application. If the law is applied uniformly, then all citizens are equal under it. In any system of government, however, there is at least a tendency for leaders, or perhaps an entire elite, to place themselves above the law, which debases the law itself. The question of whether all were equal before the law may have arisen among Chinese Communists as early as 1942, when (according to Mao) future Defense Minister P'eng Teh-huai argued that there should be no "unequal provisions" in law, and that counterrevolutionaries should have equal treatment with revolutionaries under the law.[71] If P'eng Teh-huai said anything like this, he probably meant that people accused of being counterrevolutionaries should not be dealt with arbitrarily, but rather in accordance with law. In 1949, the same directive that rescinded Kuomintang laws throughout the mainland also rejected as a manifestation of those laws the doctrine of equality before the law. "The Six Codes, like all bourgeois laws, maintained that everybody is equal before the law, but in actuality there are no true common interests between the ruling class and the ruled, between the exploiting class and the exploited, between men of property and men without property,

[68] "Completely Smash the Feudal, Capitalist, and Revisionist Legal System," *Fan P'eng, Lo hei hsien*, July 1968, translated in *CLG*, Winter 1969–70, pp. 7 f.

[69] There is little reason to believe, however, that Mao actively opposed such tendencies at this time, as this source implies.

[70] "Liu Shao-ch'i's Role in Political and Legal Work," *CLG*, Spring 1968, p. 71. For further information on the question of codification, see Arthur Stahnke, "The Background and Evolution of Party Policy on the Drafting of Legal Codes in Communist China," *American Journal of Comparative Law*, no. 15 (1966–67).

[71] Mao Tse-tung, "Letter Criticizing P'eng Te-huai's 'Talk on Democratic Education,'" translated in *CLG*, Winter 1968, p. 8.

between debtor and creditor; thus it is impossible to have truly equal rights."[72] By implication, the directive seemed to rule out equality under the law for the future, and certainly there was no equal protection for anti-Communists in the early 1950s. During the Hundred Flowers outbreak in 1957, complaints abounded about the double standard by which the law was applied, with cadres freely violating the law and failing to accord others their legal rights.[73] Not all Party leaders denied the legitimacy of such complaints. A few years later even chief-of-state Liu Shao-ch'i insisted that "it is necessary to act in accordance with the law," although he acknowledged that there should be two "phases" of law—one for the "enemy" and one for the "people."[74]

If justice is to be dispensed in an even-handed manner, it is also necessary to insulate those who make judgments from pressures which are not essential to judicial administration. The United States has made judicial independence from partisanship—and even from the primary source of formal law, the legislatures—a cardinal principle of judicial administration. This is not a regular feature of traditional political systems. In imperial China the idea of separation of the functions of government was unknown. During the republican period some steps were taken in an effort to give the courts independent standing vis à vis the other four branches. That these efforts were not very successful was only one of a number of reasons that the institution of law was largely ineffective.[75] For their part, as the Communists developed their own legal traditions, they rejected the principle of judicial independence along with other aspects of "bourgeois law." After the mid-1930s, the courts in Communist-controlled areas of northern China functioned as arms of the government and were largely dominated by the Communist party.[76] Indeed, it was not uncommon for the head of a county government to serve as the local judge.[77]

[72] Cheng P'u, "Thoroughly Destroy...," *CLG*, Fall 1968, pp. 70 f.
[73] NCNA, June 6, 1957, *SCMP*, no. 1550.
[74] "Liu Shao-ch'i's Role in Political and Legal Work," *CLG*, Spring 1968, p. 72. Quotation dated May 23, 1962.
[75] On the role of the judiciary before 1949, see Ch'ien Tuan-sheng, especially pp. 250 f.

After the Nationalists moved to Formosa, the provincial (i.e. Taiwan Province) and local courts were transferred from the Judicial Yüan to the Ministry of Justice under the Executive Yüan. This move was in violation of the constitution, as the Supreme Court (still in the Judicial Yüan) ruled (without effect).

[76] During the United Front period, however, moderate policies were followed. By means of the "three-thirds" system, some KMT and nonpartisans were consulted.

[77] Jerome Cohen, "The Party and the Courts: 1949–1959," *CQ*, April 1969, p. 128.

The constitution of 1954 reflected the general modern-world view of the need for judicial autonomy. According to Article 78, "The people's courts administer justice independently and are subject only to the law." This principle, however, was undermined by various other clauses. Article 17 stated that "all organs of the state must rely on the masses of the people, constantly maintain close contact with them, heed their opinions, and accept their supervision." At this time the word *masses* often meant "Party." The courts at any level were also made "responsible and accountable" to the legislature at that level (Art. 80). Furthermore, by virtue of Articles 81–83, a powerful procuratorate was created (not accountable to local legislatures), and judicial personnel would often be obliged to defer to a procurator's judgment. Thus, while judicial independence in any country is relative rather than perfect, and there is always pressure for political accountability, by international standards the 1954 Constitution provided for minimal autonomy of the courts.

In China the demands for political accountability have often been intense, especially since Hundred Flowers. As one writer argued in 1957:

> Noninterference in the affairs of the courts does in no way mean that the court may become an "independent state within a state." Such an assumption . . . would lead to disputes between the courts and the Party, disputes between the courts and the organs of state administration. . . . The people's courts, tools of the dictatorship, must also be implicitly subject to Party control. To deny Party control in a specific case means to deny this control in general. And if this means "interference in jurisprudence," then we are for such interference, because it is required by the cause of building socialism.[78]

Since that time almost all judicial personnel have been Party members, which means that they have been primarily responsible to their Party superiors. Even personnel whom we might loosely refer to as judges are quite frank in publicly acknowledging the need to seek instructions from and report to the Party.[79] Except for the period of the Cultural Revolution, when the Party was under too great a cloud to play such a role even if the courts had been functioning normally, this relationship

---

[78] Kang Shu-hua, "The Reactionary Essence of the Principle of 'Independence of Justice,'" *Cheng-fa yen-chiu*, 1957, quoted in I. D. Perlov, "The Departure from Democratic Principles of Justice in the Chinese People's Republic," *Sovetskoe gosudarstvo i pravo*, 1968, no. 1, translated in *CLG*, Fall 1968, p. 28.

[79] See, for example, Cohen, *Criminal Process*, pp. 501 f.

between the Party and the judiciary has remained basically unchanged since 1949.[80]

Such insistence upon Party supremacy is not simply a reflection of a cavalier disregard for the interests of justice. Rather, it is based upon the conviction that law and policy are inseparable. As the legal text quoted earlier put it, 'The people's democratic legal system can only be an instrument to serve Party policy; it cannot be anything that is above or beyond Party policy." It is acknowledged that

> in order that the policy of the Party be implemented effectively, it is still necessary to depend on the other segments of the socialist superstructure as well as to take various effective measures, among which the law that makes concrete and articulates Party policy is one of the important tools for the realization of Party policy.... [However,] the policy of the Communist party is the only basis for the state organs to enact laws and ordinances, and all regulations must be enacted in accordance with Party policy. Some people believe that "policy is prescribed by principle, and if [policy is rendered into law] it no longer is within the scope of policy." Such an interpretation is erroneous because it regards Party policy and regulations as two completely different things. ...
>
> *Not all Party policies are necessarily enacted into law.* Whether the policy of the Party is to be enacted into law must depend on the development and need of the objective situation.... Where the revolutionary movement is in a state of great convulsion, one can rely on the relatively flexible direction and policy of the Party to guide the actions of the masses.... Even if the time of revolutionary storm has passed, not all Party policies are necessarily enacted into laws.[81]

And when they are enacted into law, those laws sometimes become obsolete (i.e., Party policy changes).

> If the law is no longer suited to the needs of struggle, then we can depend only on the new policy proposed by the Party. If the bourgeois rightists should deem that this is "using policy to replace law," then it should be said that this is, in reality, what we want.... It is only natural that [law] should be replaced by Party policy when the law becomes outmoded.[82]

The notion that the courts should be sensitive to political consider-

---

[80] For demands for judicial independence, see *CLG*, Summer 1969, especially p. 50, and *CLG*, Winter 1969–70, pp. 24 ff.
[81] *CLG*, Summer 1969, pp. 5–9. Emphasis added.
[82] Ibid.

ations is hardly unique to China. Many a Western politician has won office on a pledge to affect the nature of judicial decisions. Any leader who intends either to repeal or to promote social change cannot tolerate the inherent conservativism of a judiciary that is concerned only with applying existing law. As China's leaders pursue their revolutionary course, leading the nation from primitive agricultural to modern agroindustrial status, they cannot afford to be checked by the restraining influence of the judiciary. Nor can they afford to unleash the volume of litigation that might result from people suddenly becoming aware of their legal rights and seeking to have them upheld in the courts. Such rapid legal modernization, outpacing and therefore retarding social and economic modernization, would undermine most of what is being sought for China. This is not only the perspective of the more radical Maoists; there is a general consensus on the point among the broad spectrum of Communist leaders, including the "pragmatists." All elements place the revolution ahead of considerations of individual environmental predictability, and orderliness, which are the *raisons d'être* of formal law. Although such considerations are inimical to social and cultural revolution, a technology-based economy has precisely these prerequisites. Thus, the Chinese have paid an economic price for electing to rely primarily upon informal law. This, however, is a matter beyond the scope of this book.

In one area, relations between the sexes, the Communists did attempt to legislate sociocultural change. Although we shall examine this subject further in chapter 7, we should note here that this effort to bring about revolution through formal law was not notably successful. In the more progressive regions (particularly the cities), where the role of women had been changing for decades, progress continued. In most of rural China, however, events lagged far behind the law. If laws, then, could not regulate the relations between men and women, one can understand why there was no rush to apply the technique toward other revolutionary goals. Formal law would be quite irrelevant, for example, to the elimination of elitism—and indeed would probably contribute to the problem.

Informal Law

So far we have related the various disadvantages which Chinese leaders perceive in any system of formal law. Obviously, however, any cohesive and peaceful society requires enforceable law, and the Chinese Communists are fully aware of this. On a number of occasions we have alluded to the propensity for what we have called *informal law*—law which is not precisely stated but which is backed by community sanctions. Because informal law is largely self-enforcing, the *economic* costs of maintaining such a system are probably minor compared with those of the formal model, which requires vast bureaucracies and absorbs much of what would otherwise be productive time on the part of litigants, their spokespeople, and hearers. The relative *social costs* of the two types of law are more difficult to measure, and they depend upon value judgments. From the Maoist point of view, however, the social benefits of the informal model, dispensing as it does with disliked specialists, permitting self-controlled local initiative, and fostering a sense of public spiritedness among the people, make that model infinitely superior.

Informal law is not without its own price. Not only does a complex civilization require some norms which cannot be stated in simple informal-law terms, but there are many difficulties in instituting informal law in the first place. The Communists, especially, did not necessarily select the easier path when they opted for informal instead of formal law. It might well have facilitated the curbing of traditional *li* and modern bourgeois traditions if they had simply relied upon legislation. For Mao, however, this would have been a superficial rather than a radical approach. He became increasingly convinced that simply regulating the population was not a legitimate Marxist target. Rather, the goal of the revolution should be to create a society in which, with a minimum of regulation, people would act consistently with the needs of the social and physical environments. To some extent, this could be accomplished by such expedients as the cult of personality, inciting hostility against internal and external enemies, and material incentives. These devices have all been used at one time or another, but one suspects not without some reluctance and embarrassment on Mao's part.

Thus, for a legal system to play a role in Maoist revolution, its enforcement must rely in large measure upon education and persuasion. Returning to our legal text:

> The people can see that their own legal system is based upon self-awareness and self-volition. This is because, from the standpoint of the people, our own laws and ordinances reflect the common interests of the people, are the common demand, and can be consciously observed by the people. Though there may be a few among the people who refuse to obey the law, this is usually because they do not understand

that these laws and ordinances are beneficial to their collective and permanent interests. They are bound to obey the law consciously when the reason is explained to them.[83]

Thus, whereas formal law rests upon written law and courts, informal law is dependent primarily upon the socialization process, especially education. Of course, the courts and lawmakers also play a pedagogic role. The marriage law is an outstanding example of how a statute was applied not so much as formal law but rather as a vehicle to reform popular views of what was proper in relations between the sexes.[84] For their part, courts seem to do much more to *propagate* cultural norms than they do to enforce them. Even before 1949 the Communists began developing the show trial. The word *show* is apt, for such trials were at once audience-participation dramas and classes held to illustrate for the masses the nature of their oppression and the means of remedying it.[85] In the early 1950s the art of staging such trials was perfected, and they were held frequently. Victims were generally landlords, businessmen, and former KMT officials. Thereafter, until the Cultural Revolution, trials were relatively quiet affairs, designed more to serve justice than to arouse and revolutionize the masses.[86] Nevertheless, the courts have been considered in part classrooms in which the various participants learned about cultural norms, even during periods when they were relatively minor sources of such education.

In general, however, legal socialization is accomplished through the normal institutions of socialization. This is especially true for "the people," as distinct from "the enemies of the people" whom we shall discuss shortly. For "the people," law consists of the norms communicated by the media, schoolteachers, and group leaders. Whereas in North Atlantic nations great emphasis is placed on building respect for *law in general,* in China the leadership seeks more than this; it seeks

---

[83] *CLG,* Summer 1969, pp. 34 f.

[84] Commentaries on the law were made available in popular newspapers. See, for example, answers to readers' inquiries in *Kung-jen jih-pao,* April 25, 1957, p. 3, translated in *CLG,* Spring 1969, pp. 52–59.

[85] For details of these trials during the late 1940s, see William Hinton, *Fanshen,* especially chap. 11, and Belden, pp. 180–85 passim.

[86] On the 1966 trial of Yang Kuo-ch'ing (accused of attacking foreign diplomats), see Hsia Tao-tai, "Justice in Peking: China's Legal System on Show," in *Current Scene,* January 16, 1967. A similar trial (of Yao Teng-shan, former chargé d'affaires in Indonesia) was reported in the *New York Times* on June 21, 1971. The latter trial was attended by 4,000 people (but was not reported in the Chinese press). A number of foreigners were invited, apparently so that they would be impressed with the return to "normalcy" in China's foreign relations.

to inculcate understanding and approval of the *particular norms*. This requires that the laws be simple enough for everyone to understand, and it also requires a high degree of community-mindedness, or concern that the members of one's social environment share common norms.

The ultimate paragon of this style of legal socialization is found in the "small group," of which every adult and adolescent is a member. The small group is generally comprised of between one dozen and two dozen people, and may be organized on the basis of residence, employment, or other institutional affiliation. Each week, every member will spend at least a few hours engaged in study. While not all matters taken up pertain to cultural norms, this area does comprise a large part of the small group's concern. If the leadership has launched a campaign on a particular subject, the focus of the small group will shift accordingly. Otherwise, the group's study will concern various norms or informal laws, often treated in terms of their relevance to immediate circumstances or familiar problems. The discussion will be guided (unostentatiously, if possible) by a cadre knowledgeable in matters of law and policy. A neighborhood group might discuss questions arising from appliance sharing or petty larceny; a factory group might be concerned with allocation of job assignments, authoritative roles, and so on. Not only do the small groups play a major role in legal socialization, but they are also significant enforcement agencies. Deviant acts, and even deviant thoughts, are combatted by means of group pressure, which can be so severe that the psychological and social costs of resistance are insurmountable. One's lot is cast with his group to such an extent that survival requires submission to group norms. Secret violation is unlikely, for deviant behavior is certain to draw attention from the peer group. If, for example, one illegally acquired wealth, the subsequent change in life-style would arouse suspicion.[87]

The idea that the individual is responsible for the moral and legal transgressions of those around him, and should guide his acquaintances along the proper path, is less strange to Chinese than it is to Westerners. As an American legal scholar has put it:

> If [in China] truly no man is an island and the actions of each person directly affect the lives of all others, then the "group," however defined, has a real and direct stake in controlling the actions of its members.

[87] This paragraph has drawn upon Victor Li, "Law and Penology: Systems of Reform and Correction," in Oksenberg, *China's Developmental Experience*, pp. 144–74.

This is entirely contrary to the Western approach of legally, though possibly not morally, discouraging the intrusion by one person into the lives of others, except when something very serious is involved. In place of the "officious intermeddler" rule in most Western tort law and the consequent unwillingness of bystanders to go to the aid of a person in trouble, the Chinese (and, indeed, all the Socialist countries and a few others as well) impose on the citizenry a legal duty to go to the rescue of a person in distress. Similarly, comments and criticisms made about another's life-style or work-style are regarded, in the ideal case, as proper exercises of a social duty to one's fellow man, not as invasions of privacy or as meddling in the affairs of another.[88]

In traditional China one had such responsibilities both to subordinates and to superiors (though perhaps not to equals[89]). Today, in a more egalitarian environment, this aspect of the cultural system has been transformed into one of having everyone as his brother's keeper. Whether or not admonitions are appreciated by the recipient, they are not only legitimate but *de rigueur*.

Crime and Political Crime

For most Chinese citizens, such group tactics are sufficient to achieve internalization of and compliance with the law. There are, however, elements for whom the legal socialization process is insufficient. We may say that these people fall roughly into two categories: political dissidents (of real or asserted bourgeois-capitalist inclinations) who oppose the regime, and criminals in the normal English sense of the term. Actually, although the distinction between these two categories strikes us as a natural one, in China it is generally disallowed. It is assumed that crime is a vestige of the old socioeconomic order, just as is political dissension.[90] Inasmuch as both political and nonpolitical crime are aspects of class struggle, each is dealt with by a harsh form of legal socialization, and, if that fails to reform the individual, he or she is turned over to the organs of dictatorship for long-term separation from the ranks of "the people." The first approach involves thought reform or brainwashing (*hsi-nao*). During the earliest years of the

---

[88] Ibid., p. 151.
[89] Confucianism placed emphasis on hierarchical relationships. In general, if one had a relationship to another, superior–subordinate status was established. Peers had much less responsibility for each other's behavior (except within the *pao-chia* system), and strangers had no such responsibility.
[90] See Ts'ao Tzu-tan, "On the Relationship between Crime and Class Struggle," *Cheng-fa yen-chiu*, 1964, no. 4, translated in *CLG*, Fall 1968, pp. 80 f.

regime, it was common to have errant individuals incarcerated and rendered Pavlovian rewards for improvements in attitude.[91] Until 1952 torture was not uncommon, and many incorrigibles were executed.[92] Since that period it has been the practice to place convicted (or sometimes simply accused) individuals in appropriate group situations in which extreme social pressures are applied. During the 1950s the most common setting for serious cases of deviancy was the *labor reform* camp. These were harsh institutions where labor was given much greater stress than study.[93] Beginning in 1957 the emphasis gradually shifted, and although the labor reform camps continued to exist, the *labor reeducation* camp became the more common penal institution. There is much that is not known about labor reeducation camps, but some appear to be rather in the nature of halfway houses, designed to some extent to reflect normal Chinese life. Whereas an ordinary citizen will live at home and spend only a few hours a week engaged in political discussion, camp internees live more restricted lives (often but not always forbidden to leave the grounds) and will spend perhaps fifteen hours a week engaged in political study, introspection, and group discussion. The discussions are led by a trustee appointed by the administration.[94] The difference between camp life and civilian life is thus a matter of degree. In some respects (near-normal daily work of eight to ten hours), camp existence is not very different from extramural life.[95]

The thrust of these activities is to reintegrate the individual into the society—or, more precisely, into the culture. Regular legal socialization having failed, he is given intensive "therapeutic" treatment in

---

[91] On this subject, see R. J. Lifton, *Thought Reform and the Psychology of Totalism: A Study of "Brainwashing" in China* (New York: Norton, 1961).

[92] Estimates of the number of people killed by the Chinese Communists vary greatly, and one can only give an individual impression. The KMT has claimed that 66 million died, but this figure would appear to be excessive (*Free China Weekly*, August 11, 1968, p. 1). Richard Hughes has quoted Foreign Ministry spokesperson Kung Peng as putting the figure for 1951 (presumably a peak year) at 2 million (*New York Times Magazine*, November 15, 1970, p. 128). If that figure is roughly correct, then the total would probably be between 3 and 5 million. Apparently even the Chinese leaders have not known how many executions took place. Nevertheless, there was general agreement that there were far too many. In 1962 Liu Shao-ch'i urged that the facts of the matter, however ugly, be determined and made public (*CLG*, Spring 1968, p. 73).

[93] For a participant's account, see Bao and Chelminski.

[94] Hardened (nonpolitical) criminals are not put in leadership positions, as they were in Soviet labor camps during the Stalinist era.

[95] Martin King Whyte, "Corrective Labor Camps in China," *AS*, March 1973, pp. 253–69.

a camp atmosphere. In this process, labor is an integral part, for Maoists believe that understanding derives more readily from experience than from books or intellectual discussions. Labor is compensated, but the rate of remuneration is dependent in part upon attitude. Rate of compensation is set by self-evaluation and mutual intragroup evaluation, a process which gives concrete meaning to the reform process.[96] Although prior to confinement much stress is laid upon confession, thereafter the individual is encouraged to be forward-looking, and the past is not stressed. Inmates listen to speeches and read newspapers and other materials, but in general the exercise is not passive. Each person is required to express his personal reaction to the norms outlined, and personal expression is expected to take the form of self-criticism when views are at variance with the norms which are being studied. When such self-criticism is not forthcoming, peer criticism will be. Conversely, the progress of an individual's thought reform will be in part measured by the nature and frequency of his criticisms of others.[97] *Self*-evaluation, however, is probably the most critical element in the process of internalizing informal law.[98]

The reader may have noticed that in all of this discussion of Chinese law we have said little about procedures. To the extent that these can be discerned, they would appear to be very loose and *ad hoc*. Whereas in Western law fastidious adherence to proper procedure is *sine qua non* of disposition, in China, trials are no prerequisite to long-term confinement. Right to legal counsel and to public trials were guaranteed by the 1954 Constitution, but they are not mentioned in the 1975 Constitution. At any rate, there have never been many lawyers in China, and outright defense of accused individuals has been rare.[99] It is common for final dispositions of cases to be taken by administrative rather than judicial means. Although some leaders have urged greater adherence to proper procedure, one more frequently reads of objections to the way in which procedural obstacles interfere with the dis-

[96] As this is similar to an extramural process, it also helps prepare the inmate for reintegration into society.

[97] Exceptional ability and sincerity in this regard may be rewarded by promotion to group leader.

[98] For examples of self-criticisms, see Cohen, *Criminal Process*, pp. 158–69.

[99] Some leaders are alleged to have urged that defendants' rights to counsel be taken more seriously. On P'eng Chen, see *Fan P'eng* ... (note 2 above) July 1968, translated in *CLG*, Winter 1969–70, p. 11. For a Russian account of such debates, see I. D. Perlov, "The Departure from Democratic Principles of Justice in the Chinese People's Republic," *Sovetskoe gosudarstvo i pravo*, 1968, no. 1, translated in *CLG*, Fall 1968, pp. 13–34.

THREE: *Formal Political Culture: Law*

position of cases and the reformation of culprits.[100] This points up another important difference in rationale and purpose between Chinese and North Atlantic trials. In the United States, for example, protection of the public is the official reason usually given for criminal proceedings, with emphasis also placed upon the need to provide safeguards for the rights of the accused. Neither consideration is paramount in China, where crime is not a serious threat to society.[101] Rather, penology in China has a missionary function of saving individuals from alienation.

Law, or at least formal law, better serves the cause of maintenance than innovation. For revolutionaries, this is a serious issue, but one which the Chinese hope can be circumvented by primary reliance upon informal law, and only secondary reliance upon formal law (which, ultimately, should "wither away," along with the state and Party). Even informal law's effectiveness, however, depends upon a degree of social stability and political control. These in turn presuppose skilled leadership whose legitimacy is not widely questioned and whose policies are publicly understood and accepted. It is to these aspects of politics that we now turn.

---

[100] For example, *CLG*, Summer 1969, pp. 55 ff.; and *CLG*, Winter 1969–70, p. 10.

[101] See *Main Documents of the First Session of the Third National People's Congress of the People's Republic of China* (Peking: Foreign Languages Press, 1965), especially pp. 53 and 61. The only time that nonpolitical crime was a serious problem was during the Cultural Revolution.

FOUR
Leadership and Participation

> *It is not knowing
> but acting
> which is difficult.*
>
> FU YÜEH (c. 1300 B.C.)[1]

> *I am alone with the masses.
> Waiting.*
>
> MAO TSE-TUNG (1965)[2]

THE ENGLISH WORD *leadership* can connote both the personal and the *ex officio* (institutionalized) capability to induce others to follow. In the former sense, the concept implies independence from an institutionally defined role. The dominant view among the social sciences, on the other hand, has been that meaningful leadership generally does have an institutional or at least a systemic setting, and that any scientific definition of leadership must take cognizance of that fact. Thus, leadership has been defined as "role performance whose influence is central with regard to collective action."[3]

On leadership, see Bouc; Domes, "Chinese"; Hsueh; Lindbeck (especially Johnson, "Changing"); Robinson, "Chou"; Scalapino; Schurmann (especially pts. II, IV); and Waller.

On participation, see Pfeffer; Townsend, Political Participation; and Vogel, "Voluntarism".

Also useful for comparative purposes is R. Berry Farrell, ed., Political Leadership in Eastern Europe and the Soviet Union (Chicago: Aldine, 1973).

[1] Quoted in the *Shang Shu*. James Legge, *The Chinese Classics*, 2d ed., vol. 3 (London: Frowde, n.d.), p. 258.

[2] Malraux, p. 466.

[3] Julius Gould and William L. Kolb, eds., *A Dictionary of the Social Sciences* (New York: Free Press, 1964), p. 380.

Theories of Leadership

For purposes of the study of Chinese politics, it would be appropriate to keep in mind the two facets of leadership—the *ex officio*, and the effective, self-generating, informal, opinion-molding, or what we shall call *de facto* leadership. To speak in terms of the framework established in the last chapter, we may say that institutional, or *ex officio*, leaders act within a formal law environment, whereas *de facto* leaders consider themselves free of such constraints. It may be true that even *de facto* leaders operate within what a social scientist would call a system,[4] but they operate within it as a matter of choice, and may elect at any time to dispense with institutional constraints.

We can only begin to suggest some of the reasons why, in given situations, either *ex officio* or *de facto* leaders may emerge. Perhaps the explanation in some cases will be found in the availability of leadership skills. People with such skills—i.e., the ability to lead *under existing circumstances*—are at a premium especially during periods of upheaval and institutional instability, and it is during such times that (as Max Weber pointed out) charismatic leaders are apt to emerge. Is this because existing institutionalized leadership roles are inadequate vehicles for leaders lacking personal charisma? Perhaps so, but it is undoubtedly also the case that roles are institutionally defined precisely to enhance leadership performance—a step again necessitated by the general shortage of leadership skills. Thus, that shortage seems to suggest explanations for the existence of *both* institutional and *de facto* leaders, but does not help us predict which will emerge.

Does the prior existence of viable institutions provide the answer? The American experience would tend to suggest that it is *situations* (wars, depressions) rather than the viability of institutions which foster charismatic leadership, and that institutional roles, far from obviating the need for charismatic leadership, may predetermine who can become such a leader. But here the Chinese experience gives us a quite different perspective on the matter. In Chinese history there have been two leaders whose personal charismatic qualities separate them from all others: Ch'in Shih Huang-ti and Mao Tse-tung. Both of these men were ambitious to the point of creating new offices to match the stature they sought. The former made himself the "First Emperor," and the latter became chairman initially of the Communist party, and then of the state—both new titles at the time Mao assumed them.

[4] See David Easton, *The Political System: An Inquiry into the State of Political Science* (New York: Knopf, 1953).

Unlike American presidents, some of whom were more charismatic than the first president, Chinese emperors were required to be aloof, and usually relied upon their *ex officio* roles, rather than their personalities.[5] A first emperor of any dynasty, with a serious, almost defensive concern for legitimacy, was usually cautious about appearing to behave too differently from archtypical emperors of the past. A dynastic founder's successors, who were also descendants, were constrained by the requirements of filial piety to fill faithfully the role they inherited (which rendered most of them arch conservatives). Unlike Japan, however, where cultural considerations dictated unbroken dynastic succession from prehistoric times but without preventing the sociopolitical order from undergoing profound systemic changes, China's dynastic replacement was accepted as a matter of course while the sociopolitical order remained basically intact for two thousand years. This suggests that we need to examine closely the phenomenon of legitimization—the bedrock of politics in any country.

Legitimacy

In the West, and especially in the English-speaking world, *legitimacy* has strong legalistic overtones.[6] In modern times, large bodies of constitutional law exist to legitimize governments and their conduct. Constitutions rarely are the product of popularly elected bodies, and thus it is not public opinion per se, but rather law, which determines legitimacy. If a leader gains office by popular election, it is because the *constitution* says that that is how office should be attained; the constitution is the ultimate arbiter.[7] One cannot make a scientific judgment that it is right that this should be so—that words written many years ago and now perhaps impossible to change should have precedence over public opinion; only a nation's political culture (which dictates supreme respect for constitutionalism) can make it "right."

In China, constitutions and other formal law have never been what

---

[5] Here we are concerned with typical/stereotypical emperors. Later in this chapter we shall discuss atypical ones.

[6] The word comes from the Latin *legitimare*, meaning "to declare to be lawful," and the earliest English usage continues the legalistic connotations. *Oxford English Dictionary*.

[7] There is, of course, often great tension between constitutionalism and extraconstitutional popular demands. If the constitutional rights of the opposition are denied by the government, then constitutional government is suspended, even though the government may be able to run up impressive majorities. The 1972 United States presidential election may have been a case in point.

FOUR: Leadership and Participation

validates political power. In the beginning, kings ruled by means of something akin to divine right. During Shang and early Chou times there were deities known as *Ti* and/or *T'ien*.[8] *Ti* was originally a supreme god to which only the king could appeal, thus at once enhancing and legitimizing the king's authority. Eventually *ti* became incorporated into the compound *shang-ti*, which could refer either to the supreme deity or to the priest-king himself. *T'ien* underwent an even more interesting conceptual metamorphosis. Early in the Chou period the term designated various ancestral spirits; in time it came to designate a single deity.[9] However, by the end of the Chou period *t'ien* was understood in the sense of "heaven," being a much more generalized force than *ti*. With the latter, the royal family maintained a personal relationship, and no one else could appeal to it. *T'ien*, on the other hand, could be invoked by anyone, even non-Hans.[10] Thus was born the concept of the mandate of heaven (*t'ien ming*), used by the alien Chou tribes upon overthrowing the Shang in the late twelfth century B.C. The heirs of the Chou dynasty's founder continued to rely upon the same mandate, though (if we are to believe the "histories" of this largely prehistoric period) the successors gradually fell away from his exemplary leadership. There then emerged a certain ambivalence in the Chou concept of legitimacy—a ruling dynasty, according to one way of formulating the principle, possessed the mandate of heaven so long as it continued to produce competent rulers. Eventually, the Confucian philosopher Mencius provided the definitive statement of the mandate-of-heaven doctrine. Although he insisted that it was wrong to rebel against *t'ien*, the latter nonetheless "sees as our people see and hears as our people hear."[11] An ambitious leader who sought the throne was thus promised that if the (educated) people were with him he could have his kingdom, but he was warned that if they were not—if *he* were deemed to be rebelling against heaven—then he would perish. Furthermore, although the use of force might be necessary to *found* a government, it was no way to *conduct* one. Statesmanship (*wang tao*) meant not ruling coercively (*pa tao*). Dynastic legitimacy was not

---

[8] The names *"Ti"* and *"T'ien"* sometimes referred to separate gods; at other times they were the same.

[9] On the development of the idea of *t'ien*, see H. G. Creel, *Studies in Early Chinese Culture*, 1st series (Baltimore: Waverly Press, 1937), especially p. 97 n. See also Fung Yu-lan, *A History of Chinese Philosophy* (Peiping: Vetch, 1937), p. 31, and Creel's article (in Chinese) in *Yenching Journal of Chinese Studies*, December 1935, pp. 59–71.

[10] The term *Han* denotes ethnic Chinese. Hans referred to non-Hans by various terms, some of which can be translated *barbarian*. Minority nationalities will be discussed further in chap. 7.

[11] *Mencius*, 5:5. See p. 45.

permanent, but rather contingent upon effective government and general harmony. Any social or ecological disruption would be attributed to dynastic decline, presaging the passing of heaven's mandate from one dynasty to another.[12] The ultimate test of legitimacy, then, was acceptance-inducing *effectiveness*.[13]

For the theory of legitimacy to evolve from a numinous conception to a secular one is not, of course, unique. In most Western European nations the notion of divine right of kings gave way to some form of popular sovereignty. In Europe, however, the transition was facilitated by the important rationale that "divine right" was a function of divine *law*, and that divine law legitimized temporal law. In China, the breach opened by Confucian agnosticism was not filled by law, as we saw in the previous chapter. Inasmuch as the "people" were supposed to judge whether a ruler possessed the mandate of heaven, rulers went to great lengths to demonstrate that they had done so. One way to appeal to the scholar gentry was to adhere to strict Confucian orthodoxy in matters of ideology and the conduct of state. Indeed, Confucian writers made no distinction between "legitimacy" and "orthodoxy," using the term *cheng-t'ung* to cover both. But an imperial dynasty had to impress more than just Confucian scholar-officials. For this reason, emperors conducted elaborate ceremonies, some of which (such as plowing the first furrow in the spring) touched the ordinary farmer. Through their taxes, the population also financed the lavish life-style of the imperial family, and the impressive capitals further attested to the fact that the public was in fact supporting (and thus legitimizing) the "son of heaven." Proper hallmarks, codified according to the "five agent" principles which were discussed in chapter 2 (wood, fire, earth, etc.), were also essential imperial trappings. In the absence of constitutionalism or *de facto* leadership, such elaborate mythology was essential for the legitimization of each imperial dynasty.

The parallels between traditional and recent legitimization in China

[12] Reports of natural phenomena were considered warning signals. See Wolfram Eberhard, "The Political Function of Astronomy and Astronomers in Han China," in *Chinese Thought and Institutions*, ed. John Fairbank (Chicago: University of Chicago Press, 1957). Eberhard maintains that reputed ominous occurrences such as eclipses were reported selectively, if not fictitiously. In at least one case, an upstart *ordered* portents unfavorable to the dynasty he was in the process of overthrowing. In other cases, historians during the subsequent dynastic period invented them retroactively in order to legitimize the new royal house. The system, then, provided officials with a sort of "constitutional right" to make implicit criticism of the emperor.

[13] Occasionally this was made explicit, as by Wang Fu-chih (seventeenth century), who insisted that the state serve the people and not the rulers. *ECCP*, p. 818.

can best be stated in negative terms. At no time has law played a significant legitimizing role,[14] and resort to violence has not been taken as an indication that legitimacy has been absent (notwithstanding the Chinese bias against militarism, and preference for harmony).[15] But in comparing past and recent legitimization in positive terms, we are struck by some sharp contrasts. Traditionally, the imperial family was concerned with demonstrating that they were the rightful claimants to the throne. Once this was established to the satisfaction of the world (*t'ien hsia*, i.e., "under heaven"), all of the actions of the emperor (and those acting in his name) were presumptively legitimate. Indeed, as the son of heaven (*t'ien-tzu*), whose writ was valid everywhere (*t'ien-hsia*), he was in a position to legitimize the kings of other civilized countries. In the twentieth century no such honor has been accorded Chinese rulers,[16] and indeed it is China that has been in need of the legitimacy which flows from diplomatic relations. Modern international recognition legitimates *governments* (not individual rulers, as had been the case under the old tribute system), yet it was usually the most transparent fiction that the republican "governments" which the international community recognized were the real governments of China. It was quite clear to politically aware Chinese that international recognition was not a function of legitimacy, but rather that foreign countries arrogated unto themselves the right to determine what man or clique comprised the "legitimate" government of China, and therefore whether that government would survive.[17]

Against this background, it is not surprising that the fact of a mere functioning government should not now be considered the main precondition of legitimacy. More important is whether or not the whole

[14] Note, for example, how little practical significance the constitutions of either the People's Republic of China or Formosa have had. On the latter's constitution, see Seymour, "Republic."

[15] Although most of China's traditional schools of thought abhorred war and sought harmony, war was not usually categorically rejected as illegitimate. Mencius, Mo Tzu, and Hsun Tzu all agreed that some wars were just. The determining factor was the character of the *leadership*. See Bodde, "Harmony," p. 52.

[16] The Chinese have taken it upon themselves to recognize, and in a sense legitimize, foreign revolutionary movements, which is of some importance to such movements. But in recognizing foreign governments, China is only one of over a hundred countries in a position to do so. For further discussion, see chap. 8.

[17] This system lasted until 1949 (and the United States attempted to perpetuate it through the 1960s). To say that foreign recognition was a precondition of survival is no exaggeration. In the 1920s the warlord who controlled Peking, upon being granted international recognition as the president of China, could stave off bankruptcy by taking out loans abroad which became national obligations. And the Kuomintang government in Taipei could hardly have survived without diplomatic support and massive infusions of funds to the "Republic of China" from the United States.

nation enjoys *de facto* leadership by an individual whose authority is not openly questioned. Thus, after Mao Tse-tung and his followers gained physical control of the country, *he* became the ultimate source of legitimization—in sharp contrast to the "revisionist" view that only the *Party* legitimizes. The most outrageous policies—even those reversing earlier basic lines—became legitimate not when decreed by the government or even the Party, but rather when endorsed by Mao, the *de facto* leader. The Cultural Revolution, for example, could not possibly have occurred had not Mao *personally* assumed responsibility for it.[18] Similarly, the rapprochement with the United States in the early 1970s, more than serving a legitimizing function, itself required Mao's sanction before being considered a legitimate move.[19]

Commanded by the requisites of legitimacy to be aloof and orthodox, emperors who in another political culture might otherwise have been charismatic found themselves unable to be *de facto* leaders. With the written word the preferred and almost sacred medium of communication, it was impossible to act in any but an *ex officio* capacity. The taboo against anyone's writing (in any context) a character which happened to comprise part of the emperor's personal name is an example of how the mystique of office was enhanced at the cost of removing the emperor (or republican president[20]) from the people and sometimes from politics itself.

Perhaps this tradition had something to do with Mao Tse-tung's rather cavalier attitude toward the offices he occupied. He was deter-

---

[18] On October 24, 1966, he acknowledged to the Communist party, "The fire of the great Cultural Revolution was kindled by me." Mao, *Selections*, p. 15.

[19] This was true of both the initial "Ping-Pong diplomacy" (*New York Times*, October 7, 1971, p. 4), and the invitation to President Richard Nixon to visit China. Edgar Snow, *The Long Revolution* (New York: Random House, 1972). See also the account in *Sing-tao jih-pao* (Hong Kong), February 2, 1972, p. 4, translated in FBIS I, February 10, 1972, p. A-1, relating how Chou En-lai repeatedly stressed that the invitation to Nixon had been Mao's personal decision. Of course, Chou may have said this in part to defend himself against his critics, but at the same time he was defending the policy.

In this discussion we have refrained from viewing legitimacy as a general part of political culture, which was discussed in an earlier chapter. Of course, it can be argued that political culture, and especially ideology, is what legitimates, but this is rather circular since by this reckoning legitimacy *is* culture. At any rate, we have taken the view that Mao has legitimized changes in the Chinese political culture more than he has himself been legitimized by that culture or by Marxist ideology. For a discussion of legitimacy and ideology, see Hsiung, especially pp. 93–97. On the question of how ideology itself becomes legitimized, see Schurmann, p. 25.

[20] In the Republic of China it has generally been required by law that Chiang Kai-shek be referred to by title and not by name, and that the type be arranged in a particularly honorific manner. However, emperors went much farther, in that the characters in their name could not appear in print in *any* context.

mined to avoid what he termed being treated like a buddha on a shelf. In 1959 he relinquished the title of Chairman of the Republic, possibly upon his own initiative.[21] That left him with only the position of Chairman of the Party, and before long he would provoke the near disintegration of that organization. Like Ch'in Shih Huang-ti, Mao found that he had brought more authority to the role of his creation than he was deriving from it. His response was to revert to his deinstitutionalized *de facto* leadership status. Not only did he divorce himself from his official role, but he also deinstitutionalized politics in general, leading some scholars to believe that he was more *"führerist"* than "Leninist."[22]

Marxist Views on Leadership

It was the belief of Karl Marx that leaders were more products of history than they were positive determinants of events. Genuine revolutions were leaderless. Although Engels modified this principle by saying that insurrections must be centralized, it is nonetheless fundamental to classical Marxism that leaders were at least replaceable, if not dispensable. A leader's main responsibility is to understand his times; events take care of themselves. Most of Marx's early disciples[23]

[21] Although many believe that Mao was forced out, Mao himself raised the possibility of his giving up the state chairmanship more than a year before he actually did so. On February 19, 1958, the Central Committee circulated word that Mao wanted "a preliminary exchange of views on the question of my not serving as chairman of the People's Republic of China. Mass contending and debates should be organized first among the cadres at each level and then in factories and cooperatives to solicit the views of the cadres and the masses in order to gain the concurrence of the majority. This is because in giving up the functions of the Chairman of the Republic and serving only as Chairman of the Party Central Committee, I will save a lot of time to do what the Party wants me to do. This also is more suitable to my physical condition. If in the course of debates the masses develop a mood of resistance and do not approve of this proposal, it can be explained to them that in case of national emergency in the future I will still be able to assume this national leadership post, if the Party so decides. As we are now enjoying peacetime, it is advantageous to give up one chairmanship. This request has already been agreed upon by the Political Bureau of the Central Committee and my many central and local comrades." These are not the words of a man who was fighting against being demoted. *CLG*, Spring 1972, pp. 116 f. However, there is also evidence that Mao was not fully in command of the situation in 1959. See below, note 112.

The republic chairmanship was next held by Liu Shao-ch'i, then unsuccessfully sought by Lin Piao. Finally, the position was formally abolished under the 1975 Constitution.

[22] Leonard Schapiro and John Wilson Lewis, "The Roles of the Monolithic Party under the Totalitarian Leader," in Lewis, *Party*, pp. 114–45.

[23] Bernstein, Luxemburg and to a lesser extent Kautsky, Plekhanov, and Trotsky.

continued to deemphasize the role of leadership, but the more realistic Lenin saw nothing but danger in spontaneous revolution conducted by the untutored masses. Someone had to organize the proletariat, educate them, and ignite the revolution—not necessarily in that order. The key tools, for Lenin, were the elitist party, and skilled leadership. Only after the attainment of communism would there be no need to distinguish between leaders and led; then a truly leaderless society might be possible.[24]

Most modern Marxists have, either explicitly or implicitly, attributed a central role to leadership. Herbert Marcuse, for example, argues that although there may be "necessary" historic developments, history does not unfold automatically, and human consciousness is an important input. In the Communist world the question is no longer seen as whether or not there should be leadership, but rather what is the *relative* importance of individual leaders vis à vis institutions. Within China this question has been hotly debated, but at no time has the view prevailed that neither kind of leadership was necessary. More often than not the successful conduct of the affairs of the nation is attributed directly to Mao Tse-tung's leadership.[25] Although there was a widespread hiatus in *local* leadership during the Cultural Revolution, the need for such was reemphasized in the early 1970s, and the improvement in economic conditions was often attributed directly to the improved leadership.[26]

---

[24] Lenin did not always stress the point that leadership would "wither away," and Engels had foreseen that the requirements of modern industry made this unlikely.

[25] For example, "Thanks to Chairman Mao's wise leadership and correct command," a 1948 battle had been won. Shen Chun, "Great Victory for Chairman Mao's Strategy," *HC*, 1973, no. 8, p. 15.

[26] See, for example, "Build More Tachai-Type Counties," *Honan jih-pao*, broadcast May 27, 1973. FBIS I, June 1, 1973, pp. D-4–D-5. "Hui county's grain output remained at a comparatively low level for nine consecutive years before the Great Proletarian Cultural Revolution. In the few years since then, however, it has doubled as a result of the socialist education movement in the countryside and especially as a result of the Great Proletarian Cultural Revolution. What is the reason for this? *The main reason is that the leadership has undergone a deep change in its attitude.*" Emphasis added.

Another example comes from neighboring Hunan Province. There a brigade-level Party secretary investigated a production team and "I discovered that its backwardness was caused by its leader, who did not like his work and who considered that 'a cadre's role is hard to play' and that 'it is not profitable to serve as a cadre.'" The secretary worked to raise the consciousness of the cadre, and the result reportedly was a marked increase in agricultural productivity. Mo I-chu, "Whom Should We Rely Upon to Improve Backward Production Teams?" *JMJP*, September 5, 1972, p. 2, FBIS I, October 4, 1972, pp. B-3 f.

FOUR: Leadership and Participation

This penchant for "correct leadership," and the concomitant assumption that leaders affect history, then, do not spring from classical Marxism. We might be tempted to conclude that the Soviet model is reflected here, but this is hardly a model which the Chinese now deliberately emulate. Is it a product of China's tradition?

Chinese Tradition

Earlier, we described the ideal-type emperor, and examined the basis of his legitimacy. But what were emperors *really like*? Although much research remains to be done on this subject, it is unlikely that this description (by a Chinese emigré) will ever be substantially refuted:

> The Chinese Emperor as the head of the country was a symbolic priestlike figure with an amount of power varying according to his personal character. He lived in the palace, isolated from the life of his people; he performed or was supposed to perform the daily ceremonies of filial piety as a hypothetical example for his people; he presided over the annual ceremonies of worship of Heaven and Earth for the agricultural prosperity of his land; and he received the reports and memorials of his ministers and issued edicts on the most important affairs of state. His actual power varied from nil, in the case of dissipated and feeble emperors, to absolute power, in the case of despotic and sagacious ones. The controlling factor, the personal character of the emperor, was very much left to chance: if a stupid or debauched one came to the throne the good ministers were dismissed and misrule followed.[27]

We are thus reminded of the distinction we have been making between *de facto* and *ex officio* leaders. It would appear that an emperor per se was not an important leader in the sense that *he* induced his followers to move in the direction he charted. It might be argued that the distinction is purely academic, because when an emperor really did lead, one cannot meaningfully separate his accomplishments from his imperial role. Such a reaction would be altogether appropriate were we discussing a Western political system, but it only serves to highlight this important feature of Chinese (or perhaps East Asian)[28] leadership. If a Western chief of state or premier retires from office, he no longer leads his country, and probably lives out his life

---

[27] Mu, p. 61.
[28] The Japanese example of the *genrō* (elder statesmen) comes to mind.

essentially as a museum piece. He may make a comeback, but only by resuming *office*. In China, a chief of state may relinquish that office permanently, while retaining actual control of policymaking and government machinery. Ch'ien Lung, Sun Yat-sen, Chiang Kai-shek, and Mao Tse-tung, however different they may have been in other respects, each resigned as chief of state without thereby relinquishing any of their *de facto* leadership.[29]

Even within the context of traditional Chinese culture, it might be argued, the perennial insistence that "names" be in accordance with reality demonstrates the importance placed upon reconciling *de facto* and *ex officio* leadership. But the rectification-of-names controversy can also be taken as corroborating evidence of the disparity between the two. No greater concern, nor greater failure, had Confucius. In government as in all human relations, he pleaded, the *first* order of business was to reconcile roles and reality. "The prince must be prince, minister minister, father father, and son son." Effective leadership required proper role designation.[30] Translating this into the language we have been using, Confucius was saying that a *de facto* leader must have the proper title, and an *ex officio* leader must have the authority inherent in his title. Had this situation generally *existed*, Confucius would not have made an issue of it. Nor would Lin Piao in 1970, when he allegedly argued that to "rectify the names" and restore "propriety"

---

[29] On the case of Ch'ien Lung (1796), see Harold L. Kahn, *Monarchy in the Emperor's Eyes: Image and Reality in the Ch'ien-lung Reign* (Harvard: Harvard University Press, 1971), pp. 200 *passim*.

During his attempts to establish a republican government in Canton, Sun Yat-sen withdrew from office three times, yet he was probably China's only *de facto* and nationally respected leader right up until his death (after which he became somewhat larger than life). Sharman, p. 362.

Chiang Kai-shek resigned the presidency of the Republic of China January 21, 1949, and resumed it March 1, 1950, when it was, of course, a different "Republic of China" territorially. Still, he stands as an example of the phenomenon which we are describing. During the interregnum his *de facto* leadership was not *further* impaired, as he maintained control of his armed forces and much of his personal political constituency. (It is interesting that in trying to deal with the Americans during World War II he occasionally threatened to resign if he could not have his way—much to the bewilderment of the Americans, who did not understand this peculiarity of Chinese leadership.)

Mao Tse-tung lacked full control over the government during the first few years following his 1959 resignation, but his *de facto* leadership, like Chiang's ten years earlier, did not further deteriorate (and was ultimately enhanced) as a result of his resignation as chief of state. For Mao's explanation, see "Sixty Articles," *CLG*, Spring 1972, pp. 116 f. See note 21 above.

[30] Confucius, *Lun yü*, 12:11 and 13:3.

he should become chief of state.[31] All of which should serve to remind us that neither the self-serving demands of politicians, nor the efforts of philosophers to make life tidier than it is, can prevail in the long run to overturn such a functional device (in China) as the separation of *de facto* and *ex officio* leadership. In some settings, apparently, leadership is more effective and less constrained when it is deinstitutionalized.

This notion may appear almost anarchistic, and perhaps it would be in the absence of other regulating elements. One must recall, however, that East Asian society is structured by a web of interpersonal ties—familial-style relationships, usually hierarchical, upon which are built expectancies and obligations. The tendency for this feature of the culture to color politics has been strong even in the republican period. The Kuomintang (and its factions), and the various middle-of-the-road parties were largely comprised of magnetic leaders and their personal following. One party was largely an exception to this rule. From its inception, the leaders of the Chinese Communist party were determined that it would be structured on Leninist principles, not traditional Chinese ones. As early as 1920, Mao Tse-tung wrote:

> I think our Society[32] must not remain merely a gathering of men based on personal feelings, but rather it should be transformed into an association based on a political philosophy. A political philosophy is like a banner which, once raised, gives us hope and a sense of direction.[33]

So, although Mao and his colleagues sought to depersonalize politics and thereby break with the past, the key to the new politics would still be *culture,* and this, as we know from the earlier chapters of this book, is not a new idea. Such disparate leaders as Tseng Kuo-fan, Sun Yat-sen, and Mao Tse-tung all accepted the principle that ultimately it was not individuals but ideology by which people should be led (*yi ssu-hsiang ling-tao*). And for all three, ideology's vehicle was an elite.

---

[31] Ad hoc Committee of the Central Committee,"*Chung fa,*" 1973, no. 34, *BOC,* February 14, 1974, p. 2. See also, "What Was Lin Piao's Motive in Vigorously Brandishing the Black Banner Calling For Self-Denial and the Restoration of the Sense of Propriety?" *JMJP,* January 29, 1974, FBIS I, January 31, 1974, especially p. B-5.

[32] The Communist party was not yet formed. The society referred to here is the New Citizens' Study Society, forerunner of the party.

[33] Translated (from a letter) in Jerome Ch'en, *Mao* (1969), p. 98.

Elite and Mass

In a setting in which both the traditional (Chinese) and borrowed (Leninist) systems were based upon ruling elites, it is not surprising that Chinese Communist politics, at least until the Cultural Revolution, was highly elitist. At the same time, however, Mao Tse-tung's thinking had a strong strain of populism. Thus, resolving the contradiction between elite and mass, and achieving their integration, became the chronic dilemma of the Chinese revolution.

The Role of the Elite

The political elite which emerged after 1949—Party and non-Party cadres—was roughly the same proportion of the total population as the gentry had been, although it had a broader social base.[34] The term *cadre* (*kan-pu*) came to be used very loosely, denoting almost any individual with authority over other adults. Those who were Party members comprised a smaller and more significant elite. Above the county level, the number of Party members was distilled to a few hundred thousand.[35] Although initially these people tended to be former guerrilla revolutionaries, there was an effort after 1955 to make the Party more representative of Chinese society. This meant bringing into the Party men and women from every locality, including bourgeois-intellectual types. At first there appears to have been fairly broad support within the Party for this course,[36] though people of guerrilla background naturally resented the newcomers, and radicals objected to diluting the Party's revolutionary purity. A more internally heterogen-

---

[34] It has been estimated that in the nineteenth century 2 percent of China's population belonged to the gentry. This is approximately the percentage which comprised the Communist party before the Cultural Revolution, although if non-Party cadres were included the percentage would be larger. In 1973 it was reported that the Party had 28 million members (*FEER*, October 1, 1973, p. 3), which, on the basis of a population figure of 703 million (Kyōdō, October 6, 1973, FBIS I, October 10, 1973, p. B-1), would indicate a percentage of 4.

According to Donnithorne (*China's Economic System*, pp. 66 f.), the real dividing line is between *state* (including Party) cadres, and lower local-oriented cadres. Although the latter are more subject to local pressure, a cadre's upward mobility depends on how he or she performs in the eyes of the hierarchy.

[35] According to Teng Hsiao-p'ing, the number was somewhat over 300,000 people in 1956. *Constitution*, p. 102.

[36] In his 1956 speech to the Party congress, Teng Hsiao-p'ing urged that the membership be broadened. He was more specific about the demographic qualifications new members should have than their political qualifications. *Constitution*, p. 103. He did say that "seniority" should not be unduly emphasized.

FOUR: Leadership and Participation

eous party would inevitably be a less cohesive and unified party, but at the same time it was hoped that the move would bring about a more homogeneous society as a whole, for the Party, reflecting the nation's demography, would be better integrated with society.

Although the general subject of social homogeneity will not be dealt with until later in this book, we may note here that since 1949 the Party has indeed become increasingly heterogeneous. There are at least three reasons for this. First is the simple fact of increasing size.[37] The larger the Party, the greater the tendency for broader organizational complexity and role specialization. Such tendencies are not necessarily irreversible, but the Party could not continue to be a homogeneous band of old guerrilla fighters if it were going to grow. The second reason was the perceived need of a developing economy and modernizing society for specialists. Whether old warriors were to become "experts" at new tasks, or skilled functionaries were now to become Party members, the resultant role specialization would inevitably have a fragmenting influence on the Party. Finally, as we have seen, there was the conscious effort on the part of the leadership to welcome first one then another social element into the Party.

Still, Party members did tend to develop common bonds. They came to be looked upon by both the masses and the top leadership as "special," and they enjoyed privileges—economic rewards, social prestige, and influence. The common nature of the role they played tended to countervail heterogeneity and encourage homogeneity. As Liu Shao-ch'i once observed, "It is true that not all Party members are the same. They have different abilities, both great and small; they are of different sexes, both male and female; they have different work responsibilities, and so on." The Party, therefore, must be conceived organically.

> The relationship of the Party member with the Party is a relationship of one element (the individual) with the whole collectivity, like the relationship between a cell and a human body.... Because the Party consists of various kinds of Party members, it forms various kinds of organizational units.... Generally speaking, it is the whole that determines the parts.... When a man's head is cut off, he cannot grow another one; but if the responsible persons of the Party Central Committee were seized by the enemy, it really could not put an end to our Party. If one Central Committee is destroyed, we can create another Central Committee. Furthermore, the role that single cells play in the

---

[37] In 1973 the CPC had 28 million members. In the Chinese population, about one in every thirty was a Party member. For sources, see note 34.

human body can only perform the limited function of that cell, but a Party member making an active effort not only does one person's work, but can even push the whole Party forward.[38]

When these words were first spoken (around 1940), the thinking on the subject of the role of the cadre was undergoing transition. Until then, cadres had been seen as the link *between* the leaders and the masses.[39] Then Liu told them, "You need to know how to lead people *and* how to be led by others."[40] Gradually they came to be spoken of as simply part of the leadership, with cadres leading the masses, and "leading cadres" giving orders to other cadres. By the 1950s, the line between cadres and masses had become even more rigid. Whereas once cadres had been like protective elder brothers or generous (landgiving) uncles, after 1949 they became spokesmen for a tough-minded government which to all but the very poor often seemed to take more than it gave. In the eyes of the people, cadres were transformed from "us" to "them." Although this may not have been the cadre's own perception (they more likely still saw themselves as awkwardly-positioned middlemen), the top leadership seems to have recognized the "contradiction" between leaders and led.[41]

The first time that local cadres encountered serious difficulties was around 1953—during the beginnings of agricultural collectivization. Mere land reform, however popular, had achieved little in terms of increased production or increased revenue for the state, and so the central leadership deemed it necessary to move to a "higher stage" of landholding arrangements. For the first time, cadres found themselves carrying out policies which met with widespread resistance. But the local populace was not the cadres' only constituency; it was necessary to carry out orders to the satisfaction of the Party leadership. One possible solution to the dilemma was to resign from leadership and withdraw from politics. "If we don't do a good job, we get criticized by the higher level. If our attitude isn't good, the masses complain. If we neglect our farms, the wives grumble. So the best thing is not to be a cadre."[42] This was not the usual response, of course, and

---

[38] Liu Shao-ch'i, "Self-Cultivation in Organization and Discipline," *CLG*, Spring 1972, p. 29.
[39] In the 1930s Mao distinguished between *cadres* and *leaders*. (See essays toward the end of *SW* 1.) Later, the distinction was dropped.
[40] *CLG*, Spring 1972, p. 30. Emphasis added.
[41] Mao himself spoke in these terms, although only in the 1950s.
[42] *Che-chiang jih-pao*, January 27, 1952, translated in Lewis, *Party*, p. 247 (Bernstein article).

clearly it was not the "correct" one. But what *was* correct—to listen to and serve the masses, or to follow orders from above in the presumed ultimate service of the masses' "legitimate interests"? Only after the fact (and perhaps not even then) would one know whether it was safer to err leftward or on the side of caution. In 1952–53, the implementation of official policies was occasionally so zealous that central authorities were obliged to criticize cadres for coercion ("commandism").

> In the basic-level organizations of the Party and the government... commandism and alienation from the masses prevail.... In the agricultural production and patriotic health movements directly serving the interests of the masses, the commandist style of work is quite serious, and sometimes the masses suffer tremendously.... In some places ... cadres violate laws and discipline, suppress criticism, shield counterrevolutionaries, and harm good people.[43]

Whether cadres had acted properly or errantly depended upon how successful the policies themselves proved to be, in the subsequent judgments of the leadership. And even that judgment might not be final. In the above instance, for example, two decades later the zealous cadres were vindicated.[44]

During the long intervening period, however, the grass-roots leadership felt compelled to protect itself, and it used its power to do so. More and more, it acted in a collective manner, becoming an organic body which could defend itself concertedly against outside pressures. First this group acted to limit elite circulation, by controlling entry into the elite. The Party Constitution of 1956 laid down the following procedures for acceptance of new members:

> Applicants for Party membership must each undergo the procedure of admission individually.
> New members are admitted to the Party through a Party branch. An applicant must be recommended by two full Party members, and is admitted as a probationary member after being accepted by the general membership meeting of a Party branch and approved by the next higher Party committee; he may become a full Party member only after the completion of a probationary period of a year....

[43] An Tzu-wen, *JMJP*, February 12, 1953, translated in Lewis, *Party*, pp. 258 f.
[44] For example, cadres who had insisted upon the establishment of cooperatives in 1953 in the face of the peasants' "wait-and-see" attitude were praised by NCNA, June 11, 1972, FBIS I, June 12, 1972, p. B-11.

> Party organizations at all levels may, according to each individual case, take disciplinary measures against any Party member who violates Party discipline, such as warning, serious warning, removal from posts held in the Party, placing on probation within the Party, or expulsion from the Party. . . .
>
> If he is found to be unfit for Party membership, he shall be expelled from the Party.[45]

As in other Communist countries, the purpose of such admission procedures was to create a homogeneous elite, devoid of internal tensions, and able to deal effectively and uniformly with the population. As we have noted (and as we shall explore in more detail in chap. 7), the Party could not be fully effective unless it brought together diverse types. Thus it was necessary to recruit educated people, and *create* a homogeneous Party by, for example, indoctrinating the experts so that they would also become "red," and educating the political personnel to make up for the deficiencies of their guerrilla background. By the mid-1960s the Party did indeed become a homogeneous elite at least in the sense of its being a discrete group with an understood self-interest and identity. Of course, it also had a sense of public interest and moral values, but it tended to identify the public interest with the Party interest. "Without the Communist party," it was often said, "there is no New China." This view, identified with such organization men as Liu Shao-ch'i and Lu Ting-yi, reflects the traditional Leninist view that a Socialist state must be led by an organized elite until pure communism is attained. Although this elite was stratified internally according to such criteria as Party membership (versus non-Party cadre status), length of service, salary, and job rank, these distinctions were minor in comparison with the gulf between elite membership and the masses. Consider the impression of one emigré student:

> It is meaningless to talk of any relationship between students and the Party. We had no relations with the Party. Rather, we thought of it as a powerful but secret organization. I didn't even know which teachers were members, although a few were openly identified as such. I had little idea of what went on in Party meetings. It might have been different if some *students* had been members, but this was not the case.
>
> Of course it was possible to get a line on what was going on within the Party. *Jen-min jih-pao* [*People's Daily*] and the local press were full of Party news, and these articles were usually reflected in policy announcements made by the principal. We knew there were things the

[45] *Constitution,* Articles 4 and 13.

principal could do only with the approval of higher Party authorities and certain things we could not do because we thought they would be vetoed by the higher levels. Whenever we made recommendations as school cadres, we had to take into account what we thought the Party reaction would be. We judged this on the basis of precedent and on what we could gather from the press about the present political climate. With few exceptions, there was no close relationship between Party members and students outside of school affairs. The distance between us was too great. They ordered and we obeyed.[46]

While the perceptions of someone like this who left China cannot be taken with any certainty to reflect the norm, the problem of an elite-mass gulf is often reflected in the later writings of Mao Tse-tung, who considered it one justification for launching the Cultural Revolution.

Does all of this mean that the elite that emerged in the 1950s was a self-serving New Class, with all the corruption endemic in traditional Chinese society? It is certainly possible to discover instances of ascriptive upward mobility, and of political influence based upon personal influence. The rules and culture of the Party discourage such abuses, however, and it is striking that nepotism became noticeable primarily *after* the decline of the Party due to the Cultural Revolution. Suddenly, the wives[47] and other relatives[48] of some top leaders became powerful political figures. There were also indications of favoritism on the local level, although it is unclear whether and in what way the Cultural Revolution was a factor.[49] Nonetheless, in 1972 *Red Flag* found it necessary to call attention to the problem.

---

[46] Quoted in Ronald N. Montaperto, "Revolutionary Successors to Revolutionaries," in Scalapino, p. 581.

[47] Two examples are Yeh Ch'un (Lin Piao's wife) and, more important, Chiang Ch'ing (Mrs. Mao). It is true that other wives (Mrs. Chou En-lai; Mrs. Liu Shao-ch'i) had been notable leaders prior to the Cultural Revolution, but they were considered leaders in their own right, which was in large measure true. (They were probably both affected by their husbands' prominence, but without such husbands they would still not have been "nobodies.") That the Cultural Revolution affected distaff mobility is confirmed by the fact that each of these wives disappeared from the political scene (i.e., downward mobility) with her husband's disappearance. The case of Chiang Ch'ing represents a reverse situation (unimportant before the Cultural Revolution, then becoming a major figure), also confirming that the Cultural Revolution affected distaff mobility.

[48] Lin Piao's son became air force deputy director of operations at the age of twenty-four. There are also rumors that Yao Wen-yuan is the son-in-law of Mao Tse-tung.

[49] The data are inadequate to determine whether there has been more nepotism since the Cultural Revolution than before, and if so, whether it has been a spontaneous development or a response to the example set at the center.

> There is a saying that "among colleagues, friends, superiors, and subordinates, and within one's own field, people help each other out." This kind of thinking is contrary to the viewpoint of the masses and Marxism. . . . Naturally, everyone has their own friends and relationships, and we do not oppose this. However, revolutionaries must put their relations with revolutionary comrades ahead of relationships based on friendship.[50]

This suggests that the leadership still has some difficulty with Party members who continue to be influenced by traditional loyalties toward relatives and friends, but it does not prove or even (to this writer) suggest that such corruption is pervasive.[51]

So far we have confined our discussion of leadership to the macro-elite, or the 3 or 4 percent of society who are leaders "close to the people." We have, furthermore, focused upon the period of less than two decades prior to the Cultural Revolution. Along the way, however, we have implied that the Cultural Revolution might mark a fundamental turning point for China's political elite. We have noted that the Cultural Revolution tended to heighten the role of personal or individual leadership; even at the expense of institutional (Party) leadership, that it was supposed to narrow or eliminate the gap between the elite and the masses, and that it was intended to encourage local self-reliance, so that leaders would not have an excuse to be "commandist." Finally, we have explored the possibility that the Cultural Revolution may have been marked by a lowering of ascriptive standards in leader recruitment, although this may have been temporary and largely limited to the central leadership.

The Cultural Revolution was the most disruptive movement to hit China since the wars of the 1940s. By the end of the 1960s a tremendous job of reassembly was required, and for this Mao Tse-tung relied largely upon the People's Liberation Armed Forces. Giving the army a role in economic administration and local government, however, could only be an *ad hoc* measure, not a revolutionary solution. Even the revolutionary committee (on which sat military men, Party

---

[50] Kan Ko, "*An tang de yuan-tse pan-shih*" (Attend to matters of Party principle), *HC*, 1972, no. 10, pp. 34 f.

[51] There is some evidence that personal loyalties among bureaucrats and soldiers are important. An example of this is field army loyalties within the PLA. See William Whitson, "The Field Army in Chinese Communist Military Politics,"*CQ*, January 1969, and "Statistics and the Field Army Loyalty System," *CQ*, January 1974; and (for another view) William Parish, "Factions in Chinese Military Politics," *CQ*, October 1973.

people, and "masses"[52]) was inherently unstable and might unduly interfere with central control. Ultimately, the art of politics had to be turned back to professional political leaders—i.e., local Party organs. The early 1970s saw the basic decision-making responsibilities transferred to reconstituted Party committees, to which at least 90 percent of the old basic-level cadres had been restored by 1973.[53] Revolutionary committees were not abolished, however, and although the military role steadily declined, these bodies did continue to give ordinary workers and farmers some role in administration. In general, the Party organs were supposed to make (or transmit) general policy decisions, and the revolutionary committees were to implement or enforce these decisions. But because the formulation of policy is never clearly demarked from its implementation, and also because the public was told during the Cultural Revolution that they should not blindly take orders from bureaucrats and power-holders, tensions were bound to arise between cadres and masses. This was especially true where the cadres fell back upon their old ways. A Peking textile mill provides an example of this.

> ... The Party committee's principal leading members were spending too much time at the higher level and too little time among basic level units.... They relied on holding meetings and listening to reports and performing their leadership functions. As a result, they became divorced from labor, from the masses, and from the basic-level units, thereby hindering the ideological revolutionization of Party committee members.
>
> The second reason was that there were too many meetings, many of which were held to discuss matters regardless of whether they were important or trivial. This happened because it was thought that things should not be decided by a few people.
>
> The third reason was that the Party committee had taken on too much responsibility. This included the phenomenon of assuming the work of the revolutionary committee. They held that since the princi-

[52] The word *masses* has a much less natural sound than the Chinese *"ch'ün-chung,"* but we shall use the conventional English rendering. (One could as well say *public*.) The term may connote all non-cadres (class enemies excluded), or it may be used in a more precise sense, and denote workers, poor and lower-middle farmers, and sometimes soldiers.

[53] In some cases the number of restored local leaders was greater than this, although it is unclear how many were really returned to their former positions. In Hupei, for example, 95 percent of the over four hundred leading cadres at the commune level and above were said to be either performing leadership duties "or other work which has been arranged for them." Wuhan radio, February 3, 1972, FBIS I, February 8, 1972, p. D-3.

pal leading members of the Party committee and the revolutionary committee were the same persons, it made no difference which committee assumed responsibility when work appeared. Therefore the Party committee handled almost everything. For example, such matters as family disputes . . . and water temperature in bathhouses were all handled personally by the Party committee secretary.[54]

It is clear that at least during the first year or two of the reconstituted Party committee at this mill, the questions of proper leadership style and division of responsibilities had not been satisfactorily worked out. On the one hand, the secretary and the Party committee were accused of deciding too much and trying to manage every detail. On the other hand, if they had people spend too much time in meetings they were criticized for this also. At first it had not seemed productive to rely upon the revolutionary committee, since there was a tendency for non-Party people to defer to the judgment of cadres anyway. It was nonetheless insisted that the solution did not lie in the monopolization of authority by the Party, and we are told that eventually "the new Party committee managed to give full play to the role of the revolutionary committee."[55] However, upon close examination this method sounds less than revolutionary, for "special personnel" were assigned to work in the administrative office and were given the necessary authority and power. "The responsible personnel of the administrative office under the unified leadership of the new Party committee actively carried out their work in accordance with the decisions and requirements of the Party committee or the revolutionary committee, and reported to the Party committee on its work situation at all times."[56] Far from giving the workers full control in factory management, this sounds like a rather bureaucratic solution.

Inevitably, similar problems presented themselves in the countryside. In 1972 *People's Daily* addressed itself to the question of the role of the revolutionary committee following the reestablishment of the Party committee. It cited a Kiangsu commune as a correct example of how to resolve this problem. When the Party committee had been reestablished, people had at first tended to refer all questions to it, a practice encouraged by the revolutionary committee. The Party committee, however, insisted that it was not proper:

[54] Anonymous article, "With Secretaries Taking the Lead, All Work with One Heart," Peking radio, June 18, 1970, FBIS I, July 6, 1970, p. B-1.
[55] Ibid., p. B-2.
[56] Ibid., p. B-3.

to refer everything, big and small, to the Party committee for decision. The main tasks of the Party committee were to attend to matters of line, principle, and policy, to assist basic-level leading bodies in achieving revolutionization of their thoughts and organizations, and to see that Chairman Mao's revolutionary line and policy were correctly and fruitfully carried out. The way to strengthen leadership over the revolutionary committee is not to dictate to it, but to have full trust in members of that committee, make full use of them, and lend them full support. In operational work, the Party committee should exercise its power only on important issues involving the line, principle, and policy of the Party. With regard to matters which should be decided and handled by the revolutionary committee, the Party committee should give it full support to do so.[57]

This sounds not unlike the industrial situation discussed above. In the countryside, however, Party control is somewhat more difficult to maintain. This is in part because of the economics of agriculture, and also the fact that there are fewer Party members in relation to the population (not to mention per square mile). Thus, farmers are somewhat more independent than urban workers.

But independence is not necessarily tantamount to playing a participatory role in the political life of the country. Can we say that the average Chinese citizen is in a position to take the initiative vis à vis local "leading bodies"? Or is he passive, simply following orders which flow at least ultimately from a party over which he has no influence? We now turn to the question of the extent to which popular political participation has been sought, and achieved, in China.

Mass Participation

Fu Yueh's remark about knowing being easier than acting[58] doubtless applied to kings and noblemen, but regarding the people generally the prevailing view was (to quote Confucius), "They can be made to follow; they cannot be made to understand."[59] Although it was generally assumed that Confucius did not mean that people were obliged to obey established authority under *all* circumstances, in practice the questioning of authority was discouraged, and rebellion occurred only under conditions of extreme abuse and political disintegration. Even conflict between villagers was rare and not considered proper; when

[57] *JMJP*, April 9, 1972, p. 4, FBIS I, May 10, 1972, pp. B-5 f.
[58] Chapter-head quotation. See p. 105.
[59] Confucius, *Lun yü*, 8:1.

it did occur it was resolved by mediators or authorities. As we noted in a previous chapter, resort to a magistrate meant that the petitioners had failed to properly maintain interpersonal harmony. Something in the nature of lobbying officials may have been done by gentry, but not by ordinary citizens, who simply did not participate in the governmental affairs of traditional China.[60]

We noted earlier that for the Russian Bolsheviks, spontaneous and unguided political activity was generally a fearsome prospect. The danger was that it would be more emotional than rational, and thus would, as a flooding river heading toward the delta, pursue unpredictable and perhaps dangerous directions—taking the path of least resistance rather than the most constructive course. Lenin often emphasized that spontaneity had to be controlled and channeled by 'consciousness," i.e., by the vanguard. The majority of the moment should not be allowed to prevent those with a higher level of consciousness from guiding society toward its proper historic destiny.

Most Chinese Communist leaders of the 1920s adhered closely to these Leninist principles, and while failure to involve the masses in revolution may not explain the movement's failure, nonetheless the elitism which characterized that decade's efforts naturally came in for reexamination. By 1930 it was the farmers instead of the urban workers who were deemed to comprise the most important segment of the masses. The leadership was now dominated by men of agricultural background like Mao Tse-tung and Chang Wen-t'ien, who insisted upon broad popular participation in politics.

> The soviets [this term designating areas under Communist administration] enjoy government in which the masses are able to participate directly in policymaking. The basic principle of soviet government is to provide opportunities for workers, farmers, soldiers, etc., to express their will and participate in the political process. The principle of the people's government can only be realized by means of soviet councils of workers, farmers, and soldiers.[61]

The policy of involving the masses in the revolution came to have rather broad support among the Party leadership, and even labor-oriented and organization men came to embrace it. However, many

---

[60] On these aspects of village life, see M. Yang, chap. 13, and C. K. Yang, *Village*, p. 81.

[61] *Tou-cheng* (Struggle), February 4, 1933, 1st issue. *Tou-cheng* was the organ of the Communist party in the Kiangsi soviet. It was edited by Chang Wen-t'ien, who became secretary-general of the party two years later.

difficulties arose. First, new converts to the policy among the leadership were sometimes overzealous in implementing it. This tended to generate resistance among rural people, who were sometimes reluctant to become politically involved. The intention of Mao and Chang was to keep procedures flexible and noncoercive, but with traditionally no social organization beyond the clan,[62] this could be achieved only by intensive educational efforts. Although considerable progress appears to have been made in at least giving farmers a new sense of involvement in politics, all was disrupted in 1934 when Nationalist forces drove the infrastructure out of Kiangsi.[63]

After the Long March, when the Communists settled in Shensi and other parts of China, efforts were made to benefit from the Kiangsi experiences, but the situation was not strictly comparable. The immediate effort was resisting Japanese imperialism, and this required alienating as few Chinese as possible. To obviate the divisiveness which radical policies would entail, a "united front" policy was followed. Now popular participation meant the Communists' bringing landlord and bourgeois as well as poorer elements into the political process, and so there was no landholding revolution in which farmers could participate. The important grass-roots political organization now became the guerrilla units, and leadership rather than voluntarism must characterize any military organization. Still, unit leaders were often men of humble background with no social distance from the masses. Indeed, the cadres of the 1950s were usually men who had joined the Red Army during World War II—not only farmers but also hired hands and even beggars and servants who became soldiers *faute de mieux*. The good fortune which these men enjoyed in the movement was certainly conducive to their becoming true believers in the Party, in which they continued to be leaders after the civil war. Their military backgrounds, however, had not provided the kind of experience which inclined them to subordinate themselves to the masses, or even to encourage popular political participation to a significant degree. Much has been made (primarily among Western observers) of the "Yenan syndrome," which allegedly helps explain the later Cultural Revolution. In fact, however, the Kiangsi experience was probably more

---

[62] Lack of cohesiveness within the village and among neighboring villages was in some ways a handicap to Communist organization efforts, but it at least meant that there were no competing traditional institutions of this nature which had to be resisted.

[63] For further information regarding the Kiangsi soviet, see Ilpyong J. Kim, *The Politics of Chinese Communism: Kiangsi under the Soviets* (Berkeley: University of California Press, 1973).

seminal from the point of view of the development of mobilization technique, and also more relevant to the issues and policies of the 1950s than were those of the Yenan period.[64]

Although the policies of the 1950s hark back to the 1930s, in many ways the conditions were entirely new. The most obvious new element was the fact that the Communists controlled the entire China mainland, inheriting some institutions and creating others as necessary to administer the nation. Reliance upon institutions was quite different from relying upon the incentive of redistributed land or the emotion of nationalism. Still, the new leaders of China were concerned with providing the people with a sense of involvement and identification with government, and many of the institutions existed more for the purpose of enlisting popular support than for administration. The Chinese People's Political Consultative Conference was a case in point. It embraced people from all classes, walks of life, races, and religions, and maintained organs at least down to the provincial level. Then there were the more official organs of state—the National People's Congress and corresponding local congresses to which the public elected representatives. Neither of these types of organs provided for more than the most nominal kind of participation, as the elections were manipulated by the Communist party, and the organs themselves were largely platforms for the Party to enunciate predetermined policy.

At the lowest levels, rural cooperatives and urban residents' committees often provided a kind of proximity that heightened cadre awareness of people's real sentiments, but even these were more organs of control than participation.[65] There were also the more specialized "mass organizations," such as those for farmers, workers, women, and youth. These served primarily as a means for transmitting Party intentions; they did not provide a means for the public to provide input into policymaking.[66] True, these organizations sometimes provided an avenue by which people could enter the Party and thus have some

[64] For further information on political mobilization during the 1940s, see Johnson, *Nationalism*, and William Hinton. The debate concerning whether Communist successes are attributable to substantive policies or organization/mobilization techniques is still unresolved. For an interesting discussion of the literature on the subject, see Martin Bernal, "Was Chinese Communism Inevitable," *NYRB*, December 3, 1970, pp. 43–47. (In our discussion here we are not concerned with this historical problem, but simply with the nature of Communist mass-mobilization techniques.)

[65] As was noted in chap. 3, to some degree ordinary citizens have been involved in the judicial process.

[66] We are concerned here with the question of political participation, and are thus not concerned with the consciousness-raising, welfare, and other functions of these organizations, which, of course, were very real.

political influence, but once in the Party they often lost interest in the bodies which had originally launched them on their political careers. It is also true that the subordination of mass organizations to the Communist party was sometimes more a matter of intention than of reality. For example, the Party was continually engaged in a struggle to prevent the unions from becoming autonomous.[67] But this tendency gave rise to institutional autonomy rather than worker domination. It does not appear that prior to the Cultural Revolution any of the mass organizations were in danger of succumbing to broad-based membership control.[68] On the other hand, it would be wrong to think of the mass organizations, and even the Party itself, as simply coercing and manipulating the masses. Many of the campaigns struck responsive chords, and one would have to say that there was often mobilization of genuine public sentiment.

In the Party itself, although at least throughout the 1950s there may have been reasonable equality of opportunity in terms of admission to membership, outsiders—the masses—were largely excluded from Party affairs. This was recognized as a serious shortcoming by some leaders (Mao in particular), who occasionally insisted that citizens (sometimes even including bourgeois elements[69]) should participate in the Party's internal housecleaning. The practice of "open-door rectifications," which predate 1949, has had a rocky history. That the masses should be reluctant to participate in rectifying their superiors is understandable on many grounds, especially cultural and political ones. It is even easier to understand *cadres'* lack of enthusiasm for the "open-door" policy, and why so many of them would have approved of Liu Shao-ch'i's advocating "a *little* democracy" (*hsiao min-chu,* as opposed to *kuang-fan te min-chu* or *ta min-chu*—extensive democracy). Liu wanted to see criticism among cadres, but he did not believe that they should normally be attacked by outsiders. He agreed with Maoists that rectifications were necessary, but advocated the "soft-breeze, sweet-shower" approach.[70] After 1957 the Party enjoyed nearly a decade of freedom from Mao's "great storms," but with the Cultural Revo-

[67] See Paul Harper, "The Party and the Unions in Communist China," *CQ,* January 1969.

[68] For further information on mass organizations both before and after the Cultural Revolution, see Perrin.

[69] The experience in inviting the bourgeois-democratic parties to participate in the rectification of the Communist party in 1957 is discussed in Seymour, *Parties,* chap. 5.

[70] See articles by Stuart Schram in Schram, ed., *Authority,* p. 49, and AS, April 1972, p. 285.

lution it was time again for the "open-door" approach to rectification. Maoists were determined that no skeletons should remain in the closet. As a writer in *People's Daily* acknowledged, earlier rectifications had failed "to arouse the broad masses to expose . . . the dark aspects" of the Party. Nevertheless,

> practice proves that it is the revolutionary masses who are most concerned about the rectification of the Party and best understand the situation of the Party organization and Party members. Only by carrying out the open-door Party rectification by relying on the masses, can we prevent the work of Party rectification from "taking the old road and restoring the old order," and can we better purify the Party organizationally and ideologically and build every Party branch into a strong fighting bulwark armed with the Thought of Mao Tse-tung.[71]

Even after the Cultural Revolution, as events proceeded toward relative normalcy and the reconstruction of the Party, Mao Tse-tung insisted that the masses be involved in the process. The Party branches, he said, were to be reconsolidated "in the midst of the masses" and not simply by Party members themselves. People from the masses were to attend meetings and comment upon the proceedings.[72] Whether or not this requirement was honored, no doubt the leadership was sincere; and in the wake of the Cultural Revolution pervasive noncompliance was unlikely.

Quantitative judgments in this area are extremely difficult. It may be possible, however, to make a *qualitative* evaluation. Regardless of how *much* political involvement occurs, and there is certainly some, can the role of the masses truly be termed "participation"? In traditional societies, the act of following entails highly personalized relations with little substantive input. Indeed, on any level, if loyalty is paramount, autonomous political inputs are excluded; unqualified loyalty and active participation, in this sense, are thus mutually exclusive.

This was one of the limitations of Confucianism,[73] and is one reason why in practice that philosophy was usually diluted with others. Many Chinese came to understand that statesmanship meant not only personal loyalty, but also conscientious (i.e., individually determined)

---

[71] Article by An Hsueh-kiang [sic] (October 12, 1969) quoted in Pfeffer, p. 637.
[72] This instruction was repeatedly published in the media.
[73] "Let the official give himself no respite, and let all his acts be loyal." Confucius, *Lun yü*, 12:14.

FOUR: *Leadership and Participation*

commitment to the public welfare.[74] The contradiction is hardly unique to China, of course; it created great tension in American political culture during the Vietnam war. But it does seem to be particularly conspicuous in China during times of faltering politics. Chiang Kai-shek, for example, tended to favor loyal but mediocre generals over those of greater ability and public spiritedness—with Chiang, this was simply a reflection of the culture. (Even the "modern" liberal or democratic parties of that period tended to be comprised of charismatic leaders and their personal following.) Although, as we have noted, Mao Tse-tung always intended that ideological commitment should replace traditional-style loyalty, even some of the Communists' early grassroots organizational work tended to be based upon kinship ties. In many cases this was probably due to a combination of cultural and objective conditions; that is, given the existence of civil war and enemy spies, one could trust best one's relative. But also in the more secure areas, such as the Shensi-Kansu-Ningsia border region, farmers who joined a labor exchange group were in large part relatives of the leading cadre.[75] In many villages, furthermore, a few clans (or even one) might comprise the entire population.

If after 1949 citizens continued either to ratify *ex officio* authority unquestioningly or let personal loyalties rather than independent judgment determine political decisions, then we would have to say that there has been little meaningful political participation in China. On the other hand, to the extent that governmental policy decisions are made on the basis of widespread and spontaneous public conviction, then meaningful participation would exist. And if simple mechanical *involvement* were to be equated with participation, we would have no difficulty establishing that participation was pervasive in China even during the pre-Cultural Revolution years. There were few silent, passive Chinese. Whether in small group discussions or at mass rallies, each citizen was expected to demonstrate commitment. Silence not only suggested that the individual had not been mobilized for the cause, but—and here there was some continuity with the past[76]—it might even be taken as opposition. Campaign after campaign marshaled support for Peking's various economic, social, and foreign policies. Although sometimes the issues were manufactured, and were

---

[74] See J. Liu, pp. 293 f.
[75] See, for example, Jan Myrdal, pp. 347 f.
[76] Martin Yang (p. 130) describes a political (decision-making) family discussion as follows: The father makes a little speech, probably followed by the eldest son. For the son "to say nothing would imply disagreement."

generally presented in a one-sided manner,[77] every effort was made to ensure that the public actually understood the policies and were persuaded of their utility and propriety. Indeed, campaigns often reflected genuine widespread sentiment and were characterized by emotional intensity.

All of this represents a degree of *involvement* unprecedented in Chinese history. Succumbing to one-sided propaganda, however, with no real opportunity to personally consider the merits of the issues, would have to comprise nonparticipatory, orchestrated involvement. (This does not mean that Party policies were not in the interests of the public; they were by definition, inasmuch as the Party defined those interests. And it is possible that in an open setting public support would have been forthcoming of its own accord.) But certainly the *sense* of involvement was very real, and this in itself was revolutionary. For the public to feel that it had something at stake in what went on in Peking, and that the leadership cared about public support, meant that the public had been *politicized*, whether or not it was *participating* in politics. On the question of real participation, however, our judgment concerning the 1950–65 years must be largely negative.[78]

Yet, one heard much of voluntarism in connection with Chinese politics. The indubitable enthusiasm and spontaneity of the Chinese is said to differentiate their communism from the Soviet variety. Is there —and was there before the Cultural Revolution—any truth to this? First we should note that no modern state can brook an entirely passive and disinvolved citizenry. It is possible that China required greater development in this regard than did Russia. It must also be noted that if extreme compulsion (the opposite of voluntarism) brings to mind Stalinism, then China has seen nothing of the sort. On the other hand, both Soviet and Chinese leaders have relied upon tradition of obedience to authority, to which they have added ideological indoctrination and compliance with people's needs to induce the public to obey. Whether one wants to say that people who act consistently with the desires of the leadership are doing so voluntarily becomes an almost semantic question. One could as well ask whether a Western consumer

---

[77] Chap. 5 will deal with political communications.
[78] It is true that there was often conspicuous consultation, but this was usually ritualistic. When consultation did influence the course of events, it was almost always cadres and Party functionaries whose input was influential. For example, although a draft of the 1954 Constitution was widely discussed at the grass-roots level, it appears to have been the bureaucracy which was instrumental in effecting changes. On how changes were made affecting the procuratorate, see Ginsburgs and Stahnke, "The People's Procurate . . . ," *CQ*, April 1968, pp. 83 f.

who purchases heavily advertised but otherwise unexceptional merchandise, or who votes for a lavishly promoted candidate backed by vested interests, does so voluntarily. In all instances, the individual is acting rationally in terms of his understanding, but the issue has been decided in the communications arena. (See chap. 5.)

There are, of course, differing degrees of manipulation. In the 1950s, if a cadre whipped up the enthusiasm of his neighbors to undertake a harsh task, knowing that he himself would either not have to perform with them or perhaps would receive a secret reward for doing so, then the people's "participation" was fraudulent. Under such circumstances they were not participating in what they thought they were participating in, for the facts were not as presented; the people were the state manager's tools. Likewise, if experience has taught people that failure to volunteer will result in some unknown future punishment (perhaps being struggled against during the next political campaign, or given undesirable labor), then while an individual may indeed make a personal choice to accept the leadership's suggestion, this does not mean that he had a reasonable alternative to volunteering. Still, the choice was not entirely meaningless. It was not unheard of for a small minority to refuse to go along, and this enhanced the majority's sense of voluntarism. (It also was facilitating in that it separated the malcontents from the supporters.)

We should not overemphasize negative rewards. The positive rewards for behaving in a socially accepted and constructive manner were very real, and not qualitatively different from those elsewhere (esteem, opportunities for advancement, etc.).[79] But being personally rewarded for one's conduct is not, properly speaking, a political phenomenon, and this kind of voluntarism should not be confused with political participation. Only in extreme situations, when a substantial number of people refused to volunteer, was any sort of political input effected. Prior to the Cultural Revolution, the process of volunteering did not normally reflect individual consideration of the issues, or collective aggregation of interest or interests.

This raises the issue of whether or not a fundamental contradiction inheres in our phrase "interest or interests." Even assuming that the Party has indeed reflected the public will, is it possible for that will to be amalgamated in Rousseauian fashion into a single "general will," or is it necessary, through a process of compromise and reconciliation, to formulate a public interest which takes into account the inevitable

---

[79] This subject (pre-Cultural Revolution) is discussed in Vogel, "Voluntarism."

complexity of public values and wants? There was a time when Mao accepted unquestioningly the former view. In 1948 he said, "When the masses are of one heart, everything becomes easy. A basic principle of Marxism-Leninism is to enable the masses to know their own *li-i* ['interest' or 'interests'] and unite to fight for their *li-i*".[80] As we have seen, if it is left to the Party to define the will of the masses, there is a danger that the interests of the elite will automatically be equated with the will of the masses. If this is perceived by the masses, alienation and mock affection result. Just when Mao first became concerned with this problem is unclear, but certainly by the Cultural Revolution he realized that mass demonstrativeness was not the same as mass political participation. On one occasion, for example, while watching great numbers parade through T'ien-an-men Square in Peking, he was heard to remark that one-third of the people praising him were sincere, one-third simply went along, and one-third were hypocrites.[81]

Mao was not overestimating the seriousness of the problem. He saw that political participation would be inhibited as long as true beliefs were suppressed, but, just as he had failed to anticipate the degree of disaffection which would be revealed by the intellectuals in 1957, so too would he be surprised by the intensity of anti-Party sentiment demonstrated by people after being urged to speak candidly. As he remarked at the height of the Cultural Revolution, "I did not expect that a poster, a Red Guard, and a general exchange of revolutionary experiences would produce so much trouble."[82] Events demonstrated that a way had not yet been found for the masses to participate in the political life of the nation in a manner sufficiently disciplined to avoid undermining the achievements of the revolution.

The condition of political participation is not entirely negative, however. As we have noted, there is a high degree of *identification* with national politics and leaders. (Mao may have been understating the degree of his personal popularity when he said that only a third of the people really supported him.) But perhaps more important, at the lowest level individual Chinese usually have an opportunity to interact with neighbors and cadres in a politically meaningful manner. Here, the Cultural Revolution may have provided some further impetus, but there had always been greater public political participation

---

[80] Mao, *Hsüan chi*, p. 1317. The second sentence was quoted in *HC*, 1973, no. 4, p. 3. (Yen Ch'un, "A Basic Principle of Marxism-Leninism: A Study of 'A Talk to the Editorial Staff of the *Shensi-Suiyan Jih pao*.'")
[81] Derek Davies, in *FEER*, May 7, 1973, p. 24.
[82] Speech of October 24, 1966, in Mao, *Selections*, p. 11.

FOUR: *Leadership and Participation*

in village and urban neighborhood politics than in national politics. (The same is true on Formosa.) While the nature of decisions made at this level may not seem to be of great moment, they are nonetheless important to those involved, and ultimately to the nation. They are also genuinely political—even in matters which in other societies would not be properly of political concern. Note, for example, Han Suyin's account of how family planning is arranged:

> On each street there is a committee staffed by two or more women of the neighborhood. In each quarter of the city, the committees are linked to a clinic with a visiting doctor and five or six nurses, all of whom are involved in family planning. Questionnaires were circulated some months ago throughout the population in Peking to determine the number of babies born, and to be born. Each courtyard then held "meetings" to debate the number of babies to be allowed the next year. The families have to agree whose turn it will be to have, or not to have, a baby. Thus in one courtyard with four families, family A, newly married, would be entitled to priority for a baby in 1973; family B, with four children already, was to be persuaded to stop producing and to be "mobilized" either to have the wife sterilized, or the husband vasectomized, or to carry out birth control through other methods.[83]

It is hard to believe that pressure of a coercive nature is not applied to overly prolific couples, but it also seems likely that much of the decision making is participatory, with neighbors trying both to raise each other's social consciousness, and to defend their own interests (in this case, having babies themselves).

This is an instance that probably places the concern of the cadre squarely on the side of the interest of the majority (at least in the sense that the majority believe that other people should have few children). Can an individual participate in the sense of *opposing* a neighborhood leader, factory manager, or revolutionary committee chairman? Unquestionably one can *if* one is subsequently proven politically "correct" by the superiors of the individual criticized, and this is not unusual. But obviously a critic runs great risk of becoming isolated, and perhaps victimized by the intended target. Still, the risk can be minimized through a shrewd understanding of the thrust of current Party policies and the vulnerabilities of others. If one's timing is correct, for example, it is safe to criticize a factory manager for

---

[83] *New York Times*, September 1, 1973, paraphrase.

assigning a higher priority to production than to "ideological work for the masses," for "a mandarin style of acting," and for the fact that the "enterprise has been running the masses" rather than vice versa.[84] Failing an acceptable response, one may take the case higher—to the leadership of the municipality[85] or province.[86] As one escalates the campaign, however, both the uncertainties and the risks multiply. A single dispute kept within the neighborhood or work unit is not apt to result in anyone's being sent to a labor reform camp; there is no such certainty when higher organs are brought into the situation. If the general Party line should shift, or if the bureaucrats simply decide to stand together against obstreperous subordinates, then the complainant might be in serious difficulties.[87]

In the past decade, much has transpired to embolden citizens and encourage them to participate in politics. For the present generation of adults, the memory of how the Cultural Revolution humbled the cadres remains fresh. In addition, the media often reiterate "the importance of cadres' letting all people speak out."

> Some of our comrades have shown reluctance to let all people have their say, because they consider themselves to be "superior" to others on the basis of their longer participation and greater experience in struggle. But is that a sound basis to prove one's "superiority"? Not necessarily. It is true that comrades having longer participation and greater experience in struggle can often come forward with better ideas, yet it must be acknowledged that any individual's experience and knowledge are limited at best. If one is good at one thing, one may be no good at another; and although his view may be correct today, following the development of changing events it may not be practical tomorrow. For this reason, as a leader of a party organ, one should see oneself from the viewpoint of dichotomization in order to know one's shortcomings, and see others from a similar viewpoint in order to learn from their good points. Leaders should consider themselves members of the "squad" and humbly listen to the views of all other members.

[84] This example is taken from posters in a Kunming textile mill, as reported in the *New York Times*, March 6, 1974.

[85] For example, one Shanghai resident, after failing to successfully attack a utility executive, took his case to the equivalent of mayor, through the medium of a series of twenty posters, which attracted considerable attention. The outcome of the affair is not known. *New York Times*, March 10, 1974.

[86] See, for example, the case of a group of students in Canton who, having denounced school leaders without effect, successfully appealed to the provincial Party committee. Montaperto, "Revolutionary Successors," in Scalapino, p. 585.

[87] The far northeast and northwest are some of the less desirable locations for political outcasts.

> There are comrades who pay only lip service to democracy and reliance on the masses and are impatient in listening to different views. They feel that it would be much "simpler" for them to give the final word, because "too many cooks spoil the soup." Not at all. Chairman Mao says: "*More people* means greater ferment of ideas, more enthusiasm, and more energy." The more views expressed, the more easily will comparisons be made and correct views selected to promote the continual development of the cause of the revolution.[88]

The desire for increased political participation is clear, as is the cadres' fear that impaired leadership effectiveness may result.

The hope is that leaders and followers can be integrated in a manner conducive to productive interaction, and that through consultative politics (*hsieh-shang*) cadres and masses can achieve a degree of intimacy without parochialism resulting. The organ through which this is all to be achieved is the local revolutionary committee. The revolutionary committee of a village is chosen by the people (usually annually) in a process which is not really an election, but neither is it as orchestrated as the "elections" in many Communist countries. Initially, there may be more candidates than positions to fill, but in this case the list of nominees must be reduced through consultation until it is coextensive with the positions. Then, all citizens aged sixteen and older vote for or against (by crossing out candidates' names), and candidates receiving more than fifty percent approval assume office. Obviously this is a procedure which enables the village Party committee to prevent matters from getting out of hand, but it is also one that allows villagers to make known their views, which the Party committee ignores at its peril.[89]

If the training that children have been receiving in school presages the future, it is likely that insubordination will increasingly come to characterize Chinese leader–follower relations. Students have been praised for "going against the tide"—if not by their teachers, then at least by leftist leaders. Children are told to denounce bureaucratic behavior wherever they find it, and not to let themselves be treated like "slaves." A student may not even have to accept criticism for cheating. In one instance, three high school students suffering from "nervous tension" were unable to complete a mathematics examination

---

[88] Shih Tsui-yen, "Be Good at Serving as 'Squad Leader' and Let All People Have Their Say," *JMJP*, February 17, 1973, p. 2, FBIS I, March 16, 1973, p. B-3.

[89] This process is described as it operates in Sha-shih Yü (an often exhibited village) in Alex Casella, "Mao's China 1972," *New York Times Magazine*, February 20, 1972, p. 36.

without consulting what other students had written. The teacher considered this cheating, and demanded a public confession. But the students (whose remarks were later published approvingly in *People's Daily*) responded that the teacher was in error. Said one:

> In this examination, you gave me a zero because you considered that I had cheated. That will not hurt me, because what matters is not the grade, but the mastery of practical knowledge. I succeeded in solving the problems through the inspiration I obtained during the examination. A teacher who does not allow the students to carry out a proper exchange of views is in violation of Chairman Mao's thinking on education. The prevailing examination system and method should be totally reformed.

Another student insisted that a great ship cannot be designed by engineers working in isolation, and concluded the examination system was not relevant. Surprisingly, the views of these students prevailed. According to the press acount the teacher was "deeply touched by the students' spirit," and made up her mind to emulate them. Although one suspects that we have not been told the whole story about her change of heart, the point is that this kind of independence on the part of the students has been officially encouraged. When these students become adults, it seems likely that instead of being passive citizens, they will naturally become active participants in political affairs.[90]

The Leadership Role of the Center

While our main discussion of the structural aspects of politics must wait until chapter 6, no discussion of leadership would be complete without some attention being paid to the question of how decisions are made at the apex of political authority. This can best be approached from two angles. First, there are the political organs which provide forums for top-level collective decision making. Secondly, there is the personality of the supreme individual. With these discussions, we shall round out the theoretical constructs concerning *ex officio* and *de facto* leadership with which we began this chapter. A chart depicting China's political structure appears on page 141.

[90] This article was written by three of the school's teachers, and appeared in *JMJP* on October 19, 1973, p. 2. FBIS I, November 1, 1973, pp. B-2 f. Along similar lines, see Chi Ping, "Pay Attention to the Role of Teachers by Negative Example," *HC,* 1972, no. 3, pp. 19–24, FBIS I, March 30, 1972, pp. B-5–B-11.

Collective Decision Making

In terms of the national constitution, China's supreme state organ is the National People's Congress—an unwieldy body of thousands that meets rarely and briefly.[91] The NPC which convened in 1975 was only the fourth in the history of the People's Republic, and although it made important pronouncements—and promulgated the new constitution—it was apparent that all decisions had been effectively taken beforehand. In short, the function of this body is largely communicative.

The State Council (cabinet) is an administrative organ subordinate to the political leadership. (When Chou En-lai headed this body, Chiang Ch'ing liked to say: "Chairman Mao thinks; Premier Chou acts.") Usually, the Party also controls the subordinate state organs which are nominally under the jurisdiction of the ministers. As Wang Hung-wen reemphasized at the time of the adoption of the 1973 Party Constitution, state organs are laterally responsible to the corresponding Party committee.

> As regards the relationship between various organizations at the same level, of the seven sectors—industry, agriculture, commerce, culture and education, the Army, the government, and the Party—it is the Party that exercises overall leadership; *the Party is not parallel to the others and still less is it under the leadership of any other.*[92]

People in the six other sectors doubtless provide some input for political decision making, but this process is a very inconspicuous one. Although, according to the Leninist principle of "democratic centralism," lower levels are free to make recommendations to higher organs, those levels are also bound by higher decisions. Because the higher organs may receive a variety of inputs, furthermore, in many instances the pressures may negate each other. Regardless of the nature of the feedback, however, less stress has generally been placed upon this "democracy" than upon "centralism." In a speech in 1942 (which has often been quoted in the 1970s) Mao criticized "some cadres" who "do not realize that the Communist party not only needs democracy but needs centralization even more."[93] In particular, Mao said, all

---

[91] In 1975 there were 2,885 deputies. (This was the first meeting of the NPC since 1964.)

[92] Wang Hung-wen, "Report on the Revision of the Party Constitution," *PR*, September 7, 1973, p. 32. Emphasis revised.

[93] *SW*, 3:44. Quoted in Chiang Hsueh-yuan, "Democratic Centralism in Party Committees," *PR*, November 23, 1973, p. 18.

CHINA'S POLITICAL STRUCTURE

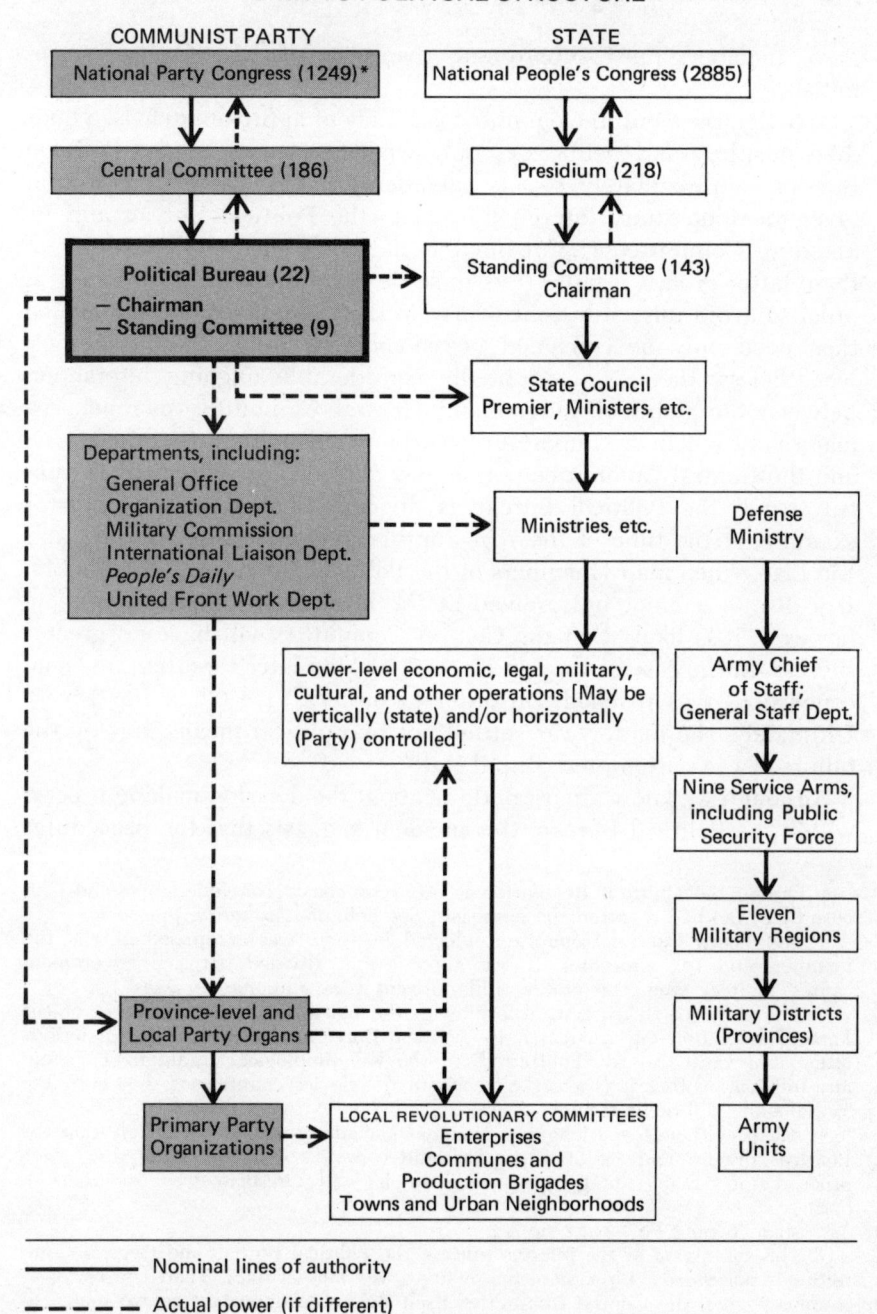

COMMUNIST PARTY

- National Party Congress (1249)*
- Central Committee (186)
- Political Bureau (22)
  - Chairman
  - Standing Committee (9)
- Departments, including:
  - General Office
  - Organization Dept.
  - Military Commission
  - International Liaison Dept.
  - *People's Daily*
  - United Front Work Dept.
- Province-level and Local Party Organs
- Primary Party Organizations

STATE

- National People's Congress (2885)
- Presidium (218)
- Standing Committee (143) Chairman
- State Council Premier, Ministers, etc.
- Ministries, etc. | Defense Ministry
- Lower-level economic, legal, military, cultural, and other operations [May be vertically (state) and/or horizontally (Party) controlled]
- Army Chief of Staff; General Staff Dept.
- Nine Service Arms, including Public Security Force
- Eleven Military Regions
- Military Districts (Provinces)
- Army Units

LOCAL REVOLUTIONARY COMMITTEES
Enterprises
Communes and Production Brigades
Towns and Urban Neighborhoods

———— Nominal lines of authority

– – – – Actual power (if different)

*Numbers in parentheses indicate the 1975 membership, excluding alternates.

Party members must subordinate themselves to the Central Committee.[94]

Actually, the Central Committee is a body of approximately two hundred people,[95] and deliberates only when convened by the Political Bureau (approximately twenty members).[96] The Party Constitution gives plenipotentiary interim powers to the Political Bureau and its Standing Committee (approximately a half-dozen people).[97] One of these latter groups usually tries to settle potentially devisive issues in order to avoid unseemly controversy in the Central Committee, which then need only be convened occasionally to ratify their decisions. Nonetheless, there is undoubtedly considerable ongoing interaction between the Political Bureau and Central Committee members (a majority of whom are important government or military functionaries), and the Central Committee per se may yet become embroiled in controversy if the Political Bureau is divided. Such was the case, for example, at the time of the 1970 rupture between Mao Tse-tung and Lin Piao, when many members of the Political Bureau sided with Lin. If a dispute cannot be resolved at the level of the Political Bureau, however, it is likely that the Central Committee will have no greater success. In the case of the Lin dispute, as Mao later reported, no "final conclusion" was reached, "in order to protect Vice Chairman Lin."[98] Ultimately, the matter was settled not by political means, but by the failure of Lin's attempted coup d'état.[99]

Although we know almost nothing about the decision-making process within the Political Bureau, this incident suggests that the procedures

[94] During the Cultural Revolution it was erroneously concluded by some Chinese that Mao had reversed the emphasis. See Schram, *Authority,* pp. 86 f.

[95] The Tenth Central Committee, elected in 1973, was comprised of 195 full members and 124 alternates. It was about evenly divided between government cadres, military men, and rank-and-file citizens ("revolutionary masses").

[96] The name of this organ, according to the official English translation of the Party Constitution (q.v., Art. 9), is "Political Bureau." However, western writers often abbreviate this to "Politburo," in the Kremlinological tradition. To avoid any implication that it is a carbon copy of the Soviet counterpart, however, the formal name will be used here.

[97] Art. 9. Although the language is somewhat ambiguous, it is unlikely that the Political Bureau and its Standing Committee would ever be opposed to each other. (Mao's major antagonists, Liu Shao-ch'i and Lin Piao, were members of both.)

[98] Mao, *"Chung Fa,"* 1972, no. 12, p. B-5.

[99] This discussion of the relative roles of the Political Bureau and Central Committee is necessarily impressionistic, owing to the lack of data. There are certainly instances when the Central Committee itself did settle important controversies, as in the case of the dismissal of a half-dozen leaders (led by P'eng Teh-huai) in 1959.

are much more brittle than in compromise-oriented Western executive groups. Studies have indicated that in the West, decisions may be hammered out about which no one is particularly enthusiastic, but with which everyone can live.[100] Whatever the effects concerning the quality of decision making, this process is highly functional from a systemic point of view (that is, the government keeps functioning, even when no one likes what the government does). In China's political bureaus, it would appear that decision making has been more of a zero-sum operation, with the "winning group" carrying out its policies, and the minority not even permitted to form a faction or comprise a "loyal opposition." This may provide for greater policy coherence, and certainly facilitates uniformity in terms of media presentations. However, decisions made in this manner are apt to labor under two serious handicaps. First, when there is no political accommodation at the highest level, then there is apt to be all the more administrative accommodation by lower-level bureaucrats sympathetic with the dissident superiors. The second problem is that the inflexibility of this decision-making process generates severe crises whenever the minority is too powerful to be overwhelmed by normal political means. Under these circumstances, there is a major disruption in the life of the Party while the dissidents are purged from its ranks.

Mao Tse-tung once recounted that there had been ten such "major struggles" in the history of the Party,[101] and they are worth listing:

1927 Ch'en Tu-hsiu, who had been identified with the policy of cooperating with the Kuomintang, replaced as Party Secretary-General by Ch'ü Ch'iu-pai (who then promoted urban uprisings). Ch'en was eventually expelled from the Party.

1928 After the failure of the Canton Commune and other debacles, Ch'ü Ch'iu-pai was removed as Party head. He spent the next few years in the USSR.

1930 Li Li-san's policy of taking cities by means of the Red Army was repudiated. He was removed from office, and spent the next fifteen years in the Soviet Union.

1931 After a struggle against "rightists" Ho Meng-hsiung, Lo Chang-lung, and others, a group of "Returned Students" (from the Soviet Union) gained control of the Party. Ho

---

[100] See, for example, G. T. Allison, *Essence of Decision: Explaining the Cuban Missile Crisis* (Boston: Little, Brown, 1972).

[101] Mao, "*Chung Fa,*" pp. B-3–B-5. For additional information, see Harrison and Boorman.

and Lo were expelled from the Party (and attempted to establish a rival movement). The transition was ratified at the Fourth Plenum of the Sixth Central Committee. Ch'en Shao-yü (Wang Ming) became Secretary-General.

1935 (January) During the Long March, a split developed among the "Returned Students," with some shifting allegiance to Mao Tse-tung (who became *de facto* leader of the Party). According to Mao's account, this is when Ch'en Shao-yü "collapsed." He was never again influential within the Chinese Communist movement (although he became a scapegoat for Mao in 1942), and he spent much of the remainder of his life in the Soviet Union.

1935 (August) Toward the end of the Long March, a logistics dispute arose betweeen Mao and his chief rival, Chang Kuo-t'ao, who took much of the Communist armed forces to Sikang, and did not join Mao at Yenan until October 1936. Although Chang remained a member of the Political Bureau, he and his supporters were frequently criticized by Mao, and he defected to the Nationalists in 1938.

1953– (Winter) A struggle developed within the Political Bureau
1954 when Kao Kang allegedly promoted northeast regional separatism. A number of Kao's followers were expelled from the Party, and he is said to have committed suicide.

1959 The conflict between Mao and P'eng Teh-huai concerning the communes, the Great Leap Forward, relations with the USSR, and so on, apparently could not be resolved within the Political Bureau, and went before the Central Committee. P'eng permanently disappeared from view. (A lesser functionary named Wu Han became the object of a national campaign after hinting that P'eng should be restored.)

1966 Liu Shao-Ch'i, Chairman of the Republic, was purged. He made three confessions, and was not heard from again.[102]

1970 Lin Piao, the second in command, apparently attempted a sort of coup d'état which failed. He was killed in a plane crash while trying to escape.

Although Mao's interest in selecting these particular crises was partisan rather than scientific, they are nonetheless of exceptional his-

---

[102] In 1974 there were reports of Liu Shao-ch'i's death.

toric importance in terms of the development of the Communist movement. They do not represent a good cross-section of important moments in policymaking; rather the list catalogs the major disruptions in the political process within the Party's upper echelons. With the exception of the Cultural Revolution, these are not "constitutional crises," or *crises de régime*. Indeed, we would almost have to say that most of these crises have been *part* of the constitutional process,[103] just as under a parliamentary system the "fall" of a government is part of the constitutional process. But is it fair to conclude that a crisis is generated within the top leadership of the Chinese Communist party whenever an important policy crossroads is reached? That would probably be overstating the case, for this sample of ten crises is self-selected in that respect. Not every major decision produced such a crisis—as in the cases of land reform, collectivization, the Korean and Indian wars. However, it could be argued that in each of these cases the question was axiomatic, or at least no Chinese Communists could take strong exception to the action taken. When fresh ground is being broken—when Marxism-Leninism or Chinese nationalism or national interests do not provide the answer, or the same answer—then there is a high probability that the relations among Political Bureau members will break down. Although the antagonists may have their constituencies, nonetheless it is the existence of serious conflict among this small group which generated such shattering crises. (This is a major difference from other political systems, where the governmental leadership is fairly unified, and political conflict is conducted on a larger scale.)

Furthermore, with almost no significant exceptions,[104] the losers in the ten crises enumerated were eliminated from the political scene. Thus, politics *within the top elite* is a zero-sum game in China, whereas in Western democracies the zero-sum game is played out between or among contending parties (rather than within elites).[105] We noted earlier that the Western process is systemically functional. Is the

---

[103] We are not, of course, making reference to the written constitutions of the Party or state, which have not functioned as constitutions.

[104] Ch'ü Ch'iu-pai made a brief comeback. Li Li-san and Ch'en Shao-yü were able to recoup modest political careers. Ho Meng-hsiung was rehabilitated posthumously. Teng Hsiao-p'ing, on the other hand, after being suspended from active politics during the Cultural Revolution, made a spectacular comeback in 1974.

[105] One problem is that notwithstanding the theory of "democratic centralism," the Political Bureau apparently does not operate by majority vote, but rather by consensus. There have been times when the minority simply would not bow to the will of the majority. As Chiang Ch'ing put it, "One could not talk about a 'minority' or a 'majority' independent of class viewpoint." PR, December 9, 1966, p. 6.

Chinese process systemically dysfunctional? Not if the "system" is defined in Leninist terms, i.e., is comprised of a plenipotentiary and unified vanguard of the proletariat. On the other hand, confining the making of crucial decisions to the chambers of the Political Bureau can produce a failure of political integration. Policy disputes become overshadowed by personal antagonisms, at heavy cost to the public which the Political Bureau is supposed to be serving. This manner of operating is also counterproductive in terms of achieving popular participation in national politics.[106] Thus, to the extent that the Chinese really want to break away from the Soviet institutional mold, they will have to open up the political process where it really counts—in the making of the important policy.

Charismatic Leadership

We have been emphasizing the role of supreme ruling *groups* in the Communist party. It should not be inferred from this that collective leadership is the natural condition of Chinese politics. Our memories of the Taiping Rebellion and the politics of the Republican period should remind us of how ineffective government can be in the absence of an individual sufficiently charismatic to control factionalism. Furthermore, if we dismiss the Kao Kang affair as relatively untraumatic, we are struck by how the one long period which was free of intra-Party crises, 1943–59, was precisely the one substantial period when Mao Tse-tung's leadership of the party was undisputed. Here we must be careful that we are not simply equating the fortunes of the leader with general political functionality. Still, it is not circular to note that the supremacy of the leader in modern China has been associated with the success of political movements and regimes to a much greater extent than is true of most modern *and* traditional political systems. We turn, then, to an examination of the individual national leader.

Mao Tse-tung became the leader of the Chinese Communist party in 1935, and for a quarter-century the movement under his direction compounded success upon success.[107] Beginning in the late 1950s, Chinese communism encountered serious difficulties, but the accompanying challenges to Mao's leadership were eventually overridden.

---

[106] As we shall note below, there is evidence of a certain sense of mystification on the part of the Chinese public regarding politics at the center.

[107] Mao apparently did not become titular head of the Party until 1943, when he permanently assumed the new title of chairman. After the founding of the People's Republic, he also became Chairman of the Republic, but as we have noted he relinquished this title in 1959. See note 21.

Mao did not simply dictate policy; obviously there were discussions within the Political Bureau in which different philosophies and interests were discussed. However, at least until 1959 Mao's associates generally agreed with him, or a consensus acceptable to Mao was hammered out. Thus, it would be misleading to think of Chinese Communist politics before 1959 as a coalition of different groups which formulated policy on the basis of compromise. In effect, there was only one interest group represented in the Political Bureau (Kao Kang excepted). Thus, this was neither coalition politics (with Mao having only one "vote") nor one-man dictatorship (with Mao having all of the "votes"). Rather, the Political Bureau seems to have functioned something like the New York City model, where the leader has more than one "vote," but must still persuade others to support his policies (or be persuaded to support theirs).

Naturally, a consensus merely within the Political Bureau was not sufficient basis for political action; the *public* must also be persuaded to accept and carry out central policies. Here, the personal role of Mao Tse-tung became crucial. First, he became the general personification of Chinese communism. This did not mean that he became a god, and in the 1950s he certainly did not supplant the state or Party, as had Stalin. (Neither Mao nor his Thought was mentioned in the national and Party constitutions of the mid-1950s.)[108] Although occasionally the word *genius* may have slipped into the rhetoric,[109] by and large Mao was portrayed as exceptionally wise but still very human.[110]

---

[108] The 1956 Party constitution contained a line which could also be interpreted as cutting Mao's image down to life size: "No ... person can be free from shortcomings and mistakes in work." However, Mao himself was not unwilling to admit his mistakes. For example, in 1959 he said that the backyard iron furnaces had been a "great disaster for which I myself must be held responsible." *CLG*, Winter 1968–69, p. 43. But Chu Teh's (perhaps self-serving) suggestion that the chairmanship rotate was not accepted. Thus, it would be anachronistic to infer that excessive adulation of the leader was generally seen as a problem in the mid-1950s.

[109] In the 1945 Party constitution, Mao had been called "the creative genius of Marxism."

[110] There were certainly many instances of unrestrained adulation. See, for example, Hu Feng's poem about Mao on the mountaintop (*CNA* 872, p. 1). On the other hand, Mao's own poems were relatively modest. Jerome Ch'en, *Mao ... Revolution*, pt. 2.

Our statement that Mao is perceived as "human" should not be construed to mean that any full accounts of Mao's personal life have been published in China. Actually, in this respect he was rather remote. Little biographical information has been made available, and although cadres often heard tape recordings of Mao's speeches, his voice was rarely heard over the radio (perhaps because of his heavy Hunan accent). Often an announcer's voice was superimposed over Mao's.

For the untutored masses, to whom the Party was an indigestible abstraction, the person of Mao was a tangible rallying point. On balance, however, the emphasis was not upon lauding Mao Tse-tung per se, but rather upon adhering to the principles set forth in his Thought. Thus, to the extent that the population came to internalize the values and goals set forth therein, Mao's leadership role served a general integrative function. Charismatic leadership made *national* totalitarian leadership unnecessary (although it made it possible for local leaders, acting in Mao's name, to be authoritarian). The Chinese took exception to the Soviet campaign against the Stalinist cult of personality. The leadership insisted that "the 'combat against the personality cult' violates Lenin's integral teachings on the interrelationship of leaders, party, class, and masses, and undermines the Communist principle of democratic centralism."[111] Thus, although Stalin had made some mistakes, excessive personalism in politics was not considered one of them.

During the 1950s, then, Chinese national leadership was characterized by what we might term a "*moderate* cult of personality." Praising Mao Tse-tung was *de rigueur*; criticizing him, treason. His early works, republished in purified form, became required reading. On the other hand, the cult of personality did not burst its bounds. Mao was now *ex officio* leader, and institutions had an organic existence independent of the person of the leader. And there was some reading fare available that was *not* based upon Mao's thought. Paying respect to Mao was never permitted to supplant political substance. Even Mao's birthday was not observed. As the decade wore on, the cult declined even further.

In 1959 it suddenly seemed that political realities more than justified this situation. Within the Central Committee Mao was barely first among equals.[112] According to one version of what happened at that year's Lushan Plenum:

> There was an emotional scene when Mao, in reply to a suggestion that the disgrace of P'eng [Teh-huai] might be the signal for revolt by the armed forces due to his popularity with them and in the country, declared with tears in his eyes that, if this happened, he would go back to the villages and recruit another army.[113]

---

[111] *On the Question of Stalin* (pamphlet reprinted from *JMJP*, September 13, 1963), p. 1, citing a June 14 letter to the Soviet Communist party.

[112] "Don't write about my wise leadership, for I have not been in control." Speech of July 23, 1959, *CLG*, Winter 1968–69, p. 39.

[113] David A. Charles [pseud.], "The Dismissal of Marshal P'eng Teh-huai," *CQ*, October 1961, p. 68.

As it turned out, the army remained loyal to Mao and continued to promote the Mao cult internally. After the Great Leap Forward, other institutions' loyalty began to flag, however, and they suspended the cult. The media ceased to be dominated by Maoist writings.[114] In particular, Liu Shao-ch'i's 1939 essay "How to Be a Good Communist" was republished in tens of millions of copies.[115] No longer evoking unquestioning devotion, unable to cope with the country's economic crises, and becoming (in the minds of some) increasingly irrelevant to the post-liberation generation of organization men, Mao seemed to be losing his charisma. By the mid-1960s both his *de facto,* and (less significantly) his *ex officio*[116] leadership positions had become eroded.

The key to recovering political power, Mao eventually concluded, was to regain his stature as China's omnipresent charismatic leader. In this process, first the army, and then the general media,[117] would be the tools, and rekindling the revolution would be the means. It became necessary to blanket the nation with every conceivable trapping of the cult of "The Great Teacher, Great Leader, Great Supreme Commander, and Great Helmsman" (as he was repeatedly called)—not only portraits, but badges, rituals, reports of near miracles, and of course the ever-read and -waved "little red book" of quotations.[118] In the book's introduction by Lin Piao (which Lin lived just long enough to regret having written), Mao was described as a man of "genius" and the "greatest Marxist-Leninist of our era,"[119] whose Thought was "an inexhaustible source of strength and a spiritual atom bomb of infinite power."[120] Small wonder that ceremonies conducted to honor Mao and his Thought often took on an almost religious character.[121]

The revived and intensified cult of personality served its purpose, at least in the short run, for the Cultural Revolution was launched, and

---

[114] See especially Merle Goldman, "The Unique 'Blooming and Contending' of 1961–62," *CQ,* January 1969, pp. 54–83.

[115] *CNA* 656, p. 2.

[116] We have emphasized the relative importance of *de facto* leadership and do not attach great importance to the fact that Mao was no longer Chairman of the Republic. (After being unsuccessfully sought by Lin Piao, this position was abolished under the 1975 Constitution.)

[117] See chap. 5.

[118] Mao, *Yü-lu.*

[119] Ibid., p. ii.

[120] Ibid., pp. vii f.

[121] Toward the end of the Cultural Revolution, many people were kneeling before the ubiquitous new plaster statues of Mao, but the practice was stopped on his direct orders. *FEER,* July 31, 1971, p. 13.

FOUR: Leadership and Participation

many of its objectives attained. Observers, including many sympathetic to China, feared that the country was leaning toward totalitarianism. Had Mao come to emulate Ch'in Shih Huang-ti, Napoleon, and Stalin, whose strengths and weaknesses he would exceed?

As it turned out, no one was more aware that total national identification with his personality would be counterproductive in terms of the real revolutionary goals. Even early in the Cultural Revolution, Mao is reported to have had reservations. To his wife he reportedly wrote: "I have self-confidence, but also some doubt. Once when I was in my teens, I said that I believed I could live two hundred years. . . . I was haughty in appearance and attitude. But now I have self-doubts, and know that when the tiger [in me] is absent from the mountain, the monkey professes himself king. I have become such a king. This is not to say that I am fickle. In my mind I am primarily a tiger, but there is also some monkey in me. . . .

> Something white is easily stained,
>   something long is easily broken:
> New fallen snow soon loses its purity,
>   a reputation is difficult to retain.[122]

These lines apply precisely to me. . . . The higher one is elevated, the harder he falls."[123] Mao thus had a highly ambivalent attitude toward the excesses of the cult of personality. It was a useful political tool—a necessary nuisance, as he told Edgar Snow[124]—but also poor Marxism.

No one had more sharply rejected such tactics than Karl Marx:

> Because of aversion to any personality cult, I have never permitted the numerous expressions of appreciation from various countries, with which I was pestered during the existence of the International, to reach the realm of publicity, and have never answered them, except occasionally by rebuke. When Engels and I first joined the secret Communist Society, we made it a condition that everything tending to encourage superstitious belief in authority was to be removed from the statutes.[125]

---

[122] Quoting a letter from Li Ku (second century A.D.) to a Han emperor.

[123] Letter to Chiang Ch'ing, July 8, 1966. *CLG*, Summer 1973, pp. 97 f. Translation revised; poem freely rendered.

[124] Harry Harding, "China," *AS*, January 1972, p. 12, citing *Life*, April 30, 1971, pp. 46–48.

[125] Letter to W. Blos, November 10, 1877, quoted in Alfred Meyer, "Historical Development of the Communist Theory of Leadership," in Farrell, *Political Leadership* (see first footnote of this chapter), p. 9.

Although this particular statement has undoubtedly not been circulated in China, nonetheless other more subtle classic statements have been studied widely and intensively. In particular, Engels's critique of Eugen Dühring's essays on revolution and science was read. In it, Engels stressed freedom and relativism, and (as emphasized in Chinese paraphrases) "the relationship between knowledge and practice." In particular, the essay is interpreted as refuting those who "spread idealist apriorism, preach the theory of genius, and maintain that knowledge and ability are innate and natural gifts."[126] Those for whom the Engels–Dühring debate was too erudite were simply reminded of the lyrics of the "Internationale": "There are no saviors; we do not rely on gods, spirits, or emperors. The happiness of mankind is our own creation."

If the expanded personality cult was a political tactic, so was its eventual negation. In 1971 the trappings of the Mao cult were either eliminated or subdued, and the most effusive slogans were discarded. This was all part of a scheme to purge the influence of the Lin Piao element, for Lin (Mao had now concluded) had used the cult for his own purposes. In rejecting Lin's claim that Mao was a "genius,"[127] Mao became the true interpreter of Marxism, and Lin, a sham Marxist. This was also a way of enhancing the status of the reconstructed Party. Whereas once it had constantly been said that people looked to *Mao* as sunflowers turn to the sun, now the simile was revised to the effect that the people looked to the *Party*.

Finally, Mao was absent from the 1975 National People's Congress, and hardly mentioned in the new constitution[128]—although his Thought was a conspicuous feature of both. There are a variety of possible explanations for his invisibility, but these developments highlight the separation of *de facto* and *ex officio* leadership. Perhaps, how-

[126] "Kiangsi Military District Cadres Study 'Anti-Dühring,'" Nanchang radio, April 27, 1973, FBIS I, May 4, 1973, p. C-1.

[127] As Chiang Ch'ing expressed it, Lin had transformed Mao into an idol to be smashed.

Actually, Lin's assertions regarding the Mao cult had been mixed. In 1968 he told army cadres: "Historically, absolute authority has only existed in slave societies.... Absolute authority can take the form of love of Chairman Mao only as a figure of speech. Romantic language of this type can still be used, but to use it in the philosophical, scientific, or political sense is incorrect and anti-Marxist." *CLG*, Summer 1973, p. 19. Translation revised.

[128] In this respect the final draft of the constitution differs markedly from earlier circulated versions. According to a draft which appeared in 1974, Mao was "the great leader of the people" (Art. 2), and the citizens' first duty was "to support Chairman Mao Tse-tung" (Art. 26). *BOC*, September 26, 1974. Such language was dropped from the final version.

152   FOUR: *Leadership and Participation*

ever, the NPC marked the beginning of the narrowing of that gulf. The *ex officio–de facto* dichotomy, after all, springs in part from the Chinese heritage, in part from China's stage of political development, and in part from Mao Tse-tung's rational response to real political situations. With Mao's passing from the scene, and China's achieving greater political development, it is possible that the culture will sustain a convergence of *de facto* and *ex officio* leadership.

FIVE
Political Communications and Socialization

> We Chinese believe that people should not know too much. Men's knowledge must not increase endlessly. If it continues to expand, it causes endless trouble, and despairs of itself. It is true that if it were to halt completely, decadence would set in; but in order really to think one must know countless ideographs, and only scholars can undertake the great labor involved. Others cannot reflect deeply, nor integrate their shapeless notions. They feel, but they cannot articulate. Their feelings inevitably remain shut within.
>
> ANONYMOUS (1895)[1]

> [We must] take the ideas of the masses (scattered and unsystematic ideas) and concentrate them (through study turn them into concentrated and systematic ideas), then go to the masses and propagate and explain these ideas until the masses embrace them as their own, hold fast to them and translate them into action. Then once again concentrate ideas from the masses and once again go to the masses so that the ideas are persevered in and carried through. And so on, over and over again, in an endless spiral, with the ideas becoming more correct, more vital, and richer each time. Such is the Marxist theory of knowledge.
>
> MAO TSE-TUNG (1943)[2]

PERSONAL AMBITIONS ASIDE, political conduct is determined on the one hand by immediate pressures and constraints, and on the other hand by experience. For the political scientist, this involves two greatly overlapping areas of inquiry. The first is political *communications*—the transmission of politically relevant information among political actors. The second is political *socialization*—the understanding of basic political concepts and the development of political skills. Because a person learns (is socialized) when information is communicated, we shall often be discussing both subjects simultaneously, and thus the chapter is not divided into two discrete sections. We begin, however, with a look at political socialization.

Political Socialization

Although there is general agreement among both Marxists and non-Marxists that people's attitudes and predispositions to behavior are shaped by their environment, the relative weight of various elements in that environment is a matter of some controversy. The classical Marxist position is that the *substructure*—the relationship of the individual to the means of production—takes precedence, and most Marxists continue to give at least lip service to this principle. Lenin altered the equation somewhat, however, by placing great emphasis upon political institutions. Mao also emphasized the role of the *superstructure*, and it appears (though many observers dispute this) that he gave primacy to education and consciousness raising, on the assumption that this affects substructural relations. To the extent that this is an accurate representation of Mao's views, he reversed classical Marxism in this respect, and reflected the idealism of Hegel, whom Marx was supposed to have "turned upside down."

The most extreme such position was taken during the early months of the Cultural Revolution. Some newspapers carried editorials proclaiming that "the key to the transformation of the objective world lies with man's ideological revolutionization." Transforming one's thinking—the "subjective world"—was a precondition to revolutionary action. Problems should still be analyzed in terms of class struggle, but classes appeared not to be defined simply in economic terms. "The change in world outlook is a basic change," and it was the place to begin. Such an emphasis certainly has not characterized all Chinese

---

Among the more important general studies relating to political communications in China are: Houn; Leyda; Alan Liu; Oliver; Solomon (both works); Wu; and Yu. On political socialization, see Levy; Price; Ridley; and C. K. Yang.

[1] Valéry. Translation revised.
[2] SW, 2:119.

Communists, and even the editorials implied that the need for the consciousness-raising approach to revolution might be peculiar to that particular time. This assertedly was because in the early stage of socialism there are remnant bourgeois elements who, deprived of their economic base, must rely primarily upon "ideological influence as a magic weapon" to oppose socialism.[3] So while the role of institutions and economic arrangements was not denied as a factor in political socialization, the view was that "spirit" can be primary. "All efforts to reform the objective world must be done by man, and all of man's activities are guided by a given world outlook."[4]

In every culture, the family is virtually always the initial instrument of socialization. Most of the socialization a child receives in his early years is not *political* socialization, but learning how to relate to others often has relevance to political behavior later in life. For example, thrusting responsibility upon children, allowing them to participate in family decisions, and encouraging a sense of self-reliance are presumably helpful in training children to become citizens in an individualistic democracy in which little support and direction will be forthcoming from government. In China, the family was traditionally collective and paternalistic, and thus not conducive to a liberal democratic spirit. On the other hand, the family was highly autonomous (at least vis à vis political authority), and the supreme object of individual loyalty. It was primarily for this reason—that the family served as a competing institution—that the Communists took various measures to curb its influence. There was no general effort to "destroy" the family, however, as sometimes alleged.[5] In some respects the family socialization process was not so inimical to Communist programs. It was in the interest of the Party, for example, that children learn collectivist attitudes and submission to authority.

Whereas the socialization the young child undergoes in the family is only implicitly political, as soon as a Chinese enters school, political socialization becomes explicit. Since 1949 not only has education been

[3] *Yang-ch'eng wan-pao*, February 3, 1966, *SCMP*, no. 3637, February 14, 1966, pp. 7 f.
[4] *Yang-ch'eng wan-pao*, April 8, 1966, *SCMP*, no. 3680, April 19, 1966, p. 9. See also *Yang-ch'eng wan-pao*, April 25, 1966, *SCMP*, no. 3692, May 6, 1966, pp. 9–12, in which the Kwangsi first secretary (Wei Kuo-ch'ing) stresses that even old revolutionaries must reform themselves. "If we do not study Chairman Mao's writings seriously ... we may lose our resistance [to embourgeoisement] through the corruption of bourgeois ideology." Ibid., p. 10.
[5] For further information on this subject, see Maurice Freedman, "The Family under Chinese Communism," *The Political Quarterly*, July 1964, pp. 342–50.

available (and compulsory) for most children,[6] its general content has been directed by the central government and made overtly political. Although relatively few students advance past primary school, during those six years much attention is paid to inculcating attitudes toward the nation, leadership, the Party, and fellow citizens. The study of what would elsewhere be nonpolitical subjects is, in China, infused with political ideology. Materials used in the teaching of reading skills are often of an openly political nature. This is as true for adult literacy education as for children. People are not only taught to approve of the political leadership and its policies, but also to be socially oriented, rather than family-oriented or individualistic.

But just as the Chinese leaders distrust the family as a socializing agent, so is there strong skepticism (especially among Maoists) about the ability of educational *institutions* to inculcate proper political attitudes and behavior. Rather, Maoist pedagogy emphasizes the role of *experience*. Knowledge and understanding that are divorced from practice are politically suspect. Thus, reading political tracts and listening to speeches is combined with political and administrative activity—campaigns, struggles, and so on. As we saw in the previous chapter, such activity often falls short of political participation in the Western sense, but it is nonetheless important as a means of socialization. In addition, the Chinese place much stress upon the relevance of economic activity for politics. All citizens, including cadres, are expected to spend at least some time engaged in productive labor, and to become aware of the social and political implications of their work. For example, white-collar workers and others may be "sent down" to work on communes to learn that the *real* China is rural China, and that real production is not what parasitic office personnel perform but rather that which involves physical labor.

Models

A favorite means of influencing social and political attitudes has a long history in China. Imperial statesmen and gentry were supposed to set high moral standards in their own lives, to be emulated by others. The supreme pacesetter in this regard was the emperor. Theoretically, his morality was transmitted downward through the ranking scholar-officials and village elders. It would be surprising,

---

[6] The Chinese were slow in providing modern education for ethnic minorities, particularly the Tibetans.

though, if there had been no gulf between the ideal and the real. Certainly the imperial image could be enhanced or marred in the course of transmission. It is also likely that the example of the emperor was more meaningful to those who could most easily identify with him—the scholar gentry. It would hardly have been apt for farmers to emulate a contrite imperial ritual after a crop failure, but a landlord might well forgive a debt or reduce rent. Likewise, if a city were engulfed in fire, modification of an emperor's life-style would have little meaning to the homeless masses unless the wealthy caught the signal and reduced their own consumption, thereby moderating prices and helping the reconstruction.[7] How important all of this was as a practical matter is impossible to judge, nor do we know whether the moral example set by the local gentry had much influence upon the conduct of the public (or how lofty that example typically was). But it is doubtful that if such a method of socialization had served no function it would have persisted throughout Chinese history as it has.[8]

Although leaders in Communist China are expected to set a very different example from that set by leaders in the past, their role as models for emulation has been strongly emphasized by both leftists and "revisionists." As Party secretary-general Teng Hsiao-p'ing said in 1956,

> Unlike the leaders of the exploiting classes in the past, the leaders of the working-class party stand not above the masses, but in their midst, not above the Party, but within it. Precisely because of this, they must *set an example* . . . in obeying the Party organizations and observing Party discipline.[9]

Although a decade later the nature of the paradigm altered, the principle of paradigmatic leadership was still considered as viable as ever. The media continue to insist that local leaders be ever mindful of the influence of their example. We are told, for instance, that a successful commune owes its achievements to exemplary leadership. "Setting an example with their own conduct, leading cadres have relied on the masses and have led them to work hard and to be self-reliant." In this

---

[7] For example, in 1201 a great fire in Hangchow destroyed 50,000 homes. The emperor published a self-critical edict, remained confined to his quarters, and had a modest table set. See Gernet, pp. 75 f.

[8] An alternative interpretation is that, as we have noted in the case of rectifying names, exemplification was stressed precisely because the socialization process was not working. However, the writer is inclined to reject this.

[9] *Constitution*, p. 82. Emphasis added.

way, public enthusiasm for socialism is said to have been aroused, with the earlier situation of "disaster and frustration" vastly improving.[10]

But these quotations point up an important contradiction inherent in leadership by example. For Teng, exemplification was a subtle method of issuing commands. The message of the examples he cited is that ordinary people, like cadres, should follow orders. Although the Cultural Revolution would constitute a reaction against this style of leadership in favor of self-reliance, until such time, just as in the case of the gentry in traditional China, what local leaders learned from their superiors was how to influence the conduct of *others*. Indeed, the field investigation of Richard Solomon among Chinese of Taiwan and Hong Kong suggests that what one learns from the *example* of a leader is how to *lead*, not how to follow or how to be independent.

> Our interview materials indicate that people do, in fact, look to superiors for guidance and initiative. Indeed, an important aspect of this system of authority relations is that initiative and precedence in communication are vested in those with power. To describe such a relationship as one of "modeling," however, would be inaccurate, for *within* the tie there is no equivalence or reciprocity; the subordinate does not copy or emulate his superior's action in response. The subordinate, rather, looks to the superior for cues or instruction as to what will be appropriate or permissible behavior on his part. Filiality requires that deference in judgment and decision making, and communication precedence, be given to the superior within the relationship. Modeling or imitation of the superior's behavior does seem to occur, however, through the subordinate's adopting his superior's style and judgments of what is proper or permissible behavior *in those other relationships in which he himself is a superior*.[11]

Among these traditional Chinese, males and seniors were socially superordinate to females and juniors, and nearly everyone became at one time or other a leader. How to lead under these conditions is an important lesson for people to learn.

On the other hand, one does not learn either to *follow* leaders, or to be a responsible *citizen*, by emulating leaders. For this reason, the Communists have made a special point of propagating a number of

---

[10] "Build More Tachai-Type Counties," *Honan jih-pao,* broadcast on Chengchow radio, May 27, 1973, FBIS I, June 1, 1973, p. D-5. Crop output is said to have doubled in a few years, the "main reason" being that "the leadership has undergone a deep change in its attitude." Ibid., p. D-4.

[11] Solomon, *Mao's Revolution,* pp. 111 f.

models who are *not* elite types but peers with whom the public can identify. The most famous such model was a young Hunanese named Lei Feng. Reportedly oppressed by the landowners and Kuomintang before the liberation, Lei first became "educated in the class struggle" in 1949 when he testified against a landlord's wife at a mass trial. He then went to school and learned that the savior was Chairman Mao and not Heaven—a message which he quickly imparted to his mother. In 1956 Lei graduated from primary school with honors, but he went directly from graduation to the agricultural front, where he made important contributions to local agricultural modernization. In time, he volunteered to go to the frigid Anshan region where his mechanical skills were in need. There, in keeping with his character, he worked with extreme diligence, ignoring suggestions that he relax his efforts. In 1959 he heard a report about military conscription, and immediately volunteered for enlistment. Although he did not meet the physical standards, he was so insistent that he was admitted into the armed services. His performance was outstanding—particularly in terms of public service—and in 1960 he was permitted to join the Communist party. He later died in an accident,[12] but was immortalized in the national media.

Not all models exemplify virtue. Some have been paragons of "evil." Often figures selected for this role had previously enjoyed official support and a large popular following. In the 1950s, the most famous such individual was Hu Feng. Hu was a leading Marxist writer who opposed what he considered to be the Party's sterile literary policies and became the target of a nationwide campaign in 1955. He was condemned as a "counterrevolutionary" and imprisoned, with the campaign against him turning into a vehicle for the repression of obstreperous intellectuals.[13] Another person who falls into the paragon-of-evil category was Liu Shao-ch'i. Liu might have been allowed to slip into oblivion had he not personified so much of what the Maoists wished to repress. As it was, he was obliged to make three public confessions, and throughout the country Party regulars were purged in his name. Even Lin Piao and his followers, though unlike the Luists in many ways, were condemned as "Liu-type swindlers." Eventually, Lin Piao became a negative example in his own right.

[12] For example, Chen Tung-lei, "Lei Feng, a Fine Example of Chinese Youth," *Evergreen*, no. 2, (April 1963); reproduced in Franz Schurmann and Orville Schell, *Communist China* (New York: Vintage, 1967), pp. 450–56, on which our account is based.
[13] On Hu Feng, see Goldman, chap. 7.

Political Communications and Chinese Culture

These models and the other didactic devices used in political socialization are effective only if actually transmitted to the public. Communications, then, are a prerequisite to political power. Indeed, what money is to an economy, words are to politics. Communications are the means by which political inputs are expressed, and by which outputs are realized. If political behavior differs in most countries today from what it was decades ago, this is probably as much due to the communications revolution as to any other factor. The information explosion has fed upon itself to the point where little remains private, with many bureaucracies and publics straining under the load.

Communications are as important for closed systems as for open ones, though for different reasons. In a true liberal democracy, leaders are accountable to an informed public. Leaders of closed systems, on the other hand, maintain their power by limiting the flow of information. In practice, of course, no system is entirely open or closed. All governments practice secrecy to some extent, and usually this enables them to manipulate public opinion. If on the next few pages the reader is struck by the degree of secrecy in Chinese politics, he should bear in mind, for example, that American politics of the early 1970s would have been entirely different had it been conducted openly. The decisions to sell grain to the Soviet Union rather than save starving Africans, to bomb and invade Cambodia, to assist Pakistan in the war against Bangladesh—decisions costing million of lives—are difficult to imagine having been made in any but a secret manner. So while political communications are more open in the United States than in China, the difference is one of degree.

Since early times, China has possessed impressive systems of political communications. During the imperial period, communications required travel, at least by messengers. The basis for empire-wide transportation was laid in the third century B.C., with the building of canals and wide thoroughfares. The political implication of the highways is suggested by the existence of a center lane reserved exclusively for imperial parties.[14] Usually, though, messages were transported by carriers, and over the centuries a remarkable pony-express-type courier system was developed, enabling the central government to communicate with the farthest reaches of the realm in a matter of days. The uniform ideo-

[14] Imperial tours were a feature of every great dynasty. They were believed to have had a precedent in prehistoric (mythical) times.

graphic writing system facilitated communication, in that written communication used a common "vocabulary" which was independent of local spoken languages. (More than any other factor, this probably accounts for China's survival as a single nation and polity.) Within the bureaucracy, written communications appear to have been the preferred means, even when distance was not a factor.

By the seventeenth century, China undoubtedly enjoyed the most sophisticated system of political communications in the world. From the palace memorial system at the center,[15] all the way down to the county-level memoranda, it was remarkably effective. But the link between the county magistrate and the public was a weak one. Efforts were made to extend political communications to that level when the Manchu government transformed the old *hsiang-yueh* (village cultural groups) into an office of political socialization. The *hsiang-yueh* (the term now designating a local scholar-sermonizer) would lecture to villagers twice monthly, basing his remarks upon imperial maxims or edicts. The following are some lecture topics (as ordered by the K'ang-hsi emperor in 1670):

> Explain the laws in order to warn the ignorant and obstinate.
> Put a stop to false accusations in order to protect the innocent and good.
> Abstain from concealment of fugitives in order to avoid being involved in their punishments.
> Pay your taxes fully in order that official urging can be dispensed with.
> Join the *pao-chia* (security organization) in order to suppress thieves and robbers.
> Expand education so that there may be improved scholarship.
> Reject false doctrines in order that education be honorable.
> Be economical; conserve money and goods.[16]

When political dissent was rife, the *hsiang-yueh* were to combat it, with remarks such as this warning on the subject of secret societies:

> Lascivious and villainous persons ... from brotherhoods bind themselves to another by oath, meet in the night and disperse at the dawn, violate the laws, ... and impose upon the people. But behold! One morning the whole thing comes to light, and they are seized and dealt

---

[15] See Wu.
[16] Hsiao, p. 187 (revised). Not all of the injunctions were as political as this selected list would suggest.

with according to law. What they vainly thought would prove the source of their felicity becomes the occasion of their grief.[17]

The content varied from reign to reign; some emperors sought to have filial obligations emphasized; others stressed the citizen's duty to the state. Sometimes praiseworthy or culpable individuals were to be singled out to stand as either emulatory or negative examples. In sum, the *hsiang-yueh* was a fairly significant medium for communicating political values and general demands from the central government to the public at large. On the other hand, it was not a means for true political mobilization.[18]

In the nineteenth century the communications system began to break down, and proved itself unable to perpetuate the integration of China in the face of Western pressures. Always better at dissemination than soliciting feedback, communications with frontier officials seem to have become almost completely ineffective during the troubles in Vietnam and during the events leading up to the Opium War. Toward the end of the century, wise leaders realized that the capital needed better access to political information, and during the abortive Hundred Days Reform the Kuang-hsu emperor decided to permit anyone in the realm to petition the throne. All such modern ideas failed, however, and no effective general system of political communications was realized until after the revolution of 1949.

Although the basis for the traditional system of political communications was the written language, over the centuries written Chinese became more and more divorced from the vernacular, and thus increasingly undemocratic. This key to power was the monopoly of the scholar-official class. A prerequisite to the institution of a modern system of political communications was language reform—reconciling the writing system with spoken language.[19] It was around 1920 that westernized intellectuals began to write in a style which reflected Pekingese, thus making literature more accessible to people who understood that dialect (with little cost to those who did not, who were largely illiterate anyway). The new style of writing was less telegraphic, more verbose than the old, but its adoption was an important

---

[17] Ibid., p. 189 (revised).
[18] There were, of course, police controls and tax collection. Ibid., chaps. 3 and 4.
[19] Pekingese, and related dialects. These are known in Chinese as *kuo-yü*, or the "national language." The term *kuo-yü* is sometimes translated "Mandarin," because the language which Ch'ing scholar officials used to communicate orally among themselves was that of the capital.

step in the direction of democratization and politicization.[20] To date, the Communists have instituted only a moderate additional reform—the simplification (reducing the number of brush strokes) of the ideographic characters.[21]

Even these limited linguistic reforms have made possible political communications on an unprecedented scale. With the modest exception of the *hsiang-yueh,* there had been little communication between imperial authorities and the public. Even the Kuomintang accomplished little in the way of developing a serviceable communications system, particularly in the countryside. The Communists, however, would place much emphasis upon working out the theoretical and practical problems of this aspect of politics.

Vertical and Horizontal Communications

There was gradually developed a theory which took account of both the vertical and horizontal dimensions of political communications.

Vertical communications are of two types: downward, which we

---

[20] Because writing continued to be done in ideographs, this was not as revolutionary a step as was taken in countries where people not only wrote in the vernacular but also with phonetic symbols, such as in Europe after the Middle Ages. The same was true of Vietnam in the 1920s, and to some extent Japan in the late nineteenth century and Korea (especially the North) after World War II. In these countries the step tended to mark both a break with the past, and a move toward national cultural autonomy—from China. Perhaps one reason why China has not moved in the same direction is that for that country, cultural autonomy is not an issue.

Although the Roman alphabet is used as a didactic device, and appears on some signs (railway stations, etc.), it is not used for general writing and publishing. There are several difficulties. The Chinese are especially proud of their language. The total break from an ideographic to a phonetic writing system would inevitably be traumatic, and indeed has rarely, with the exception of Vietnam, been accomplished anywhere in modern times. Chinese is a tonal and sound-poor language, one with many homonyms. (However, if the tones were indicated with diacritical marks, as in Vietnamese, there would probably be no more true homonyms than in English, where the problem is circumvented by arbitrary spellings). Another difficulty is that the use of Mandarin in speech is still far from universal. Thus, phoneticization is still only a distant goal. In Mao's words, "The Chinese written language must be reformed and should move in the direction of adopting a phonetic script, in common with the languages throughout the world." *KMJP,* July 10, 1973, FBIS I, August 2, 1973, page B-3. In 1973 there was considerable discussion of phoneticization. *KMJP,* May 9, 1973, FBIS I, May 11, 1973, p. B-4; *KMJP,* May 25, 1973, FBIS I, June 5, 1973, p. B-4; *JMJP,* August 24, 1973, FBIS I, August 27, 1973, p. B-5. China's non-Chinese languages will be discussed in chap. 7.

[21] See *Reform of the Chinese Written Language* (Peking: Foreign Languages Press, 1958).

shall term *dissemination*, and upward, or *feedback*. The Chinese term *mass line* (*ch'ün-chung lu-hsien*) encompasses both directions. In theory, the mass line calls for communications to be more or less balanced in each direction. Mao-Tse-tung's classic definition of the mass line, which appears as the second chapter-head quotation (p. 153), rejects the traditional Confucian idea that there can be no popular will. Mao insists that the views of the masses could not only be integrated (and most Westerners would agree but many would leave it at that) but that these views could also be consolidated, purified, and translated into action. Thus the slogan 'from the masses, to the masses"[22] became the theoretical basis for a modern system of political communications. But it soon became clear that although ultimately the masses might be allowed their political inputs, until the revolution was consummated only the center was a reliable source of "correct ideas." As Mao said in 1945:

> The political awakening of the people is not easy. It requires much earnest effort on our part to rid their minds of wrong ideas. We should sweep backward ideas from the minds of the Chinese people, just as we sweep our rooms. Dust never vanishes of itself without sweeping. We must carry on extensive propaganda and education among the masses, so they will understand the real situation and trend in China and have confidence in their own strength.[23]

Thus, the masses did not really understand their best interests, and required someone else to voice them. This was especially true of long-range and broad public concerns.

It would be wrong to take an entirely cynical view of the mass-line approach. Certainly during the period of guerrilla warfare, the masses were an important source of ideas, information (intelligence), and support for the Red Army. It is not surprising that as the military phase of the revolution drew to a close, the leadership was confident that the masses could be trusted. As Ch'en Po-ta wrote:

> The wisdom of the masses is limitless. The greatest creativity exists only with the concentration of the wisdom of the masses. In fact, any difficult problem, any matter which we cannot think out for ourselves,

---

[22] *SW*, 3:119 (1943).
[23] *SW*, 4:19. These remarks have often been quoted in the Chinese Press. See, for example, *PR*, August 13, 1965, p. 21.

can be easily managed and quickly illuminated as soon as it is discussed with the masses.[24]

As we shall see, however, such idealism led to disillusionment, and in practice much greater emphasis would be placed upon the dissemination aspect of the mass line than upon feedback.

In Chapter 2 we indicated that peer relations have constituted a sensitive area of Chinese culture, so we should not be surprised to find that horizontal communications present a special problem in politics. That this is so is underscored by the use of terms like *struggle* and *criticism* to denote such communications (although other terms, such as *discussion* and *collective leadership,* reflect a more sanguine and constructive view). Whether assembling a work team, or groups of equal-level bureaucrats from different agencies, Chinese have appeared to function less easily in such situations than do Westerners. As early as 1948, Mao wrote:

> The Party committee system is an important Party institution for ensuring collective leadership and preventing any individual from monopolizing the conduct of affairs. It has recently been found that in some (of course not all) leading bodies it is the habitual practice for one individual to monopolize the conduct of affairs and decide important problems. Solutions to important problems are decided not by Party committee meetings but by one individual, and membership in the Party committee has become nominal. Differences of opinion among committee members cannot be resolved and are left unresolved for a long time. Members of the Party committee maintain only formal, not real, unity among themselves. This situation must be changed. From now on, a sound system of Party committee meetings must be instituted in all leading bodies, from the bureaus of the Central Committee to the prefectural Party committees; from the Party Committees of the fronts to the Party committees of brigades and military areas . . .; and leading Party members' groups in government bodies, people's organizations, the news agency and newspapers offices. All important problems . . . must be submitted to the committee for discussion, and the committee members present should express their views fully and reach definite decisions which should then be carried out by the members concerned.[25]

[24] Townsend, *Political Participation*, p. 73, quoting from a 1949 Chinese collection on the mass line, edited by Liu Shao-ch'i.
[25] SW, 4:267.

Thus, Mao urged the need for improved horizontal communications at all levels.

In practice, horizontal communications appear to serve somewhat different functions at different levels. At the top the functions are largely decisional and managerial. Most important, such communications are necessary to resolve conflicts among leaders. At lower levels, horizontal communications serve to propagate and enforce norms. At the intermediate level, internal communications (i.e., intraorganizational, or interorganizational within a locality) may serve either or both functions. Interregional communications, on the other hand, are often deemed to serve no useful function at all, and are discouraged. This is largely to insure that people are not the recipients of heterogeneous communications from a variety of sources. Any outside information and directives are to come only from above.[26]

The Media

So far, our discussion has been rather abstract, and our generalizations are not without their exceptions. To be more concrete, we should briefly describe the actual media. Under some circumstances, of course, communications may be conducted without any medium, but rather on a face-to-face basis. As we saw in our discussion of the *hsiang-yueh*, China follows such a tradition. In the soviet areas before 1949, face-to-face communications also appear to have predominated. Although modern media became increasingly common after 1949, particularly in the more urbanized areas, face-to-face communications have continued to be widely used long after the revolution, especially in the countryside.

To the extent that there has been at least a relative decline in the importance of face-to-face communications, the explanation is obviously found in the worldwide revolution in communications over the last century. China was affected by these developments early. The first major newspaper, *Shun pao*, was founded in Shanghai in 1872, and distributed in many provinces. Within a few years the telegraph stretched as far as remote Szechwan and Yunnan, which facilitated the

[26] Our generalizations about the lack of horizontal communications do not apply to the period of the Cultural Revolution, when such communications were quite common. Interprovincial travel and uncontrolled posters (see below) are examples. See Lowell Dittmer, "Mass Line and 'Mass Criticism' in China: An Analysis of the Fall of Liu Shao-ch'i," AS, August 1973, pp. 772–92.

dissemination of news. Before long, the Chinese came to be thought of (with at least some justification) as a race of avid newspaper readers. During the first two decades of Communist rule, the press became the primary medium of normative pronouncements. At the same time, however, there was a decline in the amount of published cognitive information. Thus, if a top leader was purged, the press would reflect a shift in policy line, but when the individual was finally mentioned by name the incident would be a matter of history, not news. The press has been discouraged from indiscriminately publishing current events, or offhand remarks of leaders, even when the remarks are "correct." Indeed, Mao Tse-tung at least once manifested an intense aversion to reporters, insisting that they leave him alone.[27] Gradually, Mao came to perceive the entire print-media establishment as hostile to the revolution,[28] and he instigated a massive purge in 1966.[29] At first he relied upon the Shanghai press and the Liberation Army News, only gradually gaining control over the remainder of the nation's print media. After the Cultural Revolution abated, considerable variation among regional newspapers could be noted, with some, such as the Mukden *Liaoning Daily,* serving as forums for initiating national campaigns.[30] The Party organs, however—*People's Daily* and *Red Flag* (the monthly theoretical journal)—are usually the authoritative political voice.

More politically reliable than the press (from the central leadership's point of view) have been the broadcast media. Dependent upon the same news sources as the press, they nonetheless proved themselves more responsive to the Maoist leadership, and were largely immune to attack during the Cultural Revolution.[31] In China there are three broadcast media: radio (wireless), rediffusion (cable radio),

[27] For example, speech at Lushan, July 23, 1959, translated in *CLG,* Winter 1968–69, p. 41.

[28] In 1967 Mao complained that "correct" articles were "seldom seen." Mao, *Selections,* p. 39.

[29] For example, Wu Leng-hsi, head of the New China News Agency, was ousted. See his confession in *CLG,* Winter 1969–70, pp. 63–86. Years later, Wu was rehabilitated. *FEER,* January 1, 1973, p. 4.

[30] In 1971 the *Liaoning jih-pao* published the incipient attacks against Lin Piao. In 1973 it began the attacks on the examination system, and was among the first to engage in the anti-Confucian campaign. The forthrightness of the paper may be attributable to the role of provincial Party leader (and regional military commander) Ch'en Hsi-lien, or to the fact that Mao Yuan-hsin (Mao Tse-tung's nephew) is a local Party official.

[31] It was common, however, for broadcasts of local origin to be replaced by national programming.

and television[32]—the latter relatively unimportant, and available only in large cities.

At least until recently, radio has been the most important broadcast medium.[33] It would appear to be an important means of cultural integration, in terms of both ideological indoctrination and general acculturation. Most broadcasts are in Mandarin, which encourages people to gain an understanding of that language. Radio voices generally have an accomplished Peking accent, and national leaders who lack this (such as Mao Tse-tung) have rarely been heard. Although local stations may interpret national news and policies for local consumption, the content is generally similar throughout the nation, with changes in format and basic content usually taking place everywhere simultaneously.[34] Even broadcasts which originate locally tend to reflect national themes. For example, during the early 1970s a county radio station in southern China broadcast approximately a thousand programs on the lessons of the experiences of farmers in a northern production brigade (Tachai) which had become an intended model for the nation.[35] Even though regional variation in the nature of programming is minimal, events reported in the news will vary from province to province, and sometimes so will reports of priorities and degrees of success in policy implementation. Thus, listening to broadcasts from other provinces is not encouraged.[36] Needless to say, listening to foreign broadcasts is uncommon, if not actually forbidden. (They are not jammed.) Residents of southern coastal areas do sometimes listen to Hong Kong (and doubtless Formosa), but by and large the Chinese populace has not shown excessive curiosity about the outside world.[37]

Nonetheless, if the public has access to broadcasts from other provinces or states, there is always a danger that extraneous ideas will

[32] With the exception of Tibet, all province-level units have at least one television broadcasting station. FBIS I, April 20, 1973, p. B-1.

[33] Many remote parts of China could not receive radio broadcasts until recently. For example, before the Cultural Revolution only 8 percent of Yunnan's villages could receive broadcasts. By 1972, 78 percent could (apparently in conjunction with wired networks). See Radio Kunming, September 15, 1972, FBIS I, September 18, 1972, p. E-5.

[34] Generally, schedule changes have occurred twice a year, on or around the same date. See *CNA* 904, p. 6.

[35] Kunming radio, September 15, 1972, FBIS I, September 18, 1972, p. E-5.

[36] *CNA* 904, p. 6.

[37] According to a Chinese journalist quoted in the *New York Times* (November 17, 1973), "Apart from our people in Hsinhua [NCNA], few people listen to them. They aren't interested. Nonetheless, we never check up on this." Translation revised.

undermine ideological and cultural uniformity. For this reason (and also because radios are relatively expensive for farmers), in recent years a wired rediffusion network has been constructed. Nearly all villages are now connected to this system.[38] In some areas each home has a speaker, but most people listen to loudspeakers in public places. Speakers may line the streets, or be located in gathering places such as threshing grounds. Broadcasting may begin as early as 5:30 a.m. (with the playing of "The East is Red"), and continue with news, propaganda, calisthenics orchestration, and theatrical productions. When new instructions are received, people are to meet together and discuss them. Although for obvious reasons less is known about the content of rediffusion broadcasts than about radio programming, to a considerable degree the former is simply a secondary medium for the latter (similar in this respect to cable television in the United States). It is possible, however, that because of the relative "privacy" provided, the wired news is more informative than the radio news.

In China, the *arts* play a vital role in political socialization. The "message" of art is usually nonspecific, although the fact that a particular play or work of art is promoted or attacked may have concrete political significance. As early as 1942 Mao insisted that art and literature could be considered only in their political context. In a statement that has been cited countless times since he delivered it, he said:

> In the world today all culture, all literature and art, belong to definite classes and are geared to definite political lines. There is in fact no such thing as art for art's sake, art that stands above classes, or art that is detached from or independent of politics. Proletarian literature and art are part of the whole proletarian revolutionary cause; they are, as Lenin said, cogs and wheels in the whole revolutionary machine. Therefore, Party work in literature and art occupies a definite and assigned position in Party revolutionary work as a whole and is subordinated to the revolutionary tasks set by the Party.[39]

This view has often been implicitly challenged, but it has nonetheless been repeatedly emphasized. People who allegedly did not accept this principle, or who used art for the wrong political purposes, have been subject to political attack—particularly after the thaws of 1956–57 and

---

[38] In 1971 it was reported that more than 96 percent of the production brigades and about 87 percent of the production teams are wired. *PR,* September 24, 1971. Also Peking radio, September 15, 1971, FBIS I, September 17, 1971, p. B-1.

[39] *SW,* 3:86. (Probably revised by Mao.)

the early 1960s.[40] But the quest for freedom in the arts continues. Even Lin Piao has been accused of propagating the theory that art's "special characteristics" made it possible to detach it from politics.[41] Although there is little evidence that Lin himself actually advocated this view, the fact that it has been found necessary to reject this "deceptive and reactionary slogan" indicates that the view continues to enjoy currency.[42]

There are, of course, many other media of political communications. Some, such as *book publishing*, are perhaps more obvious than important.[43] China does employ some unusual media, however, which warrant mention. *Displays* of various kinds may indicate much about current political developments. Regarding portraits of leaders, for example, precise instructions are issued as to their relative size and placement.[44] *Poetry* has always been an important political medium,[45] with Mao standing tall among modern Chinese poets. Perhaps the most curious vehicle for political socialization has been the *comic book*. Featuring both historic and contemporary figures, heroes and villains, comics vividly convey political persuasions to the many who are only partially literate.[46] Finally, there is *athletics*. As in much

---

[40] An early version of the Cultural Revolution was actually concerned primarily with art and literature. See "Wen-hua chan-hsien shang ti i-ko ta ko-ming" [A great revolution on the cultural front], *HC*, 1964, no. 12, pp. 1–4. Later, the Cultural Revolution came to concern itself with culture in the broader sense of the word, as well as with various political questions. English translations of the relevant documents are contained in *A Great Revolution on the Cultural Front* (Peking: Foreign Languages Press, 1965).

[41] *JMJP*, May 17, 1973, Peking radio, May 17, 1973, FBIS I, May 21, 1973, p. B-1.

[42] The party journal *HC* frequently carries articles on this subject. See, for example, Chu Lan, "Magnificent Picturesque Presentations of Chinese Revolutionary History—On the Achievements and Significance of Revolutionary Model Theatrical Works," *HC*, 1974, no. 1, pp. 59–64, FBIS I, January 14, 1974, pp. B-4–B-10. For an excellent study of Chinese cinema, see Leyda.

[43] From 1959 until the early 1970s, book publishing in China was in a serious decline. See G. Raymond Nunn, *Publishing in Mainland China* (Cambridge: MIT Press, 1966). Recently, there has been a relative outpouring of books. See *CNA* 920, and FBIS I, May 3, 1973, pp. B-5 f. (report from Peking radio).

[44] An official directive on this subject is related in an article by Richard Hughes, *New York Times Magazine*, October 4, 1964, p. 113. In 1969 one plant alone printed 1.6 billion portraits. Broadcast of July 3, 1970, FBIS I, July 17, 1970, p. B-7.

Whose wreaths are displayed at funerals may reveal considerable information about the political fortunes of various leaders. For an interesting account by Joseph Lelyveld, see *New York Times*, May 6, 1974.

[45] See Watson.

[46] See *The People's Comic Book* (New York: Doubleday, 1973). For treatment of Confucius and Lin Piao, see the account by Joseph Lelyveld in the *New York Times*, May 1, 1974.

of the West (but in contrast to traditional China), athletics plays an important part in the socializing of youth. The "lesson" of sports varies widely from country to country, and even within a particular culture.[47] Nor are the lessons of athletics limited in terms of the number of areas of human activity to which they are applicable. As Mao once said of a writer on table tennis: "What he talks about is a ball game; what we can learn from him are theory, politics, economy, culture, and military affairs."[48]

All of the media we have discussed so far are used more for normative or hortatory purposes than to convey substantive information. There is, however, one additional medium that at times has carried considerable cognitive information—the *poster*.[49] In the previous chapter we saw how posters have been a vehicle for considerable popular involvement in politics. One reason that the Maoist leadership came to favor posters after the Hundred Flowers period is that the medium was free of the influence of professional journalism, and thus the best way to "undercut the bourgeoisie."[50] Although poster writers often labored under their own ideological imperfections, the poster became a hallmark of Chinese political communications. In 1958 many enterprises and institutions were literally papered over with posters. In universities, the halls were laced with strings, from which hung drying posters. Since that time there have been recurrent poster explosions. In 1960 they were employed in the austerity drive. During the Cultural Revolution they were the most popular (and informative) medium. In 1974 there was yet another outburst of poster politics, this time remarkably multidirectional. Although most posters were part of the anti-Confucian campaign, many writers seized the occasion to inveigh against local and national leaders, and even to vent hostility toward the police. Not surprisingly, many of the posters were removed soon after their appearance, and in some instances their authors were arrested.[51]

[47] In the United States, for example, some stress fair play, whereas for others winning is "the only thing" that counts.
[48] Quoted by Jonathan Spence in the *New York Times Book Review*, January 14, 1973, p. 5. (Review of Jonathan Kolatch, *Sports, Politics and Ideology in China*.) Translation revised.
[49] There are actually two kinds of posters, those with large characters (*ta tzu pao*), and those with smaller characters (*hsiao tzu pao*). The latter are limited-circulation newspapers, but they too are often posted on walls. They were popular during the Cultural Revolution, when they were an important source of news for outsiders.
[50] *Hsueh hsi*, June 18, 1958, quoted in Yu, p. 137. Translation revised.
[51] From accounts in the *New York Times*, June 22 and 28, 1974. (One person criticized was Hua Kuo-feng, who would soon head the internal security organization.)

Most of an individual's substantive knowledge of politics probably comes not from the above public media, but from what might be termed unpublished or *internal* communication. This differs from the published media not necessarily in that fewer people have access to it (although this is often the case), but by virtue of the fact that one can obtain such information only from a nonpublic source, such as a superior, or an in-house newsletter.

By *newsletter* we mean a small bulletin which is not circulated publicly. The best-known of these is the *Reference News* (*Ts'an-k'ao hsiao-hsi*), a four-page daily comprising relatively objective reportage of international news, with twenty to thirty news stories in each issue.[52] Until the mid-1960s such newsletters had a very limited in-house circulation. In recent years, however, there appears to have been a more general sharing of information. In 1973 *Reference News* was reported to have a circulation of nearly seven million copies, with perhaps an average of ten persons reading each copy.[53] Although not available to the entire population, people working for the government (which includes teachers and factory workers) may subscribe to it for half a yuan (U.S. $.20) per month. In short, Chinese who want to be informed about world affairs have access to information on the subject.[54] Dissemination of domestic political news is treated somewhat more sensitively, but materials (including directives,[55] documents, and tape recordings) are given such wide distribution among cadres that they frequently even find their way abroad.

Whereas communications involving middle-level bureaucrats tend to be rather formal, relations between brigade leaders and masses are more personal and communications often face-to-face.[56] The reasons for the different means of transmission involve distance, recordkeeping needs, and literacy. Numerous meetings of villagers are required for the purpose of communicating policy to them. The table on page 173 reveals the frequency of meetings (per month[57]), and the number of

[52] There is also a much larger newsletter of international affairs which is available only to high-level personages.

[53] Chu Mu-chih, NCNA director, quoted by C. L. Sulzberger, *New York Times*, November 17, 1973.

[54] See Julian Schumann's interesting account of the *Ts'an-k'ao hsiao-hsi* in *FEER*, January 22, 1972, pp. 18–19.

[55] On directives, see Oksenberg, "Methods," pp. 16–20.

[56] Reliance upon written communications within the bureaucracy increased steadily in the years after the civil war, but beginning in the late 1950s there came to be greater use of oral (face-to-face and telephonic) communications.

[57] The report used does not specify that the period covered is a month; this is inferred from the nature of other documents in the collection.

people reportedly attending the meetings in a 138-household Fukien brigade during the Socialist Education Movement.[58]

Type of Meeting	Frequency	Attendance
Party Branch	6	12
Cadres	1	88
Youth Corps	1	26
Women's Association	1	66
Militia	2	80
"Positive Elements"	7	15
Propagandists	Not Given	7
Mass Meetings	Not Given	232

Thus, meetings are a way of life for the Chinese people, especially for the more politicized Party members and "positive elements." (Although this sample is too limited for many conclusions, it is interesting that cadres per se were obliged to attend only one meeting, suggesting what must be for some a disadvantage of Party membership.) As we noted earlier, Mao Tse-tung advocated meetings at all levels as a means of achieving horizontal communication and consensus. No doubt many meetings do achieve this purpose, especially informal group tête-à-têtes (*p'eng-t'ou hui-yi*).[59] It would appear, however, that meetings are more important as a medium of vertical communications, albeit in combination with collateral discussion and feedback.

Feedback

As we noted earlier, *feedback* (*hui-pao*) is acknowledged by Chinese leaders as an important aspect of political communications, but as with the horizontal variety, involves painstaking (and often unsuccessful) efforts on the part of the leadership. Among the feedback media are documentation, certain kinds of meetings,[60] and field investiga-

[58] Data taken from C. Chen, *Lien-chiang*, pp. 174 f. These figures probably reflect a particular month in late 1962 or early 1963. It does not appear that any meeting of the entire "masses" was held during the period.

[59] The Chinese term literally means "bump-head meetings," the connotation of which is barely conveyed by our rendering above. Other types of meetings which provide a setting for horizontal (as well as vertical) communication are the work conference (*kung-tso hui-yi*), and specialist meetings (*chuan-yeh pu-men hui-yi*). See Oksenberg, "Methods."

[60] Especially the symposium (*tso-t'an hui*—literally "sit and talk meeting"), and the Experience Exchange (*chiao-liu-hui-yi*) where feedback documentation is discussed.

tions.[61] Although the institution of the meeting has been developed by the Communists largely *de novo,* documentary flow has a long established Chinese tradition. To some extent this is also true of the inspection tour,[62] but more important, field investigations occupy a hallowed position in the history of Chinese communism. Mao Tse-tung's 1927 "Report on an Investigation of the Peasant Movement in Hunan"[63] may not have had an immediate effect on the orientation and fortunes of the movement, but it continues to stand as a model of field-investigation work. In recent years, cadres not only have been encouraged to collect firsthand data, but also to take advantage of their time spent at the grass roots (which may be of months' or years' duration) to gain empathy with the masses. It is this feature of the field investigation which distinguishes it from other forms of feedback, and accounts for its popularity with the leadership.[64]

At the lowest levels, feedback may actually be criticism of cadres by citizens. Although it is difficult to judge the pervasiveness of this practice, it is not uncommon, and at times it has reflected one of the most striking efforts to improve vertical communications. Secret reports from Fukien Province, for example, reveal many instances of this kind of criticism and self-criticism of production team chiefs:

> *Criticism* (by a member of the masses): The team chief's leadership was often weak. He did not dare to supervise the Seven Personnel [lesser team leaders], and usually did not control finances. He approved the lending of materials to other teams of individuals as he pleased.
>
> *Criticism* (by another member of the masses): He did not give public notice of commune-member work-points at the proper time, and the figures were not clear. He did not have a high sense of responsibility as a cadre and did not inspect accounts at the proper time.
>
> *Self-criticism* (by the team chief): Although in June 1962 I struggled against the spirit of individual enterprise, and had not taken part in it, I was nonetheless influenced by it, and at the beginning of the rectification movement took over a few mou of land. In fact, I took over about 210 mou of land near the dam and privately planted it with sweet potatoes. I also once bought some oysters and engaged in peddling, but did not make any money and did not do it again.

---

[61] On all of these, see Oksenberg, "Methods," p. 10–28 passim.

[62] Although we would have to say that feedback was not the primary purpose of imperial tours, rotating officials to some extent had a feedback function.

[63] *SW*, 1: 23–59.

[64] This phenomenon takes many forms, including *hsia-hsiang* (mid-1950s), *hsia-fang* (since 1958), and the more recent attendance at May Seventh schools. Actual tours are known as *tiao-ch'a* (investigation) and *chien-ch'a* (inspection).

I was guilty of subjectivism in my work and did not dare to handle affairs courageously. I did not rely on the Seven Personnel and the strength of the commune members. Therefore I was not able to unite with the masses. I was not friendly enough in dealing with commune members. I had the capitalist idea of not wanting to be a cadre and of wanting to just be a laborer.[65]

Because reports of such criticism and self-criticisms are transmitted upward in the bureaucracy, it is an important vehicle of feedback.[66]

Nonetheless, feedback, like horizontal communications, has always presented problems. In large measure this is due to cultural factors. In all cultures, people prefer good news to bad. This is especially true in China, where traditionally everyone lost "face" when developments fell short of expectations. In imperial times, subordinates were obliged to be extremely discreet. If all was not well with the empire, local officials would cite real or invented portentous natural phenomena by way of warning.[67] Today, the government continues to be victimized by its own authoritarian nature, as evidenced by the repeated warnings that cadres must stop "cutting themselves off from the masses" (*t'uo-li ch'un-chung*). People know that the "organs of dictatorship" will be used against vaguely defined "counterrevolutionaries" and "capitalists"—among whom are some of the most ardent Communists in the nation. It is not surprising that people hesitate to point out the error of a particular policy or the malfunctioning of an institution. Under such circumstances, poor feedback is inevitable.[68]

The problem of feedback involves not only the matter of the leaders being in touch with the opinions and feelings of the population. Often there is difficulty in obtaining concrete, objective information about conditions around the nation. Throughout the 1950s, especially, Peking frequently received greatly exaggerated reports of "successes" at the local levels. For example, in 1952 some areas were able to per-

[65] From the records of Ch'ang-Sha Brigade, Lien-chiang County, Fukien, in C. Chen, p. 234. The translation has been somewhat revised and reorganized.

[66] As we noted earlier, criticism and self-criticism within groups is also a medium of horizontal communication.

[67] See Wolfram Eberhard, "The Political Function of Astronomy and Astronomers in Han China," *Chinese Thought and Institutions,* ed. John Fairbank (Chicago: University of Chicago Press, 1957).

[68] This is a problem which concerned Mao Tse-tung at least as early as 1941, when he complained that many functionaries "do not seek to understand things thoroughly and may even be completely ignorant of conditions at the lower levels" for which they are responsible. SW, 3:11. In 1949 he made the same point (SW, 4:378), this time (perhaps unconsciously) quoting none other than Confucius: "[A refined man] is not ashamed to ask of and learn from his subordinates." *Lun yü,* 5:14.

suade only a small minority of farmers to join in mutual aid teams, while the pressured cadres often reported to Peking that the number of participants was many times the actual figure.[69] But the most spectacular examples of inflated statistics occurred toward the end of the decade, during the Great Leap Forward. Here is how one Western economist describes that situation.

> ... Local authorities cannot afford to admit of anything but fulfillment or overfulfillment of the quota.... To admit failure is to invite the serious charge of "rightist-conservativism," the lack of faith in the efficacy of the great leap or any other basic policy of the party. As a result, the cadres and local authorities in 1958 were driven to fabricating glowing reports on accomplishments; or, in some instances, the cadres prepared two sets of figures, one higher than the other, which were at the disposal of the authorities. Finally, when interlocality emulations are held, as they frequently were in 1958, the inflating of claims by one place tends to be both the cause and effect of inflating by another.[70]

Although politically the Great Leap Forward was not without its positive aspects (and its economic failures can be attributed in part to the weather), poor communications and administration were a major cause of the debacle. Peking eventually realized this, and at the time of the Tenth Plenum (1962) insisted that "lower levels must not keep information from the higher levels.... We cannot have 'independent kingdoms.' "[71]

Notwithstanding this new emphasis upon increasing political input from below, there was the fear that "democracy," if considerable, would be at the expense of "centralism." Thus, while accuracy in upward reporting was demanded, a warning was also issued against

> the extreme of democratization, or democracy without centralization. ... [People guilty of this are those who] permit only the lower levels, not the upper levels, to talk; permit only the lower levels to criticize the upper, and not the upper to criticize the lower. It seems as if it were undemocratic to let others talk, undemocratic to let the upper levels talk; and undemocratic [for upper levels] to criticize the [lower level] cadres who leave their work posts. This condition exists at all

---

[69] See Thomas Bernstein's account in Lewis, *Party*, p. 263.

[70] Cho-ming Li, *The Statistical System of Communist China* (Berkeley: University of California Press, 1962), p. 85.

[71] Wang Hung-chih, "Implementing the Resolutions of the Tenth Plenum," in C. Chen, *Lien-chiang*, p. 109.

levels. If the upper-level Party directives suit the lower levels, then they obey them. If they do not suit them, they do not obey.[72]

Although such insubordination was attributed to only a minority of cadres, it was evidently a cause of concern. Between the problem of ordinary citizens who refused to obey cadres, and cadres who refused to follow central directives, it is clear that China was suffering serious problems of vertical political integration at the time.

At this point, some general observations about Chinese political communications are in order. First, the Chinese have been highly innovative in this area. They may not have employed computers or Madison Avenue techniques, but they have made good use of their technological resources in an effort to meet their communications needs. Problems do exist, however, deriving both from the culture and from the system. Among the cultural obstacles, some are traditional (e.g., the customary Chinese difficulties in relating to peers and superiors), and some are new (e.g., the tendency to exaggerate, or to use vague language). Presumably, those aspects of the culture which are dysfunctional will eventually atrophy, and those which are systemically reinforced will not. Thus, the communications problems which will be most chronic will be those facilitated by or conducive to the closed national information system and the tendency of elites to perpetuate their status and influence. Although Chinese politics is far from completely undemocratic, if it is to become more democratic, information will have to be presented to the public in a less bewildering manner than it has been. "How can we, people working at the basic-level units, understand the struggle if we are not aware that they are doing bad things at the upper level in the first place? Just as we failed to recognize the struggle between the two lines in the past, so we shall be unable to understand it in the future."[73] Indeed, such barriers to effective communications seem to be appreciated by the leadership, which doubtless will continue striving to improve the situation.[74]

---

[72] Ibid., p. 107.

[73] *New York Times Magazine*, January 27, 1974, p. 18. Translation revised.

[74] For examples of exhortations in this area, see Chi Yung-hung, "Conscientiously Improve Style of Writing," *HC*, 1972, no. 8, pp. 40–42, FBIS I, August 28, 1972, pp. B-1–B-3; and Chung Pin, "Learn From the Militant Writing Style of Lu Hsun's Satirical Essays," *JMJP*, August 11, 1972, FBIS I, August 24, 1972, pp. B-1–B-5. On July 26, 1972, *JMJP* carried four letters to the editor concerning the need for brevity and clarity in articles. (FBIS I, July 31, 1972, pp. B-11 f.). On July 24, 1972, *JMJP* published two model investigation reports (FBIS I, July 25, 1972, pp. B-6–B-10).

Bureaucracy

Because China's system of political communications is better geared for dissemination than for either feedback or horizontal communications, one might infer that the political system in general is designed to be highly centralized and is unresponsive to public needs. In fact, only horizontal communications are to some extent limited by design, and although communications are centralized, one should not automatically infer that all politics either is, or is supposed to be, tightly controlled from the center. Control, after all, is *facilitated*, but not mandated, by communicative access. As we shall see, the Maoist emphasis has been upon utilizing the communications media to revolutionize Chinese culture, to the end that people will behave "properly" *without centralized direction.* Just how such a system is to function in reality cannot yet be stated with any certainty; it is a question the Chinese themselves are still trying to work out. Much of the following discussion, therefore, should not be read as empirical analysis, but rather as an exploration of variations of a normative model.

During most of the civil war decades, the Chinese Communists were not cemented together by a tightly centralized and disciplined organization. The movement relied instead upon a common sense of purpose and an élan which stemmed from popular esteem and sense of mission. Under these circumstances, the far-flung pockets of entrenched revolutionaries were not dependent upon a "center" for day-to-day directions. Indeed, during the late 1920s and early 1930s the Central Committee was so out of touch with the field situation that *when it did* attempt to orchestrate events the results were disastrous. In general, the greater degree of field initiative allowed, the better the movement fared. As Mao Tse-tung described the situation:

> Because our Party and our army were long in a position in which we were cut apart by the enemy, were waging guerrilla warfare and were in the rural areas, we allowed very considerable autonomy to the leading organs of the Party and army in the different areas. This enabled the Party organizations and armed forces to bring their initiative and enthusiasm into play and to come through long periods of grave difficulties. . . .[75]

Although this loose structure was very serviceable in terms of waging guerrilla warfare against the Japanese and Kuomintang, the experi-

---

[75] October 1948 circular, SW, 4:273. This sentence continues in a contrary vein (critical of excessive decentralism), as will be discussed below.

ence of the Kiangsi soviet revealed that actual social revolution could not be effected in this manner, and in the 1950s the Communists began to turn to more centralized organizational forms.[76] Nonetheless, many continued to look with favor upon the looser and more democratic model of the earlier years, and to this day the question remains open as to whether China is to be integrated along loose "guerrilla" lines, or in the manner of the more centralized Leninist model.

In one sense, we may say that a centralized bureaucracy serves the same function as a capitalist economic system; both make possible the functional integration of specialized, differentiated units. For example, for the work of farmers and distant fertilizer manufacturers to be complementary, it must be integrated by the mechanisms either of the marketplace or of a planning system.[77] If a society's goal is modernization in the usual sense of maximizing output through specialization, then either capitalism or central planning will be necessary to integrate the differentiated units. Obviously, the Chinese Communists reject the capitalist model, because it is based upon private gain and the system responds only to money, rather than to people per se. On the other hand, they recognize that a planning system also has serious shortcomings; it requires an expensive bureaucracy, and tends to breed a parasitic elite of functionaries. These might not be of major concern to anyone who singlemindedly seeks to maximize the political and material outputs of the system. The Chinese Communists, however, are well aware of the social and ecological costs of such an orientation, and are thus much more cautious in their approach to modernization, and are also careful not to blindly copy any foreign model.

Let us first look at the question of the costs which a bureaucratically centralized, mechanically-integrated system may entail. As in the West, the term *bureaucracy* in China has strong negative connotations. But in the West, when *bureaucracy* is used pejoratively, one usually refers to some feature of the modern sector of the system which went awry. Rarely does *bureaucracy* connote old-fashionedness, and when it does it often simultaneously connotes *oriental*. (The two thoughts are combined in the term *Byzantine*.) In China, on the other

---

[76] Between 1949 and 1952 the government was characterized by powerful regional "Military and Administrative Committees," which presided over six "Great Administrative Areas." The efforts to achieve more complete centralization was met with some resistance (most notably on the part of Kao Kang of Manchuria, and Jao Shu-shih of East China, both of whom were purged in 1954).

[77] "Planning system" does not necessarily denote socialism. As John Galbraith demonstrates in *Economics and the Public Purpose* (Boston: Houghton Mifflin, 1973), American corporations in many respects comprise a planning system.

hand, the terms *bureaucracy* and *feudalism* (which in English are almost contradictory) are quite close. Both refer to the traditional means by which for thousands of years a privileged class dominated Chinese society. This helps us to understand why, long before Mao Tse-tung had any direct experience with such ills as those denoted by Parkinson's Law, he evinced great hostility toward bureaucracy.

> We must not be bureaucratic in our methods of mobilizing the masses. One manifestation of bureaucracy is slackening at work due to indifference or perfunctoriness. Bureaucratic leadership cannot be tolerated in economic construction any more than any other branch of our revolutionary work. The ugly evil of bureaucracy, which no comrade likes, must be thrown into the cesspit.[78]

True, by 1949 the realities of the international and domestic political situations dictated that the Chinese Communists orient themselves toward the Soviet model, i.e., a highly-centralized bureaucratic state. But these realities—internal dissension and external dependence—soon changed.

Within a few years it was clear that the Chinese Communists faced no serious domestic threats, and also that the Soviet tie was counterproductive both in terms of China's national interests and the leadership's moral quest.[79] By the mid-1960s Mao Tse-tung had come to believe that bureaucrats were once again reflecting the worst features of Chinese political culture. Among the "twenty manifestations of bureaucracy" which he perceived were the following:

> 1. At the highest level there is very little knowledge. Leaders do not understand the opinion of the masses; they do not investigate and study; they do not grasp specific policies; they do not conduct political and ideological work; they are divorced from reality, from the masses, and from the leadership of the party; they always issue orders, and the orders are usually wrong; they certainly mislead the country and the people; at the least they obstruct the consistent adherence to the party line and policies; and they can not meet with the people.
>
> 2. They are conceited, complacent, and they aimlessly discuss politics. They do not master their work; they are subjective and one-sided; they are careless; they do not listen to people; they are truculent and arbitrary; they force orders; they do not care about reality; they maintain blind control. This is authoritarian bureaucracy. . . .
>
> 10. They want the others to read the documents; the others read

[78] *SW*, 1:134 (1933). The author has deleted some words without indication, and the order of the sentences has been revised.
[79] Sino-Soviet relations will be discussed further in chap. 8.

and they sleep; they criticize without really looking at things: they criticize mistakes and blame people; they claim that they never make mistakes; they do not discuss things; they push things aside and ignore them; they are yes men to those above them; they pretend to understand those below them when they do not; they gesticulate; and they harbor disagreements with those on their same level. This is the lazy bureaucracy.

11. Government offices grow bigger and bigger; things are confused; there are more people than there are jobs; they go around in circles; they quarrel and bicker; people are disinclined to do extra work; they do not even fulfill their assigned duties. . . .

12. Documents abound; there is red tape; instructions proliferate; there are numerous unread reports that are not criticized; many tables and schedules are drawn up and are not used; meetings are numerous and nothing is passed on; and there are many close associations but nothing is learned. This is the bureaucracy of red tape and formalism. . . .

16. They fight among themselves for power and money; they extend their hands into the party; they want fame and fortune; they want positions, and if they get them they are not satisfied; they try to be both fat and lean; they pay a great deal of attention to wages; they are cozy when it comes to their comrades but they care nothing about the masses. This is the bureaucracy that is fighting for power and money. . . .

18. There is no organization; they employ personal friends; they engage in factionalism; they maintain feudal relationships; they form cliques to further their own private interest; they protect each other; the individual stands above everything else; these petty officials harm the masses. This is sectarian bureaucracy.

19. Their revolutionary will is weak; their politics has degenerated and changed its character; they put on official airs and pretend to be highly qualified; they exercise neither their minds nor their hands. They eat their fill every day; they easily avoid hard work; they call a doctor when they are not sick; they go on excursions to the mountains and to the seashore; they are superficial; they worry only about their individual interests, but not at all about the national interest. This is degenerate bureaucracy.[80]

We wonder if these ills are manifestations of Chinese culture, or of bureaucracy. Mao never gave a definitive statement on this matter, but from the solutions he evoked we are led to suppose that he considered both factors important. As we shall see in chapter 7, he embarked upon

[80] Mao, *Selections*, pp. 40–43. The date of this tract is unknown. (The majority of the pieces in this collection date from the 1966–67 period.)

a major effort to eliminate the bureaucratic mentality among cadres. What is even more relevant to our discussion of centralized versus decentralized integration, he decided that one way to combat bureaucratism was to reduce the size and role of the state bureaucracy itself. Bureaucrats, after all, tend to act autonomously within the purview of their responsibility. Furthermore, in a "modern" bureaucracy functionaries are highly role-specific, usually performing a small task which in some way affects the public *in general.* The words *in general* are stressed here to emphasize that bureaucrats are actually quite distant from the people, inevitably resulting in the mutual alienation of administration (bureaucrats) from politics (the people). In short, the Cultural Revolution saw a two-pronged attack on bureaucraticism. Mao sought first to debureaucratize government (insofar as this could be achieved through despecialization and decentralization), and second to debureaucratize the remaining functionaries, that is, transform their thinking so that they would be responsive to subordinate and superordinate political demands. In other words, Mao did not see anything basically wrong with the communications system; the solution to the problem of bureaucratism was to reduce the size of the bureaucracy, and resocialize the bureaucrats.

Of course, even with this accomplished, the demands from above and below may still be in conflict. There will be times when the center will have to enforce its will in spite of negative feedback. All governments do this at times—usually either perceiving or rationalizing that the government represents the real or long-term majority interest. Unbridled, however, such governmental conduct becomes tyranny, the prevention of which is the oldest problem in political science. This is a matter to which the Chinese Communists have shown some concern, as their attacks on political oppression in the Soviet Union demonstrate. The liberal alternative, which may come first to our minds, lies no deeper in Chinese political culture than Article 28 of the national constitution, which is not very deep. In fact, Mao effectively closed the door on the liberal option by the time of his 1937 essay "Combat Liberalism."[81]

Still, political communications and socialization provide only a partial answer to the problems we have discussed. Equally important is the structure of the polity, the subject to which we now turn.

---

[81] SW, 2:31–33. "... Liberalism rejects ideological struggle and stands for unprincipled peace, thus giving rise to a decadent, Philistine attitude and bringing about political degeneration in certain units and individuals in the Party and the revolutionary organizations." p. 31.

SIX

Integrative Models

> Even though we have four hundred million people gathered together in one China, in reality they are just...loose sand.
>
> SUN YAT-SEN[1]

> You say that I mix things together loosely. Well, I do.
>
> MAO TSE-TUNG[2]

WE BEGAN this study, you will recall, with an abstract discussion of political *integration*, which we defined in terms of whether political activities of individuals and groups are interdependent (fully integrated), are merely compatible (slightly integrated), or lie elsewhere on this scale. Much of the discussion in the intervening chapters has concerned the integration of the elite with the masses, an aspect of vertical integration. In imperial China the elite and the masses were defined and distinguished in the first instance in cultural terms, and because political integration requires (or is at least facilitated by) cultural homogeneity, the two classes were probably not well inte-

---

On the various aspects of political organization discussed in this chapter, see Barnett; Harding; Hofheinz, "Rural"; Schurmann; Whyte, "Bureaucracy"; and a forthcoming work on the provinces edited by Edwin A. Winckler.

[1] SCT, p. 768. The ellipsis indicates the omission of a "heap of." This is not a satisfactory translation, because it connotes three dimensions, and mutual support. Sun usually used the expression *"i p'ien san sha,"* which suggests that the grains of sand were two-dimensional and independent.

[2] Mao, *Selections*, p. 11. This is from a 1966 speech. Mao was discussing how to deal with his opposition within the Party. Translation revised.

grated politically.[3] This, however, is a subject of some debate among scholars. We did see in the preceding chapter that the communications system provided for some vertical cultural integration, and that this is much more the case today. And there can be little doubt that there has always been vertical *economic* integration, with the gentry-official class being dependent upon taxes and rents paid by the common farmers.

At this point, we shall suspend until the next chapter our discussion of culturally effected integration, and shift our attention to political *forms*. We shall also limit our concern now to the period of the People's Republic. Because this period is characterized by socialism, we shall be increasingly concerned with political economy. Under capitalism, economic integration is achieved primarily through market mechanisms; in a socialist system economic integration is a function—indeed, the primary task—of government. Political integration, in other words, becomes part of economic integration. Although we shall make no attempt to examine the condition of the Chinese economy,[4] we shall be concerned with institutional and other political relationships affecting the economy. Our goal will be an understanding of the Chinese model —or models—of structural integration.

The Maoist conception of modernization departs markedly from the Western and Soviet models, which are highly differentiated, and integrated on a wide scale with a minimum of local autonomy, especially in the economic realm.[5] Maoists have long rejected many of the assumptions of these models. In particular, they would see in the ideas of men like Talcott Parsons the very antitheses of what the Chinese revolution has been all about. According to the Parsonian developmental model, the trend is toward states which are larger and therefore increasingly complex and "differentiated in status terms." Thus emerges social differentiation "relative to the advantage-disadvantage axis," and a need for centralization.[6]

Two questions arise here. The first might be stated in popular parlance: Is the world headed toward a system of big nations? Because of the ambiguities inherent in *big* and *nation*, however, it would be more

---

[3] On the local level, it is true, gentry and commoners did interact through such institutions as the clan. On the other hand, there was little integration between the local and national political systems.

[4] On the economy of China, see Chao; Donnithorne (both works); Deleyne; Etienne; Howe; Prybyla; Richman; and Wheelwright.

[5] The once semisovereign U.S. states have in recent years become subordinated to an overarching national government, a trend that time may show to have been reversed with Watergate.

[6] Talcott Parsons, "Evolutionary Universals in Society," *ASR*, June 1964, p. 343.

scientific to rephrase the question in more analytical language: Is the trend toward a system of intrinsically integrated subcontinents? Thus stated, it is clear that we are talking about units larger than the average-sized country. More important, the concept of "integrated subcontinent" enables us to discuss integration—both political and economic—without hindrance from juridical situations pertaining to sovereignty and boundaries. One can, for example, have considerable economic and even political integration in a multicountry subcontinent such as the European Common Market. Conversely, there is virtually no political or cultural integration between Taiwan and mainland China, though the governments of both consider them to comprise a single state. The People's Republic of China itself can nonetheless be examined as a subcontinent. Finally, the term *subcontinent* frees us from the ethnic connotations of the word *nation*.

The second question to keep in mind concerns the manner in which subcontinental integration is effected. Centralized political control is one, but not the only, means of achieving such integration. Indeed, there can be highly integrated situations in which government plays little role. *Economically*, this might be by virtue of market mechanisms. Subcontinental *political* integration can exist where local units have considerable power if at the same time there is a high degree of interaction with other units of the subcontinent. These noncentralized integrative models may be termed *horizontal*.

What are the Chinese Communists' views on the subject of subcontinental integration? During much of the 1950s every effort was made to control most aspects of Chinese life from Peking. Although on a number of occasions thereafter one heard that "the whole country is one chessboard,"[7] and that "the leading organs are extremely important; the leading organs are political power,"[8] such views came to be associated with Lin Piao, and with his removal the leadership returned to waging revolution by means other than central administration. Rather, except in special fields where centralization is unavoidable, such subcontinental integration as China was to attain was to be achieved primarily by means of cultural and political socialization.

But there is more to the integration picture. Recall that Maoists (which is not to say all Chinese) are fundamentalist Marxists. They share with Marx and Engels a disenchantment with dehumanizing

[7] For example, Hunan radio, February 5, 1970, which also declared: "The whole province is one chessboard, and particularism, which looks only to the interests of a particular enterprise, is to be condemned." *CNA* 810, p. 3.
[8] Statement by Lin Piao, quoted in *Fu-chien jih-pao* (Fukien daily) editorial, August 7, 1970, *CNA* 814, p. 3.

six: *Integrative Models*

industrialization and stultifying specialization, as well as a yearning for a society in which all men and women are generalists—skilled in a wide range of activities, and able to set their life-styles accordingly. Marx and Engels believed that the enrichment of the individual should come about through the daily engagement in agriculture, animal husbandry, manufacturing, *and* intellectual pursuits.[9] Obviously, this has profound implications for social integration. For now, however, let us concern ourselves with the implications of this philosophy for politics and economics. The following (from an article in *Peking Review*) illustrates what such fundamentalist Marxism may mean for the economy:

> China's industrial construction has ... pursued the policy of integration of industry and agriculture and of town and countryside. Moreover, to prevent the emergence of revisionism [i.e., following the Soviet model] and peaceful evolution to capitalism, we have adhered to the policy of not building new cities, big cities, and high standard of living accommodations. Many newly built factories are scattered in the rural areas. This enables members of rural people's communes to take part in industrial construction and the families of workers and staff members to participate in agricultural production. Furthermore, the factories also give political, economic, and technical support to rural people's communes so that industry and agriculture can give impetus to each other and progress hand in hand.[10]

The first observation to be made is that there is no premium placed upon *subcontinental* integration. To the extent that the approach is feasible (and this must remain an open question), such a life-style can be effected on a local scale—perhaps within the commune, but certainly at no higher level than the province. And this is precisely the direction in which the Maoists have wanted to move—toward maximum intrinsic local integration, or what we shall call *subintegration*. Although, as Gunnar Myrdal has pointed out, a requirement of *national* integration is minimal lower-level integration,[11] and one would have to agree that the more intrinsically integrated the localities, the less integrated the subcontinent will be. This reservation does not disturb Mao-

---

[9] Karl Marx and Friedrich Engels, "The German Ideology," excerpted in Feuer, especially p. 254, quoted below, p. 222. For an example of the Chinese echoing such sentiments, see *JMJP*, August 1, 1966, translated in *SCMP*, no. 3754.

[10] Ti Kang, "Great Achievements in China's Socialist Construction," *PR*, September 29, 1967.

[11] Gunnar Myrdal, pp. 13 f.

ists.[12] In China, localities are repeatedly told not to look to the state for resources,[13] and production brigades (villages) are urged to be self-reliant and sometimes not even to look to neighboring brigades for such items as seed.[14] In short, a perfectly subintegrated structure possesses little vertical and horizontal integration.

Obviously, subintegration carries a price. If subcontinental complementation were to be minimized to the degree indicated in these examples, productivity would certainly be adversely affected. And although the media are replete with reports of self-sufficient, self-reliant localities and enterprises, the press reveals that this has involved considerable disputation and struggle. Here is a report concerning the automotive industry:

> Illuminated by the general line for building socialism personally formulated by Chairman Mao, more than ten provinces and municipalities trial-produced dozens of types of motor vehicles in 1958 [the year of the Great Leap Forward]. But Chairman Mao's proletarian revolutionary line was frantically opposed by the renegade, hidden traitor and scab Liu Shao-ch'i [then chairman of the Republic and number-two man in the Party] and his agents. They did their utmost to promote the slavish comprador philosophy that "making motor vehicles is not as good as buying them," and urged "buying motor vehicles from abroad while using spare parts of our own fabrication." They tried by every means to stamp out the mass movement for building a motor vehicle industry and slash down the number of newly emerging small- and medium-sized plants. This seriously suppressed the local enthusiasm to build a motor vehicle industry and hampered the growth of this industry in China.[15]

Underlying the rhetoric, the issue is apparent enough. Liu, and very likely most Party members, favored an integrated economy on a subcontinental or even larger scale. Although Mao was not opposed to a "national industry," he was more interested in fostering the growth of locally integrated industry.

In its extreme form, subintegration requires even complex industries

---

[12] There are some similarities between the Chinese and Cuban models. See Maurice Zeitlin, *Revolutionary Politics and the Cuban Working Class.* (New York: Harper, 1970), p. xxxix. In 1975 the Cubans were planning further decentralization. *New York Times,* April 30, 1975.
[13] "Hsiyang—A Tachai-Type County," *PR,* October 16, 1970, p. 26.
[14] Fukien People's Broadcasting Service, July 9, 1970, quoted in *CNA* 810, p. 6.
[15] "Rapid Expansion of Local Motor Vehicle Industry in China," *PR,* September 30, 1970, p. 14.

to be organized on a locally self-sufficient basis. The thrust of the quotation, for example, is that the motor vehicle industry should exist on a basis of subintegration, with provinces practicing "socialist coordination" cited for special praise. "A motor vehicle consists of thousands of accessories and parts. [Localities should] distribute the making of these accessories and parts to small and medium-sized plants, thereby making full use of existing equipment and bringing into play the initiative of the masses. . . ." Where necessary equipment and machinery are lacking, these should be manufactured in the same plant, using indigenous methods. In this way, even a relatively poor and backward province can build an "integrated local motor vehicle industry."[16]

One requirement of viable subintegration is local diversification. Not only must a locality be able to produce a wide range of products, but the attendant human resources must also be available. It is recommended that a commune have the capability of producing its own food and fiber, and it should manufacture its own textiles and machinery. Here again, a bitter struggle seems to have been waged between Maoists and Party regulars at various levels. For example,

> The development of sericulture in Chinshan County [near Shanghai] has witnessed a sharp struggle between the two roads and two lines. At the beginning, Liu Shao-ch'i's counterrevolutionary revisionist line greatly hampered its development. After formation of the county revolutionary committee in 1968, the broad masses criticized the revisionist line and settled accounts with Liu Shao-ch'i and company for their crimes in undermining sericulture.[17]

Whether or not the ideal of subintegration has often been attained, the point is that the message, and the model, have been made clear to the Chinese people. Repeatedly, Mao is quoted as having urged localities to retain the initiative in their own hands, and to practice self-reliant regeneration. Not infrequently are negative examples given and warnings sounded. "There are a few units," a writer in *Red Flag* once noted, "which have passively looked to higher authorities for supplies. This kind of thinking should be overcome." A difficulty such as shortage of raw materials "should actually constitute a driving force for us to do a still better job of increasing production and practicing economy."[18]

---

[16] NCNA account on Peking radio, April 17, 1971, summarized in FBIS I, April 25, 1971, p. B-1.
[17] Ibid., p. 15.
[18] Ch'eng Yü, pp. 57–60.

The argument is *not* that a commune can maximize its *efficiency* by engaging, say, in the growing of grain and production of silk. Rather, the advantages of such diversification are essentially social, psychological, ecological, and political.

The benefits of social homogenization, as well as its costs, are important subjects we shall deal with further. First, however, we should indicate in somewhat more concrete form how the problem of allocating political power among the various levels of government is handled. What we have been discussing heretofore, after all, has concerned general principles, issues, and "ideal types." One cannot automatically assume that the ideal types determine the behavior of political actors in life situations. We turn, then, to an examination of political and economic integration within and among administrative units of the various magnitudes, beginning with the nation as a whole.

The Subcontinent

Although during much of this chapter we are emphasizing the degree of local autonomy in China, the fact that there are many cultural and institutional factors which tend to forge subcontinental unity must also be stressed. For China proper, perhaps most important are the tradition of a common culture and the fact that historically there usually existed a central administration. In 1949 a central administration of unprecedented comprehensiveness was established based upon the government, Party, and armed services—and although it has occasionally been under fire, it has certainly contributed enormously to China's national cohesion. In particular, the fiscal system and major universities, both centrally controlled, have done much to weld mainland China into a single national unit. So, as we noted in the previous chapter, has the communications system. We should add that the transportation system, which not only moves goods but fosters the migrations of people, does much to break down regional differences. It might also be noted that China's single time zone is at least symbolic in this respect. Add to all this the external pressures, which foster nationalism, and we cannot but be impressed that however cellular China may be, it is still a single nation.

After a brief experiment with regional autonomy in the early 1950s, it was determined that the subcontinent should now be integrated on the basis of economic and political centralization. These decisions were taken at the February 1954 meeting of the Central Committee (and embodied in the national constitution of the following September).

Interestingly, Mao Tse-tung was not present at the meeting. Rather, the events were directed by Liu Shao-ch'i (with whom Mao would later have an open break), and Chou En-lai. Whatever were Mao's private views of the matter, for the next few years China was probably the world's most highly centralized large nation. But even for its most zealous advocates, it is doubtful that centralization was seen as an end in itself. Rather, centralization was considered a means of achieving (not necessarily for all time) subcontinental integration—i.e., an integrated state along the lines of the Soviet model. In other words, China was to provide from within its own boundaries all that was necessary to become a powerful, affluent, and politically viable nation. This would require fiscal, political, material, and ideological self-sufficiency, and to some people it also meant developing mutually interdependent sectors within the nation's economic and political structures. National autarchy, according to this view, required internal units (political organs, economic enterprises, geographic regions) themselves not self-sufficient but reliant upon each other.

Chinese philosophies of political integration are partly conditioned by foreign policy considerations—the desire for China to be truly independent of other nations and invulnerable to foreign influence and control. This concern is reflected in the motto "self-reliant regeneration" (*tsu-li keng-sheng*). The phrase has a long history in East Asia, and eventually became a ubiquitous Chinese political slogan. In 1966 Mao Tse-tung devoted a chapter to the idea in his "little red book."[19]

> On what basis should our policy rest? It should rest on our own strength, and that means self-reliant regeneration. We are not alone; all the countries and people in the world opposed to imperialism are our friends. Nevertheless, we stress self-reliant regeneration. On the basis of strength which we are able to muster on our own, we can defeat all Chinese [Nationalist] and foreign reactionaries.[20]

Whereas once the People's Republic had been dependent upon aid from the Soviet Union, Mao was now calling attention to the difference between the self-sufficient mainland and the "running dog" Nationalists, dependent for their survival upon the United States.

In the mid-1970s, after several years of embarrassing (and expensive) dependence upon Western food imports, there was renewed

---

[19] Mao, *Yü-lu*, chap. 21.
[20] Ibid., p. 364, quoting a 1945 statement.

emphasis upon national self-sufficiency. Vital industries which are inherently subcontinental in nature are treated as national assets, and in this context the slogan "self-reliant regeneration" continues to be used in the subcontinental sense (although it also has local applications).[21] Efforts have also been made to achieve self-sufficiency in non-food crops, including fiber. Whereas China once had to import such products as jute and hemp, in 1975 it was reported that the efforts in various parts of the nation to increase production had succeeded in making China "basically self-sufficient" in these two products.[22] In general, China's modest foreign trade has continued to grow, but there has been an overriding concern that China should not be so dependent upon imports that the national economy is vulnerable to foreign economic and political pressures.

Although national self-sufficiency may have always been an overriding goal in Chinese eyes, permanent subcontinental integration or centralization is not prerequisite. Only during certain periods have they been general organizing principles—as from the early 1950s until the Great Leap Forward, and again in the early 1960s. In part as a result of such policies, the subcontinent was characterized by an economically advanced (and politically underdeveloped) east coast,[23] and an economically backward (but perhaps more revolutionary) countryside. The task, as seen by the men then setting policy in Peking, was to sustain and eventually integrate these two spheres *without dissolving them*. Although it was recognized that there was a danger of inequalities emerging (urban enrichment at the expense of the countryside), it was believed that this problem could best be handled through central management of the economy. Thus, the government in Peking took direct charge of the economic life of the country during these periods. Central banking[24] and taxation were introduced from the start. Private enterprise was gradually nationalized, and before long even the most

[21] For example, on coal mining: Peking radio, October 26, 1973, FBIS I, October 31, 1973, pp. B-11 f.
[22] *PR*, February 21, 1975, p. 22.
[23] To elaborate, this urbanized sphere was comprised of two subspheres: the former treaty ports (light industry), and Manchuria (heavy industry). The whole arrangement was not new under the Communists, whose policies were as much effects as causes of the economic divisions.
[24] Local credit cooperatives were also introduced in 1951. Curiously, the vicissitudes of this institution do not follow the pattern we might expect, i.e., inversely related to the emphasis upon centralization. Instead, they were promoted primarily during 1951–58, 1961–65, and again beginning in 1973. See *CNA* 921.

detailed plant decisions required Peking's approval.[25] Although the actual degree and duration of central control is a question much debated among Sinologists,[26] there seems little doubt that through the mid-1950s provinces were strictly controlled by the center, and largely insulated from or insensitive to pressure from below. Provincial leaders had little discretionary authority or flexibility in allocating resources and managing personnel. Still, as a practical matter, the men in the Political Bureau were not able to orchestrate China's increasingly complex economy directly, and much of the decision making inevitably rested with the ministries. These sometimes functioned smoothly, but often they became serious bottlenecks, and occasionally they showed signs of becoming self-serving autarchies.[27]

The tendency toward centralization in the economic realm was typical of what was happening in politics generally. To cite one noneconomic example, the procuratorate, which initially had been organized according to horizontal principles (i.e., subject to lateral Party control) was reorganized vertically in 1954.[28] This instrument, and the various other control mechanisms, were designed to eliminate political opposition to Communist rule. In this they were quite effective, but at the price of alienating many people who might better serve the nation if given a reasonably felicitous environment in which to function.

As might be expected, such centralization led to difficulties, especially in the economic arena. Consequently, around 1957 a broad reorganization was undertaken, and the role of the central authorities declined while that of the local officials increased correspondingly. The new pattern was a "double-track" system, meaning that the old vertical lines of authority were not eliminated, but they were supplemented (and often overshadowed) by collective, *horizontal* decision making. Decisions were taken through consultation among Party, government, and managerial personnel at a given level. We shall speak more of this shortly, but here it is important to note that the decentralization was qualified in two respects. First, many matters remained within the purview of the central authorities. Output targets of key commodities, interprovincial and international trade, general policies for education,

---

[25] For example, ministries had to be consulted if an enterprise was to acquire fixed property costing more than 200 yuan (under U.S. $80). *JMJP,* November 18, 1957, cited in Chang, p. 4, n. 5.

[26] See, for example, the two contrasting articles, Chang, "Decentralization," and Falkenheim (published together).

[27] Chang, *Centralization,* p. 4.

[28] See chap. 3.

and certain other matters[29] continued to be the responsibility of the center. Second, the decentralization did not necessarily mean a corresponding reduction of subcontinental integration. On the contrary, the intention of at least some leaders (the "revisionists") was to effect the "organic integration of balancing by production branches and local balancing."[30] This meant that market forces[31] and general planning would somehow have to be meshed, and that with interdependent localities, the nation would still be integrated on a subcontinental scale.

As we have noted, there has been considerable disagreement among foreign observers concerning the nature and extent of decentralization.[32] There has been even greater disagreement within China concerning the desirability of such limited decentralization, which to some still seemed revisionistic and even capitalistic. At any rate, the trend in the 1960s was toward a system which was no longer characterized by this type of integration. The economist Audrey Donnithorne has described the resulting system as "cellular," with the role of central authority severely restricted.

> China's economic planning has been restricted mainly to the setting of targets, to drawing up lists of resolutions. It does not attempt to effect close integration of different economic sectors, nor is it much concerned with optimum allocation of resources. Throughout, and this can scarcely be stressed too much, economic planning in China is constrained by the deficiencies of the information on which it has to work, as well as by the weaknesses in the administrative and supervisory organs charged with implementation of plans and with checking this implementation.[33]

Whether all of this is *faute de mieux*, as implied by Donnithorne, or a matter of principle, as Maoist rhetoric insists, economic policy is nonetheless well characterized as *cellular*.

If we examine integration in more political terms, we find the matter complicated by the fact that provinces and the center have usually acted in harmony (the period of the Cultural Revolution excepted),

---

[29] Donnithorne, *China's Economic System*, p. 462.

[30] *Ta kung pao*, August 29, 1962, p. 3, quoted in Donnithorne, *China's Economic System*, p. 463.

[31] Donnithorne, *China's Economic System*, p. 495.

[32] See Chang, "Decentralization"; Falkenheim; and Donnithorne, *China's Economic System*, pp. 460 f.

[33] Donnithorne, *China's Economic System*, p. 457.

SIX: Integrative Models

making it difficult to determine from what levels influence has been exerted. Students of the provinces may cite low personnel turnover, lack of insubordination, and central allocations to demonstrate provincial submissiveness.[34] However, one could argue alternatively that low turnover suggests provincial autonomy, that lack of insubordination implies adequate prior consultation and feedback, and that funds and resources have been allocated according to local needs. In addition, there is the problem of interpreting the phenomenon of "overimplementation" of state plans, which might appear to be a sign of extreme loyalty but is not invariably appreciated by Peking.[35]

Another factor complicating the centralization-decentralization picture has been the subtle shifts from time to time and place to place. For example, the initial decentralization around 1957 placed authority in the hands of many cadres who were not equipped by experience or education to make appropriate judgments, and this problem, combined with poor weather, caused a serious deterioration in the economy. As a result, the "revisionist" element (Liu Shao-ch'i, Teng Hsiao-p'ing, and others) effected a partial verticalization, with reconcentration of power in the ministries. In some cases this led to a drive for ministerial self-sufficiency (the Water and Power Ministry, for example, fabricating its own machinery), a trend which was later condemned.[36] But until the mid-1960s what was feared by most Party leaders was a different kind of parochialism—subintegration. *People's Daily* inveighed against localities that insisted upon organizing distribution and transportation according to administrative boundaries, "whether or not such transport routes are appropriate."[37] And a writer in *Red Flag* argued that the interests of economic efficiency would best be served by rational methods of supply "which span county, special districts, and provinces."[38] In short, at the time subcontinental integration was sought by Peking, it was unwelcome to many. When the mayor of Shanghai asked that he be sent certain commodities from Chekiang, the province's first Party secretary replied, "Chekiang is not a colony of Shanghai." The secretary even declined to send food to areas of severe shortages, reportedly saying, "I have pigs to feed."[39] Such provincialism

[34] See Falkenheim.

[35] On this point, see Frederick C. Teiwes, "Provincial Politics in China: Themes and Variations," in Lindbeck, p. 144.

[36] Donnithorne, *China's Economic System*, p. 479.

[37] *JMJP*, March 23, 1963, quoted in Donnithorne, "China's Cellular Economy," pp. 610 f.

[38] *HC*, 1963, no. 6, quoted in Donnithorne, "China's Cellular Economy," p. 611.

[39] Chekiang provincial broadcasting service, January 13, 1969, quoted in Donnithorne, "China's Cellular Economy," pp. 616 f.

was clearly contrary to the prevailing view that China was a single integrated economic unit. It also illustrates the inadequacy (or perhaps insufficiency) of organic horizontal integration, and the need for a socialist system to have considerable centralized orchestration of the economy *if* subcontinental integration is to be realized. Thus, as late as 1965 the journal *Economic Research* was insisting that the state must control agricultural plans, and that such plans must not be revised at lower levels.[40]

Although the Cultural Revolution marked a general curtailment of efforts to centrally manage the nation, thereafter central authority was reactivated—in no small measure by the "instruments of dictatorship" —the armed services, and (to a lesser extent) the public security system.[41] Still, the state apparatus remained greatly reduced. Whereas there had been ninety ministries prior to the Cultural Revolution, after that event there were only thirty-two. And in 1970 cadres in the central government were reported to number only ten thousand, compared with sixty thousand earlier.[42] There has been renewed emphasis upon fulfilling state plans,[43] with the central government establishing targets for the provinces, but not for production units.[44] Local leaders are not supposed to blindly follow guidelines from above, but are to take into

[40] *Ching-chi yen-chiu*, 1965, no. 3, p. 33, quoted in Donnithorne, *China's Economic System*, p. 488.

[41] Jerome Cohen, in *CSM*, August 2, 1972, p. 9. An indication that the entire police force is centrally run is that all police were ordered to change their uniforms simultaneously on May 1, 1972. Peking radio, April 29, 1972, FBIS I, May 1, 1972, p. B-2.

In 1974 an interesting instance was cited. A disturbance in Hunan was quelled not by the People's Liberation Armed Services, but by armed factory workers sent from Kwangtung. The explanation (according to a middle-level party official): "With all of the factions these days, one cannot be sure where they would point their guns." *New York Times*, December 7, 1974, p. 2.

[42] Chou En-lai, in an interview with Edgar Snow, *Epoca*, February 1971, p. 23, quoted in Donnithorne, "China's Cellular Economy," p. 605.

[43] *FEER*, September 30, 1972, p. 13.

[44] At least as late as 1970, grain deliveries to the state apparently continued to be an issue among some brigades. See, for example, Hofei radio, August 2, 1970, FBIS I, August 12, 1970, p. C-8. Also grain production targets apparently continued to be inequitable. In one northern county, for example, people complained that in spite of the cold climate, they were growing more than southern counties. "Although we grow crops in the farmland *north* of the *Yellow* River, we have fulfilled the production targets set for areas *south* of the *Yangtze* River. All production potentials have been realized, and it is impossible to increase production further." However, the county Party secretary insisted that they could not rest on their laurels, and should instead "promote the further development in production and revolution." Such problems may be due to the wide discretion given local leaders. Sun Chi-chuan, "Some Impressions on Studying 'On Strengthening the Party Committee System,'" *HC*, 1973, no. 10, FBIS I, October 31, 1973, p. B-5.

consideration the overall objective situation. As a writer in *Red Flag* put it in 1972:

> In the light of the conditions prevailing in an area or a department, some things are required to be done and can be done. All the things which serve the needs of the whole country should be done; and every effort should be made to do them well. On the other hand, even though local or departmental considerations might indicate a certain course of action, a delayed or different course of action should be undertaken if the national situation so dictates.... Were local or departmental considerations to take precedence..., it would certainly adversely affect the interests of the whole.
>
> We should consciously consider what the state is considering and worry about what the state is worrying about. We should properly integrate the needs of our own areas or departments with the needs of the state as a whole. Only thus can all areas and departments have a common starting point, attain unity in action, and march in step.[45]

The burden of such language is that local leaders have considerable discretion, but in exercising it they are expected to give important weight to the interests of the nation as a whole.[46]

To the extent that there is to be integration on a subcontinental basis, then, it is hoped that it can be accomplished less by fiat of the central government than by the judgments of cadres. Some interprovincial trade is permitted, although it is not particularly encouraged.[47] On the other hand, the exchange of "experiences" with people from other parts of the nation is sometimes encouraged, and often proves very constructive.

The praise heaped upon Ch'in Shih Huang-ti during the anti-Lin Piao campaign tended to underscore China's conception of nationhood. The first emperor's main contribution to history had been not the destruction of Confucianism (which proved only temporary), but the unification of China, which he welded into a somewhat centralized, although loosely integrated, subcontinent. Beyond this—and the fact

---

[45] Chung Shih, "It Is Necessary to Take the Whole Situation into Consideration," *HC*, 1972, no. 4, FBIS I, April 13, 1972, p. B-5.

[46] Actual taxation appears to be relatively low, having always been set at 14 percent (some sources say 12 percent) of the 1953 yield, subsequent yields usually being higher. (In bad crop years, agricultural taxes often go uncollected.) See Peking radio, "Taxation in New China," FBIS I, July 8, 1971, pp. B-10 f.; *FEER*, May 21, 1973, pp. 49–51; and *CNA* 921.

[47] Interprovincial trade appears to have been increasing since the Cultural Revolution. Also, each province has a quota of foreign exchange with which to purchase foreign commodities.

that he attempted to push history into a new phase, and thus was "progressive"—Ch'in Shih Huang-ti was hardly held up as a model to emulate. His totalitarianism was not given blanket approval, and Lin Piao was concurrently being condemned for his own "fascism."[48] However exaggerated the charge,[49] the frequent reference to the threat of fascism during these years reveals that centralization of political power was still an unsettled issue. Lin reportedly had advocated the nationalization of locally held property (and eliminating wage differentials).[50] Although he had perhaps conceived of such steps as progress along the road to communism, for Mao all of this was premature, and at this stage of economic development would only entail the resurrection of the partially defunct centralized bureaucracy to administer the country. Whereas decentralization gives the people a certain amount of control over their lives and independence from national authority, excessive centralization might give rise to all of the abuses which characterized Soviet totalitarianism. By allowing sufficient local autonomy, Mao hoped to insure that after his demise China would not be ruled by a tyrant.

Regions and Provinces

The People's Republic of China, it has been said, forms a customs union but not a common market.[51] That is to say, not only is trade with other countries greatly constricted, but, as in imperial times,[52] there is no free trade among provinces. Politically, also, the history of China is in no small measure comprised of the political histories of the various provinces.[53]

The largest units within the nation are actually groups of provinces, or *regions*. Of these there has been some variety, and generally speaking their significance has been intermittent. Only the special economic regions, such as those based on river systems and hydroelectric power

---

[48] *HC*, November 1972, quoted by Leo Goodstadt in *FEER*, December 30, 1972, p. 24.
[49] This caveat is necessary because Lin Piao (or at least the "Liu Shao-ch'i-type swindler") was also accused of precisely the opposite tendencies, i.e., of "sometimes advocating the reactionary theory of many centers, or no center." Kweichow radio, February 8, 1972, FBIS I, February 10, 1972, p. E-1.
[50] See Leo Goodstadt, "Nationalizing the Communes," *FEER*, February 27, 1971, pp. 5 f.
[51] Donnithorne, "China's Cellular Economy," p. 618.
[52] During the Ch'ing dynasty there was an internal tariff known as *likin*.
[53] For historical and current analysis of the politics of each province, see the forthcoming compendium edited by Winckler.

grids, have endured, but these appear to have no autonomy and little political significance beyond strengthening the hand of central authorities vis à vis the provinces. Unlike such a body as the Port of New York and New Jersey Authority, with which they might be compared, there is little evidence that these economic regional administrations become powerful in their own right. This has not always been the case with the other main type of region, the general administrative region. Such regions actually underwent many permutations, but they were usually controlled by Party bureaus. At times they have had a strongly military character, and have been major administrative units primarily after periods of great upheaval, i.e., following the civil war, the Great Leap Forward,[54] and the Cultural Revolution. In many instances, a region has been comprised of a group of provinces with a history of administrative unity dating back as far as the Ch'ing period (and in some cases as early as the T'ang), a factor which may have been conducive to a sense of regional "kingdom" building. Whether or not this sort of regional nationalism was a factor, general administrative regions have shown a tendency to become politically independent during their periods of administrative existence, which explains why Peking has never permitted them to be of long duration.[55]

The *provinces*[56] of China have a history even more ancient than that of the regions.[57] Although continued by the Communists with only incidental reconfigurations, the provinces did not become fully realized as administrative units until after decentralization around 1957. The rationale for the change had been indicated by Mao Tse-tung in 1956, when he privately asked Party leaders at the county level and above

[54] The six regions established in 1960 were headed by Party (not military) bureaus, and were primarily to administer the economy during the period of economic difficulties.

[55] As implied above, there have been major exceptions to the generalization that the regions have been administratively unimportant. On the situation following the Cultural Revolution, see Gordon Bennett, "Military Regions and Provincial Party Secretaries," *CQ*, April 1973, pp. 294–307; and *Facts and Features* (Taipei), November 13, 1968, pp. 4 ff. The major examples of regional insubordination since 1949 involved East China and Manchuria in 1953–54, and the region comprised of Honan and Hupeh in 1967. On the latter, see Thomas W. Robinson, "The Wuhan Incident: Local Strife and Provincial Rebellion during the Cultural Revolution," *CQ*, July 1971, pp. 413–38. Finally, it should be noted that the military and strategic importance of the regions continues, regardless of any normalization in the general domestic political situation.

[56] *Sheng.*

[57] See Bodde, *China's*, pp. 140–44, 245 f.; Ssu-ma Ch'ien (Chavannes version), 2:531 f., 361, *passim;* and Wang Yü-ch'üan, "An Outline of the Central Government of the Former Han Dynasty," in Bishop, pp. 1–55 (also in *HJAS*, 1949, no. 12, pp. 134–87).

to consider the contradiction between centralism and localism, implying that increased local autonomy might be advisable.

> The provinces and municipalities have quite a few views concerning the central departments which should be expressed.... The provinces, municipalities, autonomous regions, counties, districts, and villages should have their proper enthusiasm and individuality. The center must not put them in a strait jacket.[58]

During the ensuing months a consensus was reached that the government should decentralize. In September, Liu Shao-ch'i told the Eighth Party Congress, "It is absolutely necessary for the central authority to devolve some of its administrative powers and functions onto the local authorities."

Under the new arrangement, the provincial Party committee would play a key role in the affairs of the subordinate levels. Localities would be allowed to take the initiative in the planning process, but had to formulate the plans under the guidance of the committee. The committee forwarded sample plans ("some of the best and a few of the worst") to the Party Central Committee for review.[59] The provincial committees operated on the principle of horizontal integration. Interbranch coordinating bodies made the essential decisions concerning allocation of resources, taxation, and so forth. The ministries in Peking were largely short-circuited, and with some exceptions[60] enterprises which had been administered by Peking now fell within the purview of the provinces. This included a wide range of commercial and manufacturing enterprises, and in many cases the industries that were retained by the ministries became dependent upon the new local concerns as suppliers and markets. To this day, even major economic enterprises, such as automotive plants,[61] continue to be managed at the provincial level.[62] (Small enterprises, as we shall see, have devolved

---

[58] Mao Tse-tung, "On the Ten Great Relationships," in J. Ch'en, *Mao* (1969).
[59] Mao Tse-tung, "Sixty Articles on Work Methods (Draft)," *CLG*, Spring 1972, p. 97.
[60] Heavy manufacturing, large-scale energy production, and other strategic industries remained centrally administered.
[61] Provincial automotive works are apparently rather small. See "Self-reliant Kiangsi Plant Makes 500 Cars Annually," *HC*, 1970, no. 4, pp. 36–41, FBIS I, April 14, 1970, pp. B-1–B-7. The factory is said to have manufactured 45 percent of its own machine tools, and apparently sells largely or exclusively to Kiangsi buyers. Thus, we have an example of provincial discreteness and intraprovincial integration. Also on provincial motor vehicle enterprises, see *PR*, September 30, 1970, pp. 14 f.
[62] Some enterprises are under joint central-provincial administration. See Audrey Donnithorne, "Recent Economic Developments," *CQ*, December 1974, pp. 773 f.

to the lower levels.) Indeed, the provinces, to a large extent, have been financially independent. In general, the central government does not even interfere in matters of pricing. Although provincial governments retain only about a fifth of the profits of their enterprises, they have been able to levy taxes and float bond issues almost at will. Funds generated from within the provinces have often represented many times the amount which the provinces have been allocated by Peking.[63]

This is not to suggest that the situation ever became truly stable. Until the Cultural Revolution, at least, the central bureaucracy fought, often successfully, to recover its role. On the other hand, as we shall examine shortly, Mao Tse-tung continued to fight for the devolution of power down to even more basic levels. The result has been a remarkable diffusion of decision making. Rarely, however, have the provinces been unimportant as loci of authority. To the extent that towns and villages receive specific injunctions from above, these eminate from the provincial capitals; from Peking comes only guidance of a general nature. The provinces receive directives from the center, but they enjoy considerable operational latitude. The fact that slogans are not identical among provinces and that economic plans are of varying content and length testifies to the considerable freedom which provinces enjoy vis à vis the national government.

Still, the provinces are not entirely autonomous and self-sufficient. Most of the information media continue to be dominated by Peking, and to the extent that public affairs are personalized, it is national figures who receive most of the attention. Although self-reliant regeneration continues to be the approved norm, the principle readily yields to expediency. Provinces sometimes become dependent on one another for basic supplies. For example, in 1972 Hunan grew cotton in some areas instead of grain, which can be more economically imported.[64] Such practices, which obviously run counter to provincial self-sufficiency and suggest motives of profit, are undoubtedly controversial. Thus, we are assured that Hunan redoubled its efforts in grain production, raising output by over 8 percent the following year. Not only was this cause for praise in the national media, but it was emphasized that this was accomplished in an environment of economic diversity. The operative slogan was, "take grain as the key link, ensure all-round development." But the long list of Hunan's products and activities reported by the New China News Agency all related to agriculture and fishing, suggesting that this province had decided that it could do

[63] Chang, *Centralization*, pp. 2–17 passim.
[64] *CNA* 899, p. 4, quoting a Hunan broadcast of September 8, 1972.

better selling such products as cotton elsewhere, and quietly importing manufacturers from other provinces, rather than Hunan undertaking further to "grasp industry."[65]

The provinces, then, are vital units in China's development. Interprovincial trade is only marginal, with the preponderance of trade being within each province. This intraprovincial trade is largely independent of Peking's control. Although Cultural Revolution rhetoric about each province having a "small but complete" industrial system may be played down from time to time, with the degree of provincial autonomy fluctuating, the province continues to be a key unit in Chinese politics and economics.

We have been using the term *province* rather loosely, for there are actually two types of provincial-level units in addition to those designated as provinces. One is the *autonomous region*, a term applied to large areas with substantial populations of minority nationalities. This is a subject which we shall examine in the following chapter; for now, we are treating autonomous regions as provinces. The other province-level designation is *municipality*. In 1958 the boundaries of Peking and Shanghai were expanded so as to embrace under the two administrations many towns and rural areas. In 1966 greater Tientsin became the third such province-level municipality. The dates suggest that the purpose was to make these units as self-sufficient as possible, thus rendering the three cities less parasitic and more able to participate in self-reliant regeneration. However, there have been reports that Shanghai and Tientsin have made record shipments to other parts of the country,[66] indicating that the province-level municipalities actually differ from provinces in that they have a higher degree of extrinsic integration. Certainly the cities of Shanghai and Peking played a major role in the nationwide Cultural Revolution, with the struggle between them having far-reaching repercussions for Chinese politics.[67]

[65] "Hunan Reaps Record Grain Harvest While Diversifying Economy," Peking radio, December 21, 1973, FBIS I, December 27, 1973, pp. D-4 f. Lack of energy resources is another reason why Hunan has difficulty becoming industrially self-sufficient. On this and other aspects to Hunan's reluctance to industrialize, see *CNA* 844, pp. 2, 5 f.

For an example of partial provincial-level self-sufficiency (pharmaceuticals in the Ningsia Autonomous Region), see Peking radio, June 17, 1972, FBIS I, June 20, 1972, p. H-1.

[66] Donnithorne, "China's Cellular Economy," p. 611.

[67] Between the province and county there is an additional administrative level, but this has been relatively unimportant. The most common term is *special district (chuan ch'ü)*, although many cities (*shih*) are administered at this level, as are autonomous districts (*tzu-chih chou*) and leagues (*meng*), both reserved for ethnic minorities. Although these various districts play a role in planning, they do

Localities

In traditional China, the *county*[68] government was the only point of contact, such as there was, between the populace and the imperial government. Progressive republican reformers sought to build upon this structure, making the county the unit for building a Chinese democracy. Since the Communist revolution, the importance of the county government organs has fluctuated roughly inversely with the fate of the provincial governments. In the 1950–56 period, for example, when the provinces were eclipsed by the higher levels, the county (or "banner" in Inner Mongolia) was the point at which the centralized administrative functions converged. The county Party secretary, in particular, became a powerful figure, responsible for integrating and transmitting the policies received from the center. Again in the 1960s, when Liu Shao-ch'i sought to recentralize government, the *People's Daily* declared that the county was the vital unit, and that the county Party committee was the "militant headquarters of the people."[69] During the Cultural Revolution, on the other hand, the people were called upon by Maoists to "bombard" these headquarters.[70] Since the Cultural Revolution, the counties appear to have been holding their own in a relatively balanced system in which the provinces and also the lowest levels perform important functions.

In the mid-1950s, the number of counties was reduced by means of merging the smaller ones. The purpose of this move was to insure that each county would be large enough to have an adequate economic base so that it could implement the programs charged to it. Thus, the counties generally have a population of several hundred thousand people, and some have over a million. However, when Mao developed his blueprint for local self-reliant regeneration, it was the commune which he had in mind as the ideal self-sufficient unit; as we shall see, this proved impractical. The county turned out to be the appropriate size for direct administration of light industry, and often mines and

---

not generally comprise budgetary units. The districts do have their own revolutionary committees, which may summon representatives of subordinate units to "exchange experiences." Sometimes the activities of the counties will be coordinated by the district, especially one comprised of an ethnic minority. Occasionally a district will operate a fairly large economic enterprise.

[68] *Hsien.*

[69] *JMJP*, October 12, 1965.

[70] In general, county administrations do not appear to have actually been the target of as intense attack during the Cultural Revolution, at least in comparison with other levels, but there were numerous shakeups nevertheless.

cement plants[71] (but excluding most heavy industry, which is managed at higher levels, and agriculture, which is managed at lower levels). County enterprises are typically small, and oriented toward manufacturing and repairing basic consumer goods and agricultural supplies and equipment.[72] Concerns are small, and capitalized through their own profits or loans from general county funds.[73] Counties also manage local public works, such as some of the irrigation projects.

It is important to note that not only have counties developed small industries,[74] but counties are now encouraged to develop internally integrated and externally independent economies. Although this is an ideal which can never be fully realized, impressive strides have been made. County economies have diversified even when it would be more economical to specialize and import from other areas. Thus, apiaries are sometimes maintained where the climate is less than ideal for raising bees.[75] Counties are especially applauded when they take steps to become self-sufficient in energy production. It is fairly common for counties to have their own hydroelectric stations,[76] and even these are supposed to be of local manufacture to the extent feasible. For example, 70 percent of the equipment which went into the hydroelectric stations in Tengchung County (Yunnan Province) is reported to have been manufactured by the county's own factories.[77] The same principle is applied to other industries. A county plant manufacturing rice threshers ideally operates on an entirely intracounty basis. In one case, the plant makes iron parts, and subcontracts the manufacture of wooden com-

---

[71] By the end of 1973, 80 percent of the counties had small cement plants, which apparently accounted for half of the country's output. Peking radio, December 22, 1973, FBIS I, December 27, 1973, p. B-12.

[72] "Generally speaking, the work of overhauling farm machines and tools can be handled in the county, major repairs in a commune, and minor repairs in a production brigade." *PR*, February 6, 1970, p. 11.

[73] It has been reported that in Tsunghua County (Hopei Province) loans from higher authorities are available for capitalization. *FEER*, December 31, 1973, p. 54. Because Tsunghua includes Sha-shih-yu commune, frequently visited by foreigners, it is possible that funds are more readily available from the province or central government than they would be for normal counties.

[74] Local industry is not an innovation of the 1960s; throughout the 1950s most of industrial production was localized.

[75] For example, Huma County in Manchuria. See Peking radio, February 9, 1972, FBIS I, February 9, 1972, page B-1.

[76] *PR*, February 6, 1970, p. 13. Self-sufficiency in coal is encouraged at the provincial level, but apparently not at the county level (most counties being without coal resources). However, there are some county-level coal mines (e.g. Liangshan in Szechuan). *PR*, September 24, 1971, p. 9.

[77] Peking radio, January 30, 1972, FBIS I, February 9, 1972, p. E-6.

six: *Integrative Models*

ponents out to local communes.[78] Thus, a highly integrated economy is sought, but this integration is to take the form of what we have called *subintegration*, and counties are not to become unnecessarily interdependent. The result has been a considerable degree of county independence—including some independence from provincial control.

The majority of the *cities*, not including the three province-level municipalities, are urban counterparts of the counties. They have about the same population as the counties, and are often treated alike administratively.[79] Traditionally, Chinese cities were centers of commerce and culture. Except for providing certain services, they were not noted for their productivity. Since 1949, most cities have undergone marked industrialization.[80] Furthermore, although cities are inherently non-agricultural, many of the above principles of political organization and economic self-sufficiency have been applied to cities. Mao Tse-tung even urged large industrial concerns to diversify and strive for self-sufficiency.

> Large enterprises such as Wuhan Steel can gradually be transformed into integrated multiple-purpose enterprises. Aside from producing a variety of steel products, they can engage in the production of machines, chemicals, and engage in construction. This large-scale type of

[78] Kung Yeh-ping, "It Is Necessary To Have the Concept of Viewing the Situation as a Whole," Peking radio, April 2, 1973, FBIS I, April 6, 1973, pp. B-1 f. (The *whole* in the title refers to the entire unit, whatever that unit may be.) The administrative unit here is Yungshun County (Hunan Province), and the enterprise is the Number Two Agricultural Machine Repair and Manufacturing Plant. People in this plant were said to have "a relatively high ideological consciousness in view of the situation as a whole. Chairman Mao has taught us: 'An understanding of the whole facilitates the handling of the parts.' The method used by this plant for the production of the rice threshers provides a vivid example. They made the part play a very good role for the whole.... No matter what work we do, or what task we fulfill, we must consider fraternal units which are related to our own work and tasks and consider the whole." The chess analogy is cited. "In this chess game, whether we are a small unit or a large unit, a small area or a large area, we are just a piece. Whether this piece is a pawn, a knight, a castle, or a bishop, its every move can only be fully effective when the game is played in consideration of the situation as a whole." Translation revised.

[79] Although in this study we are largely ignoring the cities, we may note in passing that many of the principles applied to provinces and counties also apply to cities. They are decentralized, i.e., divided into district of about 50,000 people. See *CSM*, September 11, 1972. Below the districts are neighborhood units, on which see *PR*, April 21, 1972, pp. 20–22. On the cities, also see Lewis (*City*, and "Political"), Schurmann, pp. 365–403, and Terrill (see Preface, note 3).

[80] For example, the small Kiangsi city of Ch'ing-chiang, which formerly had virtually no industry, today has an iron and steel mill, a tractor plant, a railway car plant, a fertilizer factory, rubber works, a cotton textile mill, and many sugar refineries.

enterprise can also engage in agriculture, commerce, education, and military affairs.[81]

Cities, in short, are intended to conform to the subintegrative pattern insofar as it is practical. While it is not necessary that they make a fetish of self-reliance (especially when it comes to luxury goods),[82] they are expected to avoid becoming unduly dependent upon other areas, and under no circumstances are they to become parasites on the countryside.[83]

With the introduction of the "people's *communes*"[84] in 1958, it was intended that these would become the focal point for most social, cultural, political and economic activities. As the Party Central Committee declared:

> In the present circumstances, the establishment of people's communes, with all-round management of agriculture, forestry, animal husbandry, side-occupations and fishery . . . is the fundamental policy to guide the farmers to accelerate socialist construction, complete the building of socialism ahead of time and carry out the gradual transition to communism.[85]

Such language reflects the ideas of Marx and Engels,[86] and suggests that the Chinese conceived of themselves as about to embark upon the transition to communism. As we have noted, however, it was ultimately determined that heavy or complex industries could usually be more efficiently managed at the higher levels.[87] (Unfortunately, this judgment was only reached after the costly Great Leap Forward.) The communes were especially inappropriate for industry in their original

---

[81] Mao, *Selections*, p. 25. Updated "Instructions."

[82] Watches, for example, are manufactured only in Shanghai and a few other cities.

[83] As indicated earlier, this book touches only lightly on China's cities. For further information, see works cited at end of note 79.

[84] *Jen-min kung-she*. For an excellent analysis, see Byung-joon Ahn, "The Political Economy of the People's Commune in China: Changes and Continuities," *JAS*, May 1975, pp. 631–58.

[85] Peitaiho Resolution, August 29, 1958, *CCPDA*, p. 454.

[86] Quoted below, p. 222.

[87] There have been instances of communes building factories even though the products could be more efficiently manufactured on a larger scale. For example, when a foreign visitor asked why a chemical fertilizer plant was being built at the same time that a neighboring commune was building the same type of plant, he was told: "They are building for their own needs, we for ours." Donnithorne, "China's Cellular Economy," p. 610.

concept. Although communes comprised of tens of thousands of people was never ruled out (and ultimately became common), the optimum size was *initially* seen as two thousand households (smaller in sparsely populated regions).[88] And as a somewhat larger size (5,000 to 15,000 people) became the usual practice, the communes became inappropriate agricultural units, except from a marketing point of view. Although there have been instances in which the commune was treated as a single unit for agricultural administrative purposes, the results have often been unsatisfactory.[89]

Nor did the communes measure up to expectations as political and administrative units. The original plan was for the township (*hsiang*) governments and Party committees to be enhanced and transformed into commune organs. Internally, the commune was to be a tightly integrated unit. According to *Red Flag*:

> In the course of their advance, the working people have put forward these slogans which are full of revolutionary spirit:
> > Get organized along military lines.
> > Do things the way battle duties are carried out.
> > Live collective lives.
>
> "Get organized along military lines," of course, does not mean that they are really organized into military barracks, nor does it mean that they give themselves the titles of generals, colonels and lieutenants. It simply means that the swift expansion of agriculture demands that they should greatly strengthen their organization, act more quickly and with greater discipline and efficiency, so that, like factory workers and soldiers, they can be deployed with greater freedom and on a large scale.... Would this breed commandism? In our opinion, for the people's communes to be organized along military lines and to arm the entire population is a completely different matter from commandism. Without the people's communes, without the organization along military lines and without soldiers, commandism can occur all the same. On the other hand, with the people's communes, with organization along military lines and with citizen soldiers, commandism can be avoided and the highest degree of democracy can be realized.[90]

Clearly, there were those who feared that the communes would become instruments of totalitarianism, for although the communes were intended as a step in the direction of decentralization, they also could

---

[88] *CCPDA*, pp. 454 f.

[89] The news media have often reported examples of centralized agricultural policymaking which was out of touch with local realities. See *CNA* 899, p. 3.

[90] *HC*, September 1, 1958, *CCPDA*, pp. 458. f. Translation revised.

mean the complete centralization of the townships themselves. As it happened, those who resisted this trend won out, and during the 1960s there was a further devolution of responsibility to the brigade and team levels (see below). Although the Party committee at the commune level did retain its authority until the Cultural Revolution, the government of almost every commune (the smallest ones excepted) has been only a shadow of its original conception. The communes are still very real, of course, but their organs serve primarily as communications conduits and allocations redividers.

Certain aspects of commune economics deserve special mention, and these may be placed under the loose heading of "services." Whereas major industry has generally been retained at the higher levels, and the agricultural accounting has devolved to the villages, the service sector is more complicated. Two important administrative functions have generally been performed by the communes: management of grain storage, and tax collection (although taxation is *controlled* by the counties). Some communes also play an important role in such fields as water conservancy,[91] and to a lesser extent banking,[92] education (especially junior high schools),[93] health services,[94] and local military security.[95] Thus, it is primarily in the service area that the continued existence of the communes tends to be justified.

During the late 1960s there was talk of the commune system evolving into a nation of 75,000 little Chinas, but such slogans quickly died out. Indeed, decentralization of this sort would probably have the effect of promoting verticalization, for it would weaken the intermediate levels

[91] See Barnett, p. 355. Also p. 392, where it is recounted that a dispute over water rights required intervention by higher (county) authorities.

[92] However, banking is generally centralized at the county level, with branch offices in the communes, and credit cooperatives at the brigade level.

[93] I.e., "lower-middle schools." However, primary schools are usually brigade-level, and high schools are often run or supervised by the county, as were primary schools before 1958.

[94] Efforts to involve the communes in health delivery have often been unsuccessful, but the general system and results have varied greatly from region to region. See David M. Lampton, *The Politics of Public Health in China: The Limits on Leadership, 1949–1969* (Chicago: Aldine, 1968).

[95] Although there is usually a militia command structure at the commune level, overall command is exercised at the county level, and the operational units are brigade-level. See Barnett, pp. 244–49. The original scheme apparently emphasized the roles of the commune and PLA. In the early 1960s, the provinces were stressed. See John Gittings, "China's Militia," *CQ*, April 1964, pp. 100–117. However, during the next few years the militia entered a period of decline. The 1970s have seen the militia's role stressed as an integral part of national defense (*PR*, February 6, 1970, p. 7), and also of local cultural and economic affairs (*JMJP*, June 19, 1972, FBIS I, June 19, 1972, pp. B-1–B-3).

of administration and thereby strengthen the center. Thus, a more balanced distribution of power appears to be emerging. But the commune has been enshrined in the 1975 Constitution, where it is defined as "an organization which integrates government administration and economic management" (Art. 7), and it thus can be expected to continue to play a significant role in China's political integration.

Inasmuch as the early efforts to maintain internally centralized communes proved unsuccessful, the key unit within the commune for all but income-distribution purposes has generally been a smaller unit of a few thousand persons. Called a *production brigade*,[96] this unit is usually comprised of several hamlets or "natural villages," but in some cases a brigade is simply a large village. General output quotas are established for the brigade by the commune authorities (whose offices are usually within an hour's bicycle ride away), but thereafter brigade authorities appear to operate relatively autonomously in day-to-day administration.

Constraints upon the brigade are largely twofold: First, it is under pressure concerning quantity of output, and it has less than a free hand in type of crops and goods produced. There is a common tendency on the part of brigades to grow the most profitable crops, regardless of obligation to the state or such normative constraints as local self-sufficiency. In the early 1970s, when some brigades sought to put more land into the growing of lucrative industrial crops, they were warned by *People's Daily* that "free sowing" would not be tolerated.

> Some production brigades pay little attention to the needs of the state, and determine what to grow simply from the point of view of how much a crop will earn. They sow cash crops on the best soil, to which they provide rich fertilizer, and they neglect crops which do not bring in much money, sowing them on poor soil and adding little fertilizer. Thus, the state plan is not fulfilled.[97]

In some cases, where the soil and climate are poor for growing grain, a village may have traditionally grown a specialty crop, such as medicinal herbs. Such a brigade is nonetheless obliged to diversify.[98] The

[96] *Sheng-ch'an ta tui.*
[97] *CNA* 899, p. 3. Translation revised.
[98] See, for example, the case of Fu-ping Brigade, in Pai-sha Commune, Hunan. Traditionally, this village specialized in *slavia Chinensis* and white paeonia; it had been able to produce only small quantities of sweet potatoes and dry-field grains. In 1973 it was reported to have produced a surplus of grain (including rice), and a wide variety of other products. "To Learn from Tachai, It Is Necessary First of All To Study the Line," *HC*, 1973, no. 6, FBIS I, June 25, 1973, pp. B-1–B-5.

second constraint upon the brigade government is that it has little financial base of its own. It can collect only a small amount of taxes (typically, a maximum of 1 percent) from the subordinate teams, and is not encouraged to seek funds from the higher levels.[99]

Thus, if a brigade per se is to be in a strong position economically, it must develop its own enterprises, and this has been widely done. It is common for a brigade to have a number of small factories (brick and tile are major products), mills (for processing of crops such as rice and sugar), storage facilities (for grain, scrap materials, etc.), and power stations. So great has been the growth of brigade industries that in many areas these have outstripped those at the commune and county level.[100] Although the brigade industry has been encouraged by national authorities, it is not supposed to interfere with agriculture. In one area the development of such production proved so successful that some people wanted to devote most of their energy to sideline occupations. At times people have complained that grain production was being overemphasized, arguing that "when money is available, there will be grain." It has been the responsibility of county Party leaders to correct such "misconceptions."[101]

With funds that the brigade does earn, it may provide various services for its teams and individual members. Probably most significant is primary education (an important part of which has been adult literacy classes). It may also maintain its own water conservancy activities, fish ponds, etc. Some services may themselves earn funds, or at least be partially self-supporting, such as health clinics[102] and stores. In the late 1950s, during an ill-fated experiment at having people eat in common dining halls, these were managed by the brigade.[103] Finally, the brigade has certain welfare responsibilities. Although in some cases this may entail placing people on an actual dole, the brigade usually finds a way to make the person self-supporting. Orphans are not placed in orphanages, but rather are taken care of by neighbors. In some cases, of course, a whole brigade may be so poor that it will require a state

---

[99] One feature for which model brigades are praised is that of being self-reliant "instead of looking to the state for money, grain, and materials." "Hsiyang—A Tachai-Type County," *PR*, October 16, 1970, p. 26.

[100] In some cases, this growth has apparently come about through the collectivization of cottage industry.

[101] Foochow radio, November 11, 1972, FBIS I, November 15, 1972, p. C-1.

[102] Typically, a farmer pays U.S. 75¢ a year, plus a nominal sum per visit, for health-care.

[103] See Barnett, p. 374.

subsidy. Needless to say, however, every effort is made to make such brigades self-supporting.[104]

Thus, notwithstanding the devolution of authority within the communes, the brigade cannot be said to be an intrinsically integrated or autonomous unit. It must accept rather strict guidelines from above, and allow considerable autonomy to the subordinate teams. The extent to which a brigade per se is able to lead a life of its own will be determined by the success it has in building local industry, the extent to which the people look to the brigade rather than other levels for leadership, and the amount of autonomy granted the brigade by the higher authorities. Although the latter criterion tended to restrict the brigades during the 1960s, in the early 1970s *Red Flag* called for greater brigade independence, at least from government authorities, who were not ordinarily to review decisions made by brigade-level Party branches.[105] Local party members, still fresh with the memory of their treatment during the Cultural Revolution, are unlikely to institute measures which have no local support. But if the Party should revert to its earlier condition as a centralized and powerful monolith, brigade autonomy would be severely restricted. Nevertheless, so far it has by no means been stressed that the masses should blindly follow Party initiatives. Indeed, here is an example of the kind of soul-searching which Party organs (in this case a commune Party committee) are encouraged to undertake:

> The masses have advanced the brilliant question: "Now that we have stood up for ourselves, what are the Party members and cadres going to do?" Accordingly, they have demanded that Party members and cadres strive to transform their subjective world while transforming the objective world and turning themselves into advanced elements of the proletariat. This is a matter of great importance.
>
> In order to revolutionize our thinking, we Party members and cadres must correctly deal with ourselves. Some comrades, while correcting the ideas of others, have failed to realize that they should also revolutionize their own thinking. The lesson which the commune Party committee has now learned is that sending higher-level cadres to engage in ideological rectification at lower levels proves that this is a most valuable practice. Why did the Party committee members once only

---

[104] For an example of a Kiangsu brigade which had perennially depended on the state for grain, but having received a capital subsidy from the county is now self-sustaining, see Nanking radio, September 8, 1972, FBIS I, September 13, 1972, pp. C-3–C-5.

[105] *FEER*, December 30, 1972, p. 25.

think of rectifying the thinking of the lower-level masses? And why have they not thought of rectifying their own thinking? This is because they have been complacent. Now, however, the comrades in the commune administration, under the supervision of the masses, have changed their attitude from believing that people at their level are in a position to correct the thinking of the lower levels, to one of upholding the revolutionary spirit of conscientiously correcting their own thinking. *This is a good lesson for those afraid to offend those in power.*[106]

In short, brigade autonomy will depend upon the mitigation of the fears of ordinary citizens toward those in power. But if history is any guide, such fears cannot be wished away by idealists such as the author of the above account.

Unlike the brigade, the *production team*[107] has an automatic safeguard protecting at least its *economic* integrity. The team is the basic accounting unit for amassing and distributing agricultural production. Taxation by higher levels is quite stable, and although required sales to the government may vary from year to year,[108] the team controls all the remaining collective output[109] and has a strong incentive to increase productivity. Most of this is returned to individual families on the basis of how much work members have done during the season, as measured in "work points."[110] Because a team is comprised of only a few dozen families, each member can see some relationship between his own effort and his end-of-season receipts. The amount of an individual's share (both in percentage and absolute terms) will of course vary from place to place, but if a team were to produce 100,000 catties (approximately 50 tons) of rice, it might be allocated somewhat as follows:

---

[106] "In Revolution, One Must Revolutionize One's Own Ideology," by a "commentator" in the PLA newspaper *CFCP*. FBIS I, August 4, 1970, pp. C-2 f. Emphasis added. Translation revised and paraphrased.

[107] *Sheng-ch'an tui*. Sometimes called "production small teams" (*shen-ch'an hsiao tui*).

[108] The brigade, within the limits of the state plan as transmitted by the commune, sets production targets and state procurement quotas at the beginning of each season. Thereafter, these are fixed, and may not be increased.

[109] One qualification due here is the possibility that the higher levels may pressure the team to allocate more funds for capital construction at the expense of consumption.

[110] *Kung fen*. Team members are also compensated for any manure which they supplied to fertilize collective land.

212   SIX: *Integrative Models*

	Catties
Taxes and compulsory sales to state	20,000
Distributed to individual members	50,000
Savings (including seed grain) and/or loan repayment	13,000
Welfare, militia, and other expenses	17,000[111]

Although these figures do not reflect the team's total income,[112] they do indicate the pattern of disposition of the gross village product.

Clearly, the production team is too small to be self-sufficient in any general sense. Nonetheless, the theme of self-reliant regeneration is applied almost as fervently to teams as to larger units. Not only do teams have their own tools, work shops, small processing shops, and granaries, but they are also urged to diversify their production somewhat. This may or may not involve light manufacturing, but it will certainly entail producing a *variety* of crops and animal products. It is stressed that the primary goal is self-sufficiency in production rather than self-sufficiency through financial means (i.e., by emphasizing high-profit crops). As a *People's Daily* discussion of a production team in Kwangsi put the matter:

> One should not judge whether a course followed by a production unit is correct *simply* on the basis of the scope of its diversified production.

---

[111] These amounts are based upon comparable 1964 figures for a team described in Barnett, pp. 421 f. Somewhat different statistics are reported by John Galbraith in the *New York Times Magazine,* November 26, 1972, p. 94. Although Barnett's figures are less up to date than Galbraith's and are limited geographically, they are nonetheless very detailed and precise, whereas Galbraith's are rather vague. (The total for Barnett's village was 77,741 catties.)

Jonathan Unger found that the average household in one *brigade* received about $340 cash a year, but that most living expenses were met by the team. Each "brigade member" also received 55 pounds of grain a month, as well as eight pounds of pork and a sack of sugar. *CSM,* June 8, 1972, p. 5.

In one (doubtless better than average) team described in *PR* (April 28, 1972, pp. 20 f.), with 105 households and 400 people, the gross income in 1971 was 111,400 yuan, and the net income (after expenses) was 93,000 yuan. Members contributed 50,000 workdays, and were paid 1.28 yuan per workday (form of payment not stated, but probably all or mostly in grain). Seventy-eight percent of net team income was distributed to members, and 22 percent went for reserves and welfare. (From our table, we can infer that probably less than 60 percent of net grain income was distributed to team members.)

[112] This would include proceeds from other collective products, private production, and proceeds from sales to the state (which should be deducted from the first figure, 20,000 catties).

If a production unit aims only at earning more money . . . it would be considered as having a capitalist tendency no matter what the scope of its diversification. By the same token, if a production unit confines its production only to grain production without diversifying its productive operations even though it had favorable conditions to do so, it would be considered wrong, because in so doing it would have failed to give more support to agriculture through side-line production when it was in a good position to do so.[113]

In other words, team diversification should not be motivated by any profit motive, nor by any utopian quest to satisfy 100 percent of its own needs, but rather this question should be considered in the overall context of priorities, of which the most important is maximizing grain production.[114] In order not to interfere with any team's productivity, there is to be little or no horizontal integration of the labor force,[115] and no vertical integration without a team's consent.

In the early 1970s there were efforts in parts of China to recentralize the brigades, and eliminate the teams as accounting units.[116] The Party put a stop to this within two years[117] because of the effect that such higher-level collectivization has in reducing incentives to produce. Although the popular model brigade at Tachai comprises an accounting unit, this brigade is a relatively small one—more comparable to a team in size. In general, the national press has stressed the importance of respecting the team's autonomy (*tzu-chu ch'üan*). It is also emphasized (perhaps primarily in the provincial media) that respecting the integrity of the team does not mean that the higher levels should stand idly by and "let things take their course freely," dubbed *tailism*.[118] In

[113] "Can That Production Team Be Considered an Exemplary Production Team?" *JMJP*, June 21, 1973, FBIS I, July 13, 1973, p. B-1. Translation revised.

[114] After weighing the various factors, this article concluded that the particular team under scrutiny was exemplary, because it had met its obligations to the state, "taken grain production as the key link," and still managed to grow five additional cash crops, raise hogs, and operate kilns, oil mills, and a grain-processing center.

[115] "After discussion among cadres, it was recognized that the number of households in the six production teams [of a Fukien brigade] is adequate to supply labor power. For this reason, further transfers will not be made. Adjustments may be made in one or two teams, but the rest need not be changed." C. Chen, *Lien-chiang*, p. 57.

[116] For example, 1970, in Chingtai County, Fukien, on which see Peking radio, "Fukien County CCP Committee Corrects Policy Violations," FBIS I, October 31, 1972, pp. C-1 f.

[117] With the exception of collectivized cottage industries, which as we have noted have often continued to be brigade operations since 1970.

[118] For example, Shantung provincial radio, June 5, 1972, FBIS I, June 8, 1972, p. C-7.

six: *Integrative Models*

recent years, however, the primary emphasis (especially in the national press) has been decidedly upon safeguarding the teams against errors such as cadres' "encroachment upon the right to self-determination of production teams by setting up impractical requirements and rules," and "being overconfident, subjective, and not having faith in the masses."[119]

Although the teams are only partially integrated into the normal governmental and economic *structures*, as we have seen there are other important dimensions to political integration. We have already emphasized the role of the media in highlighting ideal conduct and presenting models to follow. At the higher levels, we have also stressed that the Party has usually (but not always) been an important force in eliciting performance. However, at the team level the Party is not present in the same way that it is at higher levels. It is rare for a team to have more than one Party member, and common for it to have none at all. Whereas at the other levels we have been examining the Party as an important vehicle of horizontal integration (Party committees representing different organs or offices at the same level), in the team "the Party" usually means people from a *higher* level. Sometimes, when a team deteriorates seriously, the Party leaders from the brigade or commune may have no choice but to take direct control. For example, in one production team in Kiangsu Province it was discovered that only 70 percent of the able-bodied workers actually did an appreciable amount of work for the team. The Party investigated and found that work points were sometimes alloted regardless of how much labor an individual performed. When Party representatives questioned the team leader about this, he argued that to do otherwise would be "putting work points in command," a practice which had once been considered a capitalist deviation. However, the commune Party committee compelled the team to change its ways, insisting that the only correct socialist principle was "to each according to his work."[120]

Such direct Party intervention is permissible when a team is acting contrary to basic guidelines. When a team's performance is simply mediocre but it is not possible to point to a specific violation, the branch and commune Party leaders must conduct themselves more discreetly if they are to avoid opening themselves to charges of commandism. One approach is to publish comparisons between the more

---

[119] *JMJP* editor's note, Peking radio, August 24, 1972, FBIS I, August 28, 1972, p. B-4.
[120] Liu I-chao, "Specific Instructions Are Necessary for Production Teams," *JMJP*, November 11, 1972, FBIS I, December 11, 1972, pp. B-1 f.

advanced and backward teams highlighting the reasons for the latter's lack of success (wastefulness, lack of dedication, poor leadership, and so on).[121] If this does not shame the laggards into improving their performance, more drastic measures may be required. When necessary, the brigade can effect a change of team leadership. In extreme cases, police action can be taken.[122]

Although the production team is the essential unit for the administration of collective agriculture, for purposes of field labor deployment and social control the team is divided into *production groups*[123] of half a dozen households. Within the groups, the biological *family* remains the framework for child raising, domestic labor, and ultimate distribution.[124] Finally, within that the *individual* adults make the final decisions concerning income disposition, management of private property, and other family affairs. At this level, there remains considerable discretionary authority. Although sometimes there is a requirement that a certain amount of money be saved, a person is generally free to dispose of income in any legal manner. If money is deposited in a bank, however, there may be restrictions concerning how it is spent. Private land, furthermore, cannot be freely sold. This applies not only to housing, but also to private gardens.[125]

Whatever commitment the world's socialists have to socialism and its capitalists have to capitalism, when people are placed in positions of authority they virtually always find that the only viable economic system reflects elements of both ideologies. Thus China's leaders, otherwise of impeccable socialist credentials, permit about 5 percent of China's arable land to be privately farmed.[126] This means that the entire yield of these gardens redound to the benefit of the individual tillers, who decide for themselves how to utilize the land. These private gardens, roughly one-hundredth of an acre each, have been permitted since the early 1960s. They are usually devoted to the growing of vegetables, some of which are consumed by the family and some

[121] "Why Do Agricultural Production Costs of These Two Production Teams Differ So Much?" *CFCP*, September 10, 1973, FBIS I, September 13, 1973, pp. C-6 f.

[122] Although a team may not have a Party member, at least in the mid-1960s it usually did have a security officer. Barnett, p. 422.

[123] *Ch'an hsiao tsu.*

[124] Strictly speaking, the most common form of household is comprised of a "stem family," with a single couple, one or more of their parents, and the couple's children.

[125] *Tzu-liu ti.*

[126] The yield of the private gardens is worth considerably more than 5 percent of the gross national agricultural product.

of which are sold on the free market for cash. As with all mixed economies, tension develops between the public and private sectors. In terms of material incentives, the individual is inclined to invest the most work and resources (especially human manure) in his garden rather than in the team's fields. This tendency is combatted in part by rotating the gardens each year, and in part by psychic pressure, or consciousness raising. Naturally, many a cadre finds the private plots anathema, and one occasionally hears of attempts to restrict or eliminate them. The following newspaper account is interesting both for what it tells about attitudes towards private agriculture, and about the dynamics of leadership.

> Hsia Hsien-kao is secretary of the Party branch of Shuangho Production Brigade of Chingfeng Commune of Chienhu County, Kiangsu. In 1971, when he learned that a production team leader had arbitrarily forbidden members of his team to apply fertilizer to their private plots, he wanted to have a talk with that leader because he felt that such a measure was at variance with the Party economic policy for rural areas. Hearing about this, a comrade advised him: "My old friend Hsia, you had better not get involved in this, because if something goes wrong you may be accused of protecting private interests at the expense of public interests." Hsia replied: "Inasmuch as the Party has ruled that private plots may be allocated to the commune members, it is expected that they make good use of them. But how could they make good use of these private plots when they are forbidden to apply any fertilizer? This runs counter to our Party policy."
>
> But when the team leader was questioned, he remarked: "A sugarcane cannot taste sweet at both ends. By the same token, if one cares much for the crop fields under collective ownership, one must care less for his private plot, and vice versa." Hsia was not convinced by this argument, but he was unable to make the production team leader change his mind.
>
> Hsia then proceeded to review Chairman Mao's works and some documents relating to policy. He came to realize that the Party economic policy for rural areas was formulated according to the economic characteristics of the socialist period, and that if an ultra-"left" economic policy is enforced prematurely, it is bound to undermine the socialist enthusiasm of the masses, to the detriment of the cause of the revolution.
>
> On the basis of his heightened awareness, Hsia talked to the production team leader again. This time, he began with a lecture on policy and then reviewed the case of Shuangho production brigade which suffered from a breakdown of its collective economy because it went ahead to "cut off the capitalist tail" as advised by the swindlers like

Liu Shao-ch'i [i.e., Lin Piao]. This enabled the production team leader to see the light. He then took the initiative to conduct self-criticism before the masses, and made suitable arrangements for them to apply fertilizer both to crop fields under collective ownership and to private plots.[127]

So this private agriculture continues to be politically acceptable, and these gardens continue to represent an important portion of a farm family's income. Thus, some area remains for autonomy. The family is not necessarily fully integrated into its environment, but has a choice of partial or total integration.

Aside from the matter of private gardens, the production team is so small that even collective effort is such that individual effort and reward are linked, so this does not represent a purely socialist mode of production.[128] Even so, there has occasionally been pressure to make agriculture even more capitalistic by setting all production quotas at the household level. One may question whether the particular national leaders accused of this heresy were actually guilty of it,[129] but undoubtedly many pragmatists have questioned the efficacy of socialist agriculture. Around 1962 this manifested itself in "the spirit of individual enterprise," which was widely justified on several grounds. First, it was said that the interests of good management and business practices would best be served if each household would produce according to individual contracts. "Only under individual enterprise," one cadre insisted, would the Chinese farmers "redouble their efforts." There would be greater output under such a system, it was said, and the government was accused of promoting collectives because it was "afraid the masses will eat too well"—i.e., retain too high a percentage of crop yield. Even within the Party, apparently, there were those who argued for the household contract system, citing popular demands for it, and the fact that it greatly simplified the cadres' work. However, the Party leadership insisted that all such thinking was erroneous. According to one spokesperson.

> Actually, the keener the spirit of individual enterprise, the greater the decrease in production. [Specific cases and statistics are cited.] The

---

[127] "He Is Fearless Because He Is Selfless," *JMJP*, October 18, 1972, FBIS I, November 9, 1972, p. B-6.

[128] This does not apply to the state farms, located primarily in the northern border regions.

[129] One of those accused was Lin Piao. See Chung Fa, 1973, no. 34, *BOC*, February 14, 1974, p. 3.

statement... that household contract production is demanded by the masses... does not have a class basis, and investigations have found that this is not the essence of the situation. This spring [1962], in our investigation of the fourth section of Wang-chung in Tan-yang, in which the most serious movement for individual enterprise occurred, we found that of the fourteen team households, only four households (28.5%) of affluent middle peasants were actually resolutely advocating household contract production, that there were six households (43%) whose ideology was confused and who were at times irresolute, and that there were four households (28.5%) of poor peasants who resolutely opposed private contracting.

Furthermore, incentives based upon the household output had been favored only as "a pretext on the part of the affluent farmers for squeezing out poor farmers.... The Party's aim, by leading the peasants to organize, is to prevent class polarization and to insure common prosperity." Distribution according to labor, rather than output, also assured that crop-failure risks would be evenly distributed. Free enterprise meant freedom to exploit; this could not be encouraged on any grounds, least of all administrative convenience. Any argument to the contrary was worthy of Titoist revisionism.[130]

In 1975 it was again found necessary to speak out against the idea of fixing farm output quotas at the household. As Chang Ch'un-ch'iao told the Fourth National People's Congress, it was correct to be "flexible" in applying socialist principles to the point of allowing private gardens, but it would be utterly fallacious to accept the Liu-Lin heresy of going so far as to replace the garden system with general household quotas.[131]

We have seen that as the Chinese have forged their new political forms they have not only discarded the most utopian version of subintegration, i.e., self-sufficient, self-governing communes, but they have organized agriculture on such a small scale that it is, at least in structure, quasi-capitalistic. The hope is that the socialist *culture* will enable socialism to prevail over capitalism. Nevertheless, it was admitted in 1975 that "a section of the peasants still retain in varying degrees the habits of small producers," and that "the spontaneous forces of capitalism often come to the surface." Thus, "the struggle

---

[130] Wang Hung-chih, "Implementation of the Resolutions of the Tenth Plenum of the Eighth Central Committee on Strengthening the Collective Economy and Expanding Agricultural Production," in C. Chen, *Lien-chiang*, pp. 105–7. Translation revised.

[131] Chang Ch'un-chiao, "Report on the Revision of the Constitution," *PR*, January 24, 1975, p. 20.

between the socialist road and the capitalist road remains very intense."[132]

There is, of course, no single perfect unit or level around which to build socialism—or any other system. The economic facts of life determine that the commune, for example, is too large for agricultural purposes, and too small to support heavy industry. Stressing one level at the expense of others means that government will not be properly attending to important matters inherent in other levels. Thus, the Chinese now stress decentralization only to the extent that it is practical for the various functions. The goal of Maoists is to devolve authority upon the smallest unit which can effectively undertake the activity in question without reverting to capitalism, and they are willing to pay a certain price, both in terms of social theory and economics, in order to bring government within reach of the masses. For social theory, the price stems from the inherent capitalist nature of small production units. The economic price stems from the fact that if a small group is to be self-sufficient, it must get along with relatively little specialization. To make all of this work, society must be comprised of generalists with a high degree of social consciousness.

In sum, a compromise has been struck between idealism and necessity. For now, the prevailing view is that the advantages of the existing arrangements outweigh the costs. But as China's economy develops and becomes more complicated, it is possible that pressures will mount for greater integration on a subcontinental magnitude. Sophisticated technology can raise the national standard of living, but only where the economics of scale can be practiced. Furthermore, although excessive inventories have not yet become a problem, with each locality striving for self-sufficiency this could be a drag on the economy during a period of greater productivity. It is also likely that a cellular economy will in the long run exacerbate economic inequalities among localities. And for all the disadvantages of overspecialization, it has yet to be demonstrated that a nation of generalists can attain a standard of living comparable to a society characterized by specialization. As the Chinese work out the answer to such problems, they may well modify the Maoist subintegrative model in favor of greater subcontinental integration.

---

[132] Ch'ih Heng, "Conscientiously Study the Theory of the Dictatorship of the Proletariat," *PR*, February 14, 1975, p. 8.

SEVEN

Homogeneity

Equality is based upon inequality.

HSÜN TZU (3D CENTURY B.C.)[1]

Even under socialism, there have persisted three widespread disparities in society: between industrial workers and farmers, between urban and rural people, and between mental and manual workers. These three disparities are a reflection of bourgeois rights, and it is incumbent upon the dictatorship of the proletariat to restrict and narrow them.

RED FLAG (1975)[2]

DURING THE FIRST half of this book we explored the various ways in which the Chinese are bringing about political integration. In the last chapter, however, we began to see that an important way in which the integration problem is being approached is by short-circuiting the *need* for integration—through reliance upon subintegration. Now we shall examine the other way in which the need for integration is reduced, namely the "homogenizing" of society. The assumption is that great social disparities are not only unjust, they are dysfunctional. Interdependence based upon social, economic, and political "incom-

---

[1] Section 9. From Burton Watson, *Hsün Tzu: Basic Writings* (New York: Columbia University Press, 1963), p. 36. Hsün Tzu purports to be quoting the *Shu ching*, but as Watson points out (n. 5), the words are taken out of context and in the original have a very different meaning.

[2] Paraphrase based upon remarks in Ch'ih Hung [pseud.?], "Conscientiously Study the Dictatorship of the Proletariat," *HC*, 1975, no. 2, pp. 37 and 39. A translation of this article appeared in *PR*, February 14, 1975, pp. 6–10.

pleteness" leads to a kind of exploitive dependence which constitutes an unnecessary degree of integration.

Bridging Life-styles

The idea of dissolving *all* of the artificial divisions within society, and not only those stemming from "class" in the narrow sense of the word, did not originate with Mao Tse-tung. Marx and Engels argued that when an individual is forced to fulfill a specialized role in production, this has an alienating effect upon him.

> ... The division of labor implies the contradiction between the interest of the separate individual or the individual family and the communal interest of all individuals who have intercourse with one another. And indeed, this communal interest does not exist merely in the imagination, as "the general good," but first of all in reality, as the mutual interdependence of the individuals among whom the labor is divided. And finally, the division of labor offers us the first example of how, as long as man remains in natural society—that is, as long as a cleavage exists between the particular and the common interest—as long, therefore, as activity is not voluntarily but naturally divided, man's own deed becomes an alien power opposed to him, which enslaves him instead of being controlled by him. For as soon as labor is distributed, each man has a particular, exclusive sphere of activity which is forced upon him and from which he cannot escape. He is a hunter, a fisherman, a shepherd, or an intellectual,[3] and must remain so if he does not want to lose his means of livelihood; while in communist society, where nobody has one exclusive sphere of activity but each can become accomplished in any branch he wishes, society regulates the general production and thus makes it possible for me to do one thing today and another tomorrow, to hunt in the morning, fish in the afternoon, rear cattle in the evening, criticize after dinner, just as I have a mind, without ever becoming hunter, fisherman, shepherd, or intellectual.[4]

Although Marx and Engels did not deny that within the family some division of labor had a certain natural basis, applying this principle to the economy in general had tended to effect both "the separation of society into individual families opposed to one another," and "the unequal distribution (both quantitative and qualitative) of labor and

---

[3] The phrase in the Feuer translation is "critical critic," which we have changed to simply "intellectual." Mark and Engels probably meant people who use their critical faculties.

[4] Feuer, p. 254.

its products."⁵ Such specialization, then, alienated people from each other, as well as from the inherent totality of their natural personalities.⁶

Pursuant to these principles, Mao Tse-tung began promoting social homogeneity in the late 1950s. As we have noted, the communes were in part an experiment to unify the various spheres of human activity.⁷ Furthermore, this was the time of the "red-expert" campaign,⁸ when the specialists (professional people) were urged to become more "red" (politically conscious), and Party members were under pressure to develop technical competence. After the difficulties of the Great Leap Forward, critics of homogeneity became outspoken against what they ridiculed as "the doctrine of diversity."

> The doctrine of diversity occurs at all levels. It is found in the economic sector, in the Party, in the administrative sector, among the mass organizations, and in the collectives. We must resolve to correct it now. If we practice diversity, with each individual region and sector dispersing manpower, matériel, and financial power, the time required to overcome the current economic difficulties will be prolonged. This will affect the speed of socialist construction throughout the entire nation. In addition, the doctrine of diversity and the tendency toward low production may affect the faith of some people in the development of collective enterprise (as manifested in low rations), and may furnish a pretext to those promoting individual enterprise, which would be detrimental to collectivism.⁹

Advocates of homogeneity did not abandon the issue, however, and in the mid-1960s there was a renewed effort to promote it. Now Mao Tse-tung was sounding somewhat more pragmatic, no longer insisting that everyone be a jack of all trades but only reasonably well rounded.

> While the main task of the workers is in industry, they should also study military affairs, politics, and culture.... Where conditions permit, they should also engage in agricultural production and side occu-

---

[5] Ibid., p. 253.
[6] For further discussion on Marx's theory of alienation, see Bertell Ollman, *Alienation: Marx's Conception of Man in Capitalist Society* (New York: Cambridge University Press, 1971), especially chap. 24.
[7] For the initial blueprint concerning this aspect of the communes, see *CCPDA*, p. 454.
[8] This subject is analyzed in Seymour, "Policies."
[9] Wang Hung-chih. "Implementation of the Resolutions of the Tenth Plenum of the Eighth Central Committee on Strengthening the Collective Economy and Expanding Agricultural Production," in C. Chen, *Lien-chiang*, p. 108. Quotation revised and reorganized.

pations, as is done in the Taching oilfield. While the main task of the peasants in the communes is agriculture (including forestry, animal husbandry, side occupations, and fishery), they should at the same time study military affairs, politics, and culture. Where conditions permit, they should collectively run small plants. This holds for students, too. While their main task is to study, they should in addition to their studies, learn other things, that is, industrial work, farming, and military affairs. . . . The school term should be shortened, education should be revolutionized, and the domination of our schools by bourgeois intellectuals should not be allowed to continue. Where conditions permit, those working in commerce, in the service trades, and in Party and Government organization should do the same.[10]

For the armed services, where such views were first taken seriously, Mao spelled out his views in detail:

The People's Liberation Armed Services should be a great school. In this great school, our soldiers should learn politics, military affairs, and culture. They can also engage in agricultural production and side occupations, run some medium or small factories, and manufacture a number of products to meet their own needs or exchange with the state at equal values. They can also do mass work and take part in the socialist education movement in the factories and villages. After the socialist education movement, they can always find mass work to do, in order to insure that the army is always as one with the masses. They should also participate in each struggle of the Cultural Revolution as it occurs to criticize the bourgeoisie. In this way, the army can concurrently study, engage in agriculture, run factories, and do mass work. Of course, these tasks should be properly coordinated, and a difference should be made between the primary and secondary tasks. Each army unit should engage in one or two of the three tasks of agriculture, industry, and mass work, but not in all three at the same time. . . . In this way, our army of several million will be able to play a very great role indeed.[11]

This was the famous May Seven Directive. Ultimately people in all areas of life would be urged to heed it, but in 1966 Mao was only in a position to put the idea across in the armed services, which were

[10] *JMJP*, August 1, 1966, *SCMP*, no. 3754, August 5, 1966, p. 7.
[11] *CFCP*, August 1, 1966, *SCMP*, no. 3754, August 5, 1966, p. 2. Related documents can be found in: *KMJP*, May 7, 1967, *FBIS* I, May 8, 1967, p. ccc 13; *JMJP*, May 7, 1967, *FBIS* I, May 8, 1967, p. ccc 8; NCNA, August 5, 1966, *SCMP*, no. 3757, pp. 16 f; *PR*, August 5, 1966, pp. 6–14; *PR*, May 12, 1967, pp. 11 f.

under the leadership of Lin Piao. With the advent of the Cultural Revolution, the armed services were playing an outstanding role as multifunctional organizations. In 1967 their role in the economy was further stepped up. Not only did soldiers run their own farms, but they often supervised people in communes (especially urban intellectuals who had been transferred to them), sometimes providing heavy equipment and performing flood control and land reclamation duties. In industry the armed services had an even greater impact. With cadres under a cloud, soldiers stepped into supervisory positions, or at least settled disputes between cadres and workers or revolutionary elements.

Thus, the armed services were in large measure responsible for maintaining China's economy during the Cultural Revolution. One reason that it was possible for the armed services to perform such nonmilitary roles is that they had been doing so internally for years. Although soldiers were withdrawn from civilian agriculture and industrial enterprises as the Cultural Revolution wound down, it continued to be stressed that soldiers should follow Mao's motto that "politics must be integrated with economics and technology."[12] The armed services did continue to perform certain public-service functions, such as public health work and engineering projects, and, as it had done for many decades, it continued to be active in propaganda and cultural work. Indeed, Mao Tse-tung was probably not greatly exaggerating when he noted in 1972 that "by now our army is engaged only in cultural work and not in military affairs. Thus, our army has become a cultural army."[13]

There was one additional sense in which, by the mid-1960s, the armed services had come to be a paragon of social homogeneity, and this was egalitarianism. In sharp distinction with other armies (Chinese and foreign), the Red Army which Mao Tse-tung and Chu Teh began assembling in the late 1920s practiced a considerable degree of internal social equality and at least in a formal sense some democratic deliberations. Although perhaps these are natural in guerrilla warfare, they continued to be a feature of the Chinese People's Volunteers which participated in the later stages of the Korean War. Foreign intelligence observers were impressed by the generally comradely relations between officers and troops, and the lack of any officer caste system.[14] Indeed,

---

[12] Peking radio, March 15, 1972, FBIS I, March 21, 1972, p. B-2.
[13] Mao, *"Chung Fa,"* 1972, no. 12, B-7.
[14] See Alexander L. George, *The Chinese Communist Army in Action: The Korean War and Its Aftermath* (New York: Columbia University Press, 1967), especially pp. 36 ff.

only the most minor differences in dress distinguished the two categories, and it was impossible to determine soldiers' rank from their appearance. Officers were in the practice of addressing troops in polite language. Extreme forms of discipline were rarely used, and there were only moderate rank-related disparities in rations and amenities. Years later, on the eve of the Cultural Revolution, the armed services took steps to become an even more egalitarian organization. In 1965 ranks were eliminated altogether, although there is no pretense of absolute equality (unit leaders are unmistakably recognized as such). Because status differentials had been minimized for many years, the abandonment of ranks was largely a symbolic gesture, perhaps intended to provide the armed services with impeccable revolutionary credentials so that the services could be presented as a model for the nation to emulate.

Although it was within the armed services that egalitarianism was first emphasized, the more crucial arena was in the relations between civilians and cadres. Mao Tse-tung had long urged that the Party not consider itself superior to the public.

> Treat cadres and the masses with a genuine attitude of equality. It is imperative to make people feel that the relationship among human beings is truly one of equality, and to make people feel that your heart goes out to them.... There are differences in people's work and functions, but a person, no matter how high an office he or she holds, should have the demeanor of an ordinary worker among the people. On no account should one be permitted to assume arrogant airs.[15]

Why, almost a decade after the revolution, was Mao still talking almost as though no real revolution had taken place? Surely China's new ruling class was not comparable to the traditional mandarins, for the typical cadre sprang from the lowest strata of society. Apparently, though, they had come to believe that inasmuch as it had been through their foresight and good luck that they found themselves on top, they had a right to enjoy some personal benefit from their new status. A local Party secretary might rationalize that he or she could be more mobile and therefore more effective if a public bicycle were made available for the secretary's personal use. Also, secretaries might use the information which inevitably came their way to engage in profitable business activities. Through the 1950s, such people were not considered venal, nor would such conduct be considered corrupt in most

---

[15] Mao Tse-tung, "Sixty Articles" (1958), *CLG*, Spring 1972, pp. 107 f.

cultures. To Mao, however, it meant the death of the revolution. At first, this view received little real support, but one day Mao would lead others to see the light. As one local Party secretary reflected in the early 1970s, "It took me only fifteen years to be transformed from a revolutionary into a capitalist. If the Cultural Revolution had not occurred, the only people from [the village] to go to the university and to own large houses would have been my sons and the sons of my sons. My mistake was not so much that I catered to my own needs but the fact that I put my personal enrichment above the enrichment of the community."[16] Thus, instead of being an egalitarian society, China, prior to the Cultural Revolution, had been led by a socially privileged elite that enjoyed relatively high wages and other economic opportunities (including special education for their children), as well as uncommon comforts in clothing, housing, and food.

Food occupies a rather special place in Chinese civilization. For the poor (and those who can remember being poor), the preoccupation with assuring sufficient nourishment is not exceeded in intensity in any other major country. For those with an abundance of food, the culinary arts have always been given attention otherwise worthy only of the French. Dining, furthermore, is traditionally a significant occasion, when the entire household would congregate around a table for what was an important social experience. When, during the Great Leap Forward, public dining halls were instituted, it was common for cadres to eat separately, thus reinforcing their status as a social elite. In 1960 this practice was terminated, and cadres were obliged to eat with the masses. Although as it happened the popularity of public dining was short-lived and the practice was discontinued after a few years, nonetheless the attention given to the question of cadre exclusiveness was an indication of struggles to come.

More gradual, but also more enduring as a means of effecting elite-mass homogenization, was the *hsia-fang*. The term *hsia-fang* (noun or verb) denotes downward placement or demotion (not necessarily punitive), usually referring to cadres and professional people ("experts"). The term appears to have first been employed by the leadership in 1956, when Chou En-lai urged that "inflated, overstaffed" administrative offices *hsia fang* "an appropriate number of people." Some of the personnel in "nonproductive departments" were to be transferred to more productive work.[17] This was not yet promoted as a campaign to

[16] Alex Casella, "Mao's China, 1972," *New York Times Magazine,* February 20, 1972, p. 38.
[17] Speech to Eighth Party Congress. *CCPDA,* pp. 240 f.

proletarianize the elite, but simply as a pragmatic measure for streamlining the bureaucracy.

After the Hundred Flowers episode in the spring of 1957, however, *hsia fang* came to be viewed as a means of social reform. During the latter half of that year, it was decided to employ this method to reform both cadres and the educated class[18] (the two groups once having been fairly discrete, but by the late 1950s tending increasingly to overlap). Mao Tse-tung had always believed that understanding, including political understanding, comes through practice, and that the trouble with China's intellectuals and professional people was that they had traditionally considered manual labor beneath them. Thus, it was decided that they should regularly (and in certain cases permanently) work at the front lines of production. Some people could thereby gain useful experience, so that the *hsia fang* had a certain value even in purely economic terms.[19] However, it has generally been maintained that the primary purpose of demoting intellectuals was to transform their sociopolitical outlook, and that the maintenance or increasing of their special skills has little place in *hsia fang*.[20]

At any rate, at the Eighth Central Committee's Third Plenum (September–October 1957) it was decided that all "intellectual cadres" who had not yet performed labor service should do so for the purpose of engaging in mass struggle and being "tested." It was realized (and intended) that this would involve hardship, especially for the educated class of bourgeois origin. According to Chang Tzu-yi, who had recently become a deputy director of the Party's Propaganda Department, the road would be circuitous and thorny—"a path which is long and cannot be traversed without hardship and sacrifice."[21] Chang, a Party veteran from the Kiangsi days, demanded that *hsia-fanged* indi-

[18] *Chih-shih fen-tzu.*

[19] As late as February 1959, one of the chief benefits of the *hsia-fang* was considered to be the fact that it helped people in their professional work. We are told that a scientist working on the subject of parasitic insects was able to learn much during his *hsia-fang* that he had been unable to learn in the laboratory. Cadres from the Ministry of Agriculture, 171 in number, had written 235 papers, "over twenty" of which "were of great academic interest." Even musicians benefited from "closer contact with life," and from hearing work songs and folk songs. Metallurgists, engineers, broadcasters, and public health workers were among the others who were said to gain valuable practical experience. Li Fang, "Back from the Countryside," *PR*, February 10, 1959, pp. 11 f.

[20] This position was taken in *JMJP*, October 15, 1960, *CB*, no. 642, p. 37; and *KMJP*, March 24, 1965, *SCMP*, no. 3204, p. 11. More on the *hsia-fang* of intellectuals and professionals is contained in Seymour, "Policies," especially pp. 151–56.

[21] Chang Tzu-yi, "Concerning the Problem of Intellectuals in the Countryside," *Hsueh-hsi*, January 3, 1958, *ECMM*, no. 126, p. 20.

viduals fully share in the hardships of agrarian life. Intellectuals, for example, should not be billeted in the homes of the more affluent farmers, but rather should live with the poor.[22] Thus would China's elite undergo the rustication necessary for the nation to become a truly homogeneous society. In fact, millions of cadres and professional people did experience *hsia fang* during the late 1950s, and this had serious disrupting effects in terms of the economy and general governmental administration. Combined with poor weather which diminished agricultural output, China entered a period in the 1960s when such upheavals as the *hsia fang* had to be curtailed. As soon as conditions returned to relative normalcy, however, Mao sought to reemphasize the need for cadres' participation in physical labor.[23]

The year 1968 was an important one in terms of innovative efforts to effect social homogeneity. First, it was at this time that the "three-thirds" system was inaugurated, whereby a third of the county-level functionaries spend a period of time doing normal desk work, then a period engaged in study and field investigation, and finally a period engaged in physical labor in a production team. At any one time, the offices are manned by only a third of the total staff. The duration of each role has varied greatly from time to time and place to place. In one county it has been as long as a year,[24] and in another only a month.[25] Cadres at the very lowest levels spend even more than a third of their time engaged in field work.[26] In this way, cadres are supposed to be keeping in touch with their constituencies, gaining an understanding of practical day-to-day problems, and cleansing their minds of any idea that the bureaucracy should be self-serving.

Also in 1968, the May 7 cadre schools were first established. Taking their name from the date of Mao Tse-tung's 1966 pronouncement on role despecialization,[27] these boarding schools accommodate middle

[22] Ibid., p. 24.
[23] Notably Mao's directive of May 9, 1963. On the marking of the tenth anniversary of this directive, see Nanchang radio, May 9, 1973, FBIS I, May 15, 1973, pp. C-3 f. It is implied that Lin Piao had undermined the carrying out of the directive.
[24] Fenghuang County, Hunan. Peking radio, August 23, 1970, FBIS I, September 1, 1970, p. B-1.
[25] Hui County, Honan. Chengchow radio, November 12, 1973, FBIS I, November 16, 1973, p. D-1.
[26] A brigade cited in an American newspaper reported that its cadres averaged 130 field days annually, its production-team-level cadres, 280 days. *CSM*, June 8, 1972, p. 5.
[27] Quotation above, p. 224. This May 7 (1966) directive should not be confused with the "May 9" (1963) directive on physical labor referred to in note 23.

and senior cadres, and simulate the situation of a Chinese village.[28] Nearly all such cadres have now spent about six months at these, adopting the life-style of ordinary farmers, and trying to internalize the latter's progressive, nonbureaucratic outlook. This is to be achieved by living a spartan, self-reliant life. In many cases, the camps are situated on what was originally barren land, and were built by the first class of students. As far as is known, they are largely self-governing; the requirement that residents make do with what they have is sufficient deterrent against uncooperative behavior. About two-thirds of one's time is spent working—in agriculture, animal husbandry, and small industry, with the emphasis on self-sufficiency even in capital construction. Most of the remaining period is devoted to study, discussion, and soul searching. Time is also found for sports, militia training, and other activities. Men and women, young adults and their seniors, all work and study together.[29] May 7 schools exist throughout the nation, including the minority regions.[30] Thus, they serve as an important vehicle for the achievement of national integration through homogeneity—transforming cadres so that they can lead less through specialized role performance and more through identification with the general population.[31]

Like political and administrative leaders, technicians and other "experts" are similarly expected to integrate themselves with the masses, deemphasize their specialized roles, and strive to serve the true public purpose. This does not mean that specialists should cease to exist. If classical Marxism occasionally implies anything of the sort, the Chinese have nonetheless moved into the twentieth century. It is not uncommon for individuals to perform specialized tasks, but such work is usually mixed with other work such as farming; *unnecessary* monopolizing of skills is considered bourgeois professionalism. Not only should private skills not be a source of profit, but specialists are expected to impart them to others. Ideally, one

> takes the initiative in disseminating technical know-how to others rather than keeping it a secret. Previously, in [a Manchurian repair and

---

[28] The May 7 cadre school visited by Klaus Mehnert had a population of 1,255. *NYRB*, February 24, 1972, p. 4.

[29] The details in this paragraph to this point are largely taken from a description of a May 7 cadre school near Peking which appeared in *CSM*, September 11, 1972. The age range was nineteen to sixty. It was anticipated that cadres would repeat the experience every five years.

[30] One in the Sinkiang Uigur Autonomous Region was described on Urumchi radio, March 21, 1972, FBIS I, March 28, 1972, p. H-1.

[31] For other descriptions of May 7 schools, see *PR*, May 12, 1972, pp. 5–7; and Klaus Mehnert, *China Returns* (New York: Dutton, 1972).

assembly cooperative] there were some people who thought that an expert would lose his own superior position once he trained an apprentice to become an expert. Thus, they refused to pass on to the farmers even the simplest repair and maintenance technology. At present, however, they proceed from the desire to accelerate agricultural mechanization. During the past three years, they have trained more than fifty technicians for various commune and brigade industries and pumping stations by having the farmers work together with them when doing repair work or by training the farmers in the cooperative's workshop.[32]

A similar practice is sought in large-scale industries in urban centers. Insofar as is practical, personnel should be well-rounded generalists (*to-mien shou*) rather than indespensibly skilled in a narrow specialty (*i-chi chih chang*). Where specialization is unavoidable, one should cultivate some ability in other areas (*i chuan to neng*). Where technology has been confined to the eastern cities, efforts have been made to have much of it transferred to the hinterland. Although some technology will always necessarily be concentrated, integration on the Chinese model requires that it be as widespread as possible.[33]

The third program inaugurated in 1968 involved rusticating urban youth by sending them to the countryside. High school graduates were required to spend two years on a commune before they could apply for admission to college. By 1975, according to Chou En-lai's report to the National People's Congress, ten million youths had undergone the experience. The young people often had difficulty adapting to the conditions, and the villages sometimes found it difficult to absorb them. However, it doubtless has been an educational experience for all concerned, if not an invariably happy one. As with other efforts to effect

---

[32] "A Repair and Assembly Cooperative Rendering Whole Hearted Services to Agricultural Production," *HC*, 1970, no. 6, p. 100.

[33] On this subject, see Jon Sigurdson, "Rural Industry and the Internal Transfer of Technology," in Schram, *Authority*, pp. 199–232.

Also relevant to the general subject of bureaucratic specialization is Ying-Mao Kau, "The Urban Bureaucratic Elite in Communist China: A Case Study of Wuhan, 1949–1965," in A. D. Barnett, ed., *Chinese Communist Politics in Action* (Seattle: University of Washington Press, 1969), pp. 216–67. Although Kau found generalist leadership, the municipal bureaucracy otherwise was highly differentiated and specialized. However, the period under examination was one largely emphasizing specialization rather than more homogeneous institutions. How much municipal governments have changed under the Maoist influences of the past ten years is unknown. Doubtless municipal bureaucracies do not lend themselves to skill dispersion as much as communes do, which in part explains the Maoist anti-urban bias and the efforts to curb the growth of cities.

On efforts to provide workers with broad knowledge, see Jen Wen, "Road of Training Technicians from among the Workers," *PR*, August 6, 1971.

social homogeneity, the program is quite difficult to evaluate. Because of them, however, it is unlikely that China will ever be the same.

Equality

In a truly homogeneous society there should be no great social disparities based upon wealth or culture. Nonetheless, the Chinese have continued to be committed to the socialist principle of remuneration only according to work performed. Although at certain times and places variations of the communist (as distinct from socialist) principle of "to each according to his needs" have been experimented with,[34] the importance of the more realistic system continues to be generally emphasized. This means that in agriculture, for example, even though most of the land is collectivized, farmers are still paid according to the work they perform. Although their income is difficult to estimate in monetary terms because much of it is in kind, it may range from 20 to 40 yuan per month. (A bicycle costs 120 yuan; a movie ticket .10 to .20 yuan; a kilogram of rice, 1.20; a fish, 1 yuan per pound.[35]) Urban workers have been earning much greater salaries, ranging from 35 yuan for the unskilled, to 80 yuan for senior, highly skilled people. Middle management cadres in government and industry have received from 40 to 160 yuan. School teachers have earned 40 to 50 yuan; professors, 60 to 300.[36] Such disparities have usually been seen as unavoidable at China's stage of development, because of necessity to rely upon material incentives to encourage the acquisition and utilization of scarce skills. However, there have often been rumblings of discontent over the existence of such an anomaly in an egalitarian society. In 1975, Mao Tse-tung himself issued "instructions" in which he complained about the wage scales, which were "hardly different from those of the old society." Under proletarian dictatorship, he said, such inequalities should be restricted. Yao Wen-yuan argued that the wage system stemmed from the persistence of "bourgeois rights,"

---

[34] See, for example, "Dangers of Overstepping Party Policy Explained," *JMJP*, July 6, 1972, p. 4, FBIS I, August 3, 1972, pp. B-3 f.

[35] In international exchange, the yuan has been worth a little over U.S. 40¢. This figure is of no meaning in evaluating Chinese living standards, however, and one does better to consider the yuan's purchasing power within China. For very rough estimations, treating a yuan as equal to a dollar is easier and probably no less accurate than any other rate.

[36] Figures taken from various sources, including Michèle Rodière, "*Salaires et niveaux de vie,*" *NC*, June 1972, and Philippe Peemans, "*Les caractéristiques du développement,*" *NC*, April 1972.

which if not changed would generate a class of "new bourgeois elements and upstarts" who might usurp power as the revisionists had done in the Soviet Union. Although there were isolated reports of lowering of salaries, officialdom in general was slow to endorse Mao's call.[37]

Although the necessity for unequal wage scales has long been acknowledged, ascriptive factors have never been supposed to exacerbate the disparities. Thus, increasing equality for *women* has been sought, pursuant to Mao Tse-tung's injunction that "the times have changed, and today men and women are equal; whatever men comrades can accomplish, women comrades can also." Long economically and socially disadvantaged in China, women made gradual progress toward achieving equality during the decades prior to 1949,[38] and their cause was considerably advanced by the Communists in the 1950s. The best gains were made in factories, where equal work received equal pay. However, women were largely relegated to lower-paid positions, and in addition to their factory work had the continued burden of housework. Women who did not work in factories continued to be disadvantaged. This was especially true in the countryside, where as recently as 1972 the work-point system tended to be administered in a manner which favored men. In that year a campaign was begun to rectify the situation, with as yet uncertain results. The education system, whose main beneficiary had been boys, has increasingly been turning its attention to girls, an increasing number of whom are being trained for the professions, especially medicine. (In some areas, a majority of the health personnel are women.[39])

Leadership, however, continues to be predominantly male. Women have only slowly moved into positions of authority in the economy, cultural institutions, and politics generally. Recent Party central committees have been about 90 percent male, although the portion of women has been increasing slightly.[40] The only woman on the twenty-one member Political Bureau has been Chiang Ch'ing, a special

[37] These developments are breaking as we go to press. See *New York Times*, March 15, 1975.

[38] Foreign missionaries' efforts to educate women was an important beginning, and the cause of women's rights was also advanced by the May 4 (1919) movement.

[39] E.g., a commune in Kwangsi. *JMJP*, March 10, 1972, FBIS I, April 4, 1972, pp. B-2 f.

[40] The Ninth Central Committee (elected 1969) had 23 (8.2 percent) women of 279 members: the Tenth Central Committee (1973) had 41 (12.8 percent) women out of 319 members.

case which has little relevance to women's liberation.[41] During the period of the Tenth Central Committee, however, there was a drive to involve women in politics at the lower levels. Much was made of such accomplishments of an Anhwei county where 35 percent of the leadership posts were occupied by women,[42] and of a remote county populated by Chuang people in the southern mountains where 30 percent of the cadres were women.[43] In 1973 the Party itself inaugurated a major effort to build up the proportion of women in the Party.[44] Two years later, however, the National People's Congress still was only 22 percent female. Apparently, only with great difficulty is sexism, so deeply ingrained in Chinese culture, being overcome. As Mao told André Malraux in 1965, "Of course it is necessary to start by giving women legal equality, but the job of achieving real equality still remains after that. The thought, culture, and customs which brought China to where we found it must disappear, and new proletarian thought, customs, and culture must emerge."[45]

In contrast to women, China's *ethnic minorities* comprise only 6 percent of the population, and most of the groups have fewer than a million people. However, they discretely occupy more than half of the territory of the country, and at the 1975 National People's Congress no less than fifty-four different ethnic groups were officially represented. (The ethnic groups of China are shown on the map on page 235 and in the table on page 237.) But relations between these groups and the Han (ethnic Chinese) have not always been tranquil. Except for those which became absorbed by Chinese civilization, non-Hans have traditionally been poorly integrated into the life of the subcontinent. Although tolerant of and even willing to be ruled by races who adopted

---

[41] On Chiang Ch'ing (Mao Tse-tung's wife), see the forthcoming book by Roxanne Witke.

[42] *New York Times*, March 11, 1974. (The number of positions held by women was 4,680).

[43] *JMJP*, July 22, 1972, FBIS I, August 11, 1972, pp. B-3 f. The number of "minority women" among cadres was 600; apparently there were none of the Han race. The county (Hsi-lin) is located in the Kwangsi Chuang Autonomous Region, in the Yunnan-Kweichow border region.

[44] Hsia Ping, "Make Energetic Efforts to Train Women Cadres," *HC*, 1973, no. 12, FBIS I, December 3, 1973, pp. B-2–B-6; Tang Sheng-ping. "Actively Cultivate Women Party Members and Women Cadres," *JMJP*, May 18, 1973, FBIS I, June 15, 1973, pp. B-9 f.

[45] Malraux, p. 465. Translation slightly revised:
One aspect of Chinese culture was relatively independent of sexism, and that was the spoken language. Pronouns, and terms like *chairman*, do not indicate sex.
For further information on the subject of women in China, see Ruth Sidel, *Women and Childcare in China: A Firsthand Report* (Baltimore: Penguin, 1972); and M. Young, *Women in China* (Ann Arbor: University of Michigan, 1974).

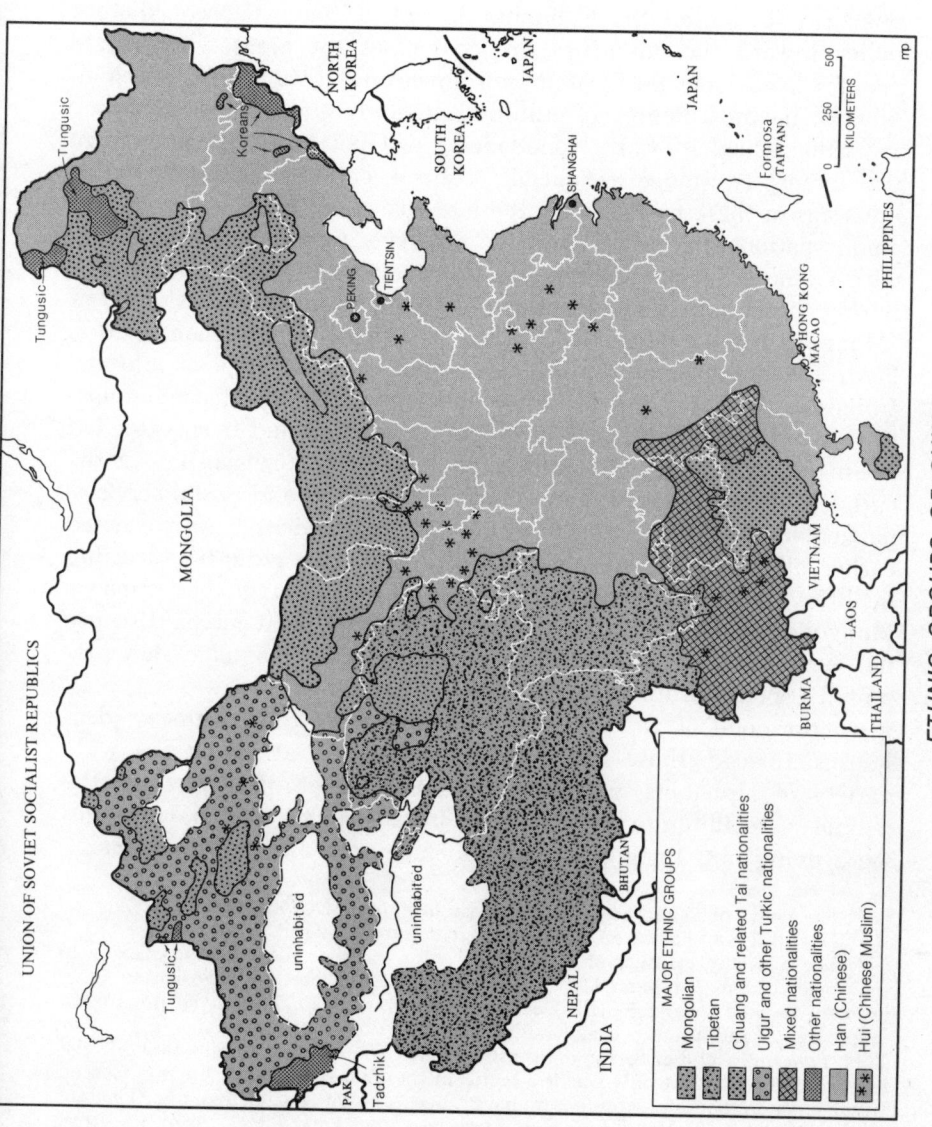

ETHNIC GROUPS OF CHINA

236   SEVEN: *Homogeneity*

Chinese culture, the Han have considered unacculturated races barbaric, and fit only to be subjugated and ruled by the Han race.[46] After the 1949 revolution the Communists took a somewhat conciliatory policy toward the minorities. In most cases the areas where these peoples lived were designated "self-governing" (*tzu chih*), which in practice meant a degree of cultural autonomy and a cautious policy regarding social reforms. Nonetheless, in Tibet[47] and Sinkiang there was intense resistance to "outside" control, culminating in the major uprisings in these two areas in the late 1950s and early 1960s.[48] Even among nationalities who have been relatively peaceful, dissatisfaction with Chinese Communist rule has been evident. In Inner Mongolia during the Hundred Flowers thaw of 1957 one heard such slogans as "Mongolia for the Mongolians," and "Sons of Genghis Khan, Unite!"

An elementary requirement of integrating these regions into the Chinese nation involves including them in the national communications system. Although air and rail transportation had been extended to Sinkiang and Inner Mongolia by the end of the 1950s, as late as the early 1970s there were still areas without transport and postal services, particularly in Tibet (which still has no rail service).[49] As we noted earlier, all provinces and autonomous regions have radio broadcasting facilities. Programs are often broadcast in local languages, such as Mongolian, Uigur, Kazakh, and Hakka.[50] Some print media also use the vernacular, but the question of local written languages has presented a special problem for the Chinese leaders.

Almost none of the minority languages ever used Chinese ideographs. Instead, those with any writing system at all used a wide variety of alphabets, generally foreign in origin. But most of the people were illiterate, and in some instances the written languages were dying out. Languages like Tibetan, on the other hand, had a

[46] The views of Wang Fu-chih are a case in point. *ECCP*, p. 818.

[47] Tibet did not become an autonomous region until 1965.

[48] The Sinkiang uprising of 1962 ended with many of the dissidents fleeing to the Soviet Union. Ten years later it was reported that there was a Turkestan "government in exile" there. *FEER*, December 12, 1972, p. 26. The Soviet press often emphasizes (and usually exaggerates) minority dissidence in China. E.g., *New York Times*, November 8, 1973. Unrest in Tibet also has had serious foreign relations implications. Not only was it a factor in the Sino-Indian war, but the Central Intelligence Agency is reported to have once brought anti-Communist Tibetans to the United States for training as guerrillas. *New York Times*, April 19, 1973, p. 2. See also chap. 8, below.

[49] Highway and postal services were extended in Tibet in 1973. NCNA, August 29, 1973, FBIS I, September 6, 1973, p. E-1.

[50] With the exception of Tibet, all autonomous regions have at least one television broadcasting station.

DEMOGRAPHIC COMPOSITION OF CHINA

Ethnic groups with more than a million people.

Ethnic Group	General Race	Million[a]	Location/Status
Han	Chinese	over 700[b]	China proper (all areas designated as provinces)
Chuang	Similar to Chinese	10[c]	Kwangsi/Autonomous Region
Uigur	Turkic	4	Sinkiang/Autonomous Region
Chinese Moslems (Hui)	Chinese-Turkic	3.5	Ningsia/Autonomous Region
Yi (formerly Lolo)		3.3	Within Szechwan and Yunnan provinces
Tibetan	Mongolian	3	Tibet/Autonomous Region (also within Yunnan, Szechwan, Tsinghai, and Kansu provinces)
Miao	Meo-Yao	2.5	Within Kweichow, Yunnan, Hunan, and Kwangtung provinces
Manchu	Tungus	2.5	Little ethnic identity. Most live in northeast and Peking area.
Mongol	Mongolian	1.5	Inner Mongolia/Autonomous Region (also in Sinkiang)
Pu-yi	Thai(?)	1.3	Within Kweichow
Korean	Tungus	1.1	Within Kirin

[a] The population figures reflect different years, and thus are not strictly comparable. Except as otherwise indicated, they are taken from Chang-tu Hu, et al., *China: Its People, Its Society, Its Culture* (New Haven, HRAF Press, 1960), pp. 70 f.

[b] In 1970 the U.S. Bureau of Census estimated China's population at about 871 million (mainland only), but the UN estimate is only 753 million. *New York Times*, February 20, 1972. Deputy Premier Li Hsien-nien has said that China has more than 750 million (not indicating whether he was including Taiwan). All three figures, of course, include the minority nationalities. Kyōdō, August 23, 1972, FBIS I, August 23, 1972, p. B-1.

[c] Agence France-Presse dispatch in the *New York Times*, October 28, 1973. This is a more recent figure than others on this chart, and represents a sharp increase over that of 1964 (7 million).

long and continuing literary tradition, and presented major difficulties for the Chinese. Tibetan literature epitomized Tibet's nationhood, and the Chinese could not tolerate Tibetan nationalism. The dilemma is being met by retaining the written language but eliminating the traditional literature and emphasizing Chinese as a second language essential to educational advancement. In the case of some other languages there was also a fair body of literature, but in Cyrillic or Arabic script. The continued use of these would foster the integration with related nationalities elsewhere in the world (especially in the Soviet Union), and the concomitant disintegration of the People's Republic of China. For these reasons, Chinese and local scholars have invented new scripts for most of the languages, based upon the Roman alphabet. In the case of the largest nationality, the Chuang of Kwangsi, the alphabet contains a mixture of Latin and Cyrillic. At one time (particularly during the Hundred Flowers thaw) it was reported that Chuang-language textbooks were to be published in large numbers.[51] However, publication efforts flagged; apparently no books are now published in the language, and it is not taught in the schools. The script does occasionally appear on signs, and it is printed on the national currency along with Tibetan, Uigur, and Mongol. But Chuang, it would appear, is gradually being replaced by Chinese.[52] In other regions, the new written languages have been promoted in recent years, particularly in Sinkiang. Tens of thousands of teachers have been trained in Uigur and Kazakh, and in at least some parts of the region virtually all youths are taught to read their native language.[53] Equally important, cadres in minority areas are urged to learn a second language. One commune near Ili proudly reported that 50 percent of the Han cadres could speak a local language, and 80 percent of the native cadres had learned Mandarin.

As we saw in chapter 5, communications and literacy are not ends in themselves; they serve important political purposes. This is as true among the minority nationalities as it is among the Han. The cultural autonomy which the minorities are permitted does not extend to the basic tenets of political culture, which is uniformly Maoist. Civics courses for Uigur children differ from those offered Han chil-

---

[51] Peking radio, March 12, 1957, FBIS I, March 15, 1957, p. ccc 7.
[52] A rare dispatch from Kwangsi, by David Bonavia of the *Times* (London), appeared in the *New York Times*, July 15, 1973.
[53] Urumchi radio, May 15, 1972, FBIS I, May 18, 1972, p. H-4. On other minority languages, see *PR*, September 20, 1974, pp. 22 f. (Mongolian books), and *PR*, September 27, 1974, p. 36 (Tibetan).

dren only in the language of instruction, not in content. Mao's works are used in literacy training in all languages.[54] Some advanced students are sent to national colleges for training as cadres. One such school, the Central Institute for Nationalities, was founded in suburban Peking in 1957. There, representatives from approximately fifty minority nationalities take various courses on ethnic studies and the special problems of leadership in these least developed parts of China.[55] Another such school exists solely for Tibetans. Founded only in 1972, it is located in Shensi, a few hundred miles from the nearest Tibetan population. The underlying purpose of such schools is the acculturation of the leaders—not to turn them into Hans but to train them as Communists and make them feel like an integral part of a multiethnic China.[56] Through such means as these it has been possible to recruit qualified minority people into the Community party, albeit in modest numbers.[57] In Tibet, which generally has been the slowest area to develop politically, Party branches at the commune level[58] have been established in a majority of cases.[59] Thus, the political infrastructure, vital both for subintegration and subcontinental integration, is slowly being constructed.

It is in the economy that development among national minorities has been most troublesome for the Chinese Communists. Recognition of the "special characteristics" of these people implied to some that the transformation to socialism could be delayed almost indefinitely. It also meant that those groups accustomed to a nomadic life and animal husbandry need not settle down in communes and diversify their economies. Not only was this offensive to Maoist ideologues, but it also meant that large areas of the nation would remain economically undeveloped, which was incompatable with the homogeneity requirement of Maoist integration. Thus, pressure began mounting in the late 1950s to bring the socioeconomic institutions of at least some of the national minorities into line with those of the Han people. The Mongol herdsmen, in particular, were required to form agricultural coopera-

[54] On education among the Hani of Yunnan, see *JMJP*, September 25, 1971, FBIS I, October 20, 1971 p. B-5.

[55] *New York Times*, July 31, 1972. See also, *CSM*, August 31, 1972.

[56] The opening of the Tibet Nationality College was reported by Lhasa radio, March 31, 1972, FBIS I, April 5, 1972, p. H-1 f.

[57] In the five autonomous regions and Yunnan, 143,000 members of minority nationalities were recruited into the Party between 1969 and 1973. NCNA, June 29, 1973, FBIS I, July 6, 1973, p. B-3.

[58] I.e. the *hsiang*. In many instances no communes had been established.

[59] T'ien Pao (Tibet Party Secretary), "Persist in Chairman Mao's Line of Party-Building," Lhasa radio, July 1, 1973, FBIS I, July 3, 1973, pp. E-1–E-5.

tives.⁶⁰ In some other areas, Han and minority peoples living in proximity were integrated into a single commune. They were expected to exchange labor at different times of year according to the different needs of the dissimilar economies, and increase their consumption of each other's produce (milk by the Han; grain by the minorities, and so on). As elsewhere in China, this kind of total integration at the commune level was not very successful. In the case of ethnically mixed communes, such attempts to homogenize the populations required a change of life-style on the part of all which was certain to be unpopular. In fact, the effort was not pressed widely, and most minority people's were probably little touched by the original commune movement.⁶¹

In 1963 there began a new drive to introduce socialism among China's ethnic minorities. No longer were the special characteristics of these peoples acknowledged. Rather, their problems were declared to be part of class struggle, and resistance to change was seen simply as an effort of the privileged classes to remain in power. As Chou En-lai told the National People's Congress in 1964,

> If the peoples of our country's various minority nationalities are to achieve their complete liberation, they must rise in revolution under the leadership of the Communist party. They must conduct and accomplish not only the democratic revolution [i.e., eliminate the "feudal" ruling class] but also the socialist revolution [i.e. eliminate the bourgeoisie], and carry them out to the end.⁶²

Chou clearly was dissatisfied with the backward economic and political condition of most of the minority nationalities. With the unhappy Great Leap Forward a not-too-distant memory, however, there was great resistance to the new campaign. When the Cultural Revolution got under way in China proper, even the *leaders* of the autonomous regions—all of impeccable Chinese Communist credentials—sought to have the minorities spared. These efforts were unavailing, and nearly all the leaders were purged (although some later returned to office). Intensive drives were waged against minority institutions, not only

---

⁶⁰ During the Great Leap Forward the number of households in APCs increased to 85 percent. June Dryer, "Inner Mongolia: The Purge of Ulanfu," *CS*, November 15, 1968, p. 5.

⁶¹ A description of such a fully integrated multi-ethnic commune in Lotu County, Ch'inghai Province, was described in an article in *JMJP*, September 13, 1958. Much of the article is translated in Schurmann, pp. 484 f.

⁶² George Moseley, "China's Fresh Approach to the National Minority Question," *CQ*, October 1965, p. 15. Translation revised.

those related to politics and production, but also the usually immune aspects of culture such as religion, art, and even dress.

Such extreme policies were carried into the Cultural Revolution. Since then relative moderation has usually prevailed, but the drive to achieve socialism and to make the minorities a more integrated part of the Chinese nation has continued. The more "advanced" regions, such as Inner Mongolia, have seen considerable industrialization among the minorities. In 1972 it was reported that both heavy and light industry were widespread in the region, and that among the workers and staff in such enterprises were 52,600 minority people. (Most of the population of Inner Mongolia is actually Han.) A sort of "affirmative action" program had been introduced to train minority workers for these jobs, so that Mongols now had a better share of technical and management jobs.[63] In other minority areas energy resources were developed, bringing important changes to the people's life-styles.[64] Communes have been introduced for the first time in many minority areas, although progress is often slow. Tibet, which had 130 communes on the eve of the Cultural Revolution, had in 1970 only 666 (34 percent of the townships). Persuading Tibetan nomads to settle down in permanent villages was obviously difficult, because of the inevitable restrictions on individual freedom. Nonetheless, there have been glowing reports of various successes.

> Instead of engaging in one undertaking, many communes are gradually developing a diversified economy of agriculture, forestry, livestock breeding, sideline occupations, and fishery. They are going in for transport, collecting medicinal herbs, fishing and hunting, and busily preparing to run industrial and handicraft shops.... The growth of the people's communes in the Tibet region has dealt powerful blows at the handful of class enemies who engaged in sabotage activities.[65]

Inasmuch as achieving ethnic homogeneity was now defined as part of the class struggle, any people who opposed Sinification were relegated to the category of class enemies.[66]

Although the 1975 Constitution reaffirmed national autonomy as an

[63] NCNA, April 27, 1972, FBIS I, April 28, 1972, p. F-2.
[64] E.g., NCNA January 30, 1972, FBIS I, February 8, 1972, pp. E-5 f. (Hydroelectric plants among the nationalities of Yunnan Province.)
[65] PR, July 31, 1970, p. 31.
[66] For an enthusiastic account of a Tibetan commune, see "Commune on the Tibetan Plateau," PR, July 13, 1973, pp. 14–17. A new Aini commune in Yunnan is described in JMJP, September 25, 1971, p. 4, FBIS I, October 20, 1971, p. B-5.

242   SEVEN: *Homogeneity*

unalienable right of ethnic minorities (Art. 4), the outlook does not appear favorable for the survival of distinctive national cultures within China. There is some evidence that the population of the more un-Chinese minorities is declining.[67] True, the largest minority, the Chuang, is increasing in numbers.[68] But these people are the most Sinified of the major minorities, and are becoming more so, a trend promoted in the education system. Officials insist that the use of the Chinese language in schools is "in accordance with the needs of the people," and that realistically speaking the disappearance of the local tongue is inevitable.[69] So it may be some day in the cases of all the nationalities, with the realization of the dream of complete ethnic homogeneity which Mao Tse-tung expressed in 1968: "Very soon China won't have either Manchus, nor Mongols, nor Tibetans—they will all have become Chinese."[70]

A word should also be said about the effort to build a more homogeneous society in terms of age. There are at least two problems here. First, a common feature of modernizing societies is the neglect of older citizens, whose old-fashioned skills are no longer needed, and who have stopped being taken care of by the extended family. In China's urban areas today, adequate welfare facilities are provided. (In the countryside such services are not so necessary because the traditional family structure is largely intact.)

The second problem concerns the authority structure. Maturing regimes tend to be dominated by elders. One might expect this to be particularly so in China, where traditionally seniority reigned supreme (even taking priority over sex). In such situations, there is always a danger that the leadership will be too concerned with old issues, and out of touch with emerging ones. When they came to power, the Communists placed the accent upon youth, but the average age of people in leadership organs tended to increase with the passage of time. In recent years emphasis has been placed upon having all ages represented in leadership bodies, avoiding the twin evils of their domination by the entrenched elder statesmen, or by the adaptable

---

[67] This is an impression; precise statistics are unavailable. Birth control is not promoted in sparsely populated regions. Claude Julien, *Le Monde,* February 6–7, 1972, p. 3, FBIS I. February 9, 1972, p. B-4.

[68] According to an Agence France-Press dispatch, the number of Chuang increased from seven to ten million between 1964 and 1973. *New York Times,* October 28, 1973.

[69] *New York Times,* July 15, 1973.

[70] *CSM,* October 4, 1968.

and malleable youngsters of uncertain revolutionary steadfastness.[71] As a means of promoting this balance, a "three-in-one" quota system has been widely promoted.[72] Pursuant to this principle, leading bodies are to be comprised of representatives from young, middle-aged, and older people. Enthused a writer in *Red Flag*:

> The three-in-one combination of the old, middle-aged, and the young offers a fine condition for giving full play to the revolutionary enthusiasm of the revolutionary cadres and continuing to strengthen the fighting capability of leading groups at all levels. Following the principle of combining the old, the middle-aged, and the young, we can continuously absorb large numbers of outstanding young cadres into the leading posts, instill new blood into the leading groups at all levels, and invigorate them. When these outstanding young people are combined with veteran cadres who have been for a long time tempered in revolutionary struggle, and with the middle-aged cadres who have possessed certain characteristics of the veteran and the new cadres, their strong points can be pooled. They can learn from each other, overcome their own weaknesses by acquiring others' strong points and unite as one for the common cause.[73]

In a society dominated first by aging mandarins and matriarchs, then youthful guerrillas, and later by septuagenarian veterans of the revolution, this attempt to achieve intergenerational homogeneity is of major significance. As with all of the other efforts to achieve homogeneity, however, it has not gone unopposed.

Is social homogeneity essential to social integration? As we noted earlier, according to the common Western conception of integration it is not, for integration thus conceived is the complementary interaction of dissimilar units. But according to the Maoist conception, the optimum form of integration is subintegration—self-sufficiency at the local level. Some efficiency is admittedly lost through the lack of

---

[71] On the question of revolutionary sentiment among youth, and efforts to improve methods of political socialization, see Ronald N. Montaperto, "The Maoist Approach," *POC*, September 1973, pp. 51–63. (Accompanied by a similar article on the Soviet Union by Joel Schwartz.)

[72] See Appendices, Party Constitution, Art. 5, and National Constitution, Art. 11.

[73] Yun Lan, "A Strategic Measure for Consolidating the Dictatorship of the Proletariat," *HC*, 1973, no. 12, FBIS I, December 6, 1973, p. B-2. On various age groups, see Tsien Tche-hao, "Législation sur l'enfance et la vieillesse," *NC*, February 1975, pp. 26–32.

regional specialization. To offset this, the human resources of a locality must be utilized to the utmost; nothing can afford to be lost through discrimination against individuals on grounds of race, sex, age, and so forth. Thus, social equality is a precondition of effective subintegration. Homogeneity, however, implies a bit more than equality. It assumes a degree of cultural similarity on a subcontinental basis to hold the nation—the *Chinese* nation—together. Other nations may be held together by economic dependence, law, or police apparatus. China does not wish to rely upon these, but rather upon a common culture. Thus it is important for no part of China to be too dissimilar from any other part, either in terms of its social system, standard of living, political attitudes, or general culture.

Clearly, China has a long way to go in these respects. Not only are the various kinds of equality we have discussed some distance from being achieved, but in certain respects the various integration models may militate *against* equality. Subintegration makes no provision for equality from one region to another. Subcontinental integration often produces concentrated wealth in the more industrial regions. Some blend of these two integrative models may help avoid social disparities. Certainly to eliminate the great discrepancies between workers and farmers, betweeen urban and rural, and between mental and manual labor, Mao Tse-tung's successors will have to do more than inherit his skepticism of Western-style modernization. To bring the benefits of the revolution to all Chinese will require the development of sophisticated and popular methods for blending cultures and spreading wealth.

EIGHT

External Politics

> *On the eastern mountain tigers eat men;*
> *On the western mountain tigers eat men too.*
>
> CHINESE PROVERB

> *The present international situation is characterized by great disorder on earth. The winds sweeping through the tower herald a rising storm in the mountains.... Relaxation is a temporary and superficial phenomenon, and great disorder will continue. This is a good thing.... It throws the enemies into confusion and causes division among them, while it arouses and tempers the people.*[1]
>
> *Whether war gives rise to revolution or revolution prevents war, in either case the international situation will develop in a direction favorable to the people, and the future of the world will be bright.*[2]
>
> CHOU EN-LAI

DOMESTIC POLITICS and external politics are probably never unrelated, and in countries with explicit ideologies an effort is usually made to accommodate all politics within a single ideological frame-

On the pre-twentieth-century history of Chinese international relations, see Fairbank, Chinese World Order. For the foreign policy of the People's Republic, see Gittings; H. Hinton; Ojha; Richer; Simmonds; and Van Ness.

[1] Chou En-lai, Address to the Tenth Party Congress, August 1973. Quoted in FEER, October 1, 1973.
[2] Chou En-lai, Address to the National People's Congress, January 13, 1975. New York Times, January 21, 1975.

EIGHT: *External Politics*

work. In this chapter we shall explore various aspects of Chinese foreign policy and international conduct, with a view to learning how these relate to general politics and values, and how the themes which we have been developing are relevant to China's external politics. We shall not stress the content of foreign policy[3] so much as style, general goals, and world view.

In foreign relations, even more than in domestic politics, the People's Republic of China usually speaks with one voice. If relations with other nations—particularly the Soviet Union and the United States—have caused some misgivings, matters of policy have nonetheless been given universal lip service, with any controversies aired in private. In this chapter, therefore, we shall take the "national actor" approach to external politics. Although this view does not lead us to every possible insight into the subject, it does help us focus upon China's *actual* foreign policy, as distinguished from the "might have beens" had the desires of dissidents (or foreign enemies' fears) been realized.

Values and Interests

Even within the "national actor" approach, we still have a variety of methods and analytical frameworks from which to choose. For example, one must consider what type of information to rely upon. If we were to emphasize government publications to the exclusion of other materials, this might cause us to overstress the influence of official norms (ideology) in international conduct. Indeed, it has been the tendency of many observers, including government analysts in the United States, to have an exaggerated view of the role that ideology plays in China's policymaking. Presidential adviser Henry A. Kissinger once remarked, "We recognize that the People's Republic is led by highly principled men whose principles are diametrically opposed to ours."[4] Certainly the Marxist convictions of these men do shape their attitudes and influence their conduct, but we must acknowledge that this leaves unstated what is meant by *Marxist* and the degree of determination to impose the creed upon others. Even if such problems did not exist, much of China's conduct would be difficult to explain if analyzed only in the context of the pursuit of Communist goals. For "ideological fanatics," the activities of the Chinese in the non-Communist world have been noted for remarkable restraint, especially

---

[3] On this, see the works cited in this chapter's lead footnote.
[4] *CSM*, December 2, 1971.

toward weak, defenseless neighbors. Washington's miscalculations concerning the Vietnam situation were based upon misconceptions in this connection. It was the view of President Lyndon Johnson's policy-makers like William Bundy that "Communist ideology as such is the single most vital element in dealing with present-day China. . . . Because of that ideology Peiping's[5] assertiveness is greatly strengthened, and extended to virtually every contiguous area and indeed beyond, down to Southeast Asia all the way down to Indonesia, to Tibet and at least to the point of wishing to neutralize a permanently weakened India."[6] Tragedy might have been avoided in Indochina if policy-makers had realized that China's orthodox national interests can be as important a determinant of her international conduct as ideological considerations.

While national interest is often difficult to define, and a less objective concept than it might first appear, there are a number of helpful, even scientific, ways of determining its scope. In the case of China, there are "controls" available to enable us to determine the probable national interests were the nation ruled by a non-Communist government. Such controls are rarely available in real politics, but the Republic of China on Formosa serves as our basis for comparison. Though staunchly anti-Communist, it is remarkable that Taipei's conception of China's national interest shows many similarities to Peking's. Both claim Tibet (to which Bundy referred) as part of China, for example. Both governments once relied upon short-lived ententes with the great northerly neighbor, Soviet Russia.[7] And today, both insist that there is only one China, of which Formosa is a part.

Because the two governments now find themselves in very dissimilar situations, however, even discounting ideology we could not expect their conduct to be identical. But where the Taipei-Peking analogy fails, history may come to the rescue. Not only did the Kuomintang once rule the mainland, but China, as an ancient empire, has seen many governments and been organized around a number of different ideologies—the law-and-order philosophy of the ancient Legalist school, then Confucianism, and in modern times republicanism and communism. Each epoch saw some expansionist tendencies or at least pretensions. Sometimes the nation was led by conquering warriors, such as Ch'in Shih Huang-ti, who in the third century B.C. brought most of what has since been China proper under his rule, and

[5] Peking.
[6] William P. Bundy, "The United States and Asia," in Buchan, p. 17.
[7] See Malraux, p. 452.

Emperor Ch'ien Lung, the eighteenth-century terror of many nations. At other times China has been pacifist, and even defeatist, as during the thirteenth century, when the nation passively waited to be overrun by the Mongols.

On the spectrum defined by these extremes, China's present rulers probably lie somewhere near the middle. They appear determined to bring under their control regions on the nation's periphery which have not clearly established themselves as independent entities under international law (Tibet, Formosa), but they show no inclination to overrun any foreign territory.[8] This is not to say that China is unconcerned about what happens abroad; indeed, China is very sensitive about developments among its neighbors—states that seem to fall into three categories: friends, neutrals, and enemies.

China's relations with adjacent *allies* are best understood in historical-national interest terms, for such countries are considered buffer states. Traditionally, China sought to surround itself with vassals to act as barriers against the more distant and less "civilized" nations. This system manifested itself in tributary terms; neighbors such as Korea and Vietnam recognized the Chinese emperor as the Son of Heaven with authority over all under heaven. China assumed responsibility for defending them against any enemies, but generally avoided direct involvement in domestic politics. Of course, the rules were occasionally broken, and the system sometimes malfunctioned because participants failed to live up to their responsibilities. Before the last Jurchen ruler was overrun by the Mongols in 1234, for example, he appealed to China for help, in these words: "We are to you as the lips are to the teeth; when the lips are gone, the teeth will feel the cold."[9] Chinese failure to heed the request led to ultimate disaster for both

---

[8] Chinese military pressure against neighbors has been rare. In the various instances of borderlands claimed by Chinese but occupied by another state, Chinese troops were sent to do battle in only two—northern India and Chen-pao (Domanski) Island in the Ussuri River. In these instances, China's legal case was quite strong. The islands of Quemoy and Matsu, which have been subjected to shelling, are similar cases. As for Formosa and the Pescadores, the legal and political issues are more complicated. Each Chinese government insists that the islands belong to "China"—*its* China. However, the issue generally stressed by Peking is simply that U.S. troops must be withdrawn. For a significant diplomatic statement, see NCNA, November 26, 1968, FBIS I, November 26, 1968, p. A-1.

In 1974 China expelled South Vietnamese (ARVN) forces from the Paracel (Hsi-sha) Islands in the South China Sea. These islands (and others in the region) are claimed by various countries, including the Republic of China. See Seymour, "Sovereignty."

[9] FitzGerald, p. 434.

states, but the lesson was permanently implanted upon the national memory.[10]

On the other hand, it was not unknown for China to become involved in the internal politics of a subordinate state. This was sometimes difficult to avoid, because the tributary relationship was, strictly speaking, between rulers, not between states. When the local ruler encountered domestic political challenge, his natural inclination was to turn to the Chinese emperor for support. In the late 1780s, for example, such a situation arose in Vietnam during an episode known as the Tayson Rebellion. Although the Chinese field command continually supplied optimistic estimates of the prospects of the military commitment, the relative political strength of the rebels rendered the Chinese position untenable. Unfortunately, by the time the home government realized this and sought to extricate itself from the conflict, events had moved beyond Peking's control.[11] Small wonder that the error has not been committed more frequently during the last thousand years. It is possible that such lessons as that learned from the Tayson affair influence Peking's conduct to this day. China appears quite satisfied with such compliant neighbors as Vietnam and North Korea; the costs of still greater subordination outweigh any possible benefits, for the primary requirement of security has already been met.

In fact, subordination may not be necessary at all if a neighbor is truly *neutral* and presents no strategic threat to China either through its activities or its alliances. Under such circumstances the People's Republic generally maintains cordial or at least "correct" relations with it. The immediate neighbors which have fallen into this category have been Burma and Afghanistan, and (less consistently) Pakistan and Laos.

Although China's relations with all of these small contiguous neighbors have been generally tranquil, since the late 1950s relations with the three *major neighbors* have been another story. The reasons in each case are very different. With India, the operative factor has been the boundary dispute.[12] There can be no doubt that China has genuinely believed that its claim to the disputed Aksai Chin and eastern Tibet-Indian frontier regions is legitimate. Possession of Aksai Chin, further-

---

[10] E.g., *New York Times*, February 15, 1971, quoting the same "lips and teeth" metaphor in reference to Laos.

[11] China's involvement in Vietnam on this occasion in many ways parallels America's adventure there in the 1960s. For example, the prisoner of war issue made extrication difficult.

[12] See Maxwell.

more, has been deemed necessary to China's security, because through it runs the major route between China's two "autonomous regions" of Sinkiang and Tibet. There are, of course, other elements underlying the antagonisms between the two nations, but many of these, such as the differing political systems, existed during the untroubled 1950s. It was the border question which brought the two to war in 1962, and has clouded their relations ever since.

To the east China faces Japan, toward whom preliberation experience is often the determining factor underlying Chinese policy. Many times was China victimized by Japanese imperialism—most notably in the Sino-Japanese wars of 1895 and 1931–45.[13] In view of this history, it is small wonder that China's leaders look across the East China Sea with apprehension.[14] Already the world's third largest economy, and apparently bent on rearming, Japan has sometimes appeared to China to be readying herself to replay her former role as conqueror in East Asia. However unrealistic these fears may seem to us in view of Japan's pacifism and devotion to internal development, it is important to understand their basis. Just as the aggressors of the 1930s were sharply etched on the minds of America's leaders of the 1960s, causing them to embark upon anachronistic adventures in Southeast Asia, so are some Chinese leaders unreasonably burdened by ancient traumas. For both China and Japan, the hope is for the emergence of younger leaders whose vision will not be distorted by such memories.

We have been saying that in these cases Peking's perceptions of her national interest, whether realistic or otherwise, determine her policies toward her neighbors. Have we gone too far in dismissing ideology as a determinant of external politics? Are not India and Japan both bourgeois democracies, the very antithesis of every principle for which the Chinese Communists stand? The answer is that they are, and that this facilitates editorial writing in *People's Daily*. It does not, however, necessarily determine the selection of enemies and friends. Friend Pakistan is even less progressive than enemy India, and with Japan, Chinese sensitivities have been more reactive to militarism than capitalism. There are, however, situations in which ideological considerations play a major role in influencing Peking's stance. This

---

[13] Also unforgotten are the Japanese attempt to invade Korea and China in the late sixteenth century, and the Twenty-one Demands of 1915.

[14] Peking has complained about Japanese "predatory trade" with Southeast Asia, citing favorable trade balances, and so on. NCNA, Febraury 15, 1973, FBIS I, February 16, 1972, p. A-1.

concerns China's relations with two groups of countries, the Soviet bloc, and (to a lesser extent) nonneighbor, third-world nations.

Relations among Socialist States

Inasmuch as the Soviet Union is an immediate neighbor of China, it would be surprising if there were no national interest considerations in the relations between the two countries. When one surveys the long history of interaction between these giants, one is struck by how rarely their interests dovetailed. However, we should make an analytical distinction among three periods. First, there was the epoch prior to the nineteenth century, when the two nations were not substantially adjacent. True, there was a partially defined common boundary (fixed about 600 miles north of China's present northern border), but it was largely academic, being in regions where neither side manifested any presence. It was not until the two nations had filled out their land masses that they came into direct confrontation. In the meantime, central Asian history had been played out largely at the expense of the nations between Russia and China. The Manchu rulers of China, until the nineteenth century more martial than typical dynasties, rivaled the Muscovite tsars in imperialistic zeal. For example, in the late 1750s Ch'ing armies carried out a genocidal war against the Dzungars, thus bringing the northern part of what is now Sinkiang permanently within the empire.

In another century the territorial spoils were exhausted, and no longer could Russia and China expand in each other's direction at the expense of third parties. During this second period—the nineteenth and first half of the twentieth century—China was the weaker power and was obliged to make major territorial concessions to Russia.[15] But by 1949, with China unified and on the road to reconstruction, the USSR found her less vulnerable. Perhaps Stalin foresaw this situation, and attempted (as Mao Tse-tung claimed) to "prevent the Chinese revolution."[16] If he failed in this, Stalin nonetheless attempted to retain

[15] The boundary between Manchuria and Siberia was fixed along the Argun and Udi rivers in an agreement signed at Nerchinsk in 1689. In 1727 a second agreement established the boundary to the west of the Argun (i.e., between Mongolia and Siberia). The line ran just south of Kiakhta where the treaty was signed). The lands north of the Amur and east of the Ussuri were lost in the Treaty of Aigun (1858), and Mongolia was given up in 1945. As a result, China today is only about three-fourths her eighteenth-century size.

[16] Mao Tse-tung, Speech at the Tenth Plenary Session of the Eighth CPC Central Committee, September 24, 1962, in CLG, Winter 1968–69, p. 88.

economic privileges in Manchuria and Sinkiang. Ultimately these had to be relinquished. Thus, the third period of Sino-Russian relations has been distinguished by China's ability to resist Soviet pressure.

Because of China's renewed power, the two nations have found themselves at a standoff. In terms of material and strategic interests, it was believed in the 1950s that nothing was to be gained by renewed conflict. Under this circumstance, one might have expected that an era of harmony between the Soviet Union and China would ensue. As it happened, the 1950s were but a lull before perhaps the stormiest period in the history of their relations. Given the apparent absence of major tangible grievances, the presumed advantages of economic integration, and the common commitment to Marxism-Leninism, why did not Sino-Soviet relations develop along, say, the U.S.-Canadian pattern? The answer is that these assumptions (once widely held by the participants and foreign observers) were unrealistic. By 1960 the Chinese concluded that in terms of their material interests, they had little to gain and much to lose through participation in an integrated Soviet bloc. And in the all-important matter of ideology, the bitter polemics of the years that followed revealed that the Soviet and Chinese versions of the canon were irreconcilable.

To begin with, it turned out that Mao and the Kremlin had very different notions about the organization of the international community. We discussed earlier Maoist attitudes toward subcontinental integration, and saw how, generally speaking, integration at the lower-levels is considered preferable to higher-level integration. If we examine the attitude toward international, or macrointegration, we find that the pattern and reasoning still hold. If it is deemed desirable for the commune to be self-sufficient, it is imperative that the nation not be dependent upon any foreign country. Here the Chinese part ways with Western economists who emphasize the benefits of international integration. According to the theory of comparative advantage, products should be produced where they can be made most cheaply. This principle is the basis for common markets,[17] including the Soviet-dominated COMECON, which China has not only declined to join but has roundly condemned.

> The Soviet revisionist renegade clique has again and again ballyhooed that "specialization and cooperation in production" is a "higher form of socialist division of labor" which can "accelerate socialist construc-

[17] Peking does approve of the European Common Market (probably for tactical reasons). See *New York Times,* August 1, 1971, p. 8.

tion." But a mass of facts shows that what the Soviet revisionists are advocating is really the turning of other member countries of COMECON into *colonies* by opposing the independent development of their national economies.

The economies of Mongolia and eastern Europe are seen as having suffered "lopsided development," in some cases being relegated to the status of permanent suppliers of raw materials or labor-intensive products for the more advanced Soviet economy.[18]

There is validity to such criticisms of COMECON, but the intensity of Chinese hostility to international economic cooperation must be understood also in terms of China's own experience as part of an international economy between the mid-nineteenth and mid-twentieth centuries. Although the oppression argument may have been somewhat overdrawn (as one economist has pointed out),[19] the unhappy experience of that period underlay the thinking of the Chinese leaders during the abortive effort at economic cooperation with the Soviet Union.[20] When one recalls that throughout Chinese history legitimate foreign trade was allowed to exist only on a very limited scale, and usually had to be disguised as "tribute," one suspects that attitudes toward trade today are in no small measure a function of national pride, and that China might be inclined to reject common market arrangements even if they were equitable.

So the difficulties between China and Russia have not been fundamentally a matter of economics. Rather, the schism has been produced by fundamental value differences, or differing interpretations about what communism is all about. The very title of a seminal statement of the Chinese position, "On Khrushchev's Phoney Communism and Its Historical Lessons for the World,"[21] suggests that the dispute concerned the nature of communism, and also that this question transcended Sino-Soviet relations. Both of these points require elaboration. First, why did Mao consider Soviet communism "phoney"? The answer is summarized in the label which detractors regularly apply to it, namely *modern revisionism*. Communism has been "revised" to make it more compatable with *modernization*. Soviet leaders long ago abandoned the atavistic or primitive communal aspects of communism,

[18] *CLG*, Fall 1969, p. 45.
[19] Chi-ming Hou, "The Oppression Argument on Foreign Investment in China, 1895–1937," *JAS*, August 1961, pp. 435–48.
[20] Comparisons are made even between COMECON and Japan's World War II "Greater East Asia Co-Prosperity Sphere." *CLG*, Fall 1969, p. 49.
[21] *PR*, July 17, 1964.

and ceased identifying with Marx's yearning for simpler, more "whole," less alienating social environment.[22] Instead, they have selected those parts of the writings of Marx and Lenin which are compatible with a more differentiated, role-specialized, structured, and even stratified society. It was this heresy on the part of both Soviet leaders and many men holding power in China which Mao undertook to expose, in the hope that it would not be repeated elsewhere.

This suggests that during the third period (since 1949) there has been an indeterminist quality about Sino-Soviet relations. And indeed, although the alliance of the 1950s and the conflict of the 1960s were viewed as natural and inevitable by many observers,[23] both developments were matters of choice, based in large measure on values and psychological needs. At first, the alliance provided the People's Republic with a desired *sense* of security, and acceptance into the Communist community provided legitimacy which Western governments sought to deny Peking by withholding diplomatic recognition. Financial credits and technical assistance were indeed useful, but on hindsight these were probably not essential. Indeed, some of the Soviet-backed projects, such as the great San-men Dam on the Yellow River, were reportedly of poor design and later had to be reconstructed by the Chinese alone.[24] In 1960, then, not only was the dispensibility of the alliance quite apparent, but the Chinese decided that it was essential to unburden themselves of their financial indebtedness and psychological reliance upon the Soviet Union.[25]

---

[22] See chap. 7.

[23] Karl Deutsch (*Nationalism*, p. 4) maintains that the split between the two nations could have been predicted on the basis of his communications theory. The split was inevitable, he says, in view of the culture gap and economic inequality. More recently, Simmonds (p. 177) argues that with one state developed and industrialized, and the other underdeveloped and agrarian, a falling out was inevitable. However, one could just as well argue that the disparate natures of the two would lead to complementation. Thus, it is not surprising that during the 1950s Westerners took at face value the solidarity of the bloc. After all, in 1954 Mao insisted that "the interests of the Soviet Union will never conflict with the interests of China's national liberation and there will always be unity between them. I regard this point as absolutely beyond doubt." *SW*, 2:51.

[24] On San-men Dam, see Theodore Shabad's account, *New York Times*, January 19, 1975.

[25] Mao may have accepted foreign aid with some reluctance, as he had long believed in self-reliance. In 1949 he had said that China should reconstruct herself without relying on aid. He seemed to imply that foreign aid would soften and corrupt the country and undermine the revolution. Rather than "beg alms," he said in 1949, the Chinese would do better to work hard, live a spartan existence, and reject "sugar-coated bullets." Eventually, this would lead to "a better life than that in most imperialist countries." *SW*, 4:374.

Although there are genuine strategic and territorial sources of Sino-Soviet tension,[26] this fact does not undermine our thesis that the dispute is in large measure ideological. The border dispute, for example, may have erupted in severe clashes, but the Chinese do not appear seriously to seek restoration of the lost territories. Rather, they often seem primarily intent upon demonstrating that the Soviet Union has strayed from socialism and that its reversion to capitalism has led it to behave imperialistically. The Chinese have kept the issue alive by insisting that Soviet troops be withdrawn from the disputed regions, a demand to which the Russians could never accede.

Indeed, since the Cultural Revolution, questions of prototypicality have been of concern in China's relations with other Communist countries. China has been very cautious in acknowledging states as "socialist." Before so endorsing them (which is to say crediting them with being properly Marxist), Peking requires that such states be in some manner ideologically acceptable. Thus, in the mid-1970s the only four "socialist" countries were Albania, which echoed Maoist ideas and (to a lesser extent) programs, Rumania, which opposed certain features of revisionism and international integration, North Korea, and Vietnam, the first being militant in word if not deed, and the second, militant in deed if not word.

China as a Model

Although it has made a general practice of restricting military and economic engagement to a minimum, China has not been uninvolved in third-world affairs. The nature of the involvement which China has emphasized may be termed cultural in the broadest sense. As we observed in chapter 1, China has practiced cultural macrointegration throughout her long history. Today, likewise, China has borrowed selectively from abroad (e.g., Marxism-Leninism), created a new synthesis, and now holds the result up for others to emulate. The content of that model is the social and political system which has been the subject of this book. Precisely what form of the model others are to emulate depends upon the stage of their revolution. In a country dominated by "feudalism" or any form of colonialism, the masses are advised to organize a popular guerrilla movement and, using the countryside as a base, overthrow the old order and set up a "new

[26] Following the Indochina wars, Sino-Soviet competition in Southeast Asia intensified. In 1975 *JMJP* accused the Soviets of having "honey on their lips and murder in their hearts," and of trying to "swallow Southeast Asia in a single gulp." *New York Times,* July 11, 1975.

democracy."[27] This process is seen as inevitably involving violence; any attempt to effect the transition peacefully is doomed to failure, as the Chilean case demonstrates.[28] During both the people's war and the new democratic periods, the "vanguard of the proletariat" (probably a Communist party) is dominant, but it at least nominally shares power with bourgeois elements, and some capitalist arrangements may continue to exist. It is important, however, that socialism gradually replace capitalism, and that steady progress be made toward one-class rule. The Chinese and Soviet experiences illustrate some of the pitfalls to be avoided. The greatest danger is that in the party and in government, complacency may replace revolutionary zeal, with revisionism ensuing.

It is also important that national revolutions be autochthonous, and that help from abroad be more political than material. China considers that its proletarian internationalist responsibility is limited, and only under the most extraordinary circumstances will China provide substantial material support for a foreign revolution.[29] Normally, acceptance of foreign support by insurgents would be counterproductive in terms of its costs in local political support and perhaps long-term economic and geopolitical obligations. Nor should such external assistance be necessary, for victory of revolution over reaction is seen as inevitable. "Although there will be setbacks in the process, this law is as certain as that the waters of the Yangtze will return to the sea."[30]

This is the formula for the "third world," as it is known in the West, or the "first intermediate zone" in Maoist terminology.[31] No formula

[27] For an account of Chinese revolutionary procedures *in loco*, see Johnson, *Peasant Nationalism*. Johnson has been criticized for giving too much attribution of the outcome to Japanese imperialism. See Martin Bernal, "Was Chinese Communism Inevitable?," *NYRB*, December 3, 1970, pp. 43–47.

[28] See Ch'iao Kuan-hua's remarks to the United Nations General Assembly, *PR*, October 5, 1973, or FBIS I, October 4, 1973, p. A-4.

[29] The only important example is the Vietnam War, which is a special case by virtue of geography. Still, China supplied only about one-tenth of the imported material.

[30] *CLG*, Fall 1969, p. 10. Some poetic license has been taken in quoting this line in the context of self-reliance. Actually, there are elements of revisionism in *KTTH*, from which this is taken. A few lines above the quoted passage it is asserted that "the might of the Soviet Union and China plays a crucial role" in revolutionary movements in the non-Communist world. This was written at a time when Mao's influence was at its nadir, and reflects the thinking of the Liuist countermodel.

[31] The notion that between the capitalist and socialist heartlands existed an intermediate zone was first alluded to by Mao in his interview with Anna Louise Strong in August 1946. See *CLG*, Fall 1969, p. 5. Later he elaborated on this subject, dividing the zone into two parts. "Talk with Members of the Japan Socialist Party," July 10, 1964, *CLG*, Fall 1969, pp. 34 f. The First International Zone comprises "Asia, Africa and Latin America." (See also note 32.)

appears to have been wrought concerning how socialist revolutions could occur in the developed capitalist world. Not only does *peaceful transition* not appear likely to the Chinese, but, because parliamentarianism and economism have so undermined the Marxist movements in these countries, *revolutions* are also unlikely. As Mao told André Malraux, revisionism might gain Western Communist party votes, "but it will make it lose teeth."[32] Looking at the world as a whole, we are provided only with the analogy of the Chinese revolution, which developed in the countryside and gradually enveloped the cities. In the future, the third world "countryside" is to surround the urbanized capitalist world and bring about its submission to revolutionary forces.[33] On the other hand, it is also said that even in the capitalist heartland, self-reliance and local initiative are the keys. Chou En-lai remarked to visiting American leftist students:

> Some of you friends have said that foreign experience cannot be mechanically brought over to your country. That's right. And Chairman Mao tells us that one must rely on one's own efforts. We cannot impose on you, nor can you just mechanically copy from us. . . . We have only our experience; we are not at all well acquainted with your situation. . . . Self-reliance proceeds from independence, and taking the initiative in your own hands.[34]

Likewise, China is disinclined to take upon itself the responsibility for purifying Russia and eastern Europe of revisionism. Although these countries' social, political, and economic systems have been sharply condemned, China has not spelled out a program for true believers in these lands.[35] Presumably, the Great Proletarian Cultural Revolution

---

[32] Malraux, p. 459. This remark was made in specific reference to the French Communist party.
There is some vagueness concerning the composition of the Second Intermediate Zone, but included are Canada, Japan, Europe, and Oceania. *CLG*, Fall 1969, p. 35. On the (only slight) possibility of peaceful transition to socialism, see "Outline of Views on the Question of Peaceful Transition," November 10, 1957, NCNA, September 6, 1963, *CB* 714, September 12, 1963, pp. 25 f. Concerning Japan, see Sheldon W. Simon, "China and Japan, Approach-Avoidance Relations," *CS*, January 7, 1972, pp. 4 f.

[33] See Lin Piao, "Long Live the Victory of People's War," *PR*, September 3, 1965. Although Lin was purged six years after the publication of this article, this analogy has not been repudiated.

[34] Text of interview in Committee of Concerned Asian Scholars, *China! Inside the People's Republic* (New York: Bantam, 1972). Quotation from p. 361. (An exchange with Paul Levine, whose interjection is deleted.)

[35] At one point China was claiming that there was an anti-Party "Stalin Group" active in the USSR, and it seemed to have Chinese endorsement. See *PR*, October 25, 1968.

has set the example, but this raises the question of whether or not a Mao-like leader would not be required. Perhaps such a movement need not be conducted by a charismatic figure, and Mao himself would probably insist that in the final analysis such movements must rely upon the consciousness of the masses. Whatever the answer, revisionism must be overthrown from within; it has never been suggested that this is a function of proletarian internationalism.

So Peking freely dispenses advice to the remainder of the world, but it is longer on rhetoric than on action. Each nation is expected to find its own road to socialism. What socialism *is* is defined in terms of the Chinese model. How it is attained depends upon the condition in which a nation finds itself. China believes that it has lit the way for the first intermediate zone, at least, but each nation is expected to carry its own revolutionary burdens.

The Primacy of Politics

By now it should be clear that China's international relations are more politicized than those of many other states. For some countries, like Japan, foreign policy is subordinated to economic considerations. For others (the Republic of China, and sometimes the United States) military considerations take precedence over politics. China, on the other hand, expects little economic or military return from external politics, for politics is almost an end in itself. This can be seen most clearly if we examine foreign *economic* relations.

Traditionally, China has placed little emphasis upon foreign trade. As Emperor Ch'ien Lung advised would-be British traders through George III,

> ... Our Celestial Empire possesses all things in prolific abundance and lacks no product within its own borders. There has therefore been no need to import the manufactures of outside barbarians in exchange for our own produce.[36]

Although Ch'ien Lung condescended to provide England certain alleged necessities which, in its "lonely remoteness," it lacked, international trade per se was not seen as basically in China's interest. As for imports, only if they came as tribute, and therefore served a political purpose, were they desirable.

Today too, China's foreign economic intercourse is very limited, accounting for only about 3 percent of the gross national product, or

[36] Quoted in Franz Schurmann and Orville Schell, *Imperial China* (New York: Vintage, 1967), pp. 108 f.

less than one-tenth of one percent of the world's international commerce. As in the past, commerce is an exceptional undertaking. Trade is often a response to momentary exigencies, as with the wheat imports from Canada, but even here politics is never pushed far into the background. It was not economically necessary for China to satisfy all of her needs from one distant source, but the diplomatic breakthrough which followed in the wake of commercial successes were of tremendous importance to China.[37]

An especially significant example of trade's political role can be found in the case of commerce between China and Japan.[38] The memorandum Trade Agreement drawn up with Japanese businessmen in 1971 stipulated that China would not trade with firms that traded with South Korea or Formosa. However, pragmatism in this case prevailed, and where China needed machinery available only from firms falling short of the political criteria, China purchased them anyway. As for Japanese businessmen visiting China, it has not been found practical to limit them to political sympathizers. As Chou En-lai told the leaders of one Japanese trade delegation, "In Japanese business circles, it would be difficult to find many leftists."[39] Indeed, cultivating relations with Japan's conservative businessmen gives China an excellent entrée into the ruling Liberal Democratic Party. Sino-Japanese trade, being more important to Japan than to China, became a lever with which China gained significant political advantage. In 1974, for example, Peking was able to force Tokyo to suspend commercial air transport arrangements with Taipei for one year—a costly step for Japan, and a political breakthrough for the People's Republic.[40]

It goes without saying that China's modest program of aid to foreign countries[41] is largely political. Although there is some economic benefit

[37] On Australia's reaction to being excluded from the wheat purchases, see *FEER*, October 2, 1971.

[38] Japan is China's most important trading partner, supplying 26 percent of China's imports in 1970, and taking about half as much in exports.

[39] *CS*, January 1972, p. 2.

[40] *New York Times*, September 30, 1974. The Tokyo-Taipei route had been Japan Air Lines' most profitable international run, serving 30,000 passengers a month. Far fewer people have been flying between Tokyo and Peking.

[41] With the exception of aid to Indochina, China's assistance has been largely of the nonmilitary variety, and is usually provided to established governments rather than emerging revolutionary forces. Only in rare instances and on a very small scale have the beneficiaries been insurgents. For them, "foreign aid is of secondary importance. Tiny rivulets flow on and on; there is no need for urgency. . . ." *KTTH*, April 25, 1961, *CLG*, Fall 1969, p. 16.

On China's foreign aid, see *FEER*, January 8, 1872; *New York Times*, October 25, 1970, and December 8, 1974.

for China (inasmuch as aid given by any country tends to "come home"), China's loan terms have generally been upon such generous terms (low interest or none at all) that politics must be the prime motive. In most instances such aid is given to established non-Communist governments who provide the People's Republic with political support in the United Nations and elsewhere.

Just as politics takes precedence over economics, so does it take precedence over *military* considerations. We know that in the late 1950s the Soviet Union pressured China to partially integrate, or at least coordinate, the armed forces of the two countries, and that Chinese resistance was a precipitating factor in the breakup of the bloc. Mao could brush off this combination of Russian generosity and intimidation because he believed that people (i.e. politics) were more important than weapons. After all, during the civil war the Red Army had outperformed better-equipped Kuomintang forces. Whether such reasoning is applicable in an era of nuclear-armed ICBMs may be problematic, but the perception is that even the United States is just as vulnerable as the Kuomintang was. As Mao said as early as 1946:

> The atom bomb is a paper tiger which the U.S. reactionaries use to scare people. It looks terrible, but in fact it isn't. Of course, the atom bomb is a weapon of mass slaughter, but the outcome of a war is decided by the people, not by one or two new types of weapons.... History will demonstrate that the American reactionaries, like all reactionaries, do not have much strength. In the United States there are others who are really strong—the American people.[42]

True, facing three nuclear powers (the Soviet Union, the United States, and potentially India) China has found it prudent to develop nuclear weapons and delivery systems. But China's ultimate weapon is probably the commune system, which would leave the country politically and economically viable after her cities had been wiped out.

There is yet another sense in which politics governs Chinese foreign relations, and that is that *internal* politics takes precedence over (and

---

[42] Mao Tse-tung, "Talk with Anna Louise Strong," *CLG*, Fall 1969, pp. 6 f. This attitude was recently reiterated by Chou En-lai, who, when asked if nuclear weapons increased a country's bargaining power, answered: "Only if the other country fears them. If the other country does not fear them, then nuclear weapons are not a deterrent, much less a decisive force in international struggles." Ross Terrill, "The 800,000,000: China and the World," *Atlantic Monthly*, January 1972, p. 45.

on occasion may actually determine) foreign policy. In other countries, particularly weak ones, domestic politics may operate in a rather tight framework circumscribed by international political and economic considerations. Conversely, a country's leaders may have such grandiose international ambitions, which they may be in a position to carry out with few internal restraints, that mobilization to meet external concerns will leave inadequate resources and attention committed to internal needs.[43] China, on the other hand, has traditionally relegated international politics to comparatively low priority, sometimes even in the face of imminent foreign invasion. The classic case was the Southern Sung dynasty. It was a period of high cultural attainments and impressive political and social development until 1279, when the country was overrun by the Mongols. Confrontation with the West in the nineteenth century saw a similar reluctance on the part of the Chinese to engage in battle. As one contemporary scholar said in the wake of the first Sino-Japanese war:

> Here everything is a part of history. All things dissolve in our mass. Conquerors lose their way in our yellow sea. Foreign armies are drowned in the flood of our descendants or crushed under the weight of our ancestors. The majestic cascades of our rivers of lives and the swelling succession of generations sweep them away.[44]

Again in the 1930s, Chiang Kai-shek was most reluctant to turn from his domestic foe and face the Japanese invaders.

For their part, the Communists have been somewhat more attentive regarding foreign military threats, as evidenced by their declaration of war on Japan in 1932, joining in the Korean War, and the more recent civil defense measures in many parts of the country.[45] The Korean conflict would appear to have been the only occasion since the establishment of the Chinese People's Republic when the Chinese lost the initiative and found themselves locked into an essentially exogenous matter. Even there, though, Peking retained a degree of flexibility by designating its troops "volunteers," which would have made it relatively easy to withdraw if the future developments dictated such a course. In any event, China has generally been successful in at least neutralizing the impact of external affairs on internal politics, and

---

[43] Examples have been the United States and Portugal, both of which took steps to correct this problem around 1974.
[44] Valéry. Translation slightly revised.
[45] On Peking's tunnels, see *New York Times*, April 15, 1973.

sometimes they have even been able to exploit foreign developments for domestic purposes.

This leads us to the sometimes exaggerated observation that Peking inflates its foreign enemies in order to marshal domestic support against opponents of the government. This technique is of only marginal value, because high-level opponents and fence-sitters are not impressed by contrived international crises, and the masses who may be more readily persuaded do not generally have much impact on central politics. Nevertheless, an enemy can be a useful thing to have at times. As *People's Daily* has stated:

> To have a ferocious enemy like U.S. imperialism glowering at us day and night will make us Chinese people always bear in mind the danger of war.... It will make us work harder to build a strong and prosperous country.[46]

Perhaps even more useful than alleged American hostility have been border clashes with major neighbors. The conflict with India in 1962 escalated just after the important Tenth Plenum of the Eighth Central Committee, and the 1969 battles with the Russians over Chen-pao Island came on the eve of the Party's Ninth Congress. Both may have been *timed* to enhance the position of Mao and Defense Minister Lin Piao, though this factor is insufficient to explain the events.

Although domestic politics generally takes precedence over external politics, foreign policy has on numerous occasions been a major issue within the Chinese leadership, and has become involved with domestic politics. One important instance was the decision to break with the Soviet Union, which entailed a rethinking of China's entire development strategy. The next major foreign policy question to arise was how to respond to the worsening situation in Vietnam in the mid-1960s. Here, the tie-in with internal politics concerned the role of the People's Liberation Armed Services. If the Vietnam War had escalated much more, China's security might have been threatened, requiring a military buildup. The problem was not that this would have enhanced the political power of the Armed Services (which was to happen anyway), but that the relatively apolitical professionals would have been in a position to recover the power that they had lost at the time of the dismissal of Defense Minister P'eng Teh-huai in 1959.[47] By now,

[46] *JMJP*, February 20, 1966, quoted in Simmonds, p. 2.
[47] For a discussion of the impact of the Vietnam War on China's internal politics, see Solomon, *Mao's Revolution*, pp. 464–74.

the army was becoming Mao's most promising instrument for waging revolution in China, the Party and government having been hopelessly "corrupted" by revisionist influences. War would require an *expert* army, and if Mao were to allow the reshaping of the army along non-Red lines, the impending Cultural Revolution could not have been carried out. Thus, the interrelatedness of internal and external politics as read by Maoists requires that foreign relations usually be subordinated to domestic political considerations.[48]

Communicating Requirements and Intentions

States cannot interact nonviolently without communicating among each other. Signals requiring transmission may concern minimum requirements, maximum wants, and negative demands (points where compromise is possible). While honesty may not always be present, by and large the statements emanating from a government, when properly interpreted, comprise a statement of the government's position. Studies have demonstrated that analysis of the verbal strategies of such nations as the United States and the Soviet Union is a meaningful and efficient way of exploring the behavior of such states.[49] Because arcane language may be used, a correct understanding of such communication requires skill, whether the analysis is conducted by detached scholars or statesmen-participants. Of course, it is helpful for the success of verbal strategy for the parties to express themselves in diplomatic language—

---

[48] During the Cultural Revolution the preoccupation with domestic politics was so great that external politics was often suspended. The tendency for the tumult of the Cultural Revolution to spill over into external affairs was, in general, kept in check except in places with large overseas Chinese communities (Burma, Hong Kong, Macao). When the Foreign Ministry came under pressure from the Red Guards, Foreign Minister Ch'en Yi told them to "go to Vietnam" if they wanted to wage revolution. Melvin Gurtov, "The Foreign Ministry and Foreign Affairs in the Chinese Cultural Revolution," in Robinson, *Cultural Revolution*, p. 326. Ch'en also defended others under fire, including his Soviet-educated vice foreign minister. "You may drag Hsu I-hsin to your struggle rallies during the day," Ch'en reportedly said, "but in the evening he will be my guest at dinner." *Report on Mainland China* (New York, Chinese [Nationalist] Information Service), January 20, 1972, p. 25.

It is widely believed that foreign policy reversals, caused in part by the excesses of the Cultural Revolution, resulted in a rethinking of foreign policy and an eventual moderation of China's attitude and activities vis à vis foreign countries. To the extent that the winding down of the Cultural Revolution can be attributed to the international situation, this would constitute an exception to our general rule regarding the primacy of internal politics.

[49] Thomas M. Franck and Edward Weisband, *Word Politics: Verbal Strategy Among the Superpowers* (New York: Oxford University Press, 1972).

that is, use the established and accepted vocabulary. And it is important that the style, content, and context of communications provide reasonable credibility.

In chapter 5 we saw that problems in communications have always been closely related to the fact that internally China has not been a highly integrated nation. It would follow that China's external politics has also labored under similar constraints. The conduct of Chinese diplomacy has rarely been characterized by perfect communications. If we look back to traditional China, we are struck by how ambiguous was some of the communication among the rulers of East Asia. When the Chinese emperor condescendingly declared a foreign ruler "king," that made the latter a vassal in the eyes of China. Was this status really accepted by the king? One suspects that in many cases his sense of subordination often lasted about as long as his visit to the Chinese capital, and was not communicated to his constituency.[50] Each foreign ruler had to reconcile the Chinese insistence upon tributary relations with his own need to be a sovereign within his domain, on the one hand, and his relations with his greater and lesser neighbors on the other. (Sometimes, nations like the Tibetans, Uigurs, or Khitans would be powerful enough to insist upon being recognized as China's equals, or better, although among Chinese the emperor continued to be thought of as presiding over "all under heaven.") Sino-Japanese relations presents an especially interesting test of the Confucian international system. Japan was never acknowledged by China as an equal. Rebuffed in 607,[51] Japan thereafter either declined to have relations with China, or artfully dodged the subordination requirement. Because of Japanese respect for Chinese culture, there was still sometimes a strong desire to maintain political relations. During the Ashikaga/Ming period, the *de facto* ruler of Japan (the shogun) permitted himself to be called king in communications between the two countries, but no mention appears to have been made of the mikado, whom the Japanese still considered their nominal sovereign.

[50] An exception here would be a very Confucian state, of which Korea may be the only example. There, investiture by the Emperor was an essential mark of legitimacy.

[51] The Japanese emperor wrote to the Chinese emperor as follows: "The Son of Heaven in the land where the sun rises addresses a letter to the Son of Heaven in the land where the sun sets. We hope you are in good health." According to the official history of the Sui dynasty, "When the emperor saw this letter he was displeased and told the official in charge of foreign affairs that this letter from the barbarians was discourteous, and that such a letter should not be brought to his attention." Ryusaku Tsunoda, et al., eds., *Sources of Japanese Tradition* (New York: Columbia University Press, 1958), p. 12.

To give a modern example of verbal imprecision we may turn to the Sino-American communiqué issued on February 27, 1972, at the conclusion of President Richard Nixon's visit to China. In some ways the document represents, as widely noted, a major healing of Sino-American relations. Less well observed has been the fact that the document was a statement of disagreements. Much of the communiqué was comprised of unilateral statements by each side. China reasserted approval of liberation movements abroad and opposition to Japanese militarism, and did not modify its position on any substantive issue. The United States made what seemed to be major concessions, although these were conditional and ambiguous. For example, on the legal status of Formosa there was an apparent departure from the official position of two decades, according to which the status of the island had been *undetermined*.[52] Now the United States acknowledged that

> all Chinese on either side of the Taiwan Strait maintain there is but one China and that Taiwan is a part of China. The United States government does not challenge that position. It reaffirms its interest in a peaceful settlement of the Taiwan question by the Chinese themselves. With this prospect in mind, it affirms the ultimate objective of the withdrawal of all United States forces and military installations from Taiwan. In the meantime, it will progressively reduce its forces and military installations on Taiwan as the tension in the area diminishes.[53]

The "objective" (it was not a promise) to withdraw militarily from Formosa carried no time limit, and was dependent upon almost inconceivable amity between Peking and Taipei. By inference, the *right* to maintain troops there was reaffirmed. There was no positive statement that the island is part of China, simply a declining to "challenge" this position held by "Chinese" on both sides of the strait. Are the Taiwanese, the disenfranchised majority on the island, "Chinese"? This may be the assumption, but one day there could emerge a Taiwanese-dominated government in Taipei which asserted Formosan statehood. Could not Washington, with complete logic and consistency, again say that it "does not challenge that position"? The communiqué, in

[52] Formosa was settled by people from China centuries ago, but has been administered by a mainland government for only brief periods, primarily during the latter part of the nineteenth century, and from 1945 to 1949. It was Japanese between 1895 and 1945, after which Japan renounced any claim to the island but did not transfer it to anyone else in particular.

[53] *New York Times*, February 28, 1972.

other words, does not seal the island's fate; it simply reasserts a hands-off attitude concerning the legal question. While some argue that the spirit of the occasion requires a more positive reading of the communiqué, that spirit cannot override the fact that Washington continued to recognize only the Republic of China (Nationalist).[54] In short, what the United States was connoting was different from what it was denoting. It *appeared* almost to meet Peking's terms, but in fact there was little if any substantive change in policy.

How is one to account for such verbal imprecision across many centuries in the relations between China and other countries? The answer lies largely in the fact that we are observing the interaction of disparate international political systems. While to some extent loose communications may prevent integration, they more generally are produced or necessitated by the fact that the systems are poorly integrated to begin with. Japan and China, for example, simply could not have conducted mutual relations without the lubrication of fictions and "agreeing to disagree." The ambiguous Sino-American formulation concerning Formosa is very much in this tradition and serves the same purpose. In order to function within its international systems (in which mutual defense treaties and trade play an important role), the United States could not abandon Taipei, for doing so would have brought into question the reliability of all its treaties and commercial relationships. China, on the other hand, did not accept the fundamental Western premise (or fiction) that the actors in international relations must be *states*, and in this case did not consider Formosa to be a state anyway. Because the underlying issues were important to both China and the United States, and had implications which went far beyond the relations between the two countries, they accommodated each other without backing away from their principles or undermining their systems. Thus, Chou En-lai did not insist upon any renunciation of the Nationalist-American security treaty, and Nixon did not insist that the Chinese promise (publicly, at least) to refrain from using force to recover Formosa. Irreconcilable positions would coexist in the interest of general harmony.

In a milieu of such imprecise verbal communications, misunderstandings may arise and lead to miscalculations. Both the Sino-American war in Korea, and the Indochina war were in large measure the result of Washington's misjudgment of China's intentions. In the

---

[54] On the other hand, by meeting with Peking officials, the President of the United States was implicitly denying Taipei's claim to be the legitimate government of mainland China.

first instance, inexperienced Washington analysts failed to read (or accept as credible) strong signals that China would not tolerate an American presence in the northern part of Korea.[55] In the case of Vietnam, the error was an *over*estimation of China's intended role in Southeast Asia. Washington was confused by its preconceptions, which were based upon an ideologically distorted view of reality. Although the quality of intelligence analysis had improved, the limited nature of China's ambitions never impressed top policymakers in Washington.[56] One reason may have been that although the substance of Peking's international plans were relatively benign, this fact was often overshadowed by the venomous tone of official pronouncements.

Considering the communications barriers and credibility gaps, it will be recognized that relations between China and foreign states cannot rely entirely upon words, and sometimes these may be of little effectiveness at all. Indeed, there are times when silence may be the more effective medium of communication. For example, Chinese boats carrying the Macartney mission on inland waterways bore the sign "Ambassador bearing tribute from England," but Macartney ignored them in order to demonstrate his determination to carry out his mission. Similarly, although the Chinese shot down several American planes in 1965 over North Vietnam (after being attacked by them), neither side publicized its own or the other's casualties. This silence was an indication to each other that both intended to localize the war and avoid confrontation. As a final example of a telling silence, in the mid-1970s the Chinese demands for progress on the Formosa issue were stated without the requirement that American troops be withdrawn or that recognition of the Taipei government end. Thus, the Chinese signaled that the situation was negotiable, without making any formal concessions. (Vice President Nelson Rockefeller may have been responding with a similar signal when he visited Formosa in April 1975 and avoided mentioning the security treaty.[57])

Another useful means of communication is what we might call "suggestive actions." Thus, foreign envoys who were given the honor

---

[55] There was no indication that the presence of South Korean troops north of the 38th parallel would require Chinese intervention.

One reason that intelligence analysis was so faulty was that right-wing elements were forcing China experts out of the government.

[56] The Pentagon Papers, covering the period to 1968, reveal little anxiety about the possibility of Chinese participation in the war. One of the important conclusions one can draw from these papers is that intelligence estimates were not heeded by the White House.

[57] *New York Times*, April 16, 1975.

268   EIGHT: *External Politics*

of an audience with the emperor were expected to perform the kowtow (three kneelings and nine prostrations) and exchange gifts.[58] No document could have so well stated the political relationship which existed. In more recent times, the question of whether and how Foreign Minister Chou En-lai and Secretary of State John Foster Dulles should greet each other assumed special importance at the 1954 Geneva Conference. Dulles believed that even shaking hands with Chou would tend to legitimize the Peking régime. When the two accidentally encountered each other, he reportedly murmured "I cannot," clasped his hands behind his back, and exited. The event had an enduring impact upon the Chinese, who accepted the act without bitterness but simply as a political statement.[59]

To illustrate the interplay between verbal and nonverbal strategies, let us examine the remarkable developments in Sino-American diplomacy which led up to the 1972 Nixon visit to China. In the history of the relations between these two countries, the 1950s marked an all-time low. The decade began with the Korean War, and was characterized on both sides by intensely ideological hostility. Although there were occasional ambassadorial talks in Geneva and Warsaw, they could not be productive in view of American refusal to speak the name Peking[60] or tolerate Communist representation in the United Nations, much less recognize the government or terminate military support for opposition Nationalist and Tibetan forces.[61] In January 1960, however, came the election of John F. Kennedy, who during his campaign, had urged a less negative policy toward China. He had recalled "our historic friendship with the Chinese people," and urged that the United

---

[58] This proved a major obstacle in the establishment of relations between China and European nations, whose envoys were often unwilling to manifest such extreme obeisance. In 1655, Dutch envoys performed the full ritual to the satisfaction of the Manchu court. Instead of gaining the desired trading privileges, however, they were told only that they could send an embassy once every eight years, accompanied by four trading ships. In 1793 the Earl of Macartney traveled to China as a royal envoy, and refused to perform the kowtow. After much negotiation, he was allowed simply to bend on one knee before the emperor, but there was no agreement on any of England's substantive requests. Morse, 1: 48, 54 f.

[59] This incident has been widely reported and does not seem to be subject to doubt. The "I cannot" remark is attributed to Dulles by a Reuters journalist, and appears in *Atlantic*, January 1972, p. 41. Full citation in note 42.

[60] *Peiping* was invariably employed. This is the name the Nationalists use, because the *-king* in *Peking* means "capital."

[61] On American activities among Tibetans, and in particular Central Intelligence Agency support for rebels in Tibet, see Allen S. Whiting, "What Nixon Must Do To Make Friends in Peking," *NYRB*, October 7, 1971, pp. 10–15.

States "work to improve at least our communications with mainland China, which might lead to cultural and economic contact."[62] In the Warsaw talks during Kennedy's presidency, however, the Chinese insisted that progress on major issues (i.e., the U.S. "occupation" of Formosa) must precede disposition of "minor matters" like the exchange of newsmen and release of prisoners. Political pressures within the United States, however, made any movement on major issues, or even Chinese admission to the United Nations, unthinkable. Nonetheless, official thinking was gradually moving ahead. Whereas during the 1960 campaign Kennedy had assumed Chinese submissiveness to Moscow, it was apparent by 1963 that this view was inaccurate, a fact which encouraged the Administration to send more signals to Peking. These came in the form of a speech by Roger Hilsman, assistant secretary of state for Far Eastern affairs. Unfortunately, even Hilsman was not free of misconceptions about the Chinese People's Republic (which, of course, was never referred to so flatteringly).[63] He alluded to Chinese aggressive impulses, and to the moderating trend of the domestic revolution. Except for the latter unwelcome praise, Hilsman was generally disparaging.[64] As in the case of Peking's propaganda, it was easier to be impressed by the hostile tone of his speech than by the expressed possibility of placing Sino-American relations on a more constructive course.

More meaningful than Hilsman's verbal signal was a silent signal by Secretary of State Dean Rusk the following April upon his arrival in Taiwan. While reaffirming the support of the Taipei government as the government of all of China, and opposing its *replacement* in the United Nations by the mainland regime, he did not, contrary to earlier administration statements, explicitly exclude the possibility of *both* governments belonging to the United Nations at some future date.[65] Again, the movement was barely perceptible and came in the context of explicit support for a rival government. And it was followed in a few months by President Lyndon Johnson's sharp reaction to China's first nuclear explosion.

> Until this week, only four powers had entered the dangerous world of nuclear explosions. Whatever their differences, all four are sober and

---

[62] *New York Times*, June 15, 1960.
[63] Until 1971, Washington usually used the term *Communist China*.
[64] *New York Times*, December 14, 1963. The statement was planned before, but delivered after, the assassination of President Kennedy.
[65] *New York Times*, April 18, 1964.

serious states, with long experience as major powers in the modern world. Communist China has no such experience. Its nuclear pretensions are both expensive and cruel to its people.[66]

At this point it was clear that if Washngton hoped to advance Sino-American relations, more than words and pregnant silences were required; an active gesture was needed. The required suggestive act came in 1965 with the Washington-approved visit of a group of American doctors, including heart specialist Paul Dudley White, to China. Unfortunately, this development came precisely at the moment of the first rumblings of the Cultural Revolution in China, and (more important) it was followed by major escalations of the war in Vietnam. Although Rusk continued to promote cultural exchanges, and offered to permit the sale of grain to China,[67] by 1967 American bombs were falling within ten miles of the Chinese border, and serious hostilities between Chinese and American forces were narrowly averted.[68] Although both sides did draw back from what would have been a catastrophic confrontation, the opportunity to normalize relations was lost, and even the Warsaw talks lapsed. Nevertheless, Washington's attitude toward China became increasingly relaxed, and in 1968 Undersecretary of State Nicholas Katzenbach came close to acknowledging *de facto* recognition of the Peking government.[69]

Domestic political developments in both countries continued to influence this dialogue. In order to prevent a yawning credibility gap while he was waging cultural revolution at home, Mao could hardly become too intimate with imperialism. Indeed, one result of the Cultural Revolution was that those who had favored any kind of accommodation with the West were removed from their positions.[70] During the racial unrest that followed the assassination of Martin Luther King, Jr., Mao issued a landmark statement in support of black and other proletarian Americans.[71] In Washington, political developments seemed uncon-

---

[66] Excerpts of document reprinted in Young Hum Kim, *East Asia's Turbulent Century: With American Diplomatic Documents* (New York: Appleton-Century-Crofts, 1966), pp. 364 f.
[67] *New York Times*, April 17, 1966.
[68] Allen S. Whiting, "How We Almost Went to War with China," *Look*, April 29, 1969, p. 77.
[69] *CSM*, May 24, 1968.
[70] The major victim of the Cultural Revolution, Chief of State Liu Shao-ch'i, is alleged to have "prostrated himself before U.S. imperialism," and to have maintained that "even within the ruling groups of the United States there are people who are more clear-minded and will gradually understand that a war policy may not be in the interests of the United States." Mao Tung-yu, Article broadcast on Hofei radio, November 19, 1969, reprinted in *CLG*, Fall 1969, p. 63.
[71] *PR*, April 19, 1968, reprinted in *CLG*, Fall 1969, pp. 41 f.

Communicating Requirements and Intentions 271

ducive to improved Sino-American relations. November 1968 saw the election of an American president of impeccable anti-Communist credentials, who in 1960 had insisted that Nationalist-held Quemoy Island, of importance only as a base for shelling the mainland, must be held as a matter of principle. Ironically, however, it was precisely the ascendancy of the undeniably conservative Richard Nixon and the undeniably revolutionary Mao Tse-tung which made a rapprochement possible, for these two men possessed a rare immunity to criticism when it came to the subject of Sino-American relations.[72]

The problem was, how could the reaching out, which had been conducted with self-defeating circumspection during the Johnson administration, be advanced? Early feelers by the Nixon administration were vehemently rejected by Peking, but this was interpreted in Washington as a smokescreen serving Peking's political requirements at home and within the Communist community of nations.[73] Undeterred, but realizing that words alone would not move Sino-American relations off of dead center, Washington once more embarked upon a series of suggestive acts. First came the announcement in Washington that the passports of certain categories of Americans would no longer be invalid for travel to mainland China.[74] More momentous was the relaxation of the nineteen-year trade embargo.[75] Although these gestures met with overt rebuke, there were indications of Chinese interest,[76] and on January 20, 1970, after a two-year hiatus, the Warsaw talks resumed.

[72] During the late 1940s and 1950s, a powerful group (known by detractors as the "China Lobby") was very influencial in the formation of Washington's anti-Communist and pro-Nationalist China policy. Most vocal was the Committee of One Million, organized in 1953. Congressional support for such groups, at first impressive, began to erode by the mid-1960s. By 1971, only a few in Congress, such as Representatives John Ashbrook (R., Ohio), opposed improved relations between Washington and Peking. Although Vice President Agnew voiced misgivings about the trend of events, the only outspoken member of the administration on the subject of Chinese communism was FBI Director J. Edgar Hoover. See "Mao's Red Shadows in America," *Veterans of Foreign Wars Magazine*, June 1971, pp 10–13. A comprehensive study of the China Lobby is Ross Y. Koen, *The China Lobby and American Politics* (New York: Harper & Row, 1975).
[73] *New York Times*, February 11, 1969.
[74] This announcement came in the summer of 1969, when the writer happened to be in Hong Kong. He immediately had American consular officials revise his passport, and then presented himself to the Chinese authorities. American citizenship, however, still precluded the issuance of a visa.
[75] The first step, which was announced on December 19, 1969, allowed overseas subsidiaries and affiliates of American corporations to sell nonstrategic goods to China. *New York Times*, December 20, 1969, and *CSM*, December 23, 1969. In 1971 the policy was extended to American-based firms. *New York Times*, June 11, 1971.
[76] *New York Times*, December 28, 1969, p. 3.

In such ways are communications problems overcome. As we have seen, however, resolving issues of substance is even more difficult.[77]

International Integration

The world appears to be becoming an increasingly integrated place. Indeed, with the advent of the multinational corporation, there are those who believe that society is experiencing a "quantum jump" comparable to the demise of feudalism and emergence of the nation state. National economies are seen as having maximized their potential in many instances, with rational economics requiring a more cosmopolitan utilization of the planet's resources and markets. Thus, multinational (or anational) corporations already account for over 15 percent of the gross world product, and that sector has been increasing at a rate of 10 percent annually. Indeed, the performance of economic entities which transcend nations is more impressive than the performance of many national economies.[78] Nor is the trend toward international integration solely economic. Culturally, the world is a far more homogeneous place than it has ever been before. Politically, great strides have been taken on certain continents. True intercontinental political integration, on the other hand, has been inhibited by the reluctance of many nations, particularly the larger ones, to relinquish any of their sovereignty.

Has China accommodated herself to "modern" times?" Do the *démarches* of the early 1970s indicate that isolationism had been a passing phase, and that China, eagerly or reluctantly, will bow to the inevitable and integrate itself into the world system? The issue is not whether Exxon signs and McDonalds' golden arches will become features of the Chinese landscape, much less whether China will compromise her sovereignty by permitting ITT and IBM to control her communications and information-storage systems. At this stage, the question is primarily whether China will acquiesce to the alleged laws of comparative advantage, and export to meet world demand while

---

[77] For other aspects of communications and external politics, see Alan P. L. Liu, "Control of Public Information and Its Effects on China's Foreign Affairs," *AS*, October 1974, pp. 936–51.

[78] On the implications of the phenomenon of multinational corporations, see Harvey Schapiro, "Giants beyond Flag and Country: The Multinationals," *New York Times Magazine*, March 18, 1973; Charles Kindleberger, ed., *The International Corporation: A Symposium* (Cambridge, MIT Press, 1972); and Raymond Vernon, *Sovereignty at Bay: The Multinational Spread of U.S. Enterprise* (New York: Basic Books, 1972).

importing that which she cannot as easily produce; or whether, on the other hand, she will give higher priority to domestic political considerations than to satisfying economic needs, and ignore the remainder of the world while concentrating on building the kind of social and political systems called for in the Maoist blueprint.

The history of the early 1970s has led many to conclude that China elected to promote and join an integrated international economy. Certainly ideology—in the sense of promoting the Maoist model and giving priority to "self-reliant regeneration"—seemed for a time not to be a constraining factor, as China's trade with the world's two largest capitalist economies—Japan and the United States—multiplied rapidly. Exuberant businessmen predicted that annual two-way trade would race past the billion-dollar mark in the case of the United States. Japan's China trade was supposed to reach $10 billion by 1980.[79] Optimists could point to the fact that the Chinese decided to import whole factories from these two countries as well as from others.[80] In 1973, fiscal conservatism gave way to deficit financing as the Bank of China began borrowing hard currency to finance imports.[81] By this time China had established trade ties with 140 countries, and with 50 of these she had formal trade agreements.[82]

Whether or not one accepts trade volume as an accurate barometer of general integration, historically the prospects for the "China trade" have nearly always been overblown. When the president of CP Air exclaimed that the Canada-China route would develop into "a real barnburner" because of China's "sheer numbers,"[83] one can only be reminded of how, a century ago, the mills of Manchester were to have been sustained indefinitely by Chinese purchasers of lengthened gowns. Very few Chinese could ever afford imported material, and today fewer still are able to afford (financially or politically) transoceanic air passage.

If one examines the development of China's trade during the early 1970s, one finds that the imports can be subsumed generally into two categories. Many imports, such as chemical plants and steel mills, are capital rather than consumption items. They are not necessarily a part of a permanent foreign trade pattern, but rather can be viewed as steps designed to facilitate China's eventual independence and self-

[79] *Journal of Commerce,* September 21, 1973, p. 5.
[80] For example, the agreement with two Japanese companies to build and deliver a $380-million steel plant. *New York Times,* November 5, 1973.
[81] *New York Times,* December 7, 1973.
[82] *FEER,* November 15, 1973, p. 41.
[83] *New York Times,* November 9, 1973.

sufficiency. The purchase of several urea plants, for example, may at first glance appear to reflect a trend toward greater foreign commerce, but in fact they are intended to enable China to meet her own fertilizer needs. The second type of imports are emergency food purchases designed to forestall hunger during bad crop years. It is true that some rice has been exported during times of wheat importation, with occasional profit accruing to the Chinese (rice being dearer than wheat). However, the volume of wheat imports have been so much greater than the volume of rice exports that there has resulted no net gain in foreign exchange.[84] Indeed, the occasional massive wheat imports have represented something of an embarrassment to the government, which has declined to report their extent to the Chinese people.

So far we have spoken primarily of imports. Obviously Chinese trade cannot be sustained in any volume on the basis of large trade deficits as was the practice in the early 1970s.[85] Logically, one might expect to see the export of crop-derived products in increasing amounts, in view of the agricultural orientation of the Chinese economy. On the contrary, however, China appears to have been deemphasizing this type of export. The products being promoted are light manufactured goods, notwithstanding the fact that these are likely to encounter the stiffest competition from the developing world. It is true that some products unrelated to agriculture, such as low-sulphur crude oil, may find ready buyers in Japan and elsewhere, but as China's own energy needs and pollution problems increase there may be less available to export.[86] In fact, China has not been behaving as a nation that is serious about exporting on a large scale. True, following the historical practice,[87] regular trade fairs are held at Canton. But while the Chinese are doubtless willing to export exhibited items, their press accounts of these fairs seem designed to impress the world not so much with what an important trading nation China is becoming as how the fairs prove

[84] See Feng-hwa Mah, *The Foreign Trade Policy of Mainland China* (Edinburgh: Edinburgh University Press, 1972).

[85] Only China's Africa trade has shown a regular surplus. (The Africa trade has amounted to approximately one-fifth of China's foreign trade in recent years.) "China's Trade with Africa," *Radio Liberty Dispatch*, September 7, 1972.

[86] See Liang Te-an, "China Will Increase Oil Exports," *Ming Pao*, November 15, 1973, FBIS I, November 27, 1973. However, to discourage such neighbors as Japan, Vietnam, and North Korea from contesting her offshore claims, China can be expected to export substantial petroleum to these countries. See article by Selig S. Harrison in *Foreign Policy*, Fall 1975 for more information on the international implications of the development of China's petroleum industry.

[87] Canton (the Chinese now prefer that its English name be changed to *Kuangchou*) was an important international trading center as long ago as the first century A.D.

what great domestic economic progress China has achieved.[88] High prices[89] and reluctance to conform to foreign marketing standards[90] likewise suggest that exporting has not been given the highest priority. While many Chinese factory managers must be impressed by the prices their products might fetch on the international market, most are sobered by the prospects of finding themselves criticized for "putting exports in command."[91]

By 1974, the two-way trade between China and the United States reached only $902 million, well below American predictions and only a small fraction of the U.S.-Formosa trade ($6,637 million).[92] The 1974 Canton spring fair was disappointing to those who arrived with inflated expectations.[93] A greater blow came in 1975, when Peking canceled contracts to buy 601,000 tons of American wheat—about two-thirds of projected grain orders through mid-1976.[94] However this step is to be interpreted, it is a striking example of how poorly China has integrated its commerce into the world economic system. Indeed, the total level of China's foreign trade cannot be large (although the precise figures are unknown), a fact which must be understood in terms of the Chinese developmental model. Except in times of food shortages, the best rationale for foreign trade would be that by exporting China can import technology. However, this is not entirely consistent with the principle of self-reliant regeneration. In the mid-1970s this slogan was reemphasized. The media reminded the nation that the superpowers could be resisted only if China sustained economic growth on the basis of its own resources and technology. *People's Daily* criticized those who advocated the importation of foreign technology. "Chinese workers," the paper pointed out, "have high aspirations and ability. . . . They can accomplish what other countries have, and will accomplish what they have not." It was fine to *learn* from foreign countries, and occasionally to import technology "on the

---

[88] *PR*, November 30, 1973, pp. 30 f.

[89] *FEER*, November 26, 1973, pp. 38 f.

[90] "We are not going to do business with those Americans who demand we put their labels on our products, complain about design and standards, and press us to give them the exclusive right to distribute an export commodity." *New York Times*, November 1, 1973. A year or so later Chinese exporters began showing more flexibility in matters of packaging and labeling.

[91] For example, *FEER*, October 2, 1971, p. 34.

[92] The volume of trade with Japan was larger ($3.3 billion in 1974). *Journal of Commerce*, March 1, 1975, p. 1. See also *Journal of Commerce*, September 9, 1974, p. 22A.

[93] *FEER*, March 20, 1974, pp. 41 f., and June 10, 1974, pp. 53 f.

[94] *New York Times*, January 28, 1975.

basis of equality and mutual benefit." But *People's Daily* held up for the highest praise those enterprises which were able to modernize *without* imported technology.[95]

The determination to be truly independent of foreign ways was reemphasized in 1975, when Chou En-lai quoted Mao Tse-tung as saying:

> We must rely mainly on our own efforts, making external assistance subsidiary. We must break down blind faith in foreigners' ways, go in for industry, agriculture and technical and cultural revolutions independently, do away with slavishness, and bury dogmatism. People should learn from both the good and bad experiences of other countries, and draw the appropriate lessons from them.[96]

Thus, both as a practical matter and as a matter of principle, integration into the world of nations is to be limited.

Politically, international relations for China serve primarily to foster and maintain *national* integration. The establishment of diplomatic relations is always conditional upon some indication on the part of the foreign government that it respects Peking's claim to the "province" of Taiwan. This, of course, is the consummate issue between China and the United States. Although the mainlanders resent the Nationalists' military provocations (allegedly 27,000 commando raids from 1950 through 1974),[97] they have indicated no serious desire to see the Nationalists give up the offshore islands of Quemoy and Matsu alone—an idea they condemn as part of a plot originating with John Foster Dulles to create Formosa as a separate national entity.[98] The continuation of the Nationalist presence on these islands within sight of the mainland maintains a dynamic between Taipei and Peking which itself represents a degree of integration, however slight.

Aside from the Formosa issue, national integration is also at stake with such neighbors as the Soviet Union and India. In both instances, a major concern of China is the protection of her borderlands as she defines them. While we have seen that this is not the only issue, history indicates that it is the one which generates armed conflict. With regard to issues not affecting China's national integrity, Peking has shown

---

[95] *FEER*, April 8, 1974, pp. 38 f.
[96] Quoted in Chou En-lai's speech to the National People's Congress, January 13, 1975. *New York Times,* January 21, 1975. Translation revised.
[97] Reported by NCNA. *FEER,* January 24, 1975, p. 25.
[98] Chou En-lai, in an interview with Marquis Childs. *Washington Post,* May 25, 1973.

great flexibility. However, one *excluded* option is the achievement of a high degree of international integration. Usually, China is content to stand as a revolutionary model.

Model considerations are important in Peking's decision whether or not to endorse a particular foreign revolution. If the revolution is more military than political, as was deemed to be the case with Che Guevara's 1967 Bolivian adventure, they will not earn Chinese support or even endorsement.[99] Emulating the Chinese model is not so much a matter of striving to set up a state similar to China's but overthrowing the old order by Maoist *means*. While it is proper and necessary for revolutionaries to promote consciousness raising, the leadership must not be too far ahead of the masses, and the situation must be allowed to ripen before overt action to overthrow the state is taken.

At any rate, China will go its own way, and conduct it's foreign policy with nations of the various "zones" according to China's national interest, even if this means arranging ententes with the capitalist heartland. Such actions may have the effect of dampening revolutionary movements in these countries, even though this may not be their intent. As Mao once remarked:

> Such compromise does not require the people of the countries of the capitalist world to follow suit and make compromises at home. The people in those countries will continue to wage different struggles in accordance with their different conditions.[100]

Thus, classical Marxist proletarian internationalism is modified to allow a new distinction regarding relations *between* socialist and capitalist states on the one hand, and revolutionary struggles *within* capitalist states on the other. Peaceful coexistence[101] means that wars between countries with different social systems should be avoided and that Peking's involvement in foreign political movements will be one of words and an occasional minor deed; it does not mean that progres-

---

[99] An example closer to China but still not within the buffer-state category was Ceylon (now Sri Lanka). The leaders of the 1971 rebellion there, according to one Chinese official, "put the gun above the party, and they did not practice the mass line." Quoted in *Atlantic*, January 1972, p. 61. Full citation in note 42.

[100] Mao Tse-tung, "Some Points in Appraisal of the Present International Situation," *SW*, 4:87. This statement was first made in 1946, and has often been quoted in official pronouncements.

[101] The 1972 Chou-Nixon communiqué contained a restatement of the five principles of peaceful coexistence, although this expression was not used. Reference to the principles represented a political gain for China.

sives in other countries should rest, but that, on the contrary, having to be self-reliant, they must redouble their efforts.[102] Peking will cheer the favored team from the sidelines, but will usually be willing to maintain correct relations with the opponents if they are equally willing.[103]

If national interest determines China's relations with capitalist and third-world governments, we have seen that ideology becomes the major factor determining relations with other Communist states.[104] Although some writers see Sino-Soviet relations as a function of national interest also,[105] the great schism between the two nations since 1960 is intelligible only as an ideological dispute. Tiny Albania, which had no strategic or economic significance, was selected as the sole eastern European ally during the 1960s because it alone was willing to embrace Mao's Thought, erect the trappings of Chinese communism, and support China in the ideological battles with the Soviet Union. Here the basic issues concern the question of which version of communism, Maoist fundamentalism or Russian modernist revisionism, is purer and more progressive. To explore in depth the basis for Chinese disenchantment with the Soviet system would be beyond the scope of this book, but we should say that it is more than a matter of aversion to bureaucracy and technology. Involved is a whole syndrome of favored life-styles, philosophical beliefs, personal antipathies, and wounded pride. Some of the wounds will heal with time, but it is unlikely that either country will soon undergo the major system and value changes required before the Communist community could again become reintegrated as a "bloc."

To go beyond this in making predictions about Chinese foreign policy would be imprudent. One does not know what specific conduct or alignments to expect. One does not know what external stimuli China will be responding to. And one does not know whether China

[102] See *The Differences between Comrade Togliatti and Us* (Peking: Foreign Languages Press, 1963), p. 25 f.

[103] "Correctness" generally requires recognition of Peking as the legitimate government of all of China, including Formosa. Even here, exceptions are sometimes made. The United States does not so recognize Peking, and formal diplomatic relations are therefore impossible, but a presidential visit is rather close to formal diplomatic relations. Canada merely needed to "take note" of Peking's claim to Formosa before ambassadors were exchanged, and Kuwait, Cameroon, and Austria did not even have to so "take note." Japan "respected" the claim.

[104] This excludes North Korea and Vietnam, which fall into the buffer-state category even though they are communist.

[105] See O. Edmund Clubb, *China and Russia: The "Great Game"* (New York: Columbia University Press, 1971). For a review by the present writer criticizing the national interest thesis, see *Soviet Studies*, April 1973, pp. 604–7.

will be led by hawks or doves. But it is unlikely that the leaders, whatever their temperament, will stray far from the parameters which we have outlined. They may adhere to them with varying fidelity, but we would do well to judge with caution behavior which first appears idiosyncratic. Within this operational framework, it is not necessarily irrational for Peking simultaneously to promote revolution and practice peaceful coexistence with capitalism. China can fulminate against SEATO, and then enter close relations with one of the pact's three Asian members (Pakistan). It can condemn the capitalist powers and then exchange pandas and doves with the most reactionary leader of them all. It can also preach self-reliant regeneration, and then build a railroad between Tanzania and Zambia. It can condemn colonialism, and then tolerate two European colonies on what is considered Chinese soil.[106] It can profess to have abandoned traditional feudal interstate politics, and then characterize its relations with Burma as based on "kinsman friendship." It can conduct proper relations with the government of a country, only to indicate a distinction between the government and the people, thus justifying party-level ties with national subversives. The byword, we may anticipate, will always be tactical flexibility. As was said in the past century, "Gentle, cruel, subtle, or barbarous—we have been what the times required."[107] Today, to a better degree than then, the Chinese have their eyes clearly fixed upon the long-range goals, but they still possess ancient patience.

---

[106] In 1975, after left-wing militarists had taken over the Portuguese government, they attempted to return Macao to China. China refused to alter the status of the city apparently fearing that this would have an unsettling effect in Hong Kong. *New York Times,* April 1, 1975, pp. 1 and 17.

[107] Valéry. Translation revised.

NINE
Conclusion: The Cellular Polity

> *The real revolution does not consist of either the initial liberation nor the stabilization of that victory; it is the mixing of the masses and cadres over a number of generations. A new culture is required, one born of the struggle and toil of the masses. In a mere fifty years, our culture must change as much as Western culture has changed since the Middle Ages. We have done our job, but who knows what will happen during the next few decades? The struggle must continue for as long as there is still a danger of a return to the past.*
>
> MAO TSE-TUNG[1]

IN TERMS OF social theory, this book has argued that integration is a valuable concept for understanding the development of a political system. Historically, however, we cannot characterize China's political development in linear terms as having evolved from a nonintegrated to a highly integrated nation. In the past, there was an ebb and flow between integration along feudal lines and integration in bureaucratic terms.[2] There was almost always considerable integration of one form or another, however, and the task of the Communists in 1949 was not to establish integration *de novo* (which might have been easier), but rather to reintegrate the polity along revolutionary lines. Although there were differing views concerning what form this reintegration should take, the Maoist perspective which eventually became dominant emphasized the need to *optimize* (rather than maximize) political

---

[1] A free paraphrase, based upon remarks by Mao quoted in Malraux, pp. 453, 465, 466.
[2] See Riggs, "Ambivalence."

integration. According to this view, it has not been the degree but rather the *quality* of integration that is important. In particular, integration is emphasized within the lowest social unit consistent with effectiveness (in terms of the particular function), and with socialist values. In lieu of systemic inducements and market mechanisms, integration is in large measure to be effected by cultural means. A high degree of local integration is to be achieved because people *understand* the advantages of cooperation. Similarly, people will be taught not to expect too much integration *among* localities.

Politics and morality are treated as indivisible, rather than separated as the result of any "modernization" process. This stress upon the role of consciousness and culture is a peculiarly *Maoist* approach. As we have indicated, however, integration has three other quadrants. Being still *Marxists*, the Chinese are careful not to make major compromises with capitalism, and to maintain productive relations which are primarily socialist. Allowing anything below the production team to serve as accounting units would clearly undermine socialism. With the exception of private plots, all means of production are publicly owned, and managed for public benefit. In addition, Chinese communism has its *Leninist* component, so organization—and particularly the organization of the Party—plays a central role in orchestrating the affairs of state and maintaining basic constitutional arrangements.

The most difficult quadrant to analyze is the *modernist* one. With the relentless campaigns against "modern revisionism" one might almost conclude that the Chinese have turned their backs on modernization, in favor of some primitive form of communism. This clearly would be too extreme a view, as the emphasis upon science and industry demonstrates. Nonetheless, the Chinese are being selective and cautious in terms of adopting various features of modernization, and are determined that the modernization quadrant should not be permitted to effect a perverted version of socialism, as they feel happened in the Soviet Union. Modernization should improve the quality of life and help integrate man into his natural environment; it should not alienate people from nature and from one another. Perhaps China has been paying a price for this approach in terms of standard of living. It is at least possible that the gross national product would have been greater under a Soviet-style corporate state, or under a capitalist system. The Soviet economic system, however, has yet to prove itself in terms of efficiency and ecology, and unrestrained capitalism would probably be an ecological disaster, resulting also in great social inequities.

Although the Chinese have evinced no intention to impose their brand of Marxism on any other nation,[3] they are convinced that theirs is the way of the future. Whether they are right or wrong, without a charismatic leader who can come forward and correct mistaken policies and compel the bureaucracy to accept his version of politics for China, it will be necessary to develop more viable political institutions there. Revolutionary committees are revolutionary at their inception, but will the new culture prevent them from eventually becoming part of a New Class? If it does not, it will be necessary to have repeated revolutions to avoid this. Mao Tse-tung once suggested as much, citing Thomas Jefferson's remark about the necessity of a revolution every twenty years. But the United States Constitution provides political mechanisms for such "revolutions." The Chinese experience suggests that unless suitable procedures are instituted in China, future revolutions will be as tumultuous and costly as the Cultural Revolution. Even more important than political mechanisms will be a cultural climate which will encourage people to hold government publicly accountable and which will effectively discourage reprisals against those who criticize official conduct. Both the national constitution[4] and *some* Maoist pronouncements are encouraging in this respect, but as long as men and women are incarcerated and obliged to undergo "reeducation," only the extraordinarily courageous will step forward to point out what they consider their leaders' errors. Equally inimical to constructive political dialogue is the tendency of Maoists to vilify those with whom they disagree, substituting moral outrage for explicit political expression. Thus, safe political activity is confined to the area defined by Mao Tse-tung's "Three Basic Principles"—that his brand of Marxism be practiced rather than revisionism, that people unite rather than cause dissension, and that no one "intrigue or conspire."[5]

The contradiction between the need for genuine politicization and the requirement that everyone's attitude always be "correct" may be the most fundamental one for the future of Chinese politics, but it is only one of many contradictions upon which the Chinese political system is built. It is difficult, therefore, to make predictions involving Chinese politics, and in this volume we have avoided making them. In the 1950s a contradiction existed—not recognized as such in the West—between national autonomy and 'leaning" toward Moscow, the center of proletarian internationalism. When this contradiction was

[3] Formosa would not be classified as "another nation."
[4] See Art. 24 of the national constitution.
[5] Quoted widely in the media, especially around 1972. E.g., *HC*, 1972, no. 7, p. 15.

resolved by leaning *away* from the Soviet Union, most Western conceptions of Chinese politics had to be reformulated. In looking to the future, one would have to consider a broad range of resolutions in such areas as *de facto* versus *ex officio* leadership, and socialism versus "capitalism." As for the problem of defining the scale of integration, this is actually more than a simple two-sided contradiction. Centralism and localism may be mutually contradictory to some extent, but the two are also mutually reinforcing, and both are more contradictory to *regionalism* than to each other. That is to say, devolving power from the intermediate levels (ministerial as well as regional) to the localities enhances rather than weakens the center. Maoists do not seek an atomized China, with each unit assuming its own form and going its own way. Rather, they seek a cellular subcontinent in which each unit remains true to basic constitutional and ideological principles. Of all of the contradictions, this is the one closest to resolution.

Does all of this make China a complete maverick? Is its developmental model unique and therefore impossible to understand except within the Chinese frame of reference? I think not.

Modern societies are apt to be characterized by *high definition* and *low participation*. That is to say, people's lives are conducted according to well-defined patterns which permit little deviation and autonomy. A good job may require the acquisition of advanced skills, but having made that investment a person is limited as to what jobs he or she can profitably undertake. The activity itself is limiting in nature; one is simply performing a role, not writing the script. In the West, more and more thought is being given to changing this situation. Many people are seeking lives with *low definition* and *high participation*. One aspect of this trend is the back-to-the-land movement. Some people are leaving the cities and building new self-sufficient lives in the countryside.[6] Most are remaining in urban areas, of course, but even the cities are showing signs of becoming more diversified and interesting for the people who live in them.[7] There has been much talk—even from conservative quarters—of democratizing the workplace.[8] Some factories have been experimenting with diversifying the

[6] Roy Reed, "Back-to-Land Movement Seeks Self-Sufficiency," *New York Times*, June 9, 1975, pp. 1 and 19.
[7] See remarks by Juan de Torres, Conference Board economist, in *New York Times*, June 14, 1975.
[8] For example, Senator Charles H. Percy, who addressed the National Conference on the Changing Work Ethic in New York on March 26, 1973. *New York Times*, March 27, 1973, p. 22.

tasks the individual performs, and involving him or her in the total production process.[9] This may ultimately involve restructuring the corporation, giving more responsibility to line workers and largely eliminating middle-management positions.[10]

The Chinese emphasis upon subintegration can also be viewed as a quest for low-definition and high-participation life-styles. The insistance upon diversification is an example of this desire to despecialize people's existences and give them a more meaningful degree of participation in the various activities which affect their lives. Likewise, the greater self-sufficiency, the less vulnerability to external forces. The Chinese consider that the ideal life-style can only be achieved in a rural setting. They view overurbanization as one of the world's chief ills and are determined to prevent it in China. Between 10 and 20 million people have been sent from the cities to the countryside in an effort to eliminate urban parasitism and put the skills and manpower where they are really needed. Many probably view this as the destruction of the most advanced sectors of civilization, and there is certainly much resentment on the part of *hsia-fang*ed intellectuals.[11] But if subintegration is to succeed, people with expertise must spread their talents among the communes. Only then will Chinese society achieve the kind of homogeneity which is prerequisite to the realization of the Maoist model of political development.

---

[9] See, for example, Agis Salpukas's feature article on changing roles in the workplace, *New York Times*, April 9, 1975, p. 24.

[10] Agis Salpukas, "Jobs Rotated to Fight Boredom," *New York Times*, February 5, 1973, pp. 1 and 57.

[11] "How could I serve in the village? Do you really think the peasants were more progressive than I? What did they know of Mao's works or of armed struggle in the Cultural Revolution?... I wanted to continue my study and then apply my knowledge in a factory." A former Red Guard, quoted in *FEER*, April 19, 1972, p. 19.

APPENDIX A
The Constitution of the People's Republic of China

Preamble

The founding of the People's Republic of China marked the great victory of the new-democratic revolution and the beginning of the new historical period of socialist revolution and the dictatorship of the proletariat, a victory gained only after the Chinese people had waged a heroic struggle for over a century and, finally, under the leadership of the Communist Party of China, overthrown the reactionary rule of imperialism, feudalism and bureaucrat-capitalism by a people's revolutionary war.

For the last twenty years and more, the people of all nationalities in our country, continuing their triumphant advance under the leadership of the Communist Party of China, have achieved great victories both in socialist revolution and socialist construction and in the Great Proletarian Cultural Revolution, and have consolidated and strengthened the dictatorship of the proletariat.

Socialist society covers a considerably long historical period. Throughout this historical period, there are classes, class contradictions and class struggle, there is the struggle between the socialist road and the capitalist road, there is the danger of capitalist restoration and there is the threat of subversion and aggression by imperialism and social-imperialism. These contradictions can be resolved only by depending on the theory of continued revolution under the dictatorship of the proletariat and on practice under its guidance.

We must adhere to the basic line and policies of the Communist Party of China for the entire historical period of socialism and persist in continued revolution under the dictatorship of the proletariat, so that our great

SOURCE: This is the official English translation of the national (state) constitution, taken from *PR*, January 24, 1975. (The constitution was adopted on January 17, 1975, by the Fourth National People's Congress.) For preliminary secret draft versions (substantially changed before promulgation), see *CLG*, Fall 1974, pp. 77–86 (1970 version) and *BOC*, September 26, 1974 (1974 version).

The previous constitution (adopted 1954) can be found in Theodore Chen, ed., *The Chinese Communist Regime: Documents and Commentary* (New York: Praeger, 1967), pp. 75–104.

motherland will always advance along the road indicated by Marxism-Leninism-Mao Tsetung Thought.

We should consolidate the great unity of the people of all nationalities led by the working class and based on the alliance of workers and peasants, and develop the revolutionary united front. We should correctly distinguish contradictions among the people from those between ourselves and the enemy and correctly handle them. We should carry on the three great revolutionary movements of class struggle, the struggle for production and scientific experiment; we should build socialism independently and with the initiative in our own hands, through self-reliance, hard struggle, diligence and thrift and by going all out, aiming high and achieving greater, faster, better and more economical results; and we should be prepared against war and natural disasters and do everything for the people.

In international affairs, we should uphold proletarian internationalism. China will never be a superpower. We should strengthen our unity with the socialist countries and all oppressed people and oppressed nations, with each supporting the other; strive for peaceful coexistence with countries having different social systems on the basis of the Five Principles of mutual respect for sovereignty and territorial integrity, mutual non-aggression, non-interference in each other's internal affairs, equality and mutual benefit, and peaceful coexistence, and oppose the imperialist and social-imperialist policies of aggression and war and oppose the hegemonism of the superpowers.

The Chinese people are fully confident that, led by the Communist Party of China, they will vanquish enemies at home and abroad and surmount all difficulties to build China into a powerful socialist state of the dictatorship of the proletariat so as to make a greater contribution to humanity.

People of all nationalities in our country, unite to win still greater victories!

Chapter One: General Principles

ARTICLE 1
The People's Republic of China is a socialist state of the dictatorship of the proletariat led by the working class and based on the alliance of workers and peasants.

ARTICLE 2
The Communist Party of China is the core of leadership of the whole Chinese people. The working class exercises leadership over the state through its vanguard, the Communist Party of China.

Marxism-Leninism-Mao Tsetung Thought is the theoretical basis guiding the thinking of our nation.

ARTICLE 3
All power in the People's Republic of China belongs to the people. The

organs through which the people exercise power are the people's congresses at all levels, with deputies of workers, peasants and soldiers as their main body.

The people's congresses at all levels and all other organs of state practise democratic centralism.

Deputies to the people's congresses at all levels are elected through democratic consultation. The electoral units and electors have the power to supervise the deputies they elect to replace them at any time according to provisions of law.

ARTICLE 4

The People's Republic of China is a unitary multi-national state. The areas where regional national autonomy is exercised are all inalienable parts of the People's Republic of China.

All the nationalities are equal. Big-nationality chauvinism and local-nationality chauvinism must be opposed.

All the nationalities have the freedom to use their own spoken and written languages.

ARTICLE 5

In the People's Republic of China, there are mainly two kinds of ownership of the means of production at the present stage: Socialist ownership by the whole people and socialist collective ownership by working people.

The state may allow non-agricultural individual labourers to engage in individual labour involving no exploitation of others, within the limits permitted by law and under unified arrangement by neighbourhood organizations in cities and towns or by production teams in rural people's communes. At the same time, these individual labourers should be guided on to the road of socialist collectivization step by step.

ARTICLE 6

The state sector of the economy is the leading force in the national economy.

All mineral resources and waters as well as the forests, undeveloped land and other resources owned by the state are the property of the whole people.

The state may requisition by purchase, take over for use, or nationalize urban and rural land as well as other means of production under conditions prescribed by law.

ARTICLE 7

The rural people's commune is an organization which integrates government administration and economic management.

The economic system of collective ownership in the rural people's communes at the present stage generally takes the form of three-level ownership with the production team at the basic level, that is, ownership by the commune, the production brigade and the production team, with the last as the basic accounting unit.

Provided that the development and absolute predominance of the collective economy of the people's commune are ensured, people's commune members may farm small plots for their personal needs, engage in limited household side-line production, and in pastoral areas keep a small number of livestock for their personal needs.

ARTICLE 8

Socialist public property shall be inviolable. The state shall ensure the consolidation and development of the socialist economy and prohibit any person from undermining the socialist economy and the public interest in any way whatsoever.

ARTICLE 9

The state applies the socialist principle: "He who does not work, neither shall he eat" and "from each according to his ability, to each according to his work."

The state protects the citizens' right of ownership to their income from work, their savings, their houses, and other means of livelihood.

ARTICLE 10

The state applies the principle of grasping revolution, promoting production and other work and preparedness against war; promotes the planned and proportionate development of the socialist economy, taking agriculture as the foundation and industry as the leading factor and bringing the initiative of both the central and the local authorities into full play; and improves the people's material and cultural life step by step on the basis of the constant growth of social production and consolidates the independence and security of the country.

ARTICLE 11

State organizations and state personnel must earnestly study Marxism-Leninism-Mao Tsetung Thought, firmly put proletarian politics in command, combat bureaucracy, maintain close ties with the masses and wholeheartedly serve the people. Cadres at all levels must participate in collective productive labour.

Every organ of state must apply the principle of efficient and simple administration. Its leading body must be a three-in-one combination of the old, the middle-aged and the young.

ARTICLE 12

The proletariat must exercise all-round dictatorship over the bourgeoisie in the superstructure, including all spheres of culture. Culture and education, literature and art, physical education, health work and scientific research work must all serve proletarian politics, serve the workers, peasants and soldiers, and be combined with productive labour.

ARTICLE 13
Speaking out freely, airing views fully, holding great debates and writing big-character posters are new forms of carrying on socialist revolution created by the masses of the people. The state shall ensure to the masses the right to use these forms to create a political situation in which there are both centralism and democracy, both discipline and freedom, both unity of will and personal ease of mind and liveliness, and so help consolidate the leadership of the Communist Party of China over the state and consolidate the dictatorship of the proletariat.

ARTICLE 14
The state safeguards the socialist system, suppresses all treasonable and counterrevolutionary activities and punishes all traitors and counterrevolutionaries.

The state deprives the landlords, rich peasants, reactionary capitalists and other bad elements of political rights for specified periods of time according to law, and at the same time provides them with the opportunity to earn a living so that they may be reformed through labour and become law-abiding citizens supporting themselves by their own labour.

ARTICLE 15
The Chinese People's Liberation Army and the people's militia are the workers' and peasants' own armed forces led by the Communist Party of China; they are the armed forces of the people of all nationalities.

The Chairman of the Central Committee of the Communist Party of China commands the country's armed forces.

The Chinese People's Liberation Army is at all times a fighting force, and simultaneously a working force and a production force.

The task of the armed forces of the People's Republic of China is to safeguard the achievements of the socialist revolution and socialist construction, to defend the sovereignty, territorial integrity and security of the state, and to guard against subversion and aggression by imperialism, social-imperialism and their lackeys.

Chapter Two: The Structure of the State

Section I. The National People's Congress

ARTICLE 16
The National People's Congress is the highest organ of state power under the leadership of the Communist Party of China.

The National People's Congress is composed of deputies elected by the provinces, autonomous regions, municipalities directly under the central government, and the People's Liberation Army. When necessary, a certain number of patriotic personages may be specially invited to take part as deputies.

The National People's Congress is elected for a term of five years. Its term of office may be extended under special circumstances.

The National People's Congress holds one session each year. When necessary, the session may be advanced or postponed.

ARTICLE 17

The functions and powers of the National People's Congress are: to amend the Constitution, make laws, appoint and remove the Premier of the State Council and the members of the State Council on the proposal of the Central Committee of the Communist Party of China, approve the national economic plan, the state budget and the final state accounts, and exercise such other functions and powers as the National People's Congress deems necessary.

ARTICLE 18

The Standing Committee of the National People's Congress is the permanent organ of the National People's Congress. Its functions and powers are: to convene the sessions of the National People's Congress, interpret laws, enact decrees, dispatch and recall plenipotentiary representatives abroad, receive foreign diplomatic envoys, ratify and denounce treaties concluded with foreign states, and exercise such other functions and powers as are vested in it by the National People's Congress.

The Standing Committee of the National People's Congress is composed of the Chairman, the Vice-Chairmen and other members, all of whom are elected and subject to recall by the National People's Congress.

Section II. The State Council

ARTICLE 19

The State Council is the Central People's Government. The State Council is responsible and accountable to the National People's Congress and its Standing Committee.

The State Council is composed of the Premier, the Vice-Premiers, the ministers, and the ministers heading commissions.

ARTICLE 20

The functions and powers of the State Council are: to formulate administrative measures and issue decisions and orders in accordance with the Constitution, laws and decrees; exercise unified leadership over the work of ministries and commissions and local organs of state at various levels throughout the country; draft and implement the national economic plan and the state budget; direct state administrative affairs; and exercise such other functions and powers as are vested in it by the National People's Congress or its Standing Committee.

Section III. The Local People's Congresses and the Local Revolutionary Committees at Various Levels

ARTICLE 21

The local people's congresses at various levels are the local organs of state power.

The people's congresses of provinces and municipalities directly under the central government are elected for a term of five years. The people's congresses of prefectures, cities and counties are elected for a term of three years. The people's congresses of rural people's communes and towns are elected for a term of two years.

ARTICLE 22

The local revolutionary committees at various levels are the permanent organs of the local people's congresses and at the same time the local people's governments at various levels.

Local revolutionary committees are composed of a chairman, vice-chairmen and other members, who are elected and subject to recall by the people's congress at the corresponding level. Their election or recall shall be submitted for examination and approval to the organ of state at the next higher level.

Local revolutionary committees are responsible and accountable to the people's congress at the corresponding level and to the organ of state at the next higher level.

ARTICLE 23

The local people's congresses at various levels and the local revolutionary committees elected by them ensure the execution of laws and decrees in their respective areas; lead the socialist revolution and socialist construction in their respective areas; examine and approve local economic plans, budgets and final accounts: maintain revolutionary order; and safeguard the rights of citizens.

Section IV. The Organs of Self-Government of National Autonomous Areas

ARTICLE 24

The autonomous regions, autonomous prefectures and autonomous counties are all national autonomous areas; their organs of self-government are people's congresses and revolutionary committees.

The organs of self-government of national autonomous areas, apart from exercising the functions and powers of local organs of state as specified in Chapter Two, Section III of the Constitution, may exercise autonomy within the limits of their authority as prescribed by law.

The higher organs of state fully safeguard the exercise of autonomy by the organs of self-government of national autonomous areas and actively support the minority nationalities in carrying out the socialist revolution and socialist construction.

Section V. The Judicial Organs and the Procuratorial Organs

ARTICLE 25

The Supreme People's Court, local people's courts at various levels and special people's courts exercise judicial authority. The people's courts are responsible and accountable to the people's congresses and their permanent organs at the corresponding levels. The presidents of the people's courts are appointed and subject to removal by the permanent organs of the people's congresses at the corresponding levels.

The functions and powers of procuratorial organs are exercised by the organs of public security at various levels.

The mass line must be applied in procuratorial work and in trying cases. In major counter-revolutionary criminal cases the masses should be mobilized for discussion and criticism.

Chapter Three: The Fundamental Rights and Duties of Citizens

ARTICLE 26

The fundamental rights and duties of citizens are to support the leadership of the Communist Party of China, support the socialist system and abide by the Constitution and the laws of the People's Republic of China.

It is the lofty duty of every citizen to defend the motherland and resist aggression. It is the honourable obligation of citizens to perform military service according to law.

ARTICLE 27

All citizens who have reached the age of eighteen have the right to vote and stand for election, with the exception of persons deprived of these rights by law.

Citizens have the right to work and the right to education. Working people have the right to rest and the right to material assistance in old age and in case of illness or disability.

Citizens have the right to lodge to organs of state at any level written or oral complaints of transgression of law or neglect of duty on the part of any person working in an organ of state. No one shall attempt to hinder or obstruct the making of such complaints or retaliate.

Women enjoy equal rights with men in all respects.

The state protects marriage, the family, and the mother and child.

The state protects the just rights and interests of overseas Chinese.

ARTICLE 28

Citizens enjoy freedom of speech, correspondence, the press, assembly, association, procession, demonstration and the freedom to strike, and enjoy freedom to believe in religion and freedom not to believe in religion and to propagate atheism.

APPENDIX A: *National Constitution* 295

The citizens' freedom of person and their homes shall be inviolable. No citizen may be arrested except by decision of a people's court or with the sanction of a public security organ.

ARTICLE 29
The People's Republic of China grants the right of residence to any foreign national persecuted for supporting a just cause, for taking part in revolutionary movements or for engaging in scientific activities.

Chapter Four: The National Flag, the National Emblem and the Capital

ARTICLE 30
The national flag has five stars on a field of red.

The national emblem: Tien An Men in the centre, illuminated by five stars and encircled by ears of grain and a cogwheel.

The capital is Peking.

APPENDIX B
Constitution of the Communist Party of China

Chapter One: General Programme

The Communist Party of China is the political party of the proletariat, the vanguard of the proletariat.

The Communist Party of China takes Marxism-Leninism-Mao Tsetung Thought as the theoretical basis guiding its thinking.

The basic programme of the Communist Party of China is the complete overthrow of the bourgeoisie and all other exploiting classes, the establishment of the dictatorship of the proletariat in place of the dictatorship of the bourgeoisie and the triumph of socialism over capitalism. The ultimate aim of the Party is the realization of communism.

Through more than fifty years of arduous struggle, the Communist Party of China has led the Chinese people in winning complete victory in the new-democratic revolution, great victories in socialist revolution and socialist construction and great victories in the Great Proletarian Cultural Revolution.

Socialist society covers a considerably long historical period. Throughout this historical period, there are classes, class contradictions and class struggle, there is the struggle between the socialist road and the capitalist road, there is the danger of capitalist restoration and there is the threat of subversion and aggression by imperialism and social-imperialism. These contradictions can be resolved only by depending on the theory of continued revolution under the dictatorship of the proletariat and on practice under its guidance.

Such is China's Great Proletarian Cultural Revolution, a great political revolution carried out under the conditions of socialism by the proletariat

SOURCE: This is the official English translation, taken from *PR*, September 7, 1973. It was adopted on August 28, 1973, by the Tenth Party Congress.

The 1928 Party constitution can be found in the Japanese work *Shina kyosanto no gaikan* [a general survey of the Chinese Communist Party] (Tokyo: Sambo Hombo, 1929), pp. 200–214. The 1945 revision appears in Conrad Brandt, et al., *A Documentary History of Chinese Communism* (New York: Atheneum, 1966), pp. 422–42. For the 1956 version, see either *Constitution* (in Bibliography), or Theodore Chen, ed., *The Chinese Communist Regime: Documents and Commentary* (New York: Praeger, 1967), pp. 127–48. Finally, the Party constitution of 1969 appeared in *CLG*, Spring 1969, pp. 64–71.

against the bourgeoisie and all other exploiting classes to consolidate the dictatorship of the proletariat and prevent capitalist restoration. Revolutions like this will have to be carried out many times in the future.

The Party must rely on the working class, strengthen the worker-peasant alliance and lead the people of all the nationalities of our country in carrying on the three great revolutionary movements of class struggle, the struggle for production and scientific experiment; lead the people in building socialism independently and with the initiative in our own hands, through self-reliance, hard struggle, diligence and thrift and by going all out, aiming high and achieving greater, faster, better and more economical results; and lead them in preparing against war and natural disasters and doing everything for the people.

The Communist Party of China upholds proletarian internationalism and opposes great-power chauvinism; it firmly unites with the genuine Marxist-Leninist Parties and organizations the world over, unites with the proletariat, the oppressed people and nations of the whole world and fights together with them to oppose the hegemonism of the two superpowers—the United States and the Soviet Union—to overthrow imperialism, modern revisionism and all reaction, and to abolish the system of exploitation of man by man over the globe, so that all mankind will be emancipated.

The Communist Party of China has strengthened itself and grown in the course of the struggle against both Right and "Left" opportunist lines. Comrades throughout the Party must have the revolutionary spirit of daring to go against the tide, must adhere to the principles of practising Marxism and not revisionism, working for unity and not for splits, and being open and aboveboard and not engaging in intrigues and conspiracy, must be good at correctly distinguishing contradictions among the people from those between ourselves and the enemy and correctly handling them, must develop the style of integrating theory with practice, maintaining close ties with the masses and pratising criticism and self-criticism, and must train millions of successors for the cause of proletarian revolution, so as to ensure that the Party's cause will advance for ever along the Marxist line.

The future is bright, the road is tortuous. Members of the Communist Party of China, who dedicate their lives to the struggle for communism, must be resolute, fear no sacrifice and surmount every difficulty to win victory!

Chapter Two: Membership

ARTICLE 1
Any Chinese worker, poor peasant, lower-middle peasant, revolutionary armyman or any other revolutionary element who has reached the age of eighteen and who accepts the Constitution of the Party, joins a Party organization and works actively in it, carries out the Party's decisions, observes

Party discipline and pays membership dues may become a member of the Communist Party of China.

ARTICLE 2

Applicants for Party membership must go through the procedure for admission individually. An applicant must be recommended by two Party members, fill out an application form for Party membership and be examined by a Party branch, which must seek the opinions of the broad masses inside and outside the Party. Application is subject to acceptance by the general membership meeting of the Party branch and approval by the next higher Party committee.

ARTICLE 3

Members of the Communist Party of China must:

(1) Conscientiously study Marxism-Leninism-Mao Tsetung Thought and criticize revisionism;

(2) Work for the interests of the vast majority of people of China and the world;

(3) Be able at uniting with the great majority, including those who have wrongly opposed them but are sincerely correcting their mistakes; however, special vigilance must be maintained against careerists, conspirators and double-dealers so as to prevent such bad elements from usurping the leadership of the Party and the state at any level and guarantee that the leadership of the Party and the state always remains in the hands of Marxist revolutionaries;

(4) Consult with the masses when matters arise;

(5) Be bold in making criticism and self-criticism.

ARTICLE 4

When Party members violate Party discipline, the Party organizations at the levels concerned shall, within their functions and powers and on the merits of each case, take appropriate disciplinary measures—warning, serious warning, removal from posts in the Party, placing on probation within the Party, or expulsion from the Party.

The period for which a Party member is placed on probation shall not exceed two years. During this period, he has no right to vote or elect or be elected.

A Party member whose revolutionary will has degenerated and who does not change despite repeated education may be persuaded to withdraw from the Party.

When a Party member asks to withdraw from the Party, the Party branch concerned shall, with the approval of its general membership meeting, remove his name from the Party rolls and report the matter to the next higher Party committee for the record.

Proven renegades, enemy agents, absolutely unrepentant persons in power taking the capitalist road, degenerates and alien-class elements must be cleared out of the Party and not be re-admitted.

Chapter Three: Organizational Principle of the Party

ARTICLE 5

The organizational principle of the Party is democratic centralism.

The leading bodies of the Party at all levels shall be elected through democratic consultation in accordance with the requirements for successors to the cause of the proletarian revolution and the principle of combining the old, the middle-aged and the young.

The whole Party must observe unified discipline: The individual is subordinate to the organization, the minority is subordinate to the majority, the lower level is subordinate to the higher level, and the entire Party is subordinate to the Ceneral Committee.

Leading bodies of the Party at all levels shall regularly report on their work to congresses or general membership meetings, constantly listen to the opinions of the masses both inside and outside the Party and accept their supervision. Party members have the right to criticize organizations and leading members of the Party at all levels and make proposals to them. If a Party member holds different views with regard to the decisions or directives of the Party organizations, he is allowed to reserve his views and has the right to bypass the immediate leadership and report directly to higher levels, up to and including the Central Committee and the Chairman of the Central Committee. It is absolutely impermissible to suppress criticism and to retaliate. It is essential to create a political situation in which there are both centralism and democracy, both discipline and freedom, both unity of will and personal ease of mind and liveliness.

ARTICLE 6

The highest leading body of the Party is the National Party Congress and, when it is not in session,* the Central Committee elected by it. The leading bodies of Party organizations in the localities, in army units and in various departments are the Party congresses or general membership meetings at their respective levels and the Party committees elected by them. Party congresses at all levels are convened by Party committees at their respective levels. The convening of Party congresses in the localities, in army units and in various departments and their elected Party committee members are subject to approval by the higher Party organizations.

Party committees at all levels shall set up their working bodies or dispatch their representative organs in accordance with the principles of close ties with the masses and simple and efficient structure.

* The words "when it is not in session" appear in the official English version, but not in the Chinese text. *HC*, 1973, no. 9, p. 27. (*Author's footnote.*)

ARTICLE 7
State organs, the People's Liberation Army and the militia, labour unions, poor and lower-middle peasant associations, women's federations, the Communist Youth League, the Red Guards, the Little Red Guards and other revolutionary mass organizations must all accept the centralized leadership of the Party.

Party committees or leading Party groups may be set up in state organs and popular organizations.

Chapter Four: Central Organizations of the Party

ARTICLE 8
The National Party Congress shall be convened every five years. Under special circumstances, it may be convened before its due date or postponed.

ARTICLE 9
The plenary session of the Central Committee of the Party elects the Political Bureau of the Central Committee, the Standing Committee of the Political Bureau of the Central Committee and the Chairman and Vice-Chairmen of the Central Committee.

The plenary session of the Central Committee of the Party is convened by the Political Bureau of the Central Committee.

When the Central Committee is not in plenary session, the Political Bureau of the Central Committee and its Standing Committee exercise the functions and powers of the Central Committee.

Under the leadership of the Chairman, Vice-Chairmen and the Standing Committee of the Political Bureau of the Central Committee, a number of necessary organs, which are compact and efficient, shall be set up to attend to the day-to-day work of the Party, the government and the Army in a centralized way.

Chapter Five: Party Organizations in the Localities and the Army Units

ARTICLE 10
Local Party congresses at the county level and upwards and Party congresses in the People's Liberation Army at the regimental level and upwards shall be convened every three years. Under special circumstances, they may be convened before their due date or postponed.

Party committees at all levels in the localities and the army units elect their standing committees, secretaries and deputy secretaries.

Chapter Six: Primary Organizations of the Party

ARTICLE 11
Party branches, general Party branches or primary Party committees shall be set up in factories, mines and other enterprises, people's communes,

offices, schools, shops, neighbourhoods, companies of the People's Liberation Army and other primary units in accordance with the requirements of the revolutionary struggle and the size of the Party membership.

Party branches and general Party branches shall hold elections once a year and primary Party committees shall hold elections every two years. Under special circumstances, the election may take place before its due date or be postponed.

ARTICLE 12

The main tasks of the primary organizations of the Party are:

(1) To lead the Party members and non-Party members in studying Marxism-Leninism-Mao Tsetung Thought conscientiously and criticizing revisionism;

(2) To give constant education to the Party members and non-Party members concerning the ideological and political line and lead them in fighting resolutely against the class enemy;

(3) To propagate and carry out the policies of the Party, implement its decisions and fulfill every task assigned by the Party and the state;

(4) To maintain close ties with the masses, constantly listen to their opinions and demands and wage an active ideological struggle so as to keep Party life vigorous;

(5) To take in new Party members, enforce Party discipline and constantly consolidate the Party organizations, getting rid of the stale and taking in the fresh, so as to maintain the purity of the Party ranks.

Bibliography

ABBREVIATIONS

APSR	*American Political Science Review*
AS	*Asian Survey*
ASR	*American Sociological Review*
BCAS	*Bulletin of Concerned Asian Scholars*
BOC	*Background on China* (Chinese [Nationalist] Information Service)
CB	*Current Background* (U.S. Consulate General, Hong Kong)
CCPDA	*Communist China, 1955-1959: Policy Documents with Analysis* (Cambridge: Harvard University Press, 1962)
CFCP	*Chieh-fang-chün pao* [Liberation Army News] (Peking)
CLG	*Chinese Law and Government*
CNA	*China News Analysis* (Hong Kong)
CQ	*China Quarterly* (London)
CS	*Current Scene* (U.S. Information Agency, Hong Kong)
CSM	*Christian Science Monitor*
ECCP	*Eminent Chinese of the Ch'ing Period* (See below, under Hummel.)
ECMM	*Extracts from China Mainland Magazines* (U.S. Consulate General, Hong Kong)

Bibliography

FBIS I	U.S. Foreign Broadcast Information Service, *Daily Report: People's Republic of China* (formerly *Communist China*)
FBIS IV	U.S. Foreign Broadcast Information Service, *Daily Report: Asia and Pacific*
FEER	*Far Eastern Economic Review* (Hong Kong)
HC	*Hung ch'i* [Red Flag] (Peking)
HJAS	*Harvard Journal of Asiatic Studies*
JAS	*Journal of Asian Studies*
JMJP	*Jen-min jih-pao* [People's Daily] (Peking)
JPRS	U.S. Joint Publications Research Service
KMJP	*Kuang-ming jih-pao* (Peking)
KTTH	*Kung tso t'ung-hsun* (Work bulletin) (See below, under J. C. Cheng.)
NC	*La Nouvelle Chine* (Paris)
NCNA	New China News Agency [Hsin Hua]
NYRB	*New York Review of Books*
POC	*Problems of Communism*
PR	*Peking Review*
SCT	*Sources of Chinese Tradition* (See below, under de Bary.)
SW	*Selected Works of Mao Tse-tung* (See below, under Mao.)
SCMP	*Survey of China Mainland Press* (U.S. Consulate General, Hong Kong)
WP	*World Politics*

THIS LIST OF BOOKS and articles is designed to provide full citations for the footnotes and is therefore comprised of a single alphabetical list. Topical guidance to the literature is provided in the footnotes, especially the first note of most chapters.

APTER, DAVID E., ed. *Ideology and Discontent.* New York: Free Press, 1964.

BAO RUO-WANG [Jean Pasqualini], and CHELMINSKI, RUDOLPH. *Prisoner of Mao.* New York: Coward, McCann & Geoghegan, 1973.

BARNETT, A. DOAK. *Cadres, Bureaucracy, and Political Power in Communist China.* New York: Columbia University Press, 1967.

BELDEN, JACK. *China Shakes the World.* New York: Monthly Review Press, 1970.

BIANCO, LUCIEN. *The Origins of the Chinese Revolution.* Stanford: Stanford University Press, 1971.

BISHOP, JOHN L., ed. *Studies of Governmental Institutions in Chinese History.* Cambridge: Harvard University Press, 1968.

BLACK, C. E. *The Dynamics of Modernization: A Study of Comparative History.* New York: Harper & Row, 1967.

BLAUSTEIN, ALBERT P. *Fundamental Legal Documents of Communist China.* So. Hackensack, N.J.: Rothman and Co., 1962.

BODDE, DERKE. *China's First Unifier: A Study of the Ch'in Dynasty as Seen in the Life of Li Ssu.* Leiden: E. J. Brill, 1938.

———. "Harmony and Conflict in Chinese Philosophy." In *Studies in Chinese Thought,* edited by Arthur Wright. Chicago: University of Chicago Press, 1953.

———, and MORRIS, CLARENCE. *Law in Imperial China: Exemplified by 190 Ch'ing Dynasty Cases.* Cambridge: Harvard University Press, 1967.

BOORMAN, HOWARD L. *Biographical Dictionary of Republican China.* New York: Columbia University Press, 1967.

BOUC, ALAIN. "La Réintegration des cadres; le cas de Deng Xiaoping." *La Nouvelle Chine* (Paris), no. 13, June 1973, pp. 4-8.

BUCHAN, ALASTAIR, ed. *China and the Peace of Asia.* New York: Praeger, 1965.

CHANG, PARRIS H. *Centralization vs. Decentralization in the Chinese Political System.* Paper delivered at the American Political Science Association convention, Chicago, September 1971.

———. "Decentralization of Power." *Problems of Communism,* July 1972, pp. 67–75.

———. *Power and Policy in China.* University Park, Pennsylvania: Pennsylvania State University Press, 1975.

CHAO, KANG. *Capital Formation in Mainland China.* Berkeley: University of California Press, 1974.

CHEN, C. S., ed. *Rural People's Communes in Lien-chiang: Documents Concerning Communes in Lien-chiang County, Fukien Province, 1962-1963.* Stanford: Hoover Institution Press, 1969.

CH'EN, JEROME, ed. *Mao.* Englewood Cliffs, N.J.: Prentice Hall, 1969.

———. *Mao and the Chinese Revolution.* London: Oxford University Press, 1965.

CHEN, PHILLIP M. *Communist China's Legal System.* New York: Dunellen Co., 1973.

CHENG, J. C., ed. *The Politics of the Chinese Red Army.* Stanford: Hoover Institution Press, 1966. A translation of a series of *Work Bulletins* (*Kung tso t'ung-hsun*). Cited in notes as *KTTH.*

CH'ENG YÜ. "*Tzu-li keng-sheng*" [Self-reliant regeneration]. *Hung ch'i* (Peking), 1970, no. 9, pp. 57–60.

CH'IEN TUAN-SHENG. *The Government and Politics of China.* Cambridge: Harvard University Press, 1961.

CH'Ü T'UNG-TSU. *Law and Society in Traditional China.* Paris: Mouton, 1961.

———. *Local Government in China under the Ch'ing.* Cambridge: Harvard University Press, 1962.

CHUGUNOV, V. E. *Criminal Court Procedures in the Chinese People's Repub-*

lic (Moscow, 1959). JPRS translation: Scholarly Book Translation Series no. 458.
COHEN, JEROME ALAN, ed. *Contemporary Chinese Law*. Cambridge: Harvard University Press, 1970.
———. *The Criminal Process in the People's Republic of China, 1949–1963: An Introduction*. Cambridge: Harvard University Press, 1968.
Communist China, 1955–1959: Policy Documents with Analysis. Cambridge: Harvard University Press, 1962. Cited in notes as *CCPDA*.
CONFUCIUS, et al. *Ssu Shu* [Four Books, including *The Analects* (*Lun yü*), and *Mencius*]. Edition cited is Hsü Po-chao, ed., *Ssu shu tu pen* (Taipei: Chung T'ai Shu Chü Yin Hang, 1960). *Note*: Verse numbering systems differ from version to version; readers seeking citations should check neighboring verses.
Constitution of the Communist Party of China. Peking: Foreign Languages Press, 1956. Contains Teng Hsiao-p'ing's report on the subject, as well as the text of the Party constitution of 1956.
CORR, GERARD H. *The Chinese Red Army: Campaigns and Politics since 1949*. New York: Schocken Books, 1974.
CREEL, H. G. *The Birth of China: A Study of the Formative Period of Chinese Civilization*. New York: Frederick Ungar, 1937.
DE BARY, WM. THEODORE, et al., eds. *Sources of Chinese Tradition*. New York: Columbia University Press, 1960. Cited in notes as *SCT*. (This is the one-volume hardbound edition. There is also a two-volume paperbound edition with different pagination.)
DELEYNE, JEAN. *The Chinese Economy*. New York: Harper & Row, 1973.
DEUTSCH, KARL W. "Communication Models and Decision Systems." In *Contemporary Political Analysis*, edited by James Charlesworth. New York: Free Press, 1967.
———. "Integration and the Social System: Implications of Functional Analysis." In *The Integration of Political Communities*, edited by P. Jacob and J. Toscano. Philadelphia: Lippincott, 1964.
———. *Nationalism and Its Alternatives*. New York: Knopf, 1969.
DITTMER, LOWELL. *Liu Shao-ch'i and the Chinese Cultural Revolution: The Politics of Mass Criticism*. Berkeley: University of California Press, 1974.
DOMES, JÜRGEN. "The Chinese Leadership Crisis." *Orbis*, Fall 1973.
———. *The Internal Politics of China, 1949–1972*. New York: Praeger, 1973.
DONNITHORNE, AUDREY. "China's Cellular Economy; Some Economic Trends since the Cultural Revolution." *China Quarterly* (London), October 1972, no. 52, pp. 605–19.
———. *China's Economic System*. New York: Praeger, 1967.
ESCARRA, JEAN. *Le Droit Chinois: Conception et évolution, institutions législatives et judiciaires, science et enseignement*. Peip'ing: H. Vetch, 1936.

ETIENNE, GILBERT. *La Voie Chinoise: la longue marche de l'économie (1949-1974)*. Paris: Presses Universitaires de France, 1974.

FAIRBANK, JOHN K., ed. *The Chinese World Order*. Cambridge: Harvard University Press, 1968.

———. *The United States and China*. 3d ed. Cambridge: Harvard University Press, 1971.

FALKENHEIM, VICTOR C. "Continuing Central Predominance," *Problems of Communism*, July 1972, pp. 75–83.

FEUER, LEWIS S. ed. *Marx and Engels: Basic Writings on Politics and Philosophy*. Garden City, N.Y.: Anchor, 1959.

FITZGERALD, C. P. *China: A Short Cultural History*. New York: Praeger, 1954.

FRIEDRICH, CARL. *Man and His Government*. New York: McGraw-Hill, 1963.

FUNG YU-LAN. *A Short History of Chinese Philosophy*. New York: Macmillan, 1960.

GEERTZ, CLIFFORD. "Ideology." In *Ideology and Discontent*, edited by David E. Apter. New York: Free Press, 1964.

GERNET, JACQUES. *Daily Life in China on the Eve of the Mongol Invasion, 1250–1276*. Stanford: Stanford University Press, 1962.

GITTINGS, JOHN. *The World and China, 1922-1972*. New York: Harper & Row, 1975.

GOLDMAN, MERLE. *Literary Dissent in Communist China*. Cambridge: Harvard University Press, 1967.

HAI FENG. *Kuang-chou ti-ch'ü Wen-ke li-ch'eng shu-lüeh* [The Cultural Revolution in Canton]. Hong Kong: Union Research Institute, 1971.

HARDING, HARRY, JR. "Maoist Theories of Policy-Making and Organization." In *The Cultural Revolution in China*, edited by Thomas W. Robinson. Berkeley: University of California Press, 1971.

HARRISON, JAMES PINCKNEY. *The Long March to Power: A History of the Chinese Communist Party, 1921–72*. New York: Praeger, 1972.

HINTON, HAROLD C. *China's Turbulent Quest*. New York: Macmillan, 1970.

HINTON, WILLIAM. *Fanshen: A Documentary of Revolution in a Chinese Village*. New York: Vintage, 1968.

HOFHEINZ, ROY, JR. "The Ecology of Chinese Communist Success: Rural Influence Patterns, 1923–1945." In *Chinese Communist Politics in Action*, edited by A. Doak Barnett. Seattle: University of Washington Press, 1969.

———. "Rural Administration in Communist China." *China Quarterly* (London), July 1962, no. 11, pp. 140–59.

HOLUBNYCHY, VSEVOLOD. "Mao Tse-tung's Materialistic Dialectics." *China Quarterly* (London), July 1964, no. 19, pp. 3–37.

HOUN, FRANKLIN. *To Change a Nation: Propaganda and Indoctrination in Communist China*. Glencoe, Ill.: Free Press, 1961.

HOWE, CHRISTOPHER. *Wage Patterns and Wage Policy in Modern China, 1919–1972*. Cambridge: Cambridge University Press, 1973.

HSIAO, KUNG-CHUAN. *Rural China: Imperial Control in the Nineteenth Century.* Seattle: University of Washington Press, 1960.

HSIUNG, JAMES CHIEH. *Ideology and Practice: The Evolution of Chinese Communism.* New York: Praeger, 1970.

HSUEH, CHUN-TU, ed. *Revolutionary Leaders of Modern China.* New York: Oxford University Press, 1971.

HUMMEL, ARTHUR W., ed. *Eminent Chinese of the Ch'ing Period.* Washington: U. S. Government Printing Office, 1943. Cited in notes as *ECCP.*

JOHNSON, CHALMERS. "The Changing Nature and Locus of Authority in Communist China." In *China: Management of a Revolutionary Society,* edited by John M. H. Lindbeck. Seattle: University of Washington Press, 1971.

———. *Peasant Nationalism and Communist Power: The Emergence of Revolutionary China, 1937–1945.* Stanford: Stanford University Press, 1962.

———, ed. *Ideology and Politics in Contemporary China.* Seattle: University of Washington Press, 1973.

KIM, ILPYONG J. "Mass Mobilization Policies and Techniques Developed in the Period of the Chinese Soviet Republic." In *Chinese Communist Politics in Action,* edited by A. Doak Barnett. Seattle: University of Washington Press, 1969.

KLEIN, DONALD W., and ANNE B. CLARK. *Biographic Dictionary of Chinese Communism, 1921–1965.* Cambridge: Harvard University Press, 1971.

LENG, SHAO-CHUAN. *Justice in Communist China: A Survey of the Judicial System of the Chinese People's Republic.* Dobbs Ferry, N.Y.: Oceana Publications, 1967.

LEVENSON, JOSEPH R. *Modern China and Its Confucian Past: The Problem of Intellectual Continuity.* Garden City, N.Y.: Anchor, 1964.

LEVY, MARION J., JR. *The Family Revolution in Modern China.* Cambridge: Harvard University Press, 1949.

LEWIS, JOHN W., ed. *The City in Communist China.* Stanford: Stanford University Press, 1971.

———. *Leadership in Communist China.* Ithaca: Cornell University Press, 1963.

———. "Political Aspects of Mobility in China's Urban Development." *American Political Science Review,* December 1966, pp. 899–912.

———. "The Study of Chinese Political Culture." *World Politics,* April 1966, pp. 509 ff.

———, ed. *Party Leadership and Revolutionary Power in China.* New York: Cambridge University Press, 1970.

LEYDA, JAY. *Dianying, Electric Shadows: An Account of Films and the Film Audience in China.* Cambridge, Mass.: M.I.T. Press, 1973.

LIN PIAO. "Long Live the Victory of the People's War." *Peking Review,* September 3, 1965.

LINDBECK, JOHN M. H., ed. *China: Management of a Revolutionary Society.* Seattle: University of Washington Press, 1971.

LIU, ALAN P. L. *Communications and National Integration in Communist China.* Berkeley: University of California Press, 1971.

LIU, JAMES T. C. "Yüeh Fei (1103-49) and China's Heritage of Loyalty." *Journal of Asian Studies,* February 1972, pp. 291-97.

LIU SHAO-CH'I. *Quotations from President Liu Shao-ch'i.* New York: Walker and Co., 1968.

MÄDING, KLAUS. *Chinesisches traditionelles Erbrecht* [Traditional Chinese inheritance law]. Berlin: Walter de Gruyter, 1966.

MALRAUX, ANDRÉ. *Anti-Memoirs.* New York: Bantam, 1967.

MAO TSE-TUNG. *"Chung Fa"* (1972), no. 12. Remarks made during an August-September 1971 inspection tour. Document published in *Sing-tao jih-pao* (Hong Kong), August 10-11, 1972; FBIS I, August 15, 1972, pp. B-2-B-9.

———. *Hsüan chi.* Peking: Jen-min Ch'u-pan-she, 1966. Chinese version of *Selected Works of Mao Tse-tung.*

———. *In Camera Statements of Mao Tse-tung. Chinese Law and Government,* Winter 1968-69. This is a special issue of *CLG,* comprised of a translation of *Mao chu-hsi tui P'eng, Huang, Chang, Chou fan-tang chi-t'uan ti p'i-p'an* (Chairman Mao's criticism of P'eng Te-huai, Huang K'o-ch'eng, Chang Wen-T'ien and Chou Hsiao-chou's anti-Party clique).

———. *Mao chu-hsi yü-lu* [Quotations from Chairman Mao]. 2d ed. Peking: Tung-fang-hung Ch'u-pan-she, 1967. This is the "little red book."

———. *Selected Works of Mao Tse-tung.* Peking: Foreign Languages Press, 1964. Cited as *SW* in footnotes.

———. *Selections from Chairman Mao.* Translated by U.S. Joint Publciations Research Service, no. 49826. The contents were taken from *Chairman Mao's Selected Writings* [*Mao chu-hsi wen-hsüan,* n.p., n.d.], information about which can be found in *CLG,* Winter 1970-71, pp. 292-97.

Note: For additional writings and speeches of Mao Tse-tung, see below under Schram.

MARX, KARL. See FEUER.

MAXWELL, NEVILLE. *India's China War.* New York: Pantheon, 1971.

MENCIUS. See CONFUCIUS, et al.

MORSE, HOSEA BALLOU. *International Relations of the Chinese Empire.* London: Longmans, Green, 1910-1918.

MU FU-SHENG [pseud.]. *The Wilting of the Hundred Flowers: The Chinese Intelligentsia under Mao.* New York: Praeger, 1962.

MULLINS, WILLARD A. "On the Concept of Ideology in Political Science." *American Political Science Review,* June 1972, pp. 498-510.

MYRDAL, GUNNAR. *An International Economy: Problems and Prospects.* New York: Harper, 1956.

MYRDAL, JAN. *Report from a Chinese Village.* New York: Pantheon, 1965.

NIVISON, DAVID S. "The Problem of 'Knowledge' and 'Action' in Chinese Thought since Wang Yang-ming." In *Studies in Chinese Thought,* edited by Arthur Wright. Chicago: University of Chicago Press, 1953.

OJHA, ISHWER C. *Chinese Foreign Policy in an Age of Transition: The Diplomacy of Cultural Despair.* Boston: Beacon Press, 1969.

OKSENBERG, MICHEL C., ed. *China's Developmental Experience.* New York: Praeger, 1973.

———. "Methods of Communication within the Chinese Bureaucracy." *China Quarterly* (London), January 1974, no. 57, pp. 1–39.

OLIVER, ROBERT T. *Communication and Culture in Ancient India and China.* Syracuse: Syracuse University Press, 1971.

PERRIN, MEILE-ROBERT, and VOLTARD, YVES. "La Reconstitution des organisations de masse." *La Nouvelle Chine* (Paris), October 1973.

PFEFFER, RICHARD M. "Serving the People and Continuing the Revolution." *China Quarterly* (London), October 1972, no. 52, pp. 620–53.

PRICE, R. F. *Education in Communist China.* New York: Praeger, 1970.

PRYBYLA, JAN S. *The Political Economy of Communist China.* Scranton, Pa.: International Textbook Company, 1970.

PYE, LUCIAN W. *Aspects of Political Development.* Boston: Little, Brown, 1966.

———. *The Spirit of Chinese Politics.* Cambridge, Mass.: M.I.T. Press, 1968.

RICHER, PHILIPPE. *La Chine et le tiers monde.* Paris: Payot, 1971.

RICHMAN, BARRY M. *Industrial Society in Communist China.* New York: Random House, 1969.

RIDLEY, C. P., et al. *The Making of a Model Citizen in Communist China.* Stanford: Hoover Institution Press, 1971.

RIGGS, FRED W. "Ambivalence of Feudalism and Bureaucracy in Traditional Societies." *The Chinese Journal of Administration,* nos. 8 and 9 (1967).

ROBINSON, THOMAS W. "Chou En-lai's Political Style: Comparison with Mao Tse-tung and Lin Piao." *Asian Survey,* December 1970, pp. 1101–1116.

———, ed. *The Cultural Revolution in China.* Berkeley: University of California Press, 1971.

SCALAPINO, ROBERT A., ed. *Elites in the People's Republic of China.* Seattle: University of Washington Press, 1972.

SCHRAM, STUART R., ed. *Authority Participation and Cultural Change in China: Essays by a European Study Group.* Cambridge: Cambridge University Press, 1973.

———. *The Political Thought of Mao Tse-tung.* New York: Praeger, 1969.

———. *Chairman Mao Talks to the People: Talks and Letters, 1956–1971.* New York: Pantheon, 1975.

SCHURMANN, FRANZ. *Ideology and Organization in Communist China.* 2d ed. Berkeley: University of California Press, 1968.
SELDEN, MARK. *The Yenan Way in Revolutionary China.* Cambridge: Harvard University Press, 1971.
SEYMOUR, JAMES D. "Communist China's Bourgeois-Democratic Parties" (M. A. thesis, Columbia University, 1960).
———. "The Policies of the Chinese Communists toward China's Intellectuals and Professionals" (Ph.D. diss., Columbia University, 1968).
———. "The Republic of China." In *Constitutions of the Countries of the World,* edited by Albert P. Blaustein and Gisbert H. Flanz. Dobbs Ferry, N.Y.: Oceana Publications, 1974.
———. "Sovereignty in the South China Sea." *Bulletin of Concerned Asian Scholars,* January 1974.
SHARMAN, LYON. *Sun Yat-sen: His Life and Its Meaning.* 1934; reprint ed., Stanford: Stanford University Press, 1968.
SHEN MOU-SSU. "*Chien-ch'ih jen-chen k'an-shu hsüeh-hsi*" [Persist in serious study]. *Hung ch'i* (Peking), 1971, no. 5, pp. 8–13.
SHIH CHÜN. "*Tu i-tien shih-chieh shih*" [Read some world history]. *Hung ch'i* (Peking), 1972, no. 4, pp. 16–21.
SIMMONDS, J. D. *China's World.* New York: Columbia University Press, 1971.
SKINNER, G. WILLIAM, and WINCKLER, EDWIN A. "Compliance Succession in Rural Communist China: A Cyclical Theory." In *Complex Organizations: A Sociological Reader,* edited by Amitai Etzioni. New York: Holt, Rinehart & Winston, 1969.
SNOW, EDGAR. *Red Star over China.* New York: Grove Press, 1961.
SOLOMON, RICHARD H. "Communication Patterns and the Chinese Revolution." *China Quarterly* (London), October 1967, no. 32, pp 88–131.
———. *Mao's Revolution and the Chinese Political Culture.* Berkeley: University of California Press, 1971.
SSU-MA CH'IEN. *Les Memoires historiques de Se Ma Ts'ien.* Paris: A. Maisonneuve, 1895–1905. Translated and edited by Edouard Chavannes.
STARR, JOHN. *Ideology and Culture.* New York: Harper & Row, 1974.
TAN, CHESTER C. *Chinese Political Thought in the Twentieth Century.* Garden City, N.Y.: Doubleday, 1971.
TAWNEY, R. H. *Land and Labor in China.* Boston: Beacon Press, 1966.
TOWNSEND, JAMES R. *Political Participation in Communist China.* Berkeley: University of California Press, 1967.
———. *Politics in China.* Boston: Little, Brown, 1974.
TREADGOLD, DONALD W., ed. *Soviet and Chinese Communism: Similarities and Differences.* Seattle: University of Washington Press, 1967.
TSIEN TCHE-HAO. "*La Politicisation du droit.*" *La Nouvelle Chine* (Paris), April 1973, pp. 27–31.
TSOU, TANG. "Western Concepts and China's Historical Experience." *World Politics,* July 1969, pp. 655–91.

Bibliography

VALÉRY, PAUL. *Collected Works.* Quotations in the present volume which cite Valéry are taken from an extract from volume 10 of *Collected Works,* reprinted in the *New York Times,* March 25, 1971, p. 39. They are the words of an unnamed nineteenth-century Chinese scholar.

VAN NESS, PETER. *Revolution and Chinese Foreign Policy: Peking's Support for Wars of National Liberation.* Berkeley: University of California Press, 1970.

VOGEL, EZRA. *Canton under Communism.* Cambridge: Harvard University Press, 1969.

———. "Voluntarism and Social Control." In *Soviet and Chinese Communism: Similarities and Differences,* edited by Donald W. Treadgold. Seattle: University of Washington Press, 1967.

WALEY, ARTHUR. *The Way and Its Power.* New York: Grove Press, 1958.

WALLER, DEREK J. "The Chinese Communist Political Elite: Continuity and Innovation." In *Comparative Communist Political Leadership,* edited by Carl Beck et al. New York: McKay, 1973.

WATSON, BURTON. "Chinese Protest Poetry: From the Earliest Times through the Sung Dynasty." *Asia* (New York), Winter 1969–70, pp. 76–91.

WEBER, MAX. *The Religion of China.* New York: Free Press, 1968.

WHEELWRIGHT, E. L., and MC FARLANE, BRUCE. *The Chinese Road to Socialism: Economics of the Cultural Revolution.* New York: Monthly Review Press, 1970.

WHITING, ALLEN S. *China Crosses the Yalu: The Decision to Enter the Korean War.* New York: Macmillan, 1960.

WHYTE, MARTIN KING. "Bureaucracy and Modernization in China: The Maoist Critique." *American Sociological Review,* April 1973, pp. 149–65.

———. *Small Groups and Political Rituals in China.* Berkeley: University of California Press, 1974.

WINCKLER, EDWIN A., ed. Forthcoming two-volume work on the politics of China's provinces.

WU, SILAS H. L. *Communication and Imperial Control in China: Evolution of the Palace Memorial System, 1693–1735.* Cambridge: Harvard University Press, 1971.

YANG, C. K. *Chinese Communist Society.* Cambridge: M.I.T. Press, 1965. Contains two earlier publications, with separate pagination: *The Chinese Family in the Communist Revolution* and *A Chinese Village in Early Communist Transition.*

———. *Religion in Chinese Society.* Berkeley: University of California Press, 1961.

YANG, MARTIN C. *A Chinese Village: Taitou, Shantung Province.* New York: Columbia University Press, 1965.

YOUNG, MARILYN, ed. *Women in China.* Ann Arbor, Mich.: University of Michigan Center for Chinese Studies, 1973.

YU, F. T. C. *Mass Persuasion in Communist China.* New York: Praeger, 1964.

Author Index

A

Ahn, Byung-joon, 205n
Ake, Claude, 5n
Allison, G. T., 143n
Almond, Gabriel A., 25n
Angell, Robert C., 4
An Hsueh-kiang, 131n
An Tzu-wen, 120n
Anonymous, 1n, 30n, 34n, 154n, 261n, 279n
Apter, David E., 61n, 62n

B

Bao Ruo-Wang, 102n
Barnett, A. Doak, 183n, 207n, 209n, 212n, 215n
Belden, Jack, 99n
Bennett, Gordon, 198n
Bernal, Martin, 129n, 256n
Bernstein, Thomas, 119n, 176n
Black, C. E., 3–4, 6n
Blaustein, Albert P., 68n
Bodde, Derke, 67n, 110n, 198n

Bonavia, David, 238n
Boorman, Howard L., 143n
Bouc, Alain, 105n
Bundy, William, 247n

C

Casella, Alex, 138n, 227n
Chai, Ch'u, 36n
Chai, Winberg, 36n
Chang, Parris H., 192n, 193n, 200n
Chang Hung-sheng, 78n
Chang Ting-ch'eng, 87n
Chang Tzu-yi, 228n
Chao, Kang, 184n
Charles, David A. (pseud.), 148n
Chelminski, Rudolph, 102n
Chen, C. S., 35n, 58n, 173n, 175n, 213n, 218n, 223n
Ch'en, Jerome, 116n, 147n, 199n
Chen, Phillip M., 68n
Chen, Theodore, 287n
Cheng P'u, 78n, 94n
Ch'eng Yü, 188n
Chen Tung-lei, 159n

Author Index

Chiang Hsueh-yuan, 140n
Ch'iao Kuan-hua, 256n
Ch'ien Tuan-sheng, 67n, 75n, 94n
Ch'ih Hung (pseud?), 219n, 221n
Childs, Marquis, 276n
Chi Ping, 139n
Chi Yung-hung, 177n
Chugunov, V. E., 68n
Chu Lan, 170n
Chu Mu-chih, 172n
Chung Pin, 177n
Chung Shih, 196n
Ch'ü T'ung-tsu, 57n, 67n
Clarity, James, 91n
Clubb, O. Edmund, 278n
Cohen, Jerome Alan, 67n, 68n, 83n, 94n, 95n, 103n, 195n
Confucius, 27n, 28n, 46n, 47n, 50n, 57n, 115n, 126n, 131n
Creel, H. G., 25n, 68n, 108n

D

Davies, Derek, 135n
De Bary, William Theodore, 17n, 51n
Deleyne, Jean, 184n
Deutsch, Karl, 5, 9, 254n
Dicks, A., 68n
Dittmer, Lowell, 166n
Domes, Jurgen, 105n
Donnithorne, Audrey, 117n, 184n, 193, 194n, 197n, 199n, 201n, 205n
Dryer, June, 240n
Dühring, Eugene, 151
Durkheim, Emile, 4, 59n

E

Easton, David, 106n
Eberhard, Wolfram, 109n, 175n
Escarra, Jean, 67n
Etienne, Gilbert, 184n

F

Fagon, Stuart, 25n
Fairbank, John K., 245n
Falkenheim, Victor C., 192n, 193n, 194n
Farrell, R. Berry, 105n, 150n
Feuer, Lewis S., 222n

Finkelstein, D., 68n
FitzGerald, C. P., 248n
Franck, Thomas M., 263n
Freedman, Maurice, 155n
Friedrich, Carl, 43n
Fung Yu-lan, 51n, 108n

G

Galbraith, John Kenneth, 179n, 212n
Geertz, Clifford, 60–61, 62n
George, Alexander L., 225n
Gernet, Jacques, 57n
Giles, Herbert A., 35n, 56n
Ginsburgs, George, 67n, 133n
Gittings, John, 207n, 245n
Goldman, Merle, 149n, 159n
Goodrich, L. C., 12n
Goodstadt, Leo, 197n
Gould, Julius, 105n

H

Han Fei-tzu, 69n
Harding, Harry, 150n, 183n
Harper, Paul, 130n
Harrison, James Pinckney, 36n, 143n
Harrison, Selig S., 274n
Hiniker, Paul J., 32n
Hinton, Harold C., 245n
Hinton, William, 99n, 129n
Hofheinz, Roy, Jr., 38n, 39n, 183n
Holubnychy, Vsevolod, 25n, 52n
Hou, Chi-ming, 253n
Houn, Franklin, 154n
Howe, Christopher, 184n
Hsiang Shih, 78n, 87n
Hsiao, Kung-chuan, 161n
Hsiao Ting, 33n
Hsia Ping, 234n
Hsia Tao-Tai, 99n
Hsieh Chueh-Tsai, 87n
Hsiung, James C., 6n, 25n, 60n, 111n
Hsu, Francis L. K., 25n
Hsueh, Chun-tu, 105n
Hu, Chang-tu, 237n
Hu, Hsien Ching, 31n
Hua Lin-mo, 35n
Huan, Cheng, 88n
Huang Mo (Mab Huang), 75n

Hu Feng, 147n
Hughes, Richard, 102n, 170n

J

Jen Wen, 231n
Johnson, Chalmers, 39n, 43n, 105n, 129n, 256n
Julien, Claude, 242n

K

Kahn, Harold L., 115n
Kang Shu-hua, 95n
Kan Ko, 123n
Kataoka, Tetsuya, 39n
Katz, Milton, 72n
Kau, Ying-Mao, 231n
Kim, Ilpyong J., 39n, 128n
Kindleberger, Charles, 272n
Koen, Ross Y., 271n
Kolatch, Jonathan, 171n
Kolb, William L., 105n
Kung Yeh-ping, 204n

L

Lampton, David M., 207n
Legge, James, 105n
Lelyveld, Joseph, 170n
Leng, Shao-chuan, 68n, 80n, 85n
Levenson, Joseph R., 25n
Levy, Marion J., Jr., 154n
Lewis, John Wilson, 25n, 38n, 87n, 112n, 119n, 120n, 176n
Leyda, Jay, 154n
Li, Cho-ming, 176n
Li, Victor, 100n
Liang Te-an, 274n
Li Fang, 228n
Lifton, Robert Jay, 32n, 102n
Lin, Fu-shun, 67n
Lindbeck, John M. H., 105n, 194n
Lin Piao, 257n
Lipson, Leon, 88n
Liu, Alan P. L., 154n, 272n
Liu, James T. C., 48n, 55n, 132n
Liu I-chao, 214n
Liu Shao-ch'i, 49n, 84n, 85n, 119n
Lubman, Stanley, 88n

M

MacIver, R. M., 41n
Mäding, Klaus, 67n
Mah, Feng-hwa, 274n
Malinowski, Bronislaw, 5n
Malraux, André, 40n, 58n, 64n, 105n, 234n, 247n, 257n, 281n
Mao Tse-tung, 18n, 38n, 47n, 50n, 57n, 61n, 64n, 93n, 111n, 135n, 142n, 149n, 181n, 183n, 190n, 199n, 205n, 225n, 226n, 251n, 260n, 277n
Mao Tung-yu, 270n
Ma Piao, 54n
Marsh, Robert M., 57n
Matthews, R. H., 55n
Maxwell, Neville, 249n
Mehnert, Klaus, 230n
Mencius, 45n, 108n
Meyer, Alfred, 150n
Michael, Franz, 75n
Mo I-chu, 113n
Montaperto, Ronald N., 122n, 137n, 243n
Moody, Peter R., Jr., 23n
Morris, Clarence, 67n
Morse, Hosea Ballou, 67, 68n, 268n
Moseley, George, 240n
Mu Fu-sheng (pseud.), 114n
Mullins, Willard A., 42n
Munro, Donald, 53n
Myrdal, Gunnar, 186
Myrdal, Jan, 132n

N

Ning Han-lin, 82n
Nivison, David S., 50n
Nunn, G. Raymond, 170n

O

Ojha, Ishwer C., 245n
Oksenberg, Michael C., 100n, 172n, 173n, 174n
Oliver, Adam, 53n
Oliver, Robert T., 154n
Ollman, Bertell, 223n
Ostroumov, G. S., 92n

Author Index

P

Parish, William, 123n
Parsons, Talcott, 4, 5, 6, 184
Pashukanis, Y. B., 80n
Peemans, Philippe, 232n
Perlov, I. D., 95n, 103n
Perrin, Meile-Robert, 130n
Pfeffer, Richard M., 105n, 131n
Price, R. F., 154n
Pruitt, Ida, 31n
Prybyla, Jan S., 184n
Pye, Lucian W., 16, 25n, 29

R

Reed, Roy, 284n
Richer, Philippe, 245n
Richman, Barry M., 184n
Rickett, W. Allyn, 81n
Ridley, C. P., 154n
Riggs, Fred W., 6n, 15n, 41n, 281n
Robinson, Thomas W., 105n, 198n
Rodière, Michèle, 232n
Ruge, Gerde, 88n

S

Salpukas, Agis, 285n
Sartori, Giovanni, 41n
Scalapino, Robert A., 105n, 137n
Schapiro, Harvey, 272n
Schapiro, Leonard, 87n, 112n
Schell, Orville, 159n, 258n
Schram, Stuart, 25n, 61n, 64n, 142n, 231n
Schumann, Julian, 172n
Schurmann, Franz, 25n, 60n, 105n, 111n, 159n, 183n, 204n, 240n, 258n
Schwartz, Benjamin, 72n
Schwartz, Joel, 243n
Selden, Mark, 39n
Seymour, James D., 75n, 110n, 130n, 228n, 248n
Shabad, Theodore, 254n
Sharman, Lyon, 115n
Shen Chun, 113n
Shen Mou-ssu, 50n, 58n, 60n, 65n

Shih Chün, 46n, 54n, 61n
Shih Tsui-yen, 138n
Shils, Edward, 4, 6
Shryock, John K., 34n
Shyu, Larry N., 17n
Sigurdson, Jon, 231n
Simon, Sheldon W., 257n
Simmonds, J. D., 245n, 254n
Snow, Edgar, 111n, 150, 195n
Solomon, Richard H., 25n, 154n, 158, 262n
Spence, Jonathan, 171n
Ssu-ma Ch'ien, 198n
Stahnke, Arthur, 93n, 133n
Starr, John Bryan, 23n, 25n
Strong, Anna Louise, 256n
Sulzberger, C. L., 172n
Sun Chi-chuan, 195n

T

Tan, Chester C., 25n
Tang Hsiao-wen, 65n
Tang Sheng-ping, 48n
Tawney, R. H., 35n
Teiwes, Frederick C., 194n
Terrill, Ross, 63n, 260n
T'ien Pao, 239n
Ti Kang, 186n
Torres, Juan de, 284n
Townsend, James R., 105n, 165n
Ts'ao Tzu-tan, 101n
Tsien Tche-hao, 91n, 243n
Tsunoda, Ryusaku, 264n

U

Unger, Jonathan, 212n

V

Van Ness, Peter, 245n
Verba, Sidney, 25n
Vernon, Raymond, 272n
Vogel, Ezra, 105n, 134n

W

Waley, Arthur, 42n

Wang Hung-chih, 176n, 218n, 223n
Wang Hung-wen, 140n
Wang Yü-ch'üan, 198n
Watson, Burton, 71n, 170n, 221n
Weber, Max, 25n, 106
Weisband, Edward, 263n
Wheelwright, E. L., 184n
Whiting, Allen S., 268n, 270n
Whitson, William, 123n
Whyte, Martin King, 102n, 183n
Winckler, Edwin A., 183n, 197n
Witke, Roxanne, 234n
Wu, John C. H., 73n, 74n
Wu, Silas H. L., 154n, 161n

Y

Yang, C. K., 25n, 28n, 29n, 154n
Yang, Martin C., 25n, 29n, 132n
Yang Hsiu-feng, 87n
Yang Jung-kuo, 22n
Yang, Lien-sheng, 30n
Yen Ch'un, 135n
Young, Marilyn, 234n
Yu, F. T. C., 154n
Yun Lan, 243n

Z

Zeitlin, Maurice, 187n

Subject Index

A

Afghanistan, 249
aged, 31, 242
Agnew, Spiro, 271n
agrarian revolts, 36–38
agriculture, 10
  collectivization, beginning of, 119
  household contract system, 217–218
  private, 215–217
  production brigades and, 208, 209
  production teams and, 211–213
  wage system, 232
  See also farmers
Aksai Chin, 249
Albania, 255, 278
apriorism, 53, 54
architecture, 16
aristocracy, 10, 14
armed services, 62n, 262–263
  Cultural Revolution and, 123, 195, 224–225
  equality in, 225–226
  Mao Tse-tung and, 148–149, 224
arts, 169–170

ascription, 44
Ashbrook, John, 271n
Ashikaga period, 264
athletics, 170–171
Austria, 278n

B

back-to-the-land movement, 284
Bernstein, Eduard, 112n
Blos, W., 150n
Bolivia, 277
book publishing, 170
Boxer Rebellion, 37
brainwashing, *see* thought reform
Buddhism
  introduction of, 16–17
  Six Dynasties period, 14n, 17
  teachings of, 28, 33, 43
Bundy, William, 247
bureaucracy, 21, 56–58, 175n, 178–182
Burma, 249, 279

C

cadres, 91, 156, 173, 214

320 Subject Index

cadres (*continued*)
  Cultural Revolution and, 137–138
  defined, 117
  feedback and, 174, 175, 177
  hsia fang and, 227–229
  May 7 schools, 229–230
  "open-door rectifications" and, 130
  Party and, 117, 119, 124
  "three-thirds" system and, 229
Cameroon, 278n
Canada, 278n
canals, 160
Canton Commune, 143
"capitalism," 7, 179, 218–219, 256, 282
Central Committee, *see* Communist Party of China, Central Committee
Ceylon, 277n
Chang Ch'un-ch'iao, 64n, 90n, 218
Chang Kuo-t'ao, 37, 144
Chang Tzu-yi, 228–229
Chang Wen-t'ien, 127, 128
charismatic leadership, 106, 146–151, 283
Chekiang province, 194
Ch'en Hsi-lien, 167n
Chen-pao Island, 248n, 262
Ch'en Po-ta, 164–165
Ch'en Shao-yü (Wang Ming), 144, 145n
Ch'en Tu-hsiu, 143
Ch'en Yi, 83, 263n
Chiang Ch'ing, 122n, 140, 145n, 150n, 151n, 233–234
Chiang Kai-shek, 73–74, 111n, 115, 132, 261
Ch'ien Lung, Emperor, 115, 248, 258
China Lobby, 271n
Chinese People's Political Consultative Conference, 19, 129
Chinese People's Volunteers, 225
Ch'ing period (1644–1912), 13, 36, 56, 57n, 161, 198, 251
Ch'in period (221–207 B.C.), 12–13, 69
Ch'in Shih Huang-ti (First Emperor), 12, 13, 68, 106, 112, 196–197, 247
Chou En-lai, 23, 190, 195n, 245–259, 276
  ethnic minorities and, 240
  hsia fang and, 227

Chou En-lai (*continued*)
  moderation of, 60
  Nixon visit and, 111n
  nuclear weapons and, 260n
  self-reliance and, 257
  State Council, head of, 140
Chou En-lai, Mrs., 122n
Chou period (1100–256 B.C.), 10–11, 14, 31n, 44, 108
Christianity, 33n, 43
Chuang (ethnic group), 238, 242
Ch'ü Ch'iu-pai, 143, 145n
Chu Teh, 147n, 225
cities, 38, 204–205
civil defense, 261
civil service examinations, 15, 55
clan system, 28, 132
coercion, 13, 59, 68, 120
collective decision making, 140, 142–146
collectivization, 19, 119
"combining two into one," *see* conjunction
comic books, 170
commandism, 120, 214
Committee of One Million, 271n
communes, 202, 219, 260
  economics of, 207
  ethnic minorities and, 239, 240, 241
  Great Leap Forward and, 20, 205
  introduction of, 19, 205
  production brigades, 208–211
  production teams, 211–215
  size of, 206
communications
  in foreign policy, 263–272
  See also political communications
communism, 17–18, 46, 47, 48, 65, 205
  See also Communist Party of China
Communist Party of China
  cadres and, 117, 119, 124
  Central Committee, 112n, 142, 148, 176, 178, 189, 199, 205, 228, 234, 262
  Eighth Congress (1956), 20
  First Congress (1921), 37n
  law and, 76–78, 84, 91–92, 94–96
  major crises of, 143–145
  membership, 117–119, 120–121

Communist Party of China (*continued*)
  National Constitution (1975), 90–91
  nepotism, 122–123
  Ninth Congress (1969), 262
  Political bureau, 142, 145, 146, 147, 233
  popular political participation and, 127–130, 135
  production teams, 214
  provincial committees, 199
  reconstituted committees, 124–125
  role specialization, 118
  unions and, 130
  See also Constitution, Party
comparative advantage, 272
compliance, affected, 31–33
compulsion, 133
confessions, 81–83
conflict, 6, 29, 126–127
Confucius (Confucianism), 13, 26–28, 33, 126, 131
  equality and, 56
  hierarchichal relationships and, 101*n*, 115
  Legalism and, 69–73
  myth and, 45
  political principles, 47–48, 55–57
  ritualism and, 32, 45–46
  See also Lin Piao and Confucius, campaign against
conjunction, 53
consciousness raising, 154, 155
Constitution, National
  1954, 20, 84, 90, 95, 103, 133*n*, 189
  1970 draft, 63*n*
  1975, 23, 89–91, 103, 112*n*, 149*n*, 151, 208, 241–242, 287–295
Constitution, Party
  1928, 297*n*
  1945, 49, 147*n*, 297*n*
  1956, 20, 120–121, 147*n*, 297*n*
  1969, 297*n*
  1973, 140, 297–302
Constitution, U. S., 283
cooperatives, 19
corruption, 57, 58
Council for Mutual Economic Assistance (COMECON), 252–253

counterrevolutionaries, 86, 88
county-level politics, 54, 202–204
courier system, 160
crime, 101–104
cultural homogeneity, 7, 46, 183
Cultural Revolution, 25, 53, 63, 65, 111, 113, 201, 202, 270, 283
  armed services and, 224, 225
  bureaucracy and, 182
  cadres and, 137–138
  cult of personality and, 149–150
  ethnic minorities and, 240–241
  foreign policy and, 263*n*, 270
  launching of, 21, 27, 64, 122
  law and, 87–88, 92, 95
  leadership and, 113, 123, 158, 195–196
  "open-door rectifications," 130–131
  popular political participation and, 131, 135
  "Yenan syndrome" and, 128
currencies, 11

D

decentralization, 192–194, 197, 199
de facto leadership, 106, 111, 114–116, 152, 284
democratic centralism, 48, 87*n*, 140
democratic dictatorship, 48, 86
depersonalization, 14
dialectic method, 52–53
dichotomization, 53, 137
dictatorship
  democratic, 48, 86
  proletarian, 48
diplomacy, 263–271
dissemination, 164, 165
dissonance, 32
diversity, doctrine of, 223
dogmatism, 64–65
Domanski Island, *see* Chen-pao Island
Dulles, John Foster, 268, 276
Dzungars, 251

E

ecology, 34–36
economic integration, 184–189, 191–193, 195, 252

Subject Index

education, 49, 99, 155–156
   ethnic minorities and, 156n, 238–239, 242
elite, role of, 117–126
elite political culture, 26, 40–65
embourgeoisement, 21, 155
emperors, 107, 109–111, 114, 156–157
energy, 203, 274
Engels, Friedrich, 112, 113n, 151, 185–186, 205
epidevelopment, 6
equality, 15, 29n, 56
   armed services and, 225–226
   ethnic minorities and, 234–242
   women and, 233–234
ethnic minorities, 15, 19, 56, 86, 156n
   Cultural Revolution and, 240–241
   demographic composition, 237
   education, 156n, 238–239, 242
   equality and, 234–242
exemplary leadership, 157–158
ex officio leadership, 106, 107, 114–116, 152, 284
extraterritoriality, 79

F

fa, 68–74
face, 31
family, 28–29, 49, 155
family planning, 136
farmers, 19, 37, 38, 126, 127, 128
   See also agriculture
fascism, 197
fatalism, 52, 60, 61
feedback, 164, 165, 173–177
"feng-shui," 35
feudalism, 10, 14, 15, 180
field investigations, 173–174
"five agent" principles, 51, 52, 109
Five Bushels Rice movement, 33n
folk religion, 27, 34, 43
food, 227
foot-binding, 39
foreign aid, 259–260
foreign influences, 2, 16–17, 18, 54n, 79, 190
foreign policy, 246–279
   communications in, 263–272

foreign policy (*continued*)
   Cultural Revolution and, 263n, 270
   foreign aid, 259–260
   foreign trade, 191, 253, 258–259, 273–275
   Formosa issue, 247, 265–267, 276
   international integration, 9n, 252, 272–279
   politics, primacy of, 258–263
   Sino-American relations, 265–271, 276
   Sino-Soviet relations, 18, 251–255, 262, 278
   values and interests, 246–250, 277, 278
foreign revolutions, 277
foreign trade, 191, 253, 258–259, 273–275
Formosa, 20, 24
   Japan and, 265n
   national interest, conception of, 247
   political participation, 136
   Sino-American relations and, 265–267, 276
"four firsts," 61–62
functionalism, 5
fundamentalism, 278
Fu Yueh, 105, 126

G

Geneva Conference (1954), 268
geomancy, 35
goal attainment, 5
granaries, 11, 55
Great Leap Forward (1958-1960), 20, 53, 86, 176, 187, 205, 240
Great Proletarian Cultural Revolution, *see* Cultural Revolution
Great Wall, 12, 68
group orientation, 29–30
Guevara, Che, 277
guilds, 30

H

Han, Eastern (A.D. 25–220), 36
Han, Western (206 B.C.–A.D. 9), 13, 14, 36
Hegel, Georg, 154

hierarchichal relationships, 30, 101n, 115
highways, 160
Hilsman, Roger, 269
ho erh erh i, see conjunction
Ho Meng-hsiung, 143, 144, 145n
homogeneity, *see* cultural homogeneity; social homogeneity
Honan province, 158
Hoover, J. Edgar, 271n
horizontal communications, 163, 165–166, 178
horizontal integration, 8–9
household contract system, 217–218
hsia-fang, 227–229, 285
hsiang-yueh, 161–162
Hsun-tzu, 71–72, 110n, 221
Hua Kuo-feng, 171n
Huang Chao, 36
Huang Tsung-hsi, 72
Hu Feng, 159
humanism, 13
Hunan province, 37, 113n, 185n, 200–201
Hundred Days Reform, 162
"Hundred Flowers" (1956–1957), 20, 228, 236, 238
  law and, 85, 92, 94

I

idealism, 52
ideology, 41–65, 246–247, 278
  behavior and, 54–56
  bureaucracy and, 56–58
  defined, 42
  distinguished from myth, 42–44
  political organization and, 47–49
  political purpose and, 60–61
  political socialization and, 49–50
  practical, *see ssu-hsiang*
  social priorities and, 61–62
  See also communism; Confucius (Confucianism); Marxism
i fen wei erh, see dichotomization
India, 249–250
industry, 186–188, 191, 201–203, 225, 231, 232
informal law, 97–101

Inner Mongolia, 236, 241
integration
  definitions of, 3–5
  economic, 184–189, 191–193, 195, 252
  functional approach to, 5
  homogeneity and, 7
  horizontal, 8–9
  international, 9n, 252, 272–279
  neutral, 8
  normative, 4
  political, 183, 185, 189–191, 193, 281–282
  political participation and, 7–8
  qualification of, 8–9
  quantification of, 8
  subcontinental, 185, 186, 189–196, 219, 239, 244
  vertical, 8, 183–184
  See also subintegration
intellectuals, 32, 85, 135, 159, 228, 229, 285
  See also "red and expert" question
international integration, 9n, 252, 272–279
internation recognition, 110, chap. 8
interprovincial trade, 197, 201

J

Jao Shu-shih, 179n
Japan, 258
  foreign influences, 16
  Formosa and, 265n
  political relations with China, 264, 266
  Sino-Japanese wars, 250, 261
  trade with China, 259, 273
Jefferson, Thomas, 283
Johnson, Lyndon B., 269–270

K

Kao Kang, 144, 146, 147, 179n
Katzenbach, Nicholas, 270
Kautsky, Karl Johann, 112n
Kennedy, John F., 268–269
Kiangsi period (1929–1934), 80, 128–129
Kiangsi soviet, 38, 81–82, 179
Kiangsu province, 125, 214

Subject Index

Kissinger, Henry A., 246
KMT, *see* Kuomintang
Korea, 16, 248
Korean War, 20, 225, 261, 266, 267, 268
Kosygin, Alexei N., 39
Kuang-hsü, Emperor, 70n
Kung Peng, 102n
Kuomintang (Nationalist Party), 39, 79–80, 116, 163
Kuo Mo-jo, 22n, 83
Kuwait, 278n
Kwangsi province, 238

L

labor, division of, 222
labor reeducation camps, 102–103
labor reform camps, 102
labor unions, 19, 130
land reform, 19, 88, 119
language, 162–163, 237, 238
Laos, 249
law, 12–13, 14, 67–104
    Communist Party and, 76–78, 80–82, 84, 91–92, 94–96
    confessions, 81–83
    crime, 101–104
    Cultural Revolution and, 87–88, 92, 95
    "Hundred Flowers" and, 85, 92, 94
    informal, 97–101
    in 1970's, 88–91
    Kiangsi period, 80
    Kuomintang laws and, 79–80, 93
    modern legal development, 79–97
    philosophical background, 68–79
    procedures, 103–104
    Six Points, 85–87
    Yenan period, 80, 82
leadership, 105–152
    age and, 242–243
    charismatic, 106, 146–151, 283
    Chinese tradition, 114–116
    collective decision making, 140, 142–146
    cult of personality, 23, 98, 148–151
    Cultural Revolution and, 113, 123, 158, 195–196

leadership (*continued*)
    de facto, 106, 111, 114–116, 152, 284
    defined, 105
    elite, role of, 117–126
    exemplary, 157–158
    ex officio, 106, 107, 114–116, 152, 284
    legitimacy, 107–112
    Marxist views on, 112–114
    mass participation, 126–139
    Shang and Chou periods, 44
    theories of, 106–116
    "three-in-one" quota system, 243
    women, 233–234
Legalism, 21–24, 68–74
legal socialization, 99–100
legislation, 75–76
legitimacy, 29n, 42, 63, 107–112
Lei Feng, 159
Lenin, V. I., 39, 40, 113, 127, 154, 254
li (propriety, rites), 33–34, 46, 55, 62, 69–71, 73
liberalism, 85
Li Hsien-nien, 237n
Li Ku, 150n
Li Li-san, 143, 145n
line, 60
Lin Piao, 60, 112n, 115–116, 257n
    defection of, 63, 142, 144
    Mao Tse-tung and, 21, 65n, 142, 149, 151
Lin Piao and Confucious, campaign against, 21–23, 61n, 65n, 151, 159, 170, 185, 196–197, 217n, 229n
Lin Piao, Mrs., *see* Yeh Ch'un
Liu Shao-ch'i, 102n, 112n, 121, 149, 199, 202, 270n
    cadres and, 119, 130
    confessions, 83, 144, 159
    "Hundred Flowers" and, 85
    ideology and, 49
    law and, 84, 92–93, 94
    Mao Tse-tung and, 49, 84, 190
    Party membership and, 118–119
    revisionist line, 187, 188, 194
Liu Shao-ch'i, Mrs., 122n
local diversification; 188–189
localism, 284
Lo Chang-lung, 143, 144

Subject Index

Lo Jui-ch'ing, 92
Long March, 144
loyalty, 55–56, 131, 132
Lu Hsün (Chou Shu-jen, 1881–1936), 25
Lu Hsün (398–417), 36
Lushan Plenum (1959), 148
Lu Ting-yi, 121
Luxemburg, Rosa, 112n

M

Macartney, Earl of, 267, 268n
Manchu period, *see* Ch'ing period (1644–1912)
Manchuria, 252
Manchus, 57n
mandate-of-heaven doctrine, 44–45, 108–109
Mao Tse-tung
  armed services and, 148–149, 224
  bureaucracy and, 57–58, 175n, 180–182
  charismatic qualities, 106, 146–151
  education, 38n
  horizontal communications and, 165–166
  ideology and, 46, 48, 49, 64, 116
  language and, 163n
  Lin Piao dispute, 21, 65n, 142, 149, 151
  Liu Shao-ch'i and, 49, 84, 190
  Long March, 144
  Marxism and, 17, 46–47, 64
  nuclear weapons and, 260
  Party organization and, 165–166, 178
  P'eng Teh-huai and, 65n, 93, 144
  political ideas of, 39–40, 46–47, 154, 283
  popular political participation and, 127, 128, 130, 131, 135
  press and, 167
  rational candor and, 33
  relinquishes Chairmanship, 112, 115, 146n
  revolution and, 39–40
  rural populace and, 37–38
  self-reliant regeneration and, 190
  Sino-Soviet relations and, 18n, 251–254

Mao Tse-tung (*continued*)
  Six Points, 85–87
  social homogeneity and, 223–229
  See also Cultural Revolution; "Hundred Flowers" (1956–1957)
Mao Tse-tung, Mrs., *see* Chiang Ch'ing
Marcuse, Herbert, 113
marriage law, 99
Marx, Karl, 205, 254
  division of labor and, 222
  on personality cult, 150
  political ideas of, 40, 185–186
  religion and, 33
  See also Marxism
Marxism
  leadership and, 112–114
  Mao Tse-tung on, 17, 46–47, 64
  See also Marx, Karl
Marxism-Leninism, 17, 64, 252, 255
mass trials, 80
materialism, 13, 59
May 4 movement (1919), 233n
May 9 Directive (1963), 229n
May 7 Directive (1966), 224, 229n
media, 166–173
meetings, 172–173
Mencius, 17, 44–45, 108, 110n
meritocracy, 47, 48
militarism, 16, 110
Ming period (1368–1644), 13, 16n, 36, 264
minorities, *see* ethnic minorities
modern revisionism, 3n, 253, 278, 282
monetization, 11
Mongols, 37, 239, 241, 248, 261
  See also Yüan period
Mo Tzu, 110n
municipalities, 201, 204
mutual aid teams, 19, 176
myth system, 41–47

N

national interest, 247–250
nationalism, 43, 54n, 129
nationalities, *see* ethnic minorities
National People's Congress, 129, 140
  1964, 240
  1975, 23, 140, 151, 234
naturalism, 35

Subject Index

natural law, 70
natural phenomena, 109n
nature, attitude towards, 34–36
negative development, 6
negativism, 85
neighborhood security groups, 29
nepotism, 57, 122–123
neutral integration, 8
newsletters, 172
newspapers, 166–167
Nixon, Richard M., 111n, 265, 268
nonascriptive offices, 14–15
norms, 4, 76
North Korea, 255, 278n
nuclear weapons, 260, 269–270

O

"one divided into two," see dichotomization
"open-door rectifications," 130, 131
Opium War, 162
orientation, 60
orthodoxy, 109
overseas Chinese, 19

P

Pakistan, 249, 250, 279
pao-chia system, 12, 161
parochialism, 29
participation, political, see political participation
parties, non-Communist, 19
Party, see Communist Party of China
Party committees, 206, 207
pattern maintenance, 5
peaceful coexistence, 277
peasants, see farmers
Peking, 201
P'eng Chen, 92, 103n
P'eng Teh-huai, 65n, 93, 144, 262
Pentagon Papers, 267n
Plekhanov, Georgi, 112n
People's Liberation Army, see armed services
Percy, Charles H., 284n
personality, cult of, 23, 98, 148–151
poetry, 170
police force, 195n

Politburo, see Communist Party of China, Political Bureau
Political Bureau, see Communist Party of China, Political Bureau
political communications, 62–63, 160–182
 bureaucracy, 178–182
 feedback, 164, 173–177
 imperial period, 160–162
 media, 166–173
 vertical and horizontal dimensions of, 163–166
political culture, formal, see law
political culture, informal, 25–65
 elite, 26, 40–65
 popular, 26–40
political development, 1–3, 10–12, 18, 36
political integration, 183, 185, 189–191, 193, 281–282
political involvement, 8
political organization, 47–49, 282
political participation, 7–8, 15, 37
 mass, 126–139
political science, 2–10
political socialization, 49–50, 154–156
 models, 156–159
 See also political communications
political structure, 139, 141
 collective decision making, 140, 142–146
 localities, 202–219
 regions and provinces, 197–201
 subcontinent, 189–197
popular sovereignty, 109
population, 117, 118n
posters, 171
practical ideology, see ssu-hsiang
pragmatism, 58–59, 259
press, 166–167
prisoners, political, 24, 75n
 See also labor reeducation camps
private gardens, 215–217
procuratorate, 192
production brigades, 208–211
production groups, 215
production teams, 211–215
proletarian dictatorship, 48
provinces, 197–201

provincial committees, 109
provincialism, 194
psychism, 59

R

radio, 167, 168–169, 236
rectification-of-names controversy, 115
rectifications, "open-door" approach to, 130, 131
"red and expert" question, 20, 48, 121, 223
  See also intellectuals
rediffusion, 167, 169
regionalism, 284
reintegration, 3
religion, 30, 50
  folk, 27, 34, 43
  foreign influences, 16–17
  reform and revolutionary movements and, 33n, 34
  use of to promote docility, 33–34
  See also names of religions
Republic of China, 258
  law and, 72–75, 79–80
  See also Formosa for post-1949
"returned students," 143, 144
revisionism, 40, 63, 64, 256–258
  modern, 3n, 253, 278, 282
revolts, agrarian, 36–38
revolution (concept), 255–257
revolution (1949), 18, 19, 37–39, 46, 93, 115, 128, 132, 162
revolutionary committees, 123–124, 138, 283
rites, see li (propriety, rites)
ritualism, 32, 45–46
Rockefeller, Nelson, 267
role specialization, 118
Rumania, 255
rural populace, Mao Tse-tung on, 37–38
Rusk, Dean, 269, 270

S

San-men Dam, 254
secret societies, 29, 161–162
self-reliant regeneration (tsu-li keng-sheng), 188, 190–191, 200, 202, 212, 257, 273, 279

semantic evolution, 44
seniority, 31, 242
Shanghai, 201
Shang period, 44, 108
Shensi, see Yenan period
show trials, 99
Shun (legendary figure), 45
Sinkiang, 236, 238, 250, 251, 252
Sino-American relations, 111n, 265–271, 276
Sino-Japanese wars, 250, 261
Sino-Soviet relations, 18, 251–255, 262, 278
Six Dynasties period (220–588), 14n, 17
Six Points, 85–87
social change, 3, 36–39
social differentiation, 15–16
social homogeneity, 118, 189
  bridging life-styles, 222–232
  equality, 225–226, 232–244
socialism, 90, 91, 155, 218–219, 240, 241, 256–258, 282
socialization, 42
  legal, 99–100
  See also political socialization
Southeast Asia Treaty Organization (SEATO), 279
Soviet Union, see Union of Soviet Socialist Republics; Sino-Soviet relations
specialization, 230, 231, 244
spiritualism, 35
Sri Lanka, 277n
ssu-hsiang, 59–60
Stalin, Joseph V., 18, 80, 147, 148, 251
State Council, 140
subcontinental integration, 185, 186, 189–196, 219, 239, 244
subintegration, 186–188, 194, 204, 218, 219, 221, 239, 243, 244, 285
Sui dynasty (589–618), 264n
Sun En, 36
Sung period (960–1279), 36, 56, 261
Sun Yat-sen, 9, 115, 116, 183
superstructure and base, 21

T

Taiping Rebellion, 33n, 37, 146

Subject Index

Taiwan, see Formosa
T'ang period (618–906), 16n, 36, 56, 71, 98
Tanzania, 279
Taoism, 27, 33, 34, 42, 43, 64
Tao Te Ching, 42
taxation, 11, 196n
Tayson Rebellion, 249
te, 44, 45
telegraph, 166
television, 168
Teng Hsiao-p'ing, 23, 117n, 145n, 157, 158, 194
Teng Ying-ch'ao, (Mrs. Chou En-lai), 122n
Tenth Plenum (1962), 176, 262
"theory," 59–60
Third Plenum (1957), 228
thought, see *ssu-hsiang*
thought reform, 19, 32, 101–103
"three-thirds" system, 229
Ti (deity), 108
Tibet, 236, 238, 239, 241, 247, 248, 250
Tibetans, 43
T'ien (heaven), 44, 108
Tientsin, 201
towns, 38
trade
  foreign, 191, 253, 258–259, 273–275
  interprovincial, 197, 201
transportation, 160, 189, 236
Trotsky, Leon, 112n
Tseng Kuo-fan, 116
Tsu-li keng-sheng, see self-reliant regeneration
Tung Chung-shu, 51, 73

U

Uigurs, 43
Union of Soviet Socialist Republics, 2, 20, 39–40
  economic system, 282
  Sino-Soviet relations, 18, 251–255, 262, 278
unions, labor, 19, 130
United Nations, 268, 269
United States of America
  Constitution, 283

Formosa issue, 265–267, 276
Sino-American relations, 111n, 265–271, 276
trade with China, 273, 275
Ussuri River, see Chen-pao Island

V

vertical communications, 163–165
vertical integration, 8, 183–184
Vietnam, 12, 20, 162, 247–249, 255, 262, 278n
villages, 38
voluntarism, 133–134
voluntary confessions, 81–83
Vyshinsky, Andrey Y., 80

W

wage system, 232
Wang Fu-chih, 109n, 236n
Wang Hung-wen, 140
Wang Kuang-mei (Mrs. Liu Shao-ch'i), 122n
Wang Ming, see Ch'en Shao-yü
waterworks, 10, 11, 12, 55
Wei, Northern (386–534), 37
Wei Kuo-ch'ing, 155n
Wen, Marquis, 11n
White, Paul Dudley, 270
women, 15
  education, 233
  equality and, 233–234
  law and, 97
  leadership, 233–234
  traditional role, 30–31
work-point system, 233
writing system, 161, 162–163, 236, 238
Wu Han, 144
Wu Leng-hsi, 167n

Y

Yang Hsien-chen, 53
Yang Kuo-ch'ing, 99n
Yao (legendary figure), 45
Yao Teng-shan, 99n
Yao Wen-yuan, 122n, 232
Yeh Ch'un, 122n
Yellow River valley, 10

Yellow Turbans, 33n
Yenan period (1935–1946), 64, 80, 82, 128, 129, 132
yin-yang, 51–52
Yo Fei, *see* Yüeh Fei
Yü (legendary figure), 44n

Yüan period, 36, 37, 56
Yüeh Fei, 56
Yunnan province, 168n, 203

Z

Zambia, 279